JOSEPH CHAMBERLAIN
A Political Study

JOSEPH CHAMBERLAIN

JOSEPH CHAMBERLAIN
A Political Study

RICHARD JAY

CLARENDON PRESS · OXFORD
1981

Oxford University Press, Walton Street, Oxford OX2 6DP

OXFORD   LONDON   GLASGOW
NEW YORK   TORONTO   MELBOURNE   WELLINGTON
KUALA LUMPUR   SINGAPORE   JAKARTA   HONG KONG   TOKYO
DELHI   BOMBAY   CALCUTTA   MADRAS   KARACHI
NAIROBI   DAR ES SALAAM   CAPE TOWN

Published in the United States by
Oxford University Press, New York

British Library Cataloguing in Publication Data

Jay, Richard
Joseph Chamberlain.
    1. Chamberlain, Joseph
    2. Statesmen—Great Britain—Biography
941.081′092′4   DA565.C4   80–40812
ISBN 0–19–822623–3

Typeset by Latimer Trend & Company Ltd, Plymouth
Printed in Great Britain by Billing & Sons Limited,
Guildford, London and Worcester

For Elisabeth and for Anna Kate

Preface

'When I was a very young man an uncle gave me a ring with a crest. I wanted a motto for it, and as there was none which the family claimed, I invented that which we all now bear: *Je tiens ferme*. It has often stood me in good stead . . .'

Joseph Chamberlain to Miss Mary Endicott (later
Mrs Joseph Chamberlain), 9 August 1888

There are great difficulties in setting out to assess one of the most controversial of modern politicians. Joseph Chamberlain aroused fierce partisan controversy, extremes of loyal devotion and bitter hatred, which extended long after his death and have since pervaded historical scholarship. Problems are compounded by the temptation to select specific events or periods from his varied career and make them bear the weight of interpretation. Some writers have extolled his early career as a Radical, tracing his progress towards a programme in 1885 which might have proved capable, had Gladstone understood its historical significance and not sought to resist its development, of advancing significantly progressive social legislation in Britain and averting Liberalism's later retreat before an independent Labour movement; others see him as a traitor to Gladstone, Parnell, and his former principles in 1886, a man who broke the back of Liberal and Irish Nationalist aspirations for a generation. Many interpreters take his later career as the reference point. During this, it has been claimed, he brought to fruition Disraelian principles of Tory Democracy and the synthesis of Imperialism and Social Reform—a vital link in Conservatism's progress from the mid-Victorian period to the present day; others, alternatively, would identify him as an alien intruder into the traditions of the Tory party, who ruined its fortunes for a decade with the inept political gamble of Tariff Reform. Hailed as a statesman, forging original solutions to great national problems, he has also been decried for making simplistic, wrong-headed and politically maladroit responses to complex issues, often from partisan motives or personal ambition. His actions have been considered as inspired by a wilful, almost destructive, energy, directed at revitalizing the society of his time, or as shrewd strategic manœuvres devised by a hard-headed, emotionless, machine politician. And finally, while his methods have been seen as a pattern for modern democratic politics, with its professional party leaders, national electoral manifestoes, and disciplined mass-based organizations, to others it marks the culmination of Victorian popular politics, a phenomenon now gone for ever.

Judicious comment is a virtue likely to emerge only with difficulty from such a plethora of views, and within the limited confines of this book it has proved impossible to do full justice to all the available interpretations. Predominant weight has been given to providing a clear narrative thread through the complex disputes of his public career, sometimes at the cost of simplifying his own motives and those of other participants in the events. But where the existing literature offers radically contrasted views on his role in contemporary affairs, or, in my view, is insufficiently clear about the issues involved, I have attempted to analyse matters in greater detail, rounding the book off with a more general survey of his contribution to the politics of his time. Non-political information has been stripped to a minimum. It is to be hoped that the character of the man has emerged from the narrative, but certain aspects of his life have suffered in consequence. Relations with his family, particularly the influence upon his sons Austen and Neville, of later fame or notoriety, have been neglected as of more relevance to their biographies than their father's; the impact of Chamberlain's continual dialogue with friends and political associates in the West Midlands has been simplified; and the character of his early friendship with Sir Charles Dilke has been treated more in the nature of a mutually advantageous political alliance than as a deep personal attachment, though it was also that.

This biography had its roots in a B. Phil. dissertation at

Oxford completed many years ago. To those who commented on that work, and on the various drafts of this which have been written, recalled, revised, laid aside, revisited with reluctance and eventually turned into a final form, I must express my deep gratitude. Particular thanks must go for comments and conversation to A. B. Cooke and V. B. Bogdanor, whose views, even when I have dissented from them, have never done anything but stimulate thought and renewed enthusiasm for the hard task of putting paper to typewriter. For the comments of Frank Wright, and of the publisher's anonymous advisers, I am also grateful. The, unfortunately not inexhaustible, patience of Chris Cook and Peter Carson must not go unacknowledged. And finally to my wife, Elisabeth, who could produce innumerable lectures, a thesis, a book and a baby in the time it took this short work to be completed, I would like to express my admiration and thanks for her patience, encouragement, and attention to the often fruitless task of ensuring that my thoughts were expressed in something approaching the English language.

Bladon, 1979

Contents

ERRATUM

Page 75, line 19 should read:

legislative inactivity, they also pointed to the need for a Radical

CHAPTER 1

A Man Worth Watching. 1836–1868

Joseph Chamberlain was born in Camberwell, London, on 8 July 1836 into a family anchored by tradition, religion and occupation in the radical middle classes of England. His father, also named Joseph, and a Unitarian by faith, organized from his City office the family's small commercial business based on shoemaking. He was a man of some local prominence, like several of his ancestors one-time Grand Master of the ancient Cordwainers Guild. In 1834 he had married Caroline Harben, daughter of a Unitarian wholesale grocer, and 'Joe' was their eldest child. The family was comfortably off, moving within a wide circle of friends and relations in the suburb of Highbury where Joe spent his early years.

Religion played an important part in the Chamberlain family life. Joseph the elder offered his three sons financial support to take up the ministry, though each finally decided to follow him into the world of commerce. Their faith, among the oldest in the English dissenting tradition, was also unique in its denial of Christ's divinity—a 'featherbed to catch a falling Christian' was one view of its beliefs—and, in Joe's case at least, the featherbed failed to support him with the onset of personal tragedies in middle age. Many Unitarians were closer to the deist beliefs prominent among many Enlightenment intellectuals than to the peculiar tenor of English Nonconformity, and within the Martineau family, famous relations of the Chamberlains, were both prominent divines and advocates of Auguste Comte's secular religion of Positivism. Religion for the Chamberlains also had powerful political overtones. They were proud of their descent from a pastor who had abandoned the Anglican ministry after 1660 rather than submit to a state-dictated theology, but religious tolerance rather than sectarian enthusiasm was considered the message imparted by this: Joe could quote his father's often-stated distaste for the political expression of orthodox Dissent as 'infinitely more illiberal than the Church in its worse times'. Like so many of their class, the Chamberlains possessed a fierce pride in their religious auto-nomy and status as independent producers of wealth, resentful of social and legal discrimination against them, and disparaging special privileges enjoyed by a parasitic upper-class establish-ment. They might rally to a patriotic war against Revolutionary France, and put up tough resistance to the economic claims of their artisan employees, but they identified themselves with a progressive struggle of 'The People' for liberty, equality, and efficient modern government against Britain's traditional Anglican landowning rulers.[1]

Until the age of fourteen Joe was educated at small private establishments, and was then sent to University College School, founded some years earlier by disciples of the radical Utilitarian philosopher, Jeremy Bentham. There he took prizes in French and Mathematics. An enjoyment of French novels, particu-larly when relaxing from the strains of speech-writing, survived throughout his life, as did an indifference to sport and un-necessary physical exertion: rising from bed of a morning he affirmed to be enough exercise for any man. In 1852 his father brought him into the family firm rather than sending him on to University College as his abilities merited, on the grounds that his finances prevented him from treating the brothers Richard and Arthur likewise, and he would not discriminate between them. Chamberlain always regretted his lack of further education—on a visit to Oxford in the 1870s he lamented the great things he could have done emerging from such a place—and contemporaries were frequently scathing about his res-tricted intellectual horizons and philistine cultural appreciation.

The year 1854 saw an important change in his life. His uncle, John Nettlefold, a Birmingham screw manufacturer, was anxious for finance to take up the patent on a new productive technique developed in America and install the necessary machinery. Chamberlain's father offered the capital, and prudently sent Joe to Birmingham to develop his budding financial acumen and safeguard the investment. The Chamberlain–Nettlefold partnership lasted for twenty years, until Joe sold out the family's share for half a million pounds, leaving the company ultimately to coalesce into the modern industrial giant of Guest, Keen and Nettlefold.

This was the formative period of Chamberlain's life. The new process eventually produced cheaper, better-quality screws which soon gave it a decided advantage over its Midlands competitors. But in the 1860s, when Chamberlain's drive and business flair began to impose itself on the other partners, much more was done. Foreign competitors also possessing the patent were challenged and the continental market itself invaded. Local rivals in difficulties were systematically taken over, though, despite later accusations, with generous compensation and some concern for safeguarding jobs. Steps were taken to guarantee supplies of raw materials through vertical integration. In the course of a decade, Chamberlain transformed a backward industry characterized by numerous competitive workshops into a prime example of modern monopoly capitalism. It was done, too, without ruthless exploitation of labour. The firm was concerned to provide a model of Victorian paternalistic industrial relations, and, though Chamberlain discovered to his political embarrassment in 1874 that union organization had been outlawed by his partners, he was frequently to be called in as an arbitrator welcome to all sides in local industrial disputes in the late 1870s. Chamberlain's particular role lay in the sales and financial side of the business: and, if the upper-class political world into which he later entered looked askance at the hard-headed, *nouveau riche* provincial screw-manufacturer (and many historians since have sought to elucidate his career in terms of his background as a dynamic industrial monopolist), it is worth observing that Chamberlain's genius, as businessman and politician, lay in selling the goods rather than making them.

During these years his family had moved from London to Birmingham and into a circle of, largely dissenting, industrialists and merchants who formed Birmingham's élite. In 1861 Chamberlain married into the Kenrick family, also Unitarians, and after his first wife, Harriet, died in childbirth, then married her cousin, Florence Kenrick, in 1868. Florence herself died in 1875, again in childbirth, within a few months of Joseph's mother and father, a man, it is reported, of reserved temperament, but who passed his proclivity for dogmatic assertion on to his son.

A weaker personality might have been broken by this succession of sudden personal tragedies, and Chamberlain was a man of strong emotions. His acquaintances were many, but his affection reserved for the few—his family, and close friends acquired in his early career like the fellow Birmingham businessman, Jesse Collings. Throughout his career he rode an emotional see-saw between periods of deep depression and high elation. 'As touchy as a schoolgirl and as implacable as Juno',[2] Chamberlain was a proud autocrat, demanding strong personal loyalty and easily moved to turn political disagreement into personal antipathy. His private grief was, if anything, a spur to his ambition and natural proclivity for action; the only solution to it, he once told a recently bereaved friend, was to 'work doubletides—to work constantly and not to think'. Personal feelings were consciously cloaked by a well-controlled public mask—'Self-mastery was his idiosyncrasy', Margot Asquith once observed—and, as close companions died or separated politically from him through his life, the high spirits and sense of fun which had characterized him in his youth were channelled into cold, ruthless determination which became a singularly daunting characteristic. Lord Salisbury once observed that Mr Gladstone, though very much hated, was also very much loved, but 'Does anyone love Mr Chamberlain?'

Political activity occupied Chamberlain little in his early years. Though prominent in a local Birmingham debating society (as well as in amateur dramatics), it was not until 1865 that he became actively involved and joined his local Liberal association. Over the next three years he attended demonstrations in favour of electoral reform, was invited to speak at meetings of his local party, and campaigned for Liberal candidates in the 1868 general election. His interest had, however, been early stimulated in a family circle where political discussion was staple fare. He was noted in Birmingham for his constant diversion of conversation to political issues—and an express ambition to become Prime Minister! In an age when politicians needed a large private income or, like Disraeli, generous friends to ensure a useful political career, Chamberlain's devotion to the creation of a personal fortune was an expedient prelude.

Of comparable importance for his career was the particular personal relationship he was eventually able to create with Birmingham's electorate. In part the product of his own political genius, it was also made possible by the specific character of the city.

By 1854 Birmingham had grown from a small market town into one of the main industrial centres of Britain, specializing in the production of finished metal goods with coal and iron from the surrounding Black Country. 'Made in Birmingham' was the characteristic mark on ironmongery, household goods, ornaments, jewellery, buttons, trinkets and general *bric-à-brac* which littered Victorian homes and were dispersed through Europe, America, and the Empire. It also contributed materials more basic to Britain's industrial pre-eminence—nails, screws, staple items in railway construction, and a small-arms trade which flourished in an era of colonial expansion and European insecurity. More civilized needs were catered for by the Cadbury family's flourishing chocolate business.

From the Georgian period the city had inherited a strong self-confidence about its place in the vanguard of material progress. A small intelligentsia in the late eighteenth century had congregated in important local scientific societies, and the harnessing of scientific knowledge to technological development achieved but its most spectacular success in Boulton and Watt's Soho Works. 'Forward', the motto of the Corporation, expressed the spirit of Birmingham's commercial enterprise, which extended into its social and political ethos.

By Chamberlain's time the commercial heart of the city had come to service the whole Midlands area. Around it lay the clutter of small factories and workshops which accommodated its massive diversity of trades, jostling for space within a maze of alleys and courts where the back-to-back housing and tenements of the labourers were located. As in other Victorian cities, successful business and professional families had gradually fled the squalor, dirt and noise of central Birmingham, although, an important factor for the city's political evolution, there were concentrations of the well-to-do in areas like Edgbaston, a carefully developed suburb barely a mile from the centre. Extremes of wealth and poverty existed as elsewhere within this geographically concentrated environment, yet there was much to obscure the unequal relationships of labour and capital. The small size of most enterprises was such that distinctions of wealth, status, and work patterns between 'masters' and 'men' were restricted: skilled artisans who predominated among the workforce had few incentives to identify themselves as members of a homogeneous exploited proletariat: if the small-scale enterprises were highly vulnerable to the vagaries of market competition and the trade cycle, the sheer variety of trades offered ready prospects for redeploying labour and capital: sub-contracting and home workshops proliferated, providing ample scope for exploiting sweated labour, but also for upward mobility among the more enterprising, or purely fortunate. The fragmentation of labour, which made the area's trade-union structure one of the weakest in industrial Britain, and the lack of any major absentee plutocracy once inspired Cobden to compare the 'more healthy and natural' condition of Birmingham society with that of Manchester because of its 'freer intercourse between all classes'.

Industrial structures which militated against sharp class cleavages encouraged, too, the creation of populist ideologies among the middle classes. Where entrenched social élites failed to generate widespread deference, and powerful industrialists could not easily discipline a large economically dependent work-force, resolving problems of social control and political leadership in the tumultuous climate of Victorian urban life was likely to be attempted through the technique of the popular alliance. Birmingham had a strong local tradition on which to build. Having housed Joseph Priestley in the late eighteenth century, it had later produced Thomas Attwood's Political Union, the most notoriously radical of the mass movements demanding economic and parliamentary reforms in the late 1820s. Joseph Sturge's Complete Suffrage Union of the 1840s had done much to mitigate locally the class conflict generated elsewhere by the rise of Chartism, and in the 1860s George Dixon, J. S. Wright and William Harris, three progressive local political leaders, had twice inspired reorganization of the local Liberal Association to incorporate separate working-class organizations on the franchise issue. In 1857

Birmingham Liberals had provided John Bright with a parliamentary seat to promote his electoral reform campaign when even Manchester turned him out. In the city he delivered his famous and, in the light of later events, unfortunate comment that Birmingham was Liberal 'as the sea is salt'.

Throughout Britain the heart of popular Liberalism lay in the chapel pulpit, and in this respect Birmingham held a singular position. Long-established as a refuge of religious freedom in the Anglican-dominated rural Midlands, its manufacturers and ministers had forged the Protestant ethic and the spirit of capitalism into a dominant ideology of progressive Dissenting radicalism, despite the numerical equality of Anglican congregations to those of Nonconformity combined. Unitarianism and Quakerism, two sects which especially cultivated a concern for social problems, had always played a major part in the city's development, and during Chamberlain's formative years here this concern was given new expression by two generations of talented local preachers. Wayward Baptists like George Dawson and Charles Vince, the Unitarian Henry Crosskey, and the Congregationalist divine Dr R. W. Dale, berated large congregations with a gospel proclaiming that the religious life was to be lived primarily through a life of social and political duty, in which the calling of Birmingham's leading citizens was to challenge the irreligion and immorality of the city populace by attacking its root sources—poverty, illiteracy, alcoholism, bad living and working conditions among the urban poor. Inculcating a sense of responsibility for moral improvement among the masses through social improvement, which was expressed elsewhere in the influential writings of the Oxford philosopher T. H. Green and the ethos of Toynbee Hall, came in Birmingham to be formalized in the 'civic gospel'. Traditions of municipal pride, improvement and self-government were tapped to support an appeal for more positive local government action to transform the city from a chaotic industrial slum into a wholesome, enlightened and humane social environment.

The civic gospel, the self-conscious democratic ethos of Birmingham life, and traditional Radical opposition to artifically maintained religious and political privileges, coalesced in Birmingham in the late 1860s around an extremely capable

generation of local political leaders. An élite of successful industrialists, Dissenting ministers, and Liberal organizers,
backed by the influential *Birmingham Daily Post* edited by a
one-time Conservative J. T. Bunce, and ultimately spearheaded by Chamberlain himself, launched a frontal assault
upon the traditional pattern of politics in the city and the
country at large.[3]

In terms of national politics, it was certainly a fortuitous
time for Chamberlain's emergence. Gladstone's successful bid
to rebuild around Irish disestablishment the Liberal alliance
splintered in the 1866–7 franchise reform debates, and his
subsequent electoral triumph, appeared to show that parliamentary majorities could be created despite, or even because
of, a lurch to the left. In the country, advocates of progressive
change looked upon the face of Liberal government and saw
that it was good. With reformers like John Bright and H. A.
Bruce in the cabinet, and others in junior offices, talented
young politicians believed they could see the way in which the
wind would blow under the new democracy. For the moment,
though, the *ancien régime* held sway. In Victorian England the
middle classes might rule, but most of the oligarchic local
committees inclined to men of traditional status and respected
professional background to represent them; and they in turn
found little to fault in cabinets dominated by their traditional
aristocratic governors, if rejuvenated periodically with new
blood from the higher professions. Men like Bright, it was clear,
were mere window-dressing. Radical intellectuals might hope,
as always, for an alternative leadership to emerge from their
marginally increased representation in 1868, but the left was
as much, in Professor Vincent's phrase, a 'coalition of convenience' as was the whole Liberal Party. Intellectual Radicals
with a broad secular ideology of social improvement and
progress could only infrequently rally reforming MPs, whose
interests generally lay in promoting single issues like disestablishment, temperance, and land reforms, or constitutional
changes and whose independence was rooted in the localiza-
tion of political issues; they were also uneasy bedfellows for the
narrow-minded provincialism of the Nonconformist conscience,
the backbone of the extra-parliamentary party, but a fissi-

parous phenomenon, dissipating its force in a host of good causes.[4]

Problems of disunity were continually to dog those of Chamberlain's generation who aspired over the following years to forge a strong Radical movement, but in 1868 the auspices could well be interpreted in their favour. Chamberlain himself entered the arena optimistic that he was riding the flood tide of inevitable progress in British political life. For Gladstone in 1877 he was 'a man worth watching', 'expecting to play an historical part, and probably destined to it'.[5] Success in industry had made him supremely self-confident of his abilities, which early political achievements in Birmingham were to confirm all the more. Shrewd, tough, aggressive, he proved able to apply his mastery in commercial dealings to the Byzantine complexities of high politics, and his marketing skills made a good preparation for the world of democratic electoral politics. 'Sensitive, indeed oversensitive as he is to the mood of public opinion', as Arthur Balfour once observed, he set out to cater for demands emerging from the consumer-elector with attractive, workable, well-packaged policy-products. An optimist possessed of big dreams and ambitions, he was never an idealist, 'not a man of imagination—a sober screw-manufacturer who wishes to extend the business. A mind without literary or artistic resources, a man of affairs; but an absolutely clear, unclouded head.'[6] He projected in public a major part of his personal character—a straightforward man, frank about his future plans, concerned to apply himself where there was 'work to be done'. His speeches were plain and prosaic, delivered with 'scrupulous economy of gesture, movement and colour',[7] or, as Disraeli put it, 'like a cheese-monger'. The audiences which packed Birmingham's Bingley Hall came to hear, not Bright's rounded oratory, nor Gladstone's convoluted pulpit rhetoric, but a workmanlike exposition of the city's next political objectives, liberally interspersed with sardonic attacks on his enemies. His characteristic sally was the sneer, delivered with a poker face broken by a distinct curl of the lip.

Chamberlain's earnestness and brash manner, his constant appeal to the gallery and obsessive devotion to politics—

growing orchids on a characteristically grandiose scale being his only major diversion—and his manifest contempt for those he considered among the 'second eleven' of politics did nothing to commend him to the political establishment. 'At least he wears his eyeglass like a gentleman', commented Disraeli on first sight, though by 1886 Gladstone was reflecting the widespread view that no gentlemanly qualities were at all detectable. Of the close friends he acquired in the early 1870s, John Morley attempted to knock the intellectual rough edges off him, while resenting that abstract discussions were always brought down to practical political issues, and Sir Charles Dilke proved largely successful as his 'arbiter elegantiarum'. In many ways, however, he always remained a provincial outsider. Though later lionized in metropolitan circles, he regarded 'Birmingham society' as superior to that of London, proving it by constructing a gothic monstrosity of a house, Highbury, in Moor Green close to his constituents and local friends. Small of stature, lean, upright in bearing, clean shaven, always impeccably dressed with his distinctive monocle and an orchid in his lapel, and an inveterate consumer of large strong cigars, his one natural point of identity with the aristocratic way of life was the gout which crippled him periodically throughout his life.

In 1868, with no political experience nor clear path of entry into the arena, Chamberlain was convinced that he had a great future before him. And in struggling up the greasy pole to secure a commanding position from which to implement his ideas, 'pushful Joe' challenged and often dislodged the conventional wisdom of his age. In the process, he twice carried a major responsibility for bringing political ruin upon the governing party of the country.

CHAPTER 2

Smashing up the Whited Sepulchre. 1868–1876

Chamberlain entered national political life as the self-appointed leader of an extremist pressure group during the educational controversy which dogged Gladstone's great reforming ministry of 1868–74. The controversy broadened his political horizons: by 1874 he was looking for ways to break up the Liberal coalition and replace it by a new political movement under his control which could more effectively tackle the problems posed by contemporary society.

Demand for educational reform had been second only to Irish disestablishment among issues canvassed by Liberals in the 1868 election. Moralists and philanthropists, increasingly sensitive to the horrors of the industrial slums, had come to see education as an initial step in converting workers from crime, irreligion, alcoholism, and squalid living. Industrialists, correlating the rapid economic development and sophisticated production methods of America and many continental countries with their extensive educational systems, were anxious for Britain to follow suit—a central consideration for the Radical educational reformer and MP for Sheffield, A. J. Mundella, like Chamberlain a major exporter and user of modern industrial techniques.[1] Most important of all in placing education on the agenda was the franchise reform of 1867. Chamberlain observed that the issue had been 'partly awakened by a desire that the extension of the suffrage . . . may find a people better prepared to exercise the privilege and fulfil the duty'. 'We must educate our masters' more tersely expressed the widespread hope that education would be an anodyne to working-class subversion; but politicians of all classes were conscious that a more sophisticated electorate was a prerequisite for greater receptiveness to the various causes they had to offer.

Finally there was the crucial religious dimension, raised because the existing voluntary school system, dominated through their large, long-standing endowments by Anglican foundations, was clearly inadequate to meet these new expectations. At root, two centuries-old motives lay behind programmes of mass education—on the one hand a religious desire to bring the Word of God to the people, on the other a secular, rationalist faith that education would extirpate religious dogma and the hold of tradition and deference. These conflicting objectives defined the two main methods by which an expansion of education could be undertaken when, in the 1860s, it became virtually inevitable that governments would have to launch a major initiative. On the one hand, public subsidies could be provided for maintenance and expansion of the existing system. This was the proposal canvassed after 1869 by the National Educational Union with support from Anglican, Catholic and select Nonconformist interests who wished to further the spirit of evangelism. Alternatively—the age-old dream of Radicals and a majority of Dissenters—a new national system could be founded, financed and run by central and local government. It was the second, in its most radical form, with which Chamberlain was to identify himself.

The specific reasons why he became involved in the question are unclear—perhaps merely that, in the years 1865–8 when he began engaging in politics locally, it was emerging as *the* central question beyond the franchise. Having long undertaken voluntary work with his own employees, in 1867 he assisted George Dixon, Birmingham's mayor and after 1868 a city MP, in founding an Education Society to investigate the scope of the local problem. The widespread interest created among a broad spectrum of local notables by the inquiry crumbled when prescriptions were offered. After a brief study of educational systems abroad, Chamberlain proposed affiliation to a respected national pressure group, the Manchester Education Society, and devised a scheme based on American experience which his close friend, Jesse Collings, subsequently published in pamphlet form. When W. E. Forster, the minister responsible for education, came later to consider them, he described the proposals as 'completely logical machinery'.[2] It was not just their logic, but the upheaval they entailed, which made

them unacceptable to the Society, for Chamberlain argued
that neither voluntary work nor independent schools could any
longer cope with problems of illiteracy: what was needed was
universal compulsory primary school attendance in a new
national system supported by government grants and local
rates.

Compulsory attendance was manifestly the crux of any major
overhaul of existing policy, yet the contemporary climate was
highly unfavourable to such an extension of state coercion of the
individual. It would entail an enormous, costly building programme; and, as one of Chamberlain's correspondents observed, working-class families would not appreciate the burden
of compulsory fees, and 'a law which the masses do not like is as
good as dead'. On this issue, Chamberlain took the bull by the
horns by arguing for a free public system; yet its likely burden
on rates, together with the implications of state doles to private
individuals, made the idea unwelcome even to some of his
closest associates. The proposal also had a further purpose. His
publicly financed system was to be entirely secular, or at least
non-sectarian in its religious teaching: private religious foundations relying on fees would thereby be beaten out of the
market. Chamberlain's philosophy dictated that the purpose of
education was to create good citizens, not good Christians.

Though such a scheme had a long historical tradition in
Britain, it remained a utopian vision, and Chamberlain had
little success propagating it in 1867. Two years later the situa-
tion had changed. Bright was in the new government, as were
Bruce and Forster, one-time parliamentary spokesmen of the
Manchester Education Society which was committed to furthering compulsory education by extending provisions of the
Factory Acts. With leaders of moderate opinion harnessed to
office and early legislation anticipated, Chamberlain saw the
opportunity to launch his own radical proposals into the arena.
After a meeting with Birmingham friends in January 1869, he,
Collings, and Dixon appointed themselves provisional officers
of a National Education League to found branch associations
and convene a conference in October. Within two months a
membership of 2,500 was being claimed, and the conference
attracted many prominent educationalists, working-class leaders, and backbench Liberals. Its proceedings displayed what

was to become Chamberlain's characteristic political style. The Birmingham junta mobilized radical delegates, partly through disproportionate representation of branches from Birmingham, to override the reservations of more moderate, and often more prominent, attenders. They gained acceptance for Chamberlain's programme and confirmed the provisional officers in their positions, with Dixon President, Collings Secretary, and Chamberlain in the key position as head of the Executive Committee. Convinced, like leaders of the Anti-Corn-Law League a generation earlier, that they were propagating a cause which was the key to social justice and progress, they began building a fund around their own large personal donations for a ten-year mass agitation, in the belief that deliberate imitation of the organization and methods of their predecessor would bring comparable results.

Dixon's first attempt to present the League scheme before Parliament early in 1870 was frustrated by a government announcement that its own proposals were in preparation. W. E. Forster, responsible for preparing it, was just the man for the task. At a time when Liberalism still had to prove that it could confront the problems of mass democracy within an alliance of the Anglican territorial aristocracy and the urban, largely dissenting, middle classes, Forster's ability to handle the hot potato of education was likely to determine not merely his own political prospects but those of the whole party. Forster, a brusque, tough, self-made businessman, initially of provincial Quaker background and impeccable Radical credentials, had created a powerful left–centre coalition in his Bradford constituency and acquired social respectability by converting to Anglicanism and marrying into the family of Dr Arnold of Rugby. Taken up by Gladstone in the mid-sixties, he promised to prove capable of rejuvenating the tradition of Peelite ministerial talents for the new era. And the reception given to his Bill in February 1870 suggested that all would be well. The existing voluntary system was to remain intact, and to be offered a year's grace to provide plans for expansion with public subsidies. If in this way educational deficiencies in the local areas into which Forster had divided the country could not be met, elected Boards were to be established to build a new school system alongside the old, financed by grants and rates.

Decision on the controversial questions of compulsory attendance, fees and religious teaching would be left to the local
School Boards.

This outline plan ultimately emerged as perhaps the most
important landmark in English educational history. It also
represented a brilliant and ingenious way of fudging the main
issues: not only was a dual educational system to be created
and state-supported, but all the controversial decisions were to
be shunted on to new elected local bodies. If everyone found
something to hate in it, most had something to gain by seeing it
approved: the Education Union was partly appeased—Dixon
and A. J. Mundella, whom Forster had carefully wooed beforehand, represented broad Radical opinion which welcomed it in
principle while having reservations on details.

Chamberlain did not. Convinced of the need for a full-
blooded reform, he was determined to force the withdrawal of
Forster's proposals. 'My hope', he told a reticent Dixon, 'is
that we may make such a show as will justify you in talking out
the Bill.' Forster's ingenuity had, however, isolated the League
scheme as the whim of a lunatic fringe: placing it on the agenda
would have to be done by ensuring that the government Bill
foundered on one or other of its key clauses. For Chamberlain,
as for Forster, who had been overridden in cabinet on the issue,
the Bill's chief defect was the absence of universal compulsory
attendance, yet this was unlikely to arouse wide political protest. More important was the potential financial support for
religious education, which instantly aroused hostility from
organized Dissent in Parliament and at the Liberal grass roots.
At a public meeting in Birmingham on 7 March, and as spokesman for a huge League delegation to Gladstone and Forster
two days later, Chamberlain catalogued the Bill's many
defects—the absence of free, compulsory education, the funds
and year of grace given to voluntary schools, and the fact that
many areas, particularly rural ones where conservative squire
and parson reigned supreme, might not receive Board schools.
His emphasis, however, was on the 'permissive sectarianism' of
the Bill—the right allowed Boards of supporting any type of
religious education. In areas where Anglican and Catholic
supporters gained control, the Nonconformist ratepayer—and
vice versa, though this little concerned such opponents—might

find himself financing creeds he condemned, an anathema both to his conscience and to his pocket. Chamberlain believed that, by exploiting this and similar clauses, he could defeat the Bill as a sectarian conspiracy, waging war under the banner 'Our choice is between the education of the people and the interests of the Church'.

This banner displayed Chamberlain's ambiguous relationship with Nonconformity, for which he was soon to become chief spokesman outside the House. Mundella was always, rightly, to refer to the League leaders as 'secularists': it was religious teaching generally, not just the Church, that Chamberlain objected to throwing on the rates, and later in Birmingham he operated an ultimately unsuccessful system in which the sects themselves organized and financed it outside school hours. The official League principle until 1873, however, was 'unsectarian' religious education, a concession to avoid alienating Dissent. Chamberlain's plan was to carry forward the League's essentially secular objectives on the shoulders of Nonconformist hostility to details of the Bill; and, in this respect, the view of Chamberlain's major biographer, J. L. Garvin, that his national, compulsory, free and unsectarian scheme was the 'Nonconformist charter' is misconceived.[3] This strategy did involve systematic ambiguity. In his address before Gladstone on 9 March he stated that he would not speak for the Nonconformists since they had their own, separate organization, but that, nevertheless, he could 'fairly claim' to be representing their views. This was hardly surprising, since it was on his initiative that Dr Dale and Dr Crosskey of Birmingham had founded a front organization, the Central Nonconformist Committee, in 1870, whose own protest against the Bill rallied two-thirds of the country's Dissenting ministers.

The progress of Forster's Bill before its final approval in August 1870 considerably undermined Chamberlain's strategy. Protest meetings in the country organized by the League, and objections in Parliament, compelled the government to compromise on a number of significant clauses, though two crucial amendments to the 'permissive sectarianism' clause were defeated by moderate Liberal and Conservative votes. To the extremists, the Bill's Anglican bias appeared amply confirmed. By accepting the Cowper–Temple amendment permitting

rate-aid only to non-sectarian education, however, the government effectively compromised with Nonconformity's chief
demand. Chamberlain had earlier believed that Forster would
not give way on this issue—which, indeed, was one of the great
virtues of exploiting it—and had been making Forster's
position as difficult as possible by launching a personal campaign against him as a traitor to Liberalism, but he was now
compelled to look around for some other issue with which to
keep up steam behind a campaign for radical alterations to the
new system. In October he urged a meeting of the Nonconformist Council to fight against the principle of grants to
the voluntary schools, increased by Gladstone in Committee to
compensate for Cowper–Temple, but soon found a much more
potent issue. Clause 25 of the new Act contained an overlooked
anomaly. Though rates might not be used to finance the
general running of schools giving denominational teaching, no
such restriction had been placed on a Board's right to subsidize
school fees. When in November the complicated cumulative
electoral system produced Anglican-dominated majorities on
the new Boards in many areas, including Birmingham, some
chose to support pupils at voluntary schools. The sums involved
were trivial, but they provided ample scope for Chamberlain
to stir up Nonconformity in the country again. For the next
eighteen months he and his colleagues toured round demanding
the repeal of Clause 25 and calling on local councils to refuse
the necessary funds to Boards which operated it in this way, a
move causing severe disruption and legal controversy.

The opposition to Clause 25 widened in scope and perpetuated the row of 1870 within the Liberal Party. Chamberlain
successfully pressed a Nonconformist conference in January
1872 to withdraw support from MPs not committed to its
repeal, and he was also making headway in harnessing the
agitation to his chief concerns. In 1871 and 1872 Dixon presented resolutions in the Commons linking repeal of the
offending clause to the imposition of universal compulsory
education, and on the second occasion 132 Liberals supported
him and only 123 the government, though Conservative votes
ensured defeat. Forster himself, encountering severe political
opposition in Bradford, was anxious to give way, and by the
beginning of 1873 Chamberlain was confident that concessions

would be forthcoming. Clause 25 had now, however, become a symbol of the government's refusal to yield to extremist pressure. Soon after its Commons defeat in March over the Irish University Bill, Forster was outvoted in cabinet and forced to go ahead with a minor Amending Bill transferring the operation of Clause 25 to Boards of Guardians.

The obvious attractions of Forster's initial proposals, and the political advantages of maintaining subsequently a middle way, had ensured a largely united cabinet front. As Chamberlain manifestly failed to make any impact upon it, his attitudes towards it and the role of the education question generally changed drastically. There were many MPs associated with the League—fifty had been the number claimed in 1870—but they were not a cohesive group and he had little direct control over their actions. Dixon, his instrument in Parliament, was both uneasy at his subjection and a minor figure compared with many MPs who had criticized government policy. The League, while claiming 300 branches in 1872, was also never strong, its influence deriving primarily from Chamberlain's decision to identify it with a campaign of sectarian bigotry. Its role increasingly lay in providing Chamberlain with platforms throughout the country from which he could harangue extreme Nonconformists with denunciations of political moderation and compromise. He had already begun condemning the government as a hypocritical group, reform *poseurs* acting just as any Tory ministry would have done, who had yet to learn 'the Liberal alphabet' and to 'spell out the first words of the Liberal creed'. By 1873 he was writing to his newly acquired parliamentary friend, Sir Charles Dilke, asking him to join in 'smashing up that whited sepulchre called the Liberal Party'. The Amending Bill he saw merely as an opportunity to create greater disruption: 'I think the Bill is doomed, but I don't care either way, as, if carried, it will be a splendid weapon for us.' Indeed it was. In the Bath by-election of June he put forward for the first time a League supporter against the official Liberal candidate and, though the move was sheer bluff, it panicked the Liberal into declaring against Clause 25. In the following months he was making preparations to repeat the exercise in every future by-election.[4]

The campaign appeared to receive important backing when

John Bright, who had resigned in 1870 for health reasons and had since been working for reconciliation, was moved in July to lay blame for the party's divided state entirely upon the government. Gladstone, however, had an ace up his sleeve. In a bid to refurbish his row of extinct volcanoes, he offered Bright cabinet office in a ministerial reshuffle. Despite desperate attempts from Chamberlain and Dale to persuade him to refuse, or at least impose tough conditions for his return, Bright, essentially concerned to rebuild the crumbling walls of Liberalism, readily accepted. He revived their hopes with a further condemnation of the Education Act during his October re-election, but was not prepared to stand up to Forster's subsequent criticisms. In this situation Chamberlain was compelled to call off his electoral campaign. For small fish such as he to fight a government upheld by Bright's tremendous popular influence was simply out of the question.[5]

His increasing hostility to the government during these years had not simply derived from frustration over the education question. Like many other Radicals, he was intensely disappointed by its failure to tackle wholeheartedly a number of other important questions; and, like any other budding politician on the left, he was also concerned to widen his net and identify himself with a wide variety of its objectives. In 1871 he chaired a Birmingham Liberation Society meeting at a time when the long campaign for disestablishment appeared to be gaining in strength after Gladstone's treatment of the Irish Church and the sectarian controversy aroused over education. In the same year he told a United Kingdom Alliance gathering that Bruce's recently introduced, and unsuccessful, temperance Bill, which was to spark off a campaign as vicious as that of the League's, did not go far enough in yielding 'the right of the community to have absolute control over [a trade] which directly affects their moral, spiritual and physical interests'. Land reform was also being widely canvassed following Gladstone's Irish legislation. J. S. Mill had founded his Land Tenure Reform Association in 1869, and in 1872 Chamberlain committed himself to its programme. At a national meeting on electoral reform which Dilke asked him to chair, he advocated an extended county franchise, redistribution of seats to the large towns, and votes for women householders. In 1871 he had

even flirted with the short-lived republican agitation in progress, telling Dilke that 'The Republic is coming, and at the
rate we are moving it will come in our time.' This indiscriminate
commitment to a rag-bag of progressive ideas reflected both his
own roots in a broad Radical tradition and the need to establish his credentials in public. But what commended him to
Dilke, an adept at cultivating useful political contacts, to John
Morley, a follower of Mill and editor of the influential *Fortnightly Review*, and through them to more intellectual, metropolitan Radical circles, was that his political horizons were
considerably wider than those of the average provincial politician. His apparent sectarianism, they appreciated, was a
studiously cultivated front, nor was he going to be content
with the customary role of backbench gadfly or advocate of
sectional causes. 'Definitely a leader for an *English* Progressive
Party,' Morley called him, meaning by 'progress' the systematic
reconstruction of society on rational lines laid down by Utilitarian and Positivist thinkers.

Increasing alienation of grass-root Liberals from the government, and its declining legislative activity and public standing
after 1870, revived among Morley and his ilk discussions on
the broad question of the future of progressive politics. While
Chamberlain was preparing his League candidates in the
autumn of 1873, he offered his own contribution to the debate
for the September *Fortnightly Review*.[6] In a savage attack upon
the Liberal Party he declared that by-election results showed it
to be exhausted as a political force, a party of 'selfishness
without organisation' headed by 'leaders without a policy and
statesmen without principle'. The intervention at Bath had
marked a climax of popular alienation, and 'the formation of a
new political party' more faithfully reflecting the popular
mood. If Liberalism wished to keep up with the times, it would
have to arouse 'the vigorous enthusiasm of those who have
something to gain by further change'. A broad political programme was needed for this purpose, and Chamberlain
offered his own suggestions—'Free Schools', 'Free Land' (the
abolition of restrictions on wider ownership placed by the laws
of entail and primogeniture), 'Free Church' (disestablishment)
and 'Free Labour' (modification of the 1871 Criminal Law
Amendment Act which had created consternation among

organized labour by restricting the right to picket). The first three he had advocated in Birmingham two years before as measures with which the government, after passing a Bill for electoral reform, might restore its popularity, but the appeal had gone unnoticed outside the city. 'Free Labour' he had reached recently, after toying with the 'Free Breakfast Table' (abolishing revenue tariffs on tea, coffee, and sugar). This partly originated in the involvement of Collings and Dilke with Joseph Arch's campaign to unionize rural labourers which spread rapidly across the country from Warwickshire in 1873:[7] it was perhaps also in anticipation of his own candidacy for Parliament. A constituency had yet to be finally determined, but Sheffield, a city strongly influenced by union politics, was high on the list. There was very little new about this programme. It represented a selection from the issues which Radicals had been canvassing throughout the century, and its origins in Bright's philosophy were reflected in a very limited approach to land reform and the exclusion of any reference to the temperance question (though perhaps this was due to difficulties in phrasing a sonorous cry—'Free Drink' would have been popular but inappropriate). Two things about the article were, however, distinctive. One was a clearly expressed aim to weld together under a common banner a long-hoped-for coalition of urban Radicals, tenant farmers and land labourers against landlordism, and Nonconformists against the Church; the other was a very un-Bright-like defence of the economic claims of labour. This he combined with a demagogic appeal on behalf of the 'masses' against the 'classes'. Contemporary agitations against industrial relations legislation and in favour of labour representation in Parliament he identified as a revolt of the working classes against the iniquities of existing society, against wealthy landowners and millionaire manufacturers: Labour saw itself as the 'victim of class legislation of an aggravated kind'. This populist appeal did not, however, represent any real departure from traditional Radicalism in the direction of class politics. Chamberlain called for a leadership to emerge which would direct proletarian discontent into constitutional channels, and offered it in active Nonconformity. Sharing a common alienation from reactionary Liberalism, the two movements could unite on the principles of his programme, and the workers would not 'forget the leaders who had been with them in all their previous struggles'. As self-appointed popular spokesman of the Nonconformist revolt he was in effect bidding for the mass appeal which his stand on Clause 25 could never give, while creating the impression that the 'new political party' which had appeared at Bath was more significant than the meagre protest it in fact was.

The article aroused considerable controversy and was used by Lord Salisbury as a peg on which to hang one of his long attacks on Liberalism as a national danger. Gladstone, not unexpectedly, ignored it, and in January 1874 threw the party into even further disarray by calling a snap election on a platform to reduce the already minute level of income tax. The result put Conservatives in a majority for the first time for a generation. With Birmingham already represented by Bright, Dixon, and Philip Muntz, Chamberlain had finally chosen to stand for Sheffield, though, with four candidates for the two seats, he was in a weak position against the two leading contenders, Mundella, with whom he was uneasily harnessed, and J. A. Roebuck, the veteran Radical agitator now firmly opposed to the 'new left'. In an age of rumbustious elections, the Sheffield contest became notorious for its bitter campaigns and consequent disruption. Chamberlain's chance lay in providing as much entertainment for the electorate as Roebuck was wont to offer, which he did with a great flourish of his *Fortnightly Review* programme. But his advocacy of temperance legislation, Republican reputation, and mild approval of Irish Home Rule were powerfully used against him. Mundella, fearing the alienation of moderate voters, had forced him to temper the campaign, and in the event Chamberlain came in a close third.[8] Intensely disappointed by the result he searched around for another suitable constituency until the problem was resolved in 1876 to his great satisfaction. George Dixon was considering retirement from the House because of his wife's illness, but wanted time to make a final decision before handing on to Chamberlain, by now his natural successor. Chamberlain called this 'childish vacillating' and got his supporters to apply strong pressure on Dixon, who finally gave way 'rather than lead such a dog's life'.[9] Chamberlain was returned unopposed in June 1876. The start of this new career, however, required abandoning another that had begun in 1873 when, elected as Birmingham's mayor, he had launched a programme of urban modernization which was to give him a reputation for constructive work unmatched by any of his contemporaries.

We have already noted the creation in Birmingham during the 1860s of the 'civic gospel' defining a programme of social improvement. Its origins lay not just in a sudden emergence of humanitarian instincts, but in specific unique local factors.[10] Despite its progressive political stance, Birmingham's urban environment had fallen very much below that of other comparable Victorian towns. Rapid and haphazard industrial development had created problems to which no adequate political response had been forthcoming. Official reports had identified the city slums as among the worst in the country: death-rates were enormous, disease prevalent, and typhoid epidemics frequent. Too many of its leading citizens had found the intense economic competition of the area and the attractions of national political questions a distraction from the petty squabbles of town politics. In the hard times of the 1840s and 1850s an economy-minded shopocracy had gained ascendancy and through its cabals at the Old Woodman tavern ran the council largely on the principle of low rates. Those who argued that the role of local government was not keeping pace with the scale of urban problems were isolated and lacked concrete plans of action. By the late 1860s things were changing. Emergence of the ideology of the 'civic gospel' coincided with increasing difficulties in the city's commercial centre as it sought to expand into the slum areas, and with the growth of the whole city, which brought its problems closer to the suburban tranquillity of the better-off.

George Dixon, William Harris, and Chamberlain, elected for the city-centre ward of St Paul's in 1869, were among a growing section of the council who felt that drastic action was required. We have already seen how their concern with local educational needs had led them into a national campaign; but there were other matters which could be dealt with on a more restricted scale, and three factors emerged in the early 1870s to provide them with the leverage they needed. One was the inquiry of a council subcommittee on which they were heavily represented, which in 1871 reported a horrific tale of squalor and disease in the slums, identified the primary cause as the health hazards of sewage disposal, and recommended building a municipal sewage works. Though accepted by a small majority on full council, it was shelved for financial reasons. The second factor was the emergence of a heady economic boom in the following years, which laid a sound basis for raising funds for municipal activities. The third had nothing inherently to do with specifically local urban problems, but was the linchpin of the enterprise. Chamberlain, elected to the School Board in 1870, had led the minority in obstructive tactics to restrict application of Clause 25. Their real defence lay, however, in the Nonconformist-dominated council's refusal to pass on rates to which the Board was entitled. Local Conservatives, mobilizing Catholic and Anglican interests, launched a powerful attack in the 1872 local elections, threatening Chamberlain's seat and ousting Francis Schnadhorst, secretary to the Central Nonconformist Committee. The challenge of this formerly weak political force following hard on failure in the 1870 Board elections drove Chamberlain's group to think hard, and, unwilling to question their policies, they sought the explanation in bad organization. For the next Board and council elections they set out to put the Liberal Association on a permanent war footing. A scheme devised by Harris, its secretary, was announced by Chamberlain in March 1873: the ward organization was restructured and expanded to ensure full representation of the mass of small subscribers, and representation of the wards on the General Committee—the '500', gradually growing in numbers to become the '2,000'—was increased. In the process a purge of the old councillors was undertaken to strengthen those wanting major changes in the city government. The reformers thereby introduced into British politics the first permanent, democratically based party machine for both national and local elections—designed, it is fair to say, less to achieve democratic control by the masses than to accumulate popular support behind a progressive social élite. In its organizational structure, the 'caucus' centralized decision-making in a small Management Committee which the Chamberlainite group dominated. In the November elections Chamberlain led the party's candidates to victory. The Board and the council were both captured with sizeable majorities and Chamberlain himself was installed as mayor.

With clear control on the council he swung into action. The sewage scheme was dusted off and in 1874, largely to finance its running, local gas companies were 'municipalized' with generous compensation. The opportunity was taken to expand the street-lighting system and bring gas supplies into many working-class homes at cheaper prices. Water companies went the same way in 1875: old, scattered and often unhygienic wells and other sources were closed up and a single distribution system created. In 1876, exploiting the extensive powers of the Conservative government's recent health legislation, Chamberlain devised plans to demolish part of a large slum area and construct a municipally owned shopping centre along the new Corporation Street. Libraries, parks, a new lawcourt, and modern street paving were planned and begun. Chamberlain summarized his exploits on leaving office: 'The town will be parked, paved, assized, marketed, Gas-and-Watered and *improved*—all as a result of three years' active work.' As with Nettlefold's, it was largely through his drive and ambition that these results could be recorded, and it was no easy victory. He displayed some of his techniques in a letter to Collings in 1876 boasting of two *coups*. The council had been persuaded to pass stringent by-laws against back-to-back housing, despite opposition from Harris, Bunce and 'all the rest of the timid ones . . . Deykin says that the resolution was carried by a majority of 47, 46 of whom voted against their consciences. I don't care about their consciences—we have got the by-laws and mean to work them.' Further, due to careful financing, he had been able to cut the rates: 'This . . . is as good as three years' lease of power. I had to use my despotic authority a little in arranging the estimates and took the matter out of the hands of the Finance Committee for the purpose, but they are *bona fide* estimates and *will wash*.'[11]

This 'despotic authority' derived, not simply from sheer force of character, but from an ability to mobilize strong popular forces behind his programme and appease the ratepayer who bore the cost of financing the large loans required. Here his business reputation counted for much—he once convinced a public meeting to accept municipalization of the gas companies by offering to run them, make a handsome profit

for the corporation and a small fortune for himself. The programme was backed by a formidable ideology. The cry which
had brought electoral success in 1873 had been 'The People
above the Priests', but this was soon superceded. In its place a
radical-democratic edge was given to the civic gospel. In proposing their vast expenditure upon urban renewal, Chamberlain's group advanced a theory of 'Municipal Socialism'—the
right of the community to own and control institutions necessary to promote communal welfare, and the responsibility of
the ratepayer to improve the lot of poorer classes. This advanced
social doctrine was reinforced by appeals to local patriotism:
'Gas-and-Water Socialism' was but the first step to putting
Birmingham on the map as a model of good government, and
of architectural and cultural development. These high-minded
objectives increasingly attracted to the work the most able and
respected local dignitaries: by the 1890s an American commen-
tator was calling Birmingham 'the best-governed city in the
world'.

Behind the myth of the 'three years' active work' there lay
inevitably a more prosaic reality. The creation of such an
advanced political ideology was largely dictated by the very
backwardness of Birmingham in undertaking the sort of public
health measures and municipal control of basic utilities which
other Victorian cities had long before implemented. Its success
was made possible by cheap loans and booming business conditions: under more difficult economic conditions in the
following decade, progress on the Corporation Street scheme
slowed dramatically, and grumblings about price rises on
municipal services and high rates became widespread. Henry
Pelling has observed how 'Municipal Socialism' could quickly
become 'Municipal Stalinism':[12] the city was gradually
adorned with expensive public buildings which had little to do
with improving the welfare of poor slum dwellers. Humani-
tarianism was not the sole motive for action. Chamberlain
presented his reforms to the ratepayer in part as a cheaper and
more effective solution to urban crime than expanding the
police force: closing down alternative water sources was a
blanket measure to impose a monopoly pricing policy by the
municipality: the development scheme smashed down slum
property but did nothing to help rehouse its residents: advance

purchase of property in the area by members of the Chamberlain clan eased the progress of slum clearance and redevelopment, but the speculative overtones of such action invite attention. Whatever else was involved, however, Municipal Socialism did achieve its central objective: disease and death-rates fell dramatically over the next few years, and for most people life in Birmingham became more pleasant and very much safer.

Upon Chamberlain himself the Birmingham experience had a deep impact. He later declared it the happiest period of his life since for once he was able to implement his ideas in full. His classic Radical identification with a strong democratic local government system was reinforced by practical experience of what it could be made to do. He long continued to work hard for anything which would elevate Birmingham's status—in the 1890s not merely a university, but even an Anglican bishopric! 'I am so parochially minded', he declared in 1880, 'that I look with greater satisfaction on the annexation of the gas and water' than upon any enterprise in the arena of colonial affairs. His success provided 'Our Joe' with a strong personal appeal in the city which, despite his perilous career, was only once ever seriously challenged. (Though it should be noted that in 1880, in the only general election he fought while Birmingham was a three-member constituency, he came third on the list behind Muntz and Bright, an indication, perhaps, of the feelings against, as well as for, him in the city.) Experience as a city boss, with the need not only to play to the gallery but to persuade, bludgeon and encourage the 'timid ones', matured his political and diplomatic talents. It confirmed also his basic intuitions about politics.

There was little specifically 'socialist' or even 'democratic' about Chamberlain's municipal improvements, which represented one instance of the universal practical response in Victorian towns to obvious problems that clearly required public rather than private initiative: there was even less about the sectarian education campaign he had launched upon the national political scene. What Birmingham had produced, however, was a distinctive rhetoric, populist and pro-working class, to carry programmes of change along. Not least in the case of 'Municipal Socialism', this rhetoric was to capture the imagination of the age, and to be applied by the next generation of municipal improvers, particularly the Progressive coalition which dominated the reformed London council after 1889, to a range of tasks that Chamberlain's generation would have found inconceivable, even, indeed, undesirable. In the case of Chamberlain himself, the rhetoric was to define his distinctive political style in the future. The lesson he had learned from Birmingham was that, in politics as in business, there was always consumer resistance even to effective products catering for an obvious need: monopolization and overselling the goods on offer were two practical methods of overcoming it.

The mayoralty had its impact also on his contemporary role in national politics. His behaviour between 1873 and 1876 did not meet with universal favour. 'I appealed to Dixon to stop Cox's proceedings at Bath,' Mundella, a fair representative of moderate Radical opinion, wrote in 1873, 'but he is weak and powerless. Chamberlain and the fanatics have the mastery, and mean to gratify their vanity and magnify their importance by showing their power to do mischief.'[13] MPs bullied over Clause 25, and pressure-group leaders, whose followers he was attempting to capture for his own ends, distrusted his ambitions and disliked his methods. The list of positive achievements in Birmingham made it hard to ignore his claims as a potential leader on the left.

CHAPTER 3
Our Best Card. 1874–1880

The Liberal Party's electoral defeat in 1874 deeply disturbed its supporters. Moralizers like Gladstone attributed it to 'gin and beer'—hostility, that is, from the drink interest: moderates blamed a too rapid pace of reform by the old government and the antics of its extreme left: to Chamberlain it was just retribution for ignoring his warnings about the alienation of working-class and Dissenting voters. Whatever the explanation, there were grounds for believing that, as many had forecast, Gladstonian Liberalism was doomed to destruction through its own internal contradictions. Chamberlain was convinced that picking up the pieces required a restructuring of the party around a new left-wing axis. The issue was whether existing Radicalism could provide anything like the necessary leadership. He was deeply contemptuous of its notorious sectionalism and of men like Forster who, he believed, had abandoned their heritage for political advancement. A new inspiration was needed to produce cohesion: how it was to be achieved was less clear. In the past, great issues like free trade, electoral reform, and Irish disestablishment had done the trick, and John Morley was arguing that disestablishment in Britain could provide a comparable issue for the 1870s. The problem though, as Chamberlain saw it, was a plethora of such candidates for the task of mass mobilization, and in August 1873 he had offered his own diagnosis and remedy to Morley:

The object just now should be to state as clearly as possible the programme of the party of the future, and to make a party thereby. At present there are only individual Radicals, each specially interested in some part of the whole, but with no connected organisation or idea of united action. There are Leagues and Associations and Unions but no party; and there never will nor can be till we choose out the most important of all the questions debated, and weld them into a connected scheme which all or most of us can accept as our programme.[1]

The story of Chamberlain's career over the next six years is that of his gradual abandonment of the strategy of nationalizing Radicalism in a new party and the '4Fs' programme with which he had intended to do it. In 1880 he elected to tread the path of personal advancement, tracing Forster's footsteps into a Gladstonian, Whig-dominated, Liberal government.

The first modification of his programme came soon after the 1874 election. Emphasizing publicly at Sheffield in March that he was looking 'for the formation of a new Liberal—a new Radical party', which required 'a more cordial and thorough union between the Nonconformists as a body and the working classes', he informed Morley that they needed to stress two items on the programme: 'Free Church and Free Labour are the best available wedges for forcing the gates of Conservative obstruction.'[2] This meant also attempting to capture the organized representatives of these two groups—the Liberation Society and the trade unions. Links with the former had been forged through his role in the education controversy: Collings and Dilke provided an *entrée* to Arch's Agricultural Union, while Dilke was at this time studiously cultivating Labour leaders in London, and writing optimistically to Chamberlain that he could 'get all the Trade Unions into a joint movement—with you for its head'.

This strategy, however, had already been revised when Chamberlain came to write a further article for the *Fortnightly Review* in September. Once again castigating the Liberal leadership, and describing Gladstone's election manifesto as 'the meanest public document that has ever, in like circumstances, proceeded from a statesman of the first rank', he offered a solution to the party's problems in its adoption of the single principle of disestablishment. This new stand reflected less the influence of Morley's ideas than Chamberlain's adaptation to changed political circumstances. Of the original four-point programme, it offered the most promising line for rapid political success.

In June 1874 most Liberal parliamentary leaders, though

not Forster, had voted for a motion demanding the repeal of
Clause 25, and effectively ended the party split on education.
'Free Education' was still highly unpopular and stood little
chance of arousing Radical forces—even in Birmingham it
took Chamberlain three years to persuade his Board colleagues
to reduce fees to a nominal level. 'Free Land', he admitted in
his article, raised highly complex problems which made agrarian reform unripe for settlement; he might also have noted that
farmers and agricultural labourers were, in 1874, too involved
in the struggle over unionization to bother much about this
issue. As for 'Free Labour', the election in 1874 of two Lib–Lab
MPs, Burt and Macdonald, had seemed to foreshadow Chamberlain's alliance, but Disraeli swiftly took the wind out of
Liberal sails by appointing Macdonald to a Royal Commission
on industrial relations law, and amending the offending 1871
Act on its recommendation. 'Free Church', however, looked
like having a promising future, not least because leading
Labour politicians were committed to it. More important was
that the 1874 session had seen an array of government Bills on
Church affairs, which moved Gladstone to comment that the
effects of 'one or two more ecclesiastical sessions . . . upon
subjects of widespread interest, will be to disestablish the
church'.[3] Many Liberals thought he might be tempted to take
up the issue, and at one stage so did he: Chamberlain was determined to plant his feet firmly in this terrain.

Most important of all Chamberlain's motives, perhaps, was
the fact that, since there was little chance of launching an
effective popular campaign until 'the great tide of commercial
prosperity which has rolled over England will begin to abate',
there was little to be gained in developing a broad electoral
programme. The crucial work for the moment lay within the
Liberal Party, where significant changes were taking place at
the grass roots. Following Birmingham's example, many local
Associations began to adopt more complex democratic structures. The impetus for this came, again as in Birmingham,
largely from extreme Nonconformists and League supporters—
R. S. Watson in Newcastle, Chamberlain's agent H. J. Wilson
in Sheffield, and Alfred Illingworth, who was plotting against
Forster in Bradford, were among the first. With the collapse of
the Clause 25 agitation, disestablishment clearly constituted

the most potent issue to mobilize those who felt themselves betrayed on education and other issues. Like disarmament in the
Labour Party during the 1950s, it constituted a clear, long-
standing issue of principle with which radicals could challenge
moderate leaderships in the constituencies, and its adoption
was, Chamberlain claimed, the crucial first step towards
eliminating that 'species of half-conscious log-rolling' which
linked Church, landlordism, the drink trade, and other
'sinister interests' to the Tory party.

His bid to lead radical Nonconformity in its campaign for
power through democracy in the constituency parties was reinforced by the help given in reorganization by Francis
Schnadhorst, Harris's successor as secretary to the Birmingham
party, and also by an attempt to draw the Liberation Society
itself into a more radical political role. His *Fortnightly Review*
article set the stage for his attendance with Morley at its special
conference in November at Manchester, but this proved a disappointing event. Their objective was persuading the Society
to abandon its role as an independent pressure group, join
forces with the League, and throw its weight behind the move
for local party reorganization. Its leaders, however, preferred
their existing role, hoping to convert the national leadership of
a party, to that of an ideological faction, though they welcomed
Chamberlain into the ranks and invited him to chair their
annual meeting in May 1876. Chamberlain's disenchantment
with its tactics was matched by dislike of its ideas. The Society
was primarily concerned for religious equality, and was as
interested in the idea of concurrent endowment of the various
sects as full disestablishment of Anglicanism. Satisfying sectarian interests was not something which appealed to secular
Radicals like Chamberlain, particularly since they were planning to pre-empt funds from disendowment for great national
projects like free education, and believed that, politically, it
was 'by citizens and not by sects that the battle must be
decided',[4] Keen observers of the new French Republic, he,
Dilke and Morley saw themselves as English Gambettas,
brandishing an English version of the cry 'le cléricalisme, voilà
l'ennemi'.

The Liberal Party at this time was as much in a state of flux
in Parliament as in the constituencies. Gladstone, lacking a

clear perception of future Liberal progress, had privately announced his intention to retire and remained locked in his study, emerging infrequently and then only to sow discord in the ranks. Sir William Harcourt, his former Attorney-General with whom he had a serious row over Disraeli's Public Worship Act, was organizing a campaign to depose him when, in January 1875, the resignation was finally announced. Two contenders for the leadership emerged, Forster, and Lord Hartington, the 'serious son of a respectable Duke' and a former Irish Secretary, whose experience, social standing and reputation for common sense made him the more likely choice. Forster's position as a Gladstonian in a Gladstonian party, however, gave him strong claims, and the crucial question was whether he appeared capable of controlling the left wing. Some could not forgive his 'betrayal' over education, but Bright and Dixon both spoke out on behalf of a majority wanting a leader of the centre–left. Morley could see little of importance in the whole question, urging Chamberlain to write an article 'defining our indifference to the hole and corner intrigues now in progress', but Chamberlain had other ideas, and was active in organizing protests from militant Nonconformists which deflated Forster's prospects and eventually induced him to stand down in Hartington's favour. Revenge was not the only motive. In his bid to create a progressive alliance Chamberlain was studiously cultivating a wildly inaccurate picture of the Liberal Party as an unnatural creature, its head a reactionary Whig oligarchy, the body a democratic Radical majority. Hartington was thus perfect for the role in which he wished to cast the leadership, while Forster—'trimming as usual', as Chamberlain described him in 1877—would have checked the left-wing reconstruction Chamberlain was intent upon.

In the confused and divided state of Liberalism after 1874, Chamberlain presented disestablishment as a principle around which to build party unity. Manifestly, this it was not, and more senior Liberals were anxious to play it down. It failed to inspire the parliamentary party, and Bright publicly condemned Chamberlain's concentration upon the issue in his presence in January 1876. At the grass roots, though, he was achieving other, more limited, aims. Since 1874 he had been planning to wind up the Education League in accordance with his broad strategy, and in June 1876 led a delegation to Hartington demanding amendments to the government's new Education Bill which brought in the principle of compulsory education. Significantly it came, not from League branches, but from Liberal Associations of the Midlands and North, marking his supporters' infiltration of the local organizations. In the bid to make Birmingham the linchpin of left-wing unity, Schnadhorst was also active in co-ordinating random agitations against unpopular government measures—its refusal to implement Samuel Plimsoll's full proposals on safety measures at sea and the Fugitive Slave Circular of January 1876, as well as the Education Bill. As Chamberlain told Morley about some scandal in India: 'There *must* be many errors made by Government, and many wrongs done by subordinates. We want to impress on the thought of the country some definite principles of conduct, and we may take advantage of isolated faults to preach our doctrines.'[5]

Given that disestablishment had, by 1876, made little impact upon the consciousness of the party, Chamberlain was inclined to turn his attention to another contentious issue. He had once committed himself to the Permissive Bill proposals of the United Kingdom Alliance under which sales of alcohol might be banned completely in areas where a poll of local ratepayers produced a two-thirds majority in favour. But the reaction during the 1874 election from opponents of temperance even to Bruce's limited Licensing Act of 1872 had been ferocious. Chamberlain had encountered severe difficulties in Sheffield, while an upsurge in the temperance campaign during 1876 promised to accentuate already existing divisions within the Birmingham party. His response to these problems was to adopt a scheme, based on the system operating in Gothenburg, Sweden, earlier proposed by the Liberal MP Sir Robert Anstruther. Under this, local authorities would be entitled to buy up publicans' licences, and either cancel them, sell the franchise on them for limited periods at a time, or run public houses under their own control. 'Municipalization' was to be complemented by compensation, a principle Chamberlain had been forced to accept in Sheffield. Chamberlain was convinced that this scheme offered a practicable middle way between the extreme positions on temperance and set out on a new campaign to attract support. Having argued in a speech in 1874 that the 'gross ignorance of the masses' and the 'horrible and shameful homes in which many of the poor are forced to live' were greater social evils than drink, he now told readers of an 1876 *Fortnightly Review* article that 'the temperance cause lies at the foundation of all social and political reform'.[6] Birmingham's party and council were persuaded to support the Gothenburg scheme after his visit to Sweden in autumn 1876 to see it in operation, and much of his first year in Parliament was spent arguing for it. Yet, though mitigating political problems in Birmingham, the proposal gained little hold among the most important groups concerned. 'Municipalization' of the drink trade laid itself open, for the temperance fanatic, to the biblical comment that he who toucheth pitch shall not remain undefiled; traditionally, too, the wages of sin had been conceived of as death, not compensation. For the publican, however, compensation was a poor alternative to his livelihood. The Alliance, like the Liberation Society, was further unwilling for Chamberlain to exploit its support for his own political purposes. Its spokesman in the Commons, Sir Wilfred Lawson, delivered the death blow with a denunciatory speech in Chamberlain's presence, at which Chamberlain, retaliating bitterly, threw over the whole question.

His attempts to force a left wing reconstruction on issues of domestic reform, though strengthening his personal reputation, and creating a large following, were not proving outstanding successes. In late 1876 they were to be thrown totally in the shade. Disraeli's decision to pursue a strong anti-Russian policy in the Middle Eastern crisis which arose in that year generated considerable hostility when news reached England of atrocities committed by Turkish troops upon the insurgent Bulgarians. While Liberal leaders remained uncertain of their policy, the Nonconformist conscience was aroused by protest meetings, and the crisis, as it unfolded, promised to benefit everyone. Disraeli was soon donning Palmerston's mantle; Forster and Hartington both rushed off to Constantinople and returned to retail their first-hand experiences of the situation; most important of all, Gladstone brought himself by pamphlets and speeches to the forefront of the anti-Turkish agitation with the aim of injecting new energy into his factious party with a great Liberal cause.

Chamberlain's reactions were more ambiguous. He failed to back the agitation between June and Gladstone's emergence in September—thought for part of this time he was away in Sweden—and then felt compelled to defend his inactivity on the grounds that he 'did not know enough of the circumstances to absolutely pronounce an opinion on them'.[7] In view of his earlier recommendation to 'take advantage of isolated faults to preach our doctrines' this seems rather strange. And, indeed, his personal position on the issue is difficult to uncover. That there was a genuinely 'nationalistic' strand to his attitudes, besides an intrinsic Radical aversion to the expansionist Tsarist autocracy, seems clear from his subsequent career and his early life. Years before he had organized a local Volunteer force when the French Emperor Napoleon III's 'imperialism' threatened war with England, and he opposed Bright's election for the city in 1857 because of his stand on the Crimea. The initial reaction of what A. J. P. Taylor has called the 'intellectual Radicalism of Bright and Cobden'[8] to the Bulgarian agitation was largely one of suspicion based upon fear of involvement in a war whether for or against Turkey. This does not appear to have been the source of Chamberlain's parallel coolness. He always declared his opposition to the pacifism of the Peace Society and sections of the 'Little England' school, which he termed a 'policy of selfish isolation . . . fatal to the best interests of the country'. Morley, an advocate of a Little England if ever there was, had earlier been 'alarmed at the ease with which "un homme comme vous" prepares to sanction' British involvement in Egypt; and, disclaiming the common Radical horror, Chamberlain had regarded Disraeli's purchase of the Suez Canal shares as 'a clever thing', since, whether desirable or not, 'we have a finger in the Egyptian pie . . . and that is the point of view from which the purchase ought to be regarded.'[9] The moral stance and tone adopted by Radicals and Gladstonians towards the Eastern Question appears to have been alien to his mind, and a great oration later delivered by Bright on the ethics of international affairs he called an 'inferior speech', 'peace-at-any-price—Crimean War *ad nauseam* and nothing to the point and to the present occasion'.[10]

A number of writers have attributed to Chamberlain during this period the kind of views on imperial expansion and uni-

fication which characterized the later part of his career. Such
attributions are anachronistic in relation not merely to Chamberlain's ideas but also to the whole range of attitudes adopted
in Britain towards 'imperialism' in the 1870s. It does, however,
seem clear that Chamberlain should not be identified with
what is often regarded as the characteristic position of the
British Radical or Nonconformist conscience towards foreign
affairs, defined as it usually is in terms of doctrines of internationalism, anti-colonialism and non-intervention. There was
a strand of patriotic nationalism inherent in Chamberlain's
Radicalism, a phenomenon rather more noteworthy of French
and American than of British Radical history, though perhaps
more widespread among the middle classes from which
Chamberlain sprang than inheritors of Gladstonian and Manchester School doctrines have been prepared to recognize.

Apart from this, however, there are two clear reasons which
might account for Chamberlain's reticence towards the Eastern
Question. One was the obvious fact that in the 1857 election
Palmerston had decimated Radical critics of his foreign policies
and the politically astute Chamberlain may well have been
wary of repeating Bright and Cobden's errors at that point. A
second was that the Eastern Question cut straight across his
strategy of reconstructing progressive politics and polarizing
Liberalism on issues of domestic reform. Yet, once his Radical–
Nonconformist base had set off in full cry against Turkey,
Chamberlain, aspiring to be their leader, had no option but to
follow. He soon also saw major advantages in doing so. Dilke
was informed in October that 'I don't believe I am more
Gladstonian than you, but at this time I can't help thinking he
is our best card', and 'if he were to come back for a few years (he
can't continue in public life for very much longer) he would
probably do much for us and pave the way for more . . . [I]t
would be almost equivalent to a victory, and would stir what
Bright calls "the masses of my countrymen" to the depths.'[11]
Chamberlain's idea of propelling himself forward under Gladstonian steam initially encountered difficulties, since Mundella
and Sheffield Liberalism had already seized the initiative by
organizing a huge conference in St James's Hall, London, for
December. Mundella shared Gladstone's aim of building a
great campaign involving prominent national figures: 'I don't

intend that any Radicals shall speak *if I can help it*. I want to fire off the Bishops, the Parsons, the Peers, the Literati, etc., not those who have been the actors heretofore but *a new set*.'[12] Chamberlain, however, had specifically rejected this approach in his first speech on the crisis. The opposition to Disraeli's policy should be an essentially partisan one, he argued, so long as commitment to party involved commitment to great principles. Since the Conservatives were acting against the 'national will', it was the duty of all Liberals to unite behind Gladstone (to whom 'we all owe loyal submission') and force a dissolution.[13] Mundella, sounding Chamberlain out on his proposed conference, was rebuffed, complaining that 'nothing seems to go down with Birmingham that is not of *home manufacture*', and received the alternative suggestion, in its turn rejected, for a meeting of Liberal Associations and MPs. Chamberlain's clear aim was to turn the Eastern Question into an intra-party battle, replacing disestablishment as the crucial test question of the moderates and Whigs.

His proposal, though postponed, was not abandoned. The December Conference having produced little save a rather feeble Eastern Question Association, he decided that the time was ripe to regain the initiative, and in January 1877 dissolved the moribund Education League on the grounds that it was now unfitted to propagate its only outstanding commitment, free education.[14] Speaking to a newly reorganized Association in Leeds, he announced his intention of forming 'some sort of general union of these bodies with periodical meetings and occasional meetings in cases of national emergency and great crisis'. On 31 May at Birmingham the National Liberal Federation, comprising initially some forty of the 100 associations, was inaugurated.[15]

In his speech to the first meeting and in subsequent articles defending 'The Caucus', Chamberlain expounded its character and aims. It was a federal organization of local Liberal Associations, but designed neither to control the federated bodies nor to mobilize electoral support for the party. '[T]he caucus does not make opinion, it only expresses it', was his view: 'no programme could be imposed on such an organisation, as each member will attend its meetings because he is a representative Liberal . . . Besides, Liberalism should not be narrowed by any

stereotyped creed: it is an open trust.' Its tasks were rather to
ascertain constituency opinion on issues of the day, and hence
avert 'misconceptions' on the part of parliamentary leaders
about 'the mood of the country'.[16] This was the Federation's
public ideology to attract the unwary, though Chamberlain
expected much more of it. If its aim was co-ordination, Mundella noted, 'appeals to the associations will be made or neglected as Birmingham deems desirable, and Chamberlain
moves Birmingham.' His suspicions of monopolistic control are
confirmed by Chamberlain's request in March to Harris,
architect and convenor of the Federation, for postponement of
the initial meeting to avoid Manchester and Leeds becoming
joint hosts, since 'they will claim equal representation on all the
Committees'. The meeting was in fact as well-organized as that
of the League in 1869, and the Federation's headquarters were
set in Birmingham, with Schnadhorst as secretary and Chamberlain president. His disclaimer of a common programme for
the caucus was also disingenuous. The attenders at a business
meeting on the afternoon of 31 May all belonged, he noted, 'to
what they believe to be the party of progress', and he advocated
three reforms worthy of adoption by the Liberal Party—a
national education system, Bright and Cobden's scheme for
land reform, and religious equality. These, he observed, bore a
striking resemblance to his own '3Fs'—one he expected to increase with time! Finally, Chamberlain saw the caucus as an
instrument against the parliamentary leadership: 'I think this
may become a very powerful organisation and proportionately
detested by all Whigs and Whips,' he told Morley. Hartington,
though invited to the initial meeting, refused, probably for
reasons which disturbed Lord Granville: 'it is not the Eastern
Question but the hope of breaking up the party which excites
[Chamberlain, whose] object is not to reorganise the whole
Liberal party, but to strengthen the young Liberal, and more
advanced, portion of it.'[17]

Granville had been attempting to dissuade Gladstone from
attending and hence legitimizing Chamberlain's activities, but
failed. Gladstone in mid-May was looking for a new public
platform when, having presented resolutions to Parliament
supporting Russia's recent declaration of war against Turkey
on behalf of the mismanaged Balkan states, he was persuaded

to avoid a Liberal split by putting only the mildest of his five points. Chamberlain, having spared no effort in arranging demonstrations in the country and whipping up support in Parliament to force the breach which Gladstone was determined to avoid, was suitably annoyed by the 'cave in', as he called it. Gladstone's urge to unmuzzle himself, however, provided a perfect opportunity for the favourable reception of an invitation to address the inaugural Federation meeting. Here the contrasting aims of the two major participants were clearly reflected in their speeches. Gladstone delivered a great oration on the Eastern Question, Chamberlain stressed the virtues of grass roots co-ordination and domestic reform. This inherent tension over the future tasks of Liberalism was gradually to be resolved in Gladstone's favour, but his apparent 'capture' by Birmingham was to provide Chamberlain's projects with a major boost in status.

But the 'Radical Programme' was in no way as clear as it had been. The Federation indeed soon lived up to Chamberlain's claim of incorporating a broad span of Liberal opinion, and he was careful at subsequent annual meetings to confine his speeches to safe topics and the moderate recommendation of minor reforms. A large part of his time was spent addressing the inaugural meetings of recently 'democratized' Associations, where the programme could be given greater weight. Yet it was being gradually pruned. Free education he increasingly regarded as an issue 'for which this country is certainly not yet prepared'. At Rochdale in November 1878 he could announce that 'For myself, I care little which of the great questions we first attack—the Church or the land', but events were conspiring against the former. The Liberation Society, like the United Kingdom Alliance, refused to follow the Education League's example of dissolving itself into the NLF, while problems in the rural areas were beginning to attract attention on the domestic scene. A deepening crisis in agriculture after 1877 generated strong political demands from the farmers for assistance, increased emigration of labourers to the towns, and began to stir up serious discontent in Ireland. Chamberlain followed other Liberals in turning his mind to the problem and in 1877 was working out with the Radical, Shaw Lefevre, a new scheme of land reform. Equally important was that, while he had been canvassing disestablishment and temperance, others, in particular G. O. Trevelyan and Forster, had been more successful in proposing electoral and local government reform for the counties as the party's next major task, a view that was accepted by Hartington in 1877. Chamberlain had initially rejected it, claiming that it posed the danger of Disraeli pre-empting the ground and ignoring a major redistribution of seats as he had in 1867.[18] Yet by May 1877—though admittedly this was at a meeting of Arch's Union—he had reverted to his 1872 priorities: county franchise was first on the list of Liberal measures, to be succeeded by county government and agrarian reform, and finally disestablishment. This ordering was to be stressed increasingly in his speeches over the next few years. Yet even they began to take second place to a growing concentration upon foreign affairs.

Initially he had attempted to avoid falling entirely under the Gladstonian umbrella, referring to the Eastern Question in his speeches only in the opening passage or a casual aside. In November 1877, as excitement over the Russo-Turkish war was reaching its peak, he could tell Morley that 'I am full of Free Land, Free Church and Liberal organisation.' But when, to tension in the Middle East, was added annexation of the Transvaal in 1877, an initially disastrous war launched by Britain's High Commissioner, Sir Bartle Frere, against the Zulus, and the wars of 1878–9 to limit Russian influence in Afghanistan, Radical passion grew increasingly inflamed against Disraeli's adventurist 'imperialism'. Chamberlain began trimming himself to Gladstonian moral indignation: Disraeli was pursuing a policy of 'brag and bluster', backed by 'a declamatory appeal to British bunkum'; the Zulu War was 'as iniquitous and unjust as any in which this country has yet been engaged', and the Afghan crisis 'the natural consequence of Jingoism, Imperialism, "British interests", and all the other phrasing of this mountebank government'. As taxation increased and the economic depression he had been hoping for since 1874 set in during 1879, and particularly when Gladstone moved to Midlothian, Chamberlain began to recognize that the coming election had to be fought on foreign policy: 'We want to din into the constituencies that the Government policy is one of *continual*, petty, fruitless, unnecessary, and inglorious squabbles—all due to their bullying nagging ways', he told Dilke.[19]

In the country he was building up his personal reputation as a red-hot, 'Little England' Radical through demonstrations organized by the Federation, and speeches as its president, against the government. In Parliament his position was more complex, even though he could write to Bunce in late 1878 that 'Dilke and I together have been the real triumphs of the session' with their co-ordinated attacks on the government. His close personal adherents were few. A Radical 'cave' that he formed on entering the House contained only five MPs, which a split on Bulgaria soon reduced to the insignificant Welsh MP, Dillwyn, and Dilke. Dilke for his part, though sharing Chamberlain's desire for an independent Greece and dislike of government policy in South Africa, was no Gladstonian and strongly in favour of standing up to Russia over Afghanistan. Nor were Chamberlain's relations with Gladstone satisfactory. Left-wing backbenchers looked for their strategy to Bright and Gladstone, who were concerned to avoid splitting the party and isolating it from broad opinion in the country, and Chamberlain had to warn enthusiastic Birmingham supporters in April 1878 that 'the position is a hopeless one . . . I do not believe that . . . there is one single person besides myself who thoroughly desires that any amendment to the address should be moved.' Increasingly, too, he dropped his old hostility to the 'Whig' leadership. He was not prepared to try and unseat Hartington, he told Collings in 1878, since 'he keeps the place out of worse hands. Except Gladstone, there is no other possible leader; and Gladstone . . . is erratic and cannot be relied on with absolute confidence.'[20] Hartington refused to attend the 1879 Federation meeting, but in his absence Chamberlain stressed the need to rebuild party unity. In November 1879 he invited Harcourt to Birmingham to counter rumours of major disagreements in the party, and in February 1880 offered merely 'suggestions' of a moderate reform programme for a future Liberal government, refraining from drawing out any divergences on overall policy. There were the occasional sallies. He and Dilke secretly co-operated with the increasingly truculent Irish Nationalist MPs to oppose official Liberal policy on several issues, though Parnell was later to claim that this was because Chamberlain was too frightened to do the work himself. In a debate on flogging in the armed forces, however, he caused a stir by turning on Hartington and referring to him as 'lately the leader of the Opposition, but now the leader of a section only'. The incident arose from Hartington's misunderstanding of agreed party tactics, and later he apologized for causing it, but it illustrates two points. Dilke's shrewd comment was that 'If Chamberlain were to have fought Hartington on any question on which he had not the Liberal constituencies with him, he would have got the worst of it; but then he was too wise to stir on any question on which he could not at least carry all the active elements of the party in the large towns.'[21] The paucity of incidents on which he was 'stirring' in clear opposition to the leadership marks his shift from the strategy of party reconstruction to one of delivering isolated pinpricks. Further, many Liberals had wanted Hartington to force an apology from Chamberlain after the incident: wiser councils had made Dilke's point. Chamberlain's plan of 1874 to form a 'new Radical Party' had not been realized, but he had at least established a commanding position in a far more influential Liberal left wing. How commanding, the election which Disraeli called for March 1880 was to test.

The Liberals secured a clear majority of forty-two over all other parties, the Irish Nationalists, though divided, returning sixty-five strong. Radicals could expect the new government to give them a fair share of offices, but not to be fundamentally different in structure and outlook from that of 1868. There was no 'Radical programme' to heave them into positions of power, and the most prominent Liberal issues in the election had been Gladstonian foreign policy, county franchise and county government reform. The first allowed Gladstone himself to force Hartington from leadership of the party, but a left-of-centre Prime Minister militated against strong Radical presence in government: the other matters were agreed party policy—G. J. Goschen refused office for this reason. The choice for the Radicals lay between seeking office in these unpromising circumstances and remaining on the backbenches in the hope of improving their position by exploiting possible future government failures. Neither was an appealing prospect: Chamberlain was conscious that Gladstone would be 'King

Stork, and that some of us Radical frogs will have a hard time of it under him', while Dilke at one stage in the squabbling over offices was to fret that 'to be out now is to be out for ten years certain'. The situation was ripe for personal ambition to dominate collective Radical interests, and Harcourt could observe with his usual wry amusement that Chamberlain, Dilke and Fawcett (the blind Cambridge professor) were 'mutually jealous' and 'jostling' for position.

All might expect that the government would need reinforcing by their occupation of junior offices, but the crucial question was whether cabinet seats would be made available. Here Dilke was at a major advantage compared with Chamberlain. His respectable social background, long membership of the Commons compared with Chamberlain's four years, his reputation as a solid parliamentarian willing to get along with all shades of opinion, and his almost Gladstonian capacity to comprehend and discourse upon complex issues of policy, made him the more obvious candidate. Chamberlain could see his chances further deflated by the probable entry of Bright as representative of popular Radicalism and, during the election, he wrote to Dilke suggesting an 'offensive and defensive' alliance between them under which, unless both were in the cabinet, they should each refuse any office and threaten to form a back-bench cave against the government.[22] Dilke, not wishing to risk his own chances in a ministry he still expected would be formed by Hartington or Granville, replied that one seat was all that the 'young Radicals' could hope for, and it would be sufficient. He was warned of the possible consequences: 'I feel you may have a difficult question to decide, viz., whether you can safely take the *sole* representation of the Radical element . . . For myself . . . I will take no responsibility which does not carry with it some real power.'

Gladstone's premiership changed the post-election prospects. To restrict Radical representation, he invented the principle that cabinet place would be given to no one without previous government experience. Dilke's first inclination was to refuse any junior office he might be offered, but, informed by Harcourt that he would be an early candidate for the cabinet if he accepted, then sent out a desperate call for Chamberlain's help. Though feigning indifference to the situation and reluctance to leave his Birmingham observation post for the intrigue of London, Chamberlain agreed to move, and then swung into action. Conscious that his earlier hope for two cabinet seats was now impossible, he adopted Dilke's view that one was sufficient, and Gladstone was informed through intermediaries that the two Radicals were intent upon blackmailing him for it with the threat of future trouble in the Commons. In this situation, Dilke began to lose the initiative. He was soon offered a post as Under-Secretary at the Foreign Office, but his firmly-held republican views, which Chamberlain for his part had carefully laid to rest during a royal visit to Birmingham in 1874, were causing trouble with the Queen. Chamberlain himself, notoriously a far more truculent personality than Dilke, was in turn building up his own importance as chief threat to any government of which he was not a member, and drawing attention to his influence in the country through the Federation with a letter to *The Times* exaggerating its role in the recent election victory.[23] Bright, Harcourt and Hartington began to impress upon Gladstone that safety lay in appeasing Chamberlain. Most important, Dilke was put in the position of having to reply to Gladstone's offer with the Radical ultimatum of at least one in the cabinet. Ethics dictating that he could not ask for the post himself, he was forced to insist that Chamberlain be promoted over his head. Though greatly annoyed, Gladstone eventually succumbed. Chamberlain was offered the Board of Trade and a cabinet seat, and accepted when Dilke agreed to make do with his lowly position.

Chamberlain's expressed surprise at this reversal of fortunes was perhaps less than frank. Exploiting Dilke's opinion when rejecting his "two in the cabinet" offer, he had pushed Dilke into his final ultimatum, and made no effort in dealings with Gladstone's intermediaries to press Dilke's claims in preference. Dilke in turn made two errors of judgement. He could have insisted that both receive their offers of office and present their ultimatum jointly, before Gladstone was forced to choose between them, rather than putting himself in the position of devil's advocate; and he had earlier called upon Chamberlain's weight to heave himself forward. And once their respective weights were placed in the balance, Dilke was found wanting: he commanded good repute but no battalions. Chamberlain's strength lay as self-appointed spokesman for opinion in the large urban constituencies, and for the Liberal leaders this was a vital factor. They might suspect the extent of his personal following, the electoral significance of the Federation, and his influence over it, but they lacked the means to make a definite assessment. With consummate skill, Chamberlain had taken up issues and dropped them as they acquired temporary prominence or disrepute among the rank and file, and carefully refrained from open challenges which would test his claims to independent leadership of radical-democratic forces in the party. When he declined to play the game of cabinet formation like a gentleman, it was too much of a gamble to leave him roaming free on the backbenches.

CHAPTER 4

Responsibility Without Power. 1880–1885

Despite his aversion to taking any office which carried no real power, Chamberlain was to find that this was very much what he had done. His new cabinet colleagues were predominantly experienced Whigs and Gladstonians, unsympathetic to the personality, methods, and policies of this *arriviste* who had 'neither from his parliamentary experience nor from his party conduct deserved such a lift', as Edward Hamilton, Gladstone's private secretary, observed.[1] The other cabinet Radical, Bright, was a declining force, with neither the will nor the capacity for the politics of governing, who kept Chamberlain firmly at arm's length, while deep, long-standing, personal differences separated him from Forster, now Irish Secretary. Only the Home Secretary, Harcourt, showed any real personal liking for him, and in politics Harcourt was a law unto himself. Most ministers shared the view of Gladstone, who had taken the Exchequer and placed his minions Lords Granville and Kimberley respectively at the Foreign and Colonial Offices, that the government's task was to restore sound administration: Disraeli's financial profligacy was to be rectified, and the alarums and excursions of his foreign policy replaced by pacific settlements of outstanding problems.

Gladstone himself was the crucial figure. Towering over all his subordinates, he provided a bastion for the moderates against Radical enthusiasm, and for the left a guard against reaction. Everyone for the moment needed the Gladstonian 'umbrella'. Yet, while he remained, the leaders of neither wing could hope fully to realize their ambitions. The tension between these two positions, however, combined with growing suspicion of Gladstone's competence and real value to the party, was continually to tax the loyalty of both Chamberlain and

Hartington, now, with the premiership seized from him, increasingly inclined to take the lead of conservative forces within Liberalism.

Chamberlain himself was inclined to see the ministry essentially as an unsatisfactory stop-gap. At the first cabinet of 3 May he confirmed his colleague's suspicion of his capacities by demanding the instant recall of Sir Bartle Frere and reversal of the Transvaal annexation to symbolize a break with Disraeli's imperialism, and then the introduction of a franchise Bill for the counties. Gladstone quashed him. He wanted temporary retention of the old South Africa policy to promote an autonomous federation of the colonies there; and, knowing franchise to be a potentially divisive issue in the party, insisted on its delay. For Chamberlain, its divisiveness was its most attractive feature. During the election Harcourt had been told of his hope for agrarian and electoral reforms to be pushed through early 'to keep the fire alive'.[2] The fire contemplated in this theory of permanent revolution was designed not only to warm Liberal hearts but also to consume the Whigs in its flames. Chamberlain saw himself leading a great popular campaign which would overshadow or alienate the moderate leaders and drive them into oblivion once enfranchised rural workers had given their hoped-for support to the Liberal left. Land reform would rally tenant farmers and labourers against the landowning classes and eventually provide urban Radicals with the leverage to seize ultimate political power.

These considerations reinforced Chamberlain's basic lack of commitment to the ministry's survival. When Lloyd George, his successor as leader of popular Radicalism, entered the Board of Trade in 1905, he is reported to have ransacked it for measures to make his name and bring colour to an essentially pallid administration. Chamberlain gained credit by steering through the important Employer Liability Act of 1880 on industrial accidents, and followed it with minor Bills to protect the finances and safety of merchant seamen, improve railway travel for commuting workmen, allow local authorities to install electric street lighting, and revise patent and bankruptcy laws. In 1884 he attempted to turn a Merchant Shipping Bill into a showpiece of modern Radical measures, but this collapsed. Useful legislation was not his prime concern: 'What is the good of bothering about Bankruptcy or Local Government when our real business is to outbid Chaplin and Co. with the farmers,' he told Dilke in September 1881. The same message reached Morley in 1883, with a recognition of the limited coherence he had been able to impose on progressive politics: 'The time is coming when our Party (of three or four) must have a programme and know exactly what it is aiming at . . . It is no use trying to elevate Bankruptcy and Patents into a new dispensation.'[3]

His entry into government, however, had imposed responsibility for confronting its problems over South Africa, Ireland and Egypt, *inter alia*. These problems assumed wider significance. Each offered prospects of strengthening his position through ministerial reconstructions or even, on occasions, the government's collapse: each also created risks of becoming isolated from the Liberal rank and file to whom he owed his place on the greasy pole. The result was a series of dubious ventures in cabinet and on the platform which accentuated the ministry's troubles.

They were also to tax his relations with Dilke and Morley. In the 1870s these three promised to offer complementary talents within a new Radical élite, Chamberlain mobilizing mass support, Dilke supplying the parliamentary skills Chamberlain had yet to develop, and Morley the leadership of intellectual opinion through his editorship of the *Fortnightly Review* and, from 1880 to 1883, the *Pall Mall Gazette*. The definition of these roles soon became less clear. Though they were close personal friends, policy disagreements had already created tensions within the triumvirate. Chamberlain had leapfrogged over Dilke into the cabinet; and, though he continued to consult him secretly over cabinet policy and pressed his claims for higher office, an element of personal competition inevitably came to permeate their differences of opinion. Relations with Morley were to prove far more of a difficulty, particularly when, with Chamberlain's help, he won the Newcastle by-election in 1883 and began to develop political ambitions of his own. Morley, a sensitive and complex man, displayed rather more intellectual sophistication than political nous: he was inclined to too rigid an adhesion to political principle in the face of practical problems, and displayed a marked proclivity for hero-worshipping men of action with whom he could identify these principles. Chamberlain's preoccupation with cabinet politics was to provide him with less opportunity to shape Morley's ideas; the latter's disillusion with his hero grew, to culminate in an almost overnight conversion in 1885 to Gladstone and the Home Rule cause.

Beyond these connections, Chamberlain, despite resigning its presidency on entering the cabinet, still had the Liberal Federation in his grip and Schnadhorst's office was to be used to apply pressure upon backbench MPs over the next few years. But it too became a less malleable instrument, particularly as more moderate associations like that in Leeds assumed greater influence in its councils. As Chamberlain twisted and turned to create a coherent Radical response to the unprecedented problems of the ministry, he found increasing difficulties in operating within the political framework which had brought him high office in 1880.

Ireland was the chief problem in the first two years. Chamberlain's approach to the question proved too complex and convoluted for easy summary, but in 1880 at least he had a clear line, if no detailed policies.[4] To the Irish Land League's campaign for the immediate objectives of reduced rents and the protection of tenants from ejection during the agricultural depression, his views reflected the classic Radical solution of land tenure reforms at the landlords' expense. That some changes were advisable most of the cabinet accepted, and in 1880 a Compensation for Disturbance Bill, guaranteeing compensation to certain classes, particularly poorer ones, of evicted tenants, was introduced to hold the line in anticipation of major legislation in 1881. Again like most of his colleagues, Chamberlain rejected any idea of renewing the Conservatives' coercive legislation. Before 1880, however, his attention had been focussed primarily upon the political relations between Westminster and Ireland. Having expressed support in 1874 for the aspirations of Isaac Butt's Home Rule movement, he told Morley in 1879 that he was working on 'a modified form of Home Rule', and during squabbles over the Liberal candidacy for Liverpool in 1880 publicly advocated an extended franchise in Ireland and an assembly in Dublin—hinting also that, if this failed to reconcile Ireland, some greater reform might be needed.[5] In Parliament he had tried to reach accommodation with Parnell and his disruptive Nationalist group (though chiding Morley for sentimental attachment to 'these rascally Irishmen' who would cause more trouble yet), in part to further the general strategy of drawing under his banner all elements politically active on the fringes of Liberalism.

Parnell's bid to strengthen Irish Nationalism through agrarian discontent meant, however, that the land problem was first on the agenda after 1880. Chamberlain was soon attempting to turn it into a major issue. He suggested to Forster a joint resignation if the cabinet failed to press the Compensation Bill against opposition, and, when the Lords rejected it in August, demanded its reintroduction in a special, autumn session backed by a great agitation against the Upper House. Simultaneously he prepared a wide programme of public works to tackle problems of unemployment and under-development in Ireland. Both ideas were rejected. The latter was an imaginative but long-term measure with limited relevance for the immediate crisis, as he realized, and the Bill, despite his perhaps not unjustified later claim that it might have stemmed the tide of discontent, offered nothing in the way of catering for the Land League's main objective of reforms in the land tenure system. Rejection of the strategy was also inevitable. It entailed confronting the Irish landlords and the peers, 'unmuzzling' the Liberal left, and directly threatening party cohesion. The absence of either coercive or remedial legislation, however, accentuated disorder in Ireland during the autumn around Parnell's campaign of 'boycotting'. Forster, awaiting the report of a land Commission, could respond only with a proposal to prosecute the chief 'agitators', with the threat of calling a special session to suspend Habeas Corpus were it not accepted. Prosecution was regarded as a pointless exercise, necessary only to appease British public opinion, and failure of the case in the new year damaged the government's credibility: but Chamberlain followed Gladstone in reluctantly consenting to it. Many Radicals were very upset, and Dilke, assessing after the appointments fiasco that truculence might now pay where sweet reasonableness had failed (a tactic he was to deploy systematically over the next two years), protested strongly. Chamberlain had to defend his acquiescence as the only alternative to coercion, especially since 'Parnell is doing his best to make Irish legislation unpopular with English Radicals. The workmen here do not like to see the law set at defiance, and a dissolution on the "Justice for Ireland" cry would under present circumstances be a hazardous operation.'[6]

More important to him, perhaps, than public opinion was his temporary isolation in cabinet, a situation which had changed by late autumn. Despite his earlier cabinet success, Forster reopened the case for a special session for coercion. Gladstone remained hostile, and his stand was strongly backed. In mid-November Chamberlain and Bright spoke out at Birmingham against coercion without prior remedial measures, and came to a cabinet on the 18th with the threat of their own and Dilke's resignation—countered by one from Hartington on Forster's behalf. Dilke considered this a risky venture since they would 'incur temporary unpopularity, as . . . public opinion . . . was running strongly in favour of coercive legislation', but Chamberlain more optimistically observed that 'if, as I expected, the split with Whiggery had to come, it had better be this split, so that we should have the great names of Gladstone and Bright on our side.' A left–right collision on Ireland would probably break the ministry, but it might leave them a heartbeat from the leadership of the bulk of Liberal forces. Such an upset of the party balance held no attractions for Gladstone, nor indeed for Forster, who yielded before the Radical threat.

These disagreements, publicized through cabinet leaks from the chief participants, were but a preliminary skirmish to the real battle of 1881, which placed Chamberlain in far greater difficulties. In January the cabinet discussed proposals for detention without trial, a Land Bill, and an Arms Bill legalizing wide powers of search conceived by Harcourt, a hard-liner on law and order. Suspension of Habeas Corpus, Forster insisted, must have priority. Already in November 1880 Chamberlain had been willing to acquiesce in coercion, conditional upon the early introduction of remedial legislation, accepting it as inevitable given the state of public opinion while complaining that it 'would be like firing a rifle at a swarm of gnats'. Now he put up little opposition. The parliamentary disruption which it stirred up from the Radical and Nationalist benches, indeed, made his case for the widest possible measure of land reform all the stronger, and he attempted to block moves to impose special closure rules on debate by a forceful threat of resignation.

Land reform was the central bone of contention, offering a number of broad alternatives. Though many landlords and MPs might protest against any threat to existing rights of ownership and free contract, no Liberal government could afford purely to maintain the *status quo*, particularly with the legislative precedents available. The logical alternative in an age dominated by the fetish of private property was the transfer of ownership to the Irish tenants, which would entail state loans to finance land purchase and compensate existing owners. This was the proposal Bright had made on anti-landlord grounds as an alternative to Gladstone's 1870 Land Act, when he had succeeded in embodying the principle in the 'Bright clauses', though the practice remained a dead letter. It was also the ultimate aspiration of large sections of the Irish tenantry, and future Conservative governments were to accept it as the only way of creating stability in Ireland and rescuing the landlords from the consequences of their own folly. Late in 1880 Bright and Chamberlain began canvassing this option, but when they presented a proposal to Gladstone in December he described it as 'wild' and naif', holding, said Edward Hamilton, 'very un-Radical ideas on anything touching landed property.'[7]

The final alternative, rooted in a long tradition of tenant right movements in Ireland, was for legislation guaranteeing and extending the often unclear principles of the 'Ulster custom' of land tenure—the '3Fs' of 'free sale' by tenants, 'fair rents' (to be set, it was hoped, by a land court), and 'fixity of tenure', which established a form of 'dual ownership' in the land. The degree to which legislation should explicitly cover all three items was, however, controversial. Gladstone's 1870 Act had taken a minimalist line, establishing 'free sale' and compensation determined by courts for improvements to their holding made by departing tenants, which, though some way along the road, had had only limited impact. In 1880, Gladstone was inclined to build on his earlier principle, but Forster, fortified by the land Commission's report, had determined to go the whole hog. Though in 1880, and later, he showed considerable indecision and was soon to acquire the reputation for a hard line on Ireland, Forster had been appointed Irish Secretary to symbolize the government's good intentions, and for the time being at least firmly believed that land reform was the key to the problem.

His proposals were far less drastic than Chamberlain had been wanting, and Dilke's first reaction when news of it and coercion were leaked to him in January was to propose their joint resignation. Chamberlain had little to gain from this impetuous course. Forster had won over Gladstone and Bright to a draft Bill embodying the '3Fs', despite the former's continuing reluctance about the 'fixity of tenure' principle, and Chamberlain's main hope lay in ensuring that its detailed clauses were as pro-tenant as possible. In cabinet he called for inclusion of the defunct 1880 Bill, and clauses extending the Land Bill's provisions to tenant leaseholders as well as copyholders, and to those in arrears of rent—those, that is, most in need of protection. All were rejected, ultimately to become the main targets of Nationalist attempts to destroy the Bill and prevent the land agitation being undermined. Though Chamberlain's instincts warned him against hasty resignation, he was sufficiently unhappy with the government's course to remain on the look-out for a means of escape. A cabinet meeting of late February turned the tide. On 19 February Forster proposed delaying the Land Bill until Harcourt's Arms Bill had been introduced, a measure and a timetable which Chamberlain, believing that the Irish solution lay in rapid concessions to the tenantry, rejected. So too did the cabinet. A week later, however, the decision was reversed in Gladstone's absence due to an accident. Chamberlain, 'very angry', became set on confrontation.

The issue could not, however, be Ireland. Gladstone was still ready to stand behind his Irish Secretary, and Bright, finding himself a prime target of Nationalist abuse in the House, was rapidly moving towards a unconciliatory line. The Radicals had to find an issue capable of producing stronger cabinet support, and this they did in South African policy.

After failing to sway the May 1880 cabinet, Chamberlain and Dilke had worked for a change of mind towards the Transvaal by surreptitious co-operation with Radical backbenchers. A sop had been given in June with the recall of Sir Bartle Frere, the plan for a South African federation having foundered; and, though annexation remained, further trouble was pre-empted by Chamberlain's appointment as government spokesman in the Commons. Gladstone and Kimberley's reading of the Transvaal problem was, however, defective. Disappointed in their expectation of an early return to independence, the Boers rose up in rebellion in December 1880. Confident of easy victory, the cabinet rejected demands from Bright and Chamberlain for negotiations to be opened, despite their ostentatious withdrawal from the chamber with Dilke and the Little England Under-Secretary, Leonard Courtney, during a critical vote on 21 January 1881. The malcontents' position was strengthened when Afrikaner opinion in the Cape and Orange Free State grew restive over the hostilities and Gladstone began looking for a negotiated settlement. Majuba Hill disrupted the initiative. When the British commander, Colley, bungled his instructions and launched an unsuccessful attack on Boer troops at the cost of his own life, a bellicose mood erupted in Britain. Kimberley came under severe criticism and pressure to reinforce the military effort.

This was strongly resisted in cabinet. Dilke and Chamberlain set to work on Bright and persuaded him to present their joint resignations, with the expectation of Courtney's additional support, unless further peace overtures were made immediately. But, as Dilke privately observed,[8] this was not the real issue. His and Chamberlain's prime consideration was their general weakness in cabinet and their inability to obtain a satisfactory Irish policy. Resignation under Bright's mantle, impossible on Ireland, would save them from growing suspicion among the rank and file, and provide them with freedom to regroup malcontents on the left and work for that alliance with the Nationalists they had attempted in 1879. Gladstone's acceptance of their ultimatum, on the other hand, might force out Kimberley, a conservative over Ireland, and leave a cabinet spot for someone like Dilke to fill. Crude conspiracies like this rarely succeed, particularly with men of Gladstone's calibre in charge. He persuaded Kimberley to offer peace terms to the Boers rather than succumb to the jingoistic pressures to which he was being primarily subjected, and the outcome, only marginally satisfactory for Chamberlain, was an agreement on extensive internal self-government for the Transvaal at the

Pretoria Convention in October. The *fracas* had once again displayed Chamberlain's continuing weakness in cabinet, and his need to rely on backing from far more powerful figures to obtain even minor portions of his proposals.[9]

The failure of his subterfuge did little to ease the basic problem. The Arms Bill was rushed through the Commons despite strong opposition from Radicals, Nationalists, and the 'Fourth Party', Lord Randolph Churchill's adventurist group who were bidding for high places in the Conservative Party by their brilliant attacks on government policy and their own leaders. The Land Bill, introduced in April and managed personally by Gladstone, encountered an even tougher response. Chamberlain's own continuing discontent was channelled into secret backing for amendments acceptable to Nationalist opinion, and pressure from the Liberal Federation was applied to MPs. Complaints about its interference were met with his suggestion to Schnadhorst of an expansion of propaganda in what might be 'the starting point in a new campaign in which Birmingham would once more take the lead.' ('Do not use my name more than is necessary and treat this letter as private', he added.)[10] But growing Radical discontent needed a more dramatic public response. To reports of disaffection in Birmingham during February he had given a limp reply condemning Conservative neglect of Ireland and Nationalist intransigence,[11] but local difficulties were so grave that by May he had decided on a major speech to the mass Birmingham party.

It was delivered on 7 June in a defensive mood. The government was by no means perfect, he noted, but surely preferable to Conservative 'meddlesome interference and wanton aggression'. It had made early mistakes over the Transvaal, but was now pursuing an honourable course in relation to a people with an 'unconquerable love of freedom and liberty'. The Land Bill, too, was an honourable response to legitimate Irish grievances, though Tories and Parnellites might be opposing it for sectional purposes. And, until its effectiveness was established, coercion was necessary: 'I hate the name. I hate the thing . . . But then we hate disorder more.'

The speech was singularly effective in quelling rebellious elements among his followers and was praised by Gladstone, though he had sharp words for the nicely calculated rejection of collective responsibility for past South African policy. It also marked an important switch in Chamberlain's approach. Like most of the government, he was putting his money on the Land Act's success in ending agrarian discontent and in the speech he effectively disowned the Parnellites, identifying them as the central obstacle to resolving the problem. Whether this was a rational procedure the autumn would tell, for Parnell announced in September that cases would be brought before the newly established land courts to prove, so he said, the Act's inadequacy. Forster and the Prime Minister were determined to stop any such challenge to their policy, and a public interchange of taunts between Gladstone and Parnell was used as an excuse to intern the Land League principals and then proscribe the League when a No-Rent manifesto was issued from Kilmainham gaol.

The winter marked a long struggle between the government and League supporters for the allegiance of the Irish tenantry's attitudes on rents, violence and the operation of the new Act. The government had steered a consistent course throughout 1881 between the extreme advocates of repression and appeasement: they had to make the new policy work or face another year of parliamentary disruption with unpredictable risks to party cohesion. Whig discontent had already been marked by the resignations of Lords Lansdowne and Argyll, while the Liberal left was muttering about betrayed principles. In the government camp there could be no waverers, and Chamberlain threw himself into the fray. Forster's application of his special powers he justified as a policy of 'In for a penny, in for a pound. I hope it will be a clean sweep. The electors will better stand a crushing blow than coercion by driblets. There is no other alternative except new legislation—and from that may Heaven defend us.'[12] At the October Federation conference in Liverpool he spoke in a tone which the local newspaper editor, Edward Russell, called 'conciliating our John Bulls', but which was designed essentially to convince the Radicals that coercion was inevitable. Here, and in Birmingham and the Commons in the new year, he went even further than in June in separating the 'legitimate grievances' of the Irish tenants, whose cause the government was furthering, from exploitation of them by the Parnellites for other purposes. Yet his hard-line stand was

dictated less by conviction than by confusion and lack of alternative ideas: 'I am clear that we were right in resisting coercion
last year,' he told Dilke, 'and I even wish that we had gone out
upon it. But what is to be done now? Can we go on drifting
without a policy? We cannot go back . . . Altogether it is a
horrible imbroglio, and for the moment I do not see my way
out of the fog.'[13]

The mist began to clear with the coming of spring. The
struggle in Ireland was drawing to a stalemate, each side
gaining successes unevenly through the province. Rents were
being paid in many places; tenants were going to the land
courts, though thereby bringing the arrears problem to prominence; the Land League was in disarray; and coercion was
biting, though Parnell believed that its more efficient application could have stopped 'outrages' entirely. At Westminster
new positions were being adopted. Under Churchill's prompting the Conservatives were bidding for Nationalist and Radical
support by criticizing the use which Dublin Castle under
Forster and the Viceroy, Lord Cowper, were making of their
special powers, cutting the government's customary large
majority to thirty-nine on 30 March 1882. Forster, on the other
hand, having difficulty in securing convictions of suspected
lawbreakers, had since December been urging the abolition of
jury trials, while Gladstone was looking to complete the Land
Act by compelling Forster to prepare an Arrears Bill and, unsuccessfully, canvassing the idea of democratic local government reforms in Ireland. His aim was to mitigate what
promised to be the major problem of 1882—a decision over the
one-year coercion Act due to expire in August.

In late March Forster threw the cat among the pigeons by
unilaterally announcing in the Commons his expectation of its
renewal during the year. Gladstone was furious at this attempt
to force the government's hand, and it immediately drove the
Radicals towards a new course of action. After a meeting with
Chamberlain and Dilke, John Morley wrote in early April an
article for the *Pall Mall Gazette* calling for the abandonment of
coercion and Forster's replacement. Chamberlain considered
the publication counter-productive when support rose for
Forster against this bid to make him a scapegoat for the government: 'I doubt whether the British public is ready for a change

of policy just yet—let alone a change of persons,' he told Morley, but added frankly that 'you have set them thinking, and they will get used to both ideas in time.'[14]

It was important for the Radicals to initiate a new departure at this point. Chamberlain's original plans for settling Ireland by extending local autonomy and buying out the landlords had proved impracticable once law and order became the dominant issue. On this, the Liberal left had been thrown into confusion, and its traditional links with reformist opinion in Ireland undermined. By burying coercion, and the minister most responsible for applying it, what was now the major source of antagonism would be allayed, and conditions created for reforging the old links and re-establishing the issue along more familiar lines. There was, however, one major precondition for this strategy becoming viable—that incarceration in Kilmainham had taught Parnell and his followers a lesson. Since agitation on the land question was the only thing which had given Nationalism a firm popular base, it was unclear whether its leaders could even afford to behave themselves if special powers were relaxed and the carrot of possible future reforms were dangled before them, but some prior knowledge of their intentions was needed, which involved the dangerous political tactic for the government of discussions with men it had detained for advocating illegal activities.

These barriers to conciliation were regarded by Forster, it soon emerged, as insurmountable. At a cabinet on 22 April he outlined the terms of a new coercion Bill, more restricted in some respects than the old but incorporating the abolition of jury trials, and an Arrears Bill which he saw primarily as a palliative necessary to appease Gladstone and the Radicals. And, though recommending release of the Land League leaders, he imposed clear conditions: prior to it, either Ireland should have returned to normalcy, or coercion must have been passed, or the detainees must give the usual assurances demanded of those released to offer no future support for civil disobedience. For the first time, however, Forster was presented with a coherent challenge in cabinet. Independently, Chamberlain had been developing an alternative strategy.

On 10 April Forster had paroled Parnell to visit a sick relative, allowing him to visit his mistress, Kitty O'Shea, on the birth of their child. Captain O'Shea, her husband, an Irish MP with large ambitions, seeing advantages for himself in arranging a Liberal–Nationalist *rapprochement*, contacted Gladstone with news that Parnell was anxious to leave prison and restore control over the 'wild men' in his organization. He was rebuffed, but on 15 April approached instead Chamberlain as 'a Minister without political pedantry'. For Chamberlain it was a godsend. If O'Shea's information that Parnell wanted a reasonable arrangement with the government involving his release proved accurate, he might be able to fight Forster's coercion proposals on the grounds that Parnell's statement of his good intentions made them unnecessary. He secured approval from Forster and Gladstone for further negotiations and an offer to extend Parnell's parole. Chamberlain needed consent to avert suspicion of his intentions—Forster gave it to avoid appearing intransigent—Gladstone, though unwilling to compromise himself in direct negotiations, had no objection to his junior colleague so doing. Parnell, averting possible charges of collusion, refused the parole offer but on 23 April passed on through O'Shea to Chamberlain the basis of a possible agreement. In return for a satisfactory Arrears Bill, he was prepared to advocate the end of boycotting and a general return to legality in Ireland.

This seemed to justify Chamberlain's stand at the previous day's cabinet where, in a long memorandum, he accepted Forster's arrears proposals, pressed again for his public works scheme of 1880, but rejected the need for anything other than a very limited coercion Bill. A final decision was postponed for further discussion to avoid a cabinet split, but Forster was now beginning to worry about his position. The resignation of Lord Cowper was being rumoured, and Gladstone's clear aim would be to appoint a replacement more capable of standing up to the autocratic Irish Secretary. (On 28 April the appointment of the experienced Gladstonian, Lord Spencer, was announced.) Forster had already been compelled to water down his coercion proposals because of Parnell's initiative, which greatly appealed to a worried cabinet, and he made it clear that release of the detainees must be accompanied by a public statement of future good behaviour, shrewdly calculating that Parnell's position in Ireland would make this very difficult and thus undermine his credibility with the cabinet. This was also what Chamberlain had discovered from O'Shea: Parnell, apparently, would be willing to try and stop the campaign of lawbreaking, but was reticent about making a compromising public declaration.[15]

Events were hastened by the parliamentary situation. On 26 April Gladstone responded favourably, in accordance with agreed cabinet policy, to a well-behaved Nationalist appeal for legislation on arrears which showed that they had come to accept the principles of the Land Act; a motion was also laid down for 2 May protesting against the use of coercion, which it seemed advantageous to meet with some concessions in the absence as yet of agreement on future legislation. In addition, Chamberlain had received an important letter on 28 April, written for the Nationalist MP, Justin McCarthy, by Parnell just before his return to Kilmainham on the 23rd. Parnell, it has been suggested,[16] recognized O'Shea's tendency to subordinate accuracy to expediency and had decided to clarify his position through other channels. The offer he made, which Chamberlain had received verbally from McCarthy on the 24th but then ignored, was to meet an Arrears Bill by revoking the No-Rent manifesto—a more limited concession than O'Shea had first suggested, and one which the government, having correctly perceived that the League's 'no-rent' policy was failing and that it had little relationship to the 'outrages' still extensively occurring, might regard as of little consequence. Parnell's willingness to have his letter shown to the cabinet, though not beyond, perhaps convinced Chamberlain that he might be pushed into a more satisfactory declaration. With Forster's approval, he immediately sent O'Shea off to Kilmainham, against Parnell's express wish, to see if this were possible.

Why he did so is not entirely clear. Parnell's offer on the No-Rent manifesto might well have contented a cabinet weary of fighting the land war and increasingly anxious to enter the approaching debate with a conciliatory gesture but, since it failed to meet Forster's condition of a prior publishable commitment to abide by the law, Chamberlain may well have been aiming to overcome the last obstacle to an arrangement. But there was a further consideration. In the discussions so far,

coercion had been playing the role of the dog which significantly did not bark. Neither Chamberlain nor Parnell dared
commit themselves to a position on it to the other, yet it was
hostility to Forster's advocacy of tough measures that, for the
former at least, lay at the heart of the new initiative. Forster
distrusted Parnell's word and, believing strong coercion necessary despite the Land League leaders' incarceration, was
apparently using his condition tactically to promote it:
Chamberlain, seeing that the cabinet's relief at any satisfactory move from Parnell would weaken its enthusiasm for
coercion, had to counter by securing Forster's condition and
thereby outflanking his whole position.

This was precisely what happened when O'Shea returned
on 30 April with a letter in his own hand confirming the earlier
proposal of Parnell's attempt to end outrages and intimidation
in return for an Arrears Bill. There was also a further offer, to
'co-operate cordially for the future with the Liberal party in
forwarding Liberal principles and measures of general reform'.
The hint at parliamentary collusion, though an additional
boon, made publication of the letter impossible—a consideration probably not absent from Parnell's mind—and Chamberlain might well have treated it warily for this reason. O'Shea,
however, hoped to seal his *coup* by ditching Chamberlain and
showed the letter first to Forster, who promptly declared it inadequate. This was not Gladstone's view. He set to work on the
cabinet, and on 2 May announced to the Commons the release
of the detainees, throwing in the additional bombshell that
Forster had resigned.

Commentators then and since have suggested that he was
anxious to abandon the Irish Office which had caused him so
much anxiety and loss of reputation. Undoubtedly there is
truth in this. But Forster was shaken by Gladstone's readiness
to accept his loss. Unaware that the Prime Minister was tired of
dealing with a difficult colleague, who had asked for Parnell's
promise of good behaviour and then balked when he got it, he
surely delivered his threat as a last-ditch effort to retain the
control of Irish affairs which Chamberlain's negotiations had
undermined. Chamberlain must have considered this a possible
consequence, and he welcomed it with open arms. As the chief
architect of what was soon being seen as a new departure, he

could anticipate strengthening his hold on Irish affairs, and was confidently telling friends and Irish MPs of his expectation of succeeding Forster and going to Ireland to 'smash the Dublin Castle system'. Gladstone was determined, however, that he and Spencer would alone steer Ireland through the remaining problems. He appointed Lord Frederick Cavendish, an amiable acolyte, who, as Hartington's brother, offered the additional benefit of reconciling conservative Liberals to the new departure. The euphoria vanished when Cavendish and his chief civil servant, T. H. Burke, were assassinated in Phoenix Park, Dublin, on 7 May. The likelihood that the public reaction would force tougher coercion proposals upon the government, however irrational a response this might be, placed a premium on finding Cavendish's replacement among the Liberal left. Chamberlain's claims, however, were once more ignored. Later, Gladstone avowed that he was unaware of Chamberlain's interest in the office, while Chamberlain himself subsequently rationalized the 'oversight' by stating his own unwillingness to assume a post which had been the graveyard of so many English political reputations. When Dilke was offered the appointment, however, Chamberlain applied strong pressure for him to accept. This embarrassed Dilke and led him to nurse a resentment for some years, for Gladstone declined to attach a place in the cabinet to the post and Dilke would make no move from the Foreign Office which did not bring real promotion. Eventually the Radical G. O. Trevelyan took the post.

Though Parnell kept his promise to revoke the No-Rent manifesto, the new departure was off to a bad start. Chamberlain still insisted in cabinet on a limited coercion measure which would not antagonize Radicals and Nationalists and would allow early introduction of the Arrears Bill, but failed to sway his colleagues. Introducing the new Crimes Act, which Forster regarded as the most stringent measure yet proposed and was to last for three years, Harcourt made matters worse with a tub-thumping law and order speech. Forster himself did the greatest damage. He forced a public reading of the full text of Parnell's letter despite O'Shea's clumsy attempt to omit the passage offering future co-operation. Accusations levelled at the 'Kilmainham Treaty' now made such co-operation a hazardous venture.

Chamberlain, however, was ready to take the risk. Gladstone warned against overt relations with the Nationalists (while himself keeping contact with Parnell through Mrs O'Shea), but Chamberlain set out during the two months of parliamentary obstruction to the Bill secretly to reach agreement with them on satisfactory amendments.[17] He pushed hard in cabinet for changes, periodically threatening resignation and instigating counter-threats from Harcourt and his supporters. Gladstone, however, was able to keep the sides together, and by 11 June had persuaded a majority to accept some at least of Chamberlain's amendments.

It did little to allay Chamberlain's now almost total disenchantment with the direction of government policy. Coercion risked destroying the good standing he and the ministry had reacquired among progressive and Nationalist opinion by his role in the Kilmainham negotiations, and his resignation threats can be seen as a further attempt like that of February 1881 to produce a solution to his political difficulties. And just as the intrusion of South African affairs had provided him then with a useful issue to exploit, so now events in Egypt promised to produce an equally attractive weapon. On 14 June, three days after his limited success in cabinet on coercion, he threw himself into head-on conflict with Gladstone by presenting a memorandum backing demands from Dilke and Hartington for immediate military intervention in Egypt and reparations from its government for recent riot damage in Alexandria.

As in Ireland and South Africa, the British government's problem in Egypt was the mobilisation of local grievances under nationalist banners. The Egyptian army leaders, headed by Arabi, had roused a popular campaign against the puppet Khedive installed by Britain and France in the late 1870s, and against the joint Financial Control through which they regulated his finances to guarantee repayment of the state's massive overseas debts. Facing this threat Britain and France were each anxious to uphold the *status quo* without direct intervention, or any action which might allow the other increased influence over a country spanning the strategic Suez Canal route.[18]

Chamberlain had initially approached this problem from the Little England standpoint taken earlier over the Transvaal, and in January 1882 joined Bright in protesting against an

Anglo-French note reaffirming support for the Control against Arabi's opposition. But when Gladstone, after first taking their side, succumbed to Granville's insistence, the Radicals retired into sulky silence—Granville complained later that neither had commented on a cabinet circular and were boycotting a problem they found unpalatable.[19] Meanwhile he and Gladstone searched for ways of regulating a situation exacerbated rather than calmed by the Note. In planning to overawe Arabi, their prime aim was to gain international support for the threat of either joint Anglo-French, or Turkish, intervention. But when Bismarck set out to exploit the situation to separate France and Britain, the plan soon collapsed: Turkey was inspired to withdraw from a conference at Constantinople on Egypt's debts, and France to revoke her commitment to Turkish intervention when an Anglo-French fleet sent to Alexandria strengthened rather than reduced Arabi's influence. The fading appeal of Gladstone's internationalist strategy, undermined by Bismarck's shrewd manœuvres and by delays which had allowed the consolidation of Arabi's position, received a major setback with reports of riots in Alexandria on 11 June which resulted in several deaths and much damage to foreign property.

This strengthened the hand of Dilke and Hartington who had consistently opposed Gladstone's line. Arabi's threat to the Suez Canal and the Control, they believed, would eventually entail direct intervention: early and, if necessary, unilateral action could alone contain the crisis and avert pre-emptive moves by France.

Before 14 June Chamberlain had taken a back seat on the issue, torn perhaps between Dilke and Bright's radically different views on a crisis on which he had few qualifications to speak. Later he was to claim that his change of tune originated in recognizing Arabi to be a military adventurer rather than a nationalist leader;[20] but since Gladstone himself was tending to the same view, this fails fully to explain Chamberlain's transformation from a Little Englander into what Granville called 'almost the greatest Jingo' in cabinet, and his readiness to join forces with Hartington in challenging his customary allies. Dilke's growing intransigence was perhaps a further factor. He was now attending the cabinet to argue out his disagreement with Granville and, appealing to outraged opinion over the riots—'our side in the Commons are very Jingo . . . They badly want to kill somebody'—threatened that 'Either Arabi goes or I do'.

Chamberlain's reaction to the political crisis in the week following Friday 7 July perhaps adds something further. On that day several Whigs joined the Conservatives to defeat the government on an amendment to Clause 14 of the Crimes Bill which, coming on top of the Nationalist obstruction, persuaded the cabinet to impose a closure on the Bill. The Arrears Bill had been introduced on 5 July, though Hartington still strongly disagreed with Gladstone and Chamberlain on several clauses, and serious trouble was threatened when on 10 July Lord Salisbury announced that he would recommend its rejection by the Lords. Egypt formed a backdrop to these domestic events. On 21 June Gladstone had carried a compromise in cabinet of reinforcing the Alexandria fleet but, when the fleet was threatened by Egyptian reinforcement of a fortress overlooking its moorings, disagreements re-emerged. Despite Bright's strong opposition, Gladstone deferred to his 'jingos' and agreed on 3 July to demand cessation of work on the fort. Refusal was met by the British admiral's decision on the 11th to bombard it, despite the French fleet's withdrawal. Arabi deposed the Khedive in a *coup* and threatened the Canal route. On the 20th the cabinet agreed to request a Vote of Credit for unilateral military intervention to restore control.

In the midst of this tense situation Gladstone twice—on 7 and 11 July—issued the explosive news that he was intent on his immediate resignation. This prospect, long forecast, was conveniently to be raised on several future occasions when Gladstone had his back to the wall against a divided or insurgent cabinet. Ultimately, the value of the Gladstonian umbrella lay in the threat that it would be rolled up, and perhaps converted into an offensive weapon against insubordinate colleagues.

Chamberlain, however, saw the threat as a solution to his problems. His response to the first announcement was to persuade Dilke that resignation with Gladstone, with Irish policy as the pretext, would ease their position on the same grounds as in February 1881. However, their ally Trevelyan was loath to abandon his new office, and Dilke himself, pushing a strong Egyptian policy in part to establish his claims upon a cabinet seat, was reticent about missing the chance. On the 11th Chamberlain turned to a more appealing line: if Gladstone could be persuaded to retire to the relative obscurity of the Lords, the Radicals should consider serving in a Granville or Hartington ministry with tough conditions over offices 'on the grounds that a Liberal Government with a Whig Prime Minister must be Radical'. With Courtney, whom Dilke said they had wanted in cabinet for some time, Dilke himself and Trevelyan in high places, policy towards Ireland and Egypt could be moulded into what they believed would be a more acceptable shape.[21]

This attractive strategy failed to get off the ground. Gladstone had made his threat to impose not abandon control; and, though Hartington anticipated the succession, he and the cabinet right wing were not prepared to let Gladstone go if there were any prospect of an 'unmuzzling' like that of 1876. They agreed to a closure on 8 July after the Whig backbench rebellion over coercion, and to a statement from Gladstone on the 11th that no amendments to the Arrears Bill would be accepted, thereby effectively nullifying Salisbury's resistance.

Furthermore, Gladstone took the wind out of his opponents' sails on Egypt by swinging round to a bellicose position. Convinced now of the improbity of Arabi's conduct—or perhaps acknowledging Courtney's view that 'At last we have done a popular thing: we have bombarded Alexandria'—he pressed for an invasion and accepted, though unwillingly, Bright's resignation in protest at the events. Bright sacrificed office to save his conscience, but his withdrawal in the contemporary climate posed little threat to Chamberlain's decision to stay on, even though Schnadhorst later found it expedient to restrain Bright's circulation of an inflammatory statement through the Federation.

Chamberlain's 'jingo' mood over Egypt requires some comment both because it has been taken as the first real sign of that nationalist, imperialist philosophy he was to expound later in his life, and because the transformation in his stand from January to June was so rapid and so drastic. Certainly he had good grounds for abandoning his customary role as Gladstone's lieutenant. As someone whose instinctive reaction to any débâcle was to search for a new rabbit to pull out of the hat and restore the situation, he could quite well have decided after the Alexandria riots hit the headlines that Dilke and Hartington had shown a better appreciation of the situation than the Prime Minister and must henceforward be supported. Perhaps, too, as his late start over the Bulgarian agitation had shown, he had little instinctive sympathy with Gladstone's Liberal internationalism; and if his first preference for the total non-intervention which Bright advocated could not be met—and certainly after 11 June it was not practical politics—then, with the enthusiasm of a convert, he might have been inclined to go full-steam for unilateral intervention. Even so, the conversion should be seen in a wider context. On Ireland, the dominant contemporary issue, he had just seen his improvised plans for taking over control of government policy collapse in ruins, creating a significant personal rift with Dilke in the process. Added to the subsequent parliamentary confusion, Egypt had brought the ministry's reputation down to rock bottom. In this climate, and with Gladstone apparently increasingly incapable of keeping a firm grasp on his party, it was not unreasonable to consolidate relations with Dilke and work for some alignment that might effect either the remaking or the breaking of a government from which he could see few advantages emerging. The attempt failed, but was still significant: it represented Chamberlain's recognition that on some issues Gladstone's instincts were not to be trusted, and that it might be possible, temporarily, to find common ground with his natural political opponents in the party. The seeds of 1886 had been laid.

As it was, Gladstone held his cabinet intact through the summer by taking a firm line on both Arrears and Egypt. And when he initiated official celebrations for Sir Garnet Wolseley's victory over Arabi at Tel-el-Kebir in September, the paradox of his handling of Egypt was complete: a carefully constructed international operation had materialized in a nationalist jamboree. The boost to the government's reputation was all the greater for Conservative confusion and a politically mistaken bid for Radical defections through opposition to unilateral intervention.

The attitude of the left to this imperialist venture was, however, a source of serious discomfiture to Chamberlain and his change of tack in June had been accompanied by an attempt to change the public justification for intervention. He persuaded Dilke to drop from his memoranda any reference to 'British interests' and to stress instead British responsibilities for restoring peace and the rule of law. The Financial Control and the interests of foreign creditors—the essential issue on which Arabi had clashed with the European governments, but the prime source of Radical suspicion of government policy—were to be downgraded, and Gladstone expressed bewilderment at Chamberlain's speech on the Vote of Credit which argued that intervention would have been necessary had the Control never existed. In a cabinet paper of 21 June, indeed, Chamberlain had invented a new principle of British policy to replace that of upholding the *status quo*: intervention 'should be directed not to impose on Egypt institutions of our choice but to secure for the Egyptian people a free choice for themselves so far as this may not be inconsistent with the permanent interests of other Powers'. Britain's tasks were to restore order, depose Arabi, obtain reparations for the riots, hand over complete control to a reformed Chamber of Notables, Egypt's oligarchic legislature, and then retire. With Gladstone's weighty backing, this general line was accepted, and Chamberlain and Dilke could remove from a dispatch of 13 July references to the interests of foreign creditors.

Egypt, however, proved a running sore over the next three years. It caused Chamberlain severe problems, and he was soon admitting to Bright that intervention had been an error. Though the government's declared aims were along Gladstonian and Little England lines with which he could satisfy his followers, it proved an ambiguous policy, difficult to implement. In October Granville proposed a plan, acceptable he believed to the European powers, to restore the deposed Khedive, appoint a single European financial adviser representing a special council on the public debt in place of the old dual Control, and provide British guarantees for Egyptian independence. Chamberlain, strongly opposed to any outside control of Egyptian finances, called it 'childishly insincere' and demanded again a democratic Chamber which would deal directly with foreign creditors. Hartington too was hostile, though from the contrary position that Britain should assume greater unilateral control. Both, however, as in June, were

implicitly agreed that the Gladstonian attempt to lower international tension by pandering to France's resentment at the
invasion and increasingly obstructionist tactics was an unholy
policy. It would be better, Chamberlain put it, if the government were 'defeated by the selfishness of other nations concerned than that we should sacrifice our principles . . . beforehand. . . . We shall at any rate have discharged our responsibilities and have a fair record with which to appeal to our own
supporters.'[22] For the moment, though, he was not prepared to
push his arguments to the limit. During the last months of 1882
he, Granville, and Hartington thrashed out in committees a
modified version of Granville's scheme, but France's refusal to
accept abolition of the old control broke up the Constantinople
conference, leaving the British cabinet in the lurch with the sole
responsibility which few wanted, for a deeply indebted country.
A new line was called for. Hartington and Chamberlain urged
outflanking France's opposition by appealing for German
support of the agreed plan, while Lord Dufferin was sent off
to Egypt and reported in February 1883 that Britain should
not expect to be out in under twelve months. Changes in the
civil service and army, the education, taxation, and land
systems, and the building of stable political institutions would
all in the meantime have to be undertaken. A year was to prove
an optimistic deadline for a complete social revolution.

Chamberlain was perhaps not unhappy at this postponement of a final decision, which might have entailed choosing
between acceptance of an unpopular policy or resignation. He
was anticipating a new course of government activity in 1883
for which his presence in the cabinet might be vital and which
might allow him to cover over his difficulties. For problems
there were. Despite earlier reticence, he gave full approval to a
special autumn session for enacting disciplinary rules against
Irish parliamentary disruption, but this gave Liberal backbenchers an extra chance to air their grievances. Ireland was
gradually returning to normalcy but the Maamtrasna murders
of August led Spencer to use his powers under the Crimes Act
to the full. Morley began stirring up trouble from the *Pall Mall
Gazette*, but with public opinion largely favourable to Spencer's
régime and the Arrears Bill passed Chamberlain had little
interest in Radical qualms. 'The more I think of the prosecu-

tions . . . the less I like them. But I have said nothing of this to Morley,' he told Dilke, instead working to abate Morley's attacks on the government.[23] In any case, Egypt had to a large extent replaced Ireland as the Radical bugbear, and the con-spiratorial backbench MP, Henry Labouchere, was warning that Churchill was angling for Radical defections with the cry of 'restoring the liberties of the Egyptian people', for which the only antidote was a policy of 'snubbing the bondholders'.[24] Though troops were withdrawn in October 1882, an amend-ment to the 1883 Address was defeated by only thirty-five votes, despite a powerful speech from Dilke.

By the winter of 1882–3 Chamberlain had become very restive. His generous and constructive plans for Ireland had been shunted aside in favour of half-measures that had only just averted catastrophe; he had seen Gladstone fumbling and back-tracking on controversial foreign and colonial issues; the domestic reforms which he regarded as the stuff of politics had so far been checked by successive crises. That the electorate shared his disillusion he believed confirmed by poor by-election results since 1880. Attempts to assert himself in cabinet had produced mixed, though largely unsatisfactory, results, and his supporters outside could well be wondering whether his accept-ance of office had contributed anything to furthering reform causes. It was a situation calculated to lead him into a new initiative. The party, he told Dilke, was 'ripe for a new depar-ture in constructive Radicalism'. Perhaps more accurately, it was a chance to strengthen his position in the leadership by appealing outside the cabinet to the rank and file on clear issues of left-wing principle. Pressing Dilke in November 1882 to 'introduce a distinctly Radical note into your speeches', he himself raised the standard at the Ashton-under-Lyme Liberal Federation meeting later in the month, thereby exciting Spencer's suspicions that 'the way is being paved for a new party on Gladstone's retirement, and that J.C. will try and split us up on the two subjects of Education and Ireland.'[25]

This was not an implausible interpretation. Gladstone's departure in the wake of his taxing Irish labours was being widely rumoured, not least by Gladstone himself. A complete split, however, was probably less in Chamberlain's mind than a reconstruction on the lines suggested in July, though events during the winter made the former a possibility. But Gladstone was not yet ready to abandon his hold on Liberalism. In December he reshuffled his government, making a concession to his age only by giving up the Exchequer to Childers. Due deference was paid to the Radicals by promoting Dilke to the Local Government Board and a cabinet seat, though the overall balance remained largely as before. These changes were in line with Chamberlain's view that the ministry needed to present a new face after living essentially from hand to mouth over the previous two years, and, for the first time, Gladstone instituted cabinets to plan the next session's legislation in advance.

The proposals it considered were a mixed bag. On Chamberlain's patent and bankruptcy measures there was no disagreement, and the important Corrupt Practices Bill caused only minor rumblings. London government reform was seen as an important priority, but cabinet squabbles were so intense that it was eventually shelved indefinitely in 1884. Extensions of tenant right in Britain Chamberlain wanted urgently since it would be 'a great stroke of business. Without it we shall lose the farmers for a certainty.'[26] Collings, his counsel on agrarian matters, was now advocating big plans of land purchase, but for the 1883 session Chamberlain accepted a non-controversial measure extending earlier legislation on compensation for improvements to retiring tenants. Ireland and franchise were Chamberlain's chief interests. He and Gladstone pressed for democratic Irish local government reforms to contain the challenge of Nationalism, but Harcourt and Hartington were as firmly opposed as Forster had been earlier. Ill health compelled Gladstone to rest in France between January and March, leaving Granville to exert well-meaning but weak control over a divided cabinet. The participants tried to impose their views in disharmonious publicity—Hartington at Bacup, Chamberlain at Swansea, and Gladstone in a French newspaper interview—but Hartington emerged successful. Warned by Schnadhorst that 'Justice for Ireland' would not stir the electorate at this stage,[27] Chamberlain refused to force the issue, especially when Gladstone shied away from a confrontation in the unfavourable climate of Fenian bombings in London, capture of the Phoenix Park murderers, and subsequent revelations of Irish underground activities.

On the issue of franchise, which Chamberlain pressed strongly for the first time, Hartington and the moderates also had their way. They resisted him on two lines. One was that English county government reform had been long promised and a further delay imposed by franchise would be a breach of faith. Though the Radicals disapproved, partly through apprehension of a limited measure which would enable old county élites to establish themselves in the new machinery before the labourers had been mobilized on franchise, Dilke was eventually compelled to prepare a scheme which was ultimately dropped through pressure of time. The second point was that franchise should be accompanied by a redistribution measure. Liberal moderates echoed Conservative views, expecting seat redistribution under existing parliamentary conditions to be more restricted than under a reformed House of Commons. Precisely for this reason, and to prevent squabbles over redistribution from weakening party unity on franchise, Chamberlain wanted to separate the two issues. He also had a third reason: it was 'entirely a matter of tactics . . . The very fact that the Tories bitterly oppose the separation of the two questions points conclusively to the probability that this course would be the most advantageous for us to take.'[28] A good agitation against the Tories and the Lords promised to 'unmuzzle' him and 'keep the fire alive'. But Gladstone was again not ready to steer his way through a further whirlpool after the previous two turbulent years. Chamberlain was persuaded to hold fire with a commitment that the issue would definitely be tackled in 1884, but its absence meant that 1883, intended as a year of Liberal revival, dribbled away inconclusively behind a patched-up façade of party unity.

Rebuffed in cabinet, Chamberlain was now straining at the leash. At Swansea on 1 February 1883 he asked Radicals not to forsake continued co-operation with the moderates, but also made clear his unhappiness with a legislative programme which 'errs on the side of moderation'. More significantly, at Birmingham on 30 March he returned to his populist style of the 1870s with a violent attack on Lord Salisbury who had recently spoken in the city. He quoted Shakespeare's 'See what a desperate homicide this Salisbury is' to denounce Conservative policy in Ireland and abroad, and attacked him as chief representative of a degenerate aristocratic influence in politics, the 'spokesman of the class . . . who toil not neither do they spin'. The gibe came from a speech he had delivered a decade before, but, levelled now by a cabinet minister, it created an outcry. Gladstone had already recognized that Chamberlain would soon be trying to build up the franchise issue, and on the same day as the speech promised Dilke that he would stay on to introduce a wide Bill in 1884. Chamberlain was not reassured. On 13 June he flouted the spirit of Bright's jubilee celebrations in Birmingham with an aside against the trappings of monarchy, a call for early settlement of the franchise question, and the expressed hope that the near future would see household replaced by manhood suffrage, payment of MPs and equal electoral districts. Gladstone attempted subsequently to impose discipline, but was rebuffed a fortnight later in a speech at the Cobden Club in which Chamberlain asserted his right to independent declarations on future possibilities.

Though franchise and the possibility of an agitation and election on it were in the forefront of his mind during 1883 Chamberlain was also thinking further ahead. After his speech to the Federation in November 1882 in which free education had been resurrected, he commented to a correspondent that 'It is clear that Socialism is in the air: there was such a ready response to the hint I gave,' and was soon beginning to propound the view that 'the politics of the future are social politics'.[29]

New ideas were indeed afloat, though little influenced by Chamberlain's present politics. In 1883 Andrew Mearns published *The Bitter Cry of Outcast London*—a catalogue of the squalor and overcrowding in London's slums which became an immediate best-seller. It persuaded Lord Salisbury to propagate the housing question, forced Chamberlain to rethink the problems of his municipal days, and led to a great showpiece commission in 1884. Many observers, however, had already been disturbed by events in 1882. Agitations against overcrowding and high rents had arisen in many cities, and the panaceas of high land taxation and land nationalization purveyed respectively by Henry George and Alfred Wallace gained strong support among working-class Radicals. When Morley informed him that 'In London, "Nationalisation of the Land" is the one subject that would furnish a basis for agitation', Chamberlain was compelled to consider how a 'new Radical' leadership, appealing to democratic principles and ostentatiously expressing its objectives in terms of social improvement and the satisfaction of popular grievances, could respond. Questions posed by urban discontent were compounded by Collings's growing insistence that past agrarian legislation and the old Radical panacea of 'free land' were insufficient to deal with contemporary problems of declining agricultural production and rural depopulation.

These factors gave a sharp edge to the franchise campaign which could be claimed, not merely as 'justice to the rural labourer', but as a democratic assault upon the political power of those whose rents came neither from toiling nor from spinning and were the cause of such social distress. In a year marked by sharp contrasts between popular discontent and Liberal 'legitimate grievances' of 'The People' to the conventional ideo-leadership which expected to emerge very much strengthened from the campaign to define its future activity. This was the task Chamberlain set himself in 1883, when he arranged for the publication of a series of articles in the *Fortnightly Review*, co-ordinated by its editor T. H. S. Escott. Escott himself wrote three pieces calling for more democratic government and defining a 'new Radicalism', well-disciplined and popular-democratic in nature, which this would entail; Morley wrote on disestablishment and disendowment; Collings on land reform and measures to improve rural wages and housing; Francis Adams, former secretary of the Education League, on free education and on taxation and finance; and housing was discussed, poorly by the later infamous journalist Frank Harris, and with some force by Chamberlain himself. The articles formed the core of the *Radical Programme* published in July 1885.[30]

Throughout the year, Chamberlain's opponents were denouncing him as a revolutionary Jack Cade or Robespierre, and a socialist wolf in Liberal clothing. Such exaggerated accusations are the common stuff of conservative attempts to discredit reform governments through their more radical ministers, and Chamberlain, like many radicals before and since, rather relished his notoriety as the enemy's prime target. But these shots fell far wide of the mark. 'Socialism' in the 1880s was, admittedly, an even more imprecise concept than today, but there was little socialism, even municipal socialism, in the *Fortnightly*'s pages. There was much talk of 'social politics', society's responsibilities for the welfare of its underprivileged, and a greater role for the state in contrast to the dominant ideology of *laissez-faire* and protection of property rights; but the alternative ideology which loosely bound together the proposals was largely that of classical radical-democracy. The 'new Radicalism' was the old Radicalism's assault on privilege, traditionalism, and the irresponsible social power of 'sinister interests', couched in the context of the 'new democracy' to be created in 1884. 'Free education' was argued for in the same terms as in 1869—Morley's article was a revised version of one he had written in the 1870s. Collings's plans were more original, involving extensive compulsory purchase powers to be allocated to reformed local governments in the counties and designed to replace 'free land' as the Radical method of creating an independent yeomanry in the rural areas. More extensive compulsory purchase powers were also part of Chamberlain's proposals for urban problems, together with Collings's idea for stronger local authority powers to force landlords into housing improvements. He also adopted the scheme devised by J. S. Mill in the 1860s for taxing 'unearned' increments of land value as a financial basis for local authority slum clearance and housing improvements, an imaginative proposal on which one item in Lloyd George's later 'People's Budget' was to be based. These housing measures were the only ones which really lived up to any claim for a concern with 'social politics', and they represented, not so much any ideological transformation on Chamberlain's part, as extended implications of his earlier concern with municipal improvement. And, like municipal socialism and the civic gospel, a mixture of motives lay behind them. Primarily Chamberlain argued a practical case for making slum-clearance easier and throwing the financial burdens of improvement more on to slum landlords, and those who benefited from slum-clearance, than on to the ratepayer: at the same time he commended to

Radical friends the political expediency of taking 'the wind out of Salisbury's sails'.[31]

If Radicalism made no ideological breakthrough in 1883, neither did it become 'revolutionary'. Chamberlain and his colleagues were as much 'old parliamentary hands' as Gladstone, perennially conscious that they were selling Radicalism to an electorate in which the average working-class Liberal voter was as much a respectable, constitutional adherent to Victorian middle-class values as the middle-class activist who ran the constituency associations. Indeed, one recent biographer has seen Chamberlain's programme as essentially counter-revolutionary, aimed at pre-empting fundamentalist attacks on private property from the working-class support which George, Wallace, and H. M. Hyndman's Marxist Social Democratic Federation acquired in the 1880s.[32] Killing class agitations with kindness was perhaps an inspiration for Salisbury's concern with housing at this time, but, though Chamberlain had strong objections to truly socialist or confiscatory proposals which he considered politically impracticable and unrelated to the immediate issues of rural decline and urban overcrowding, at the forefront of his mind in forming his own plans was the central political task—how to harness the 'legitimate grievances' of 'The People' to the conventional ideologies of the Liberal left, and thereby promote a *coup* in the party which would still inherit the centrist opinion which had made Liberalism the dominant force for a generation.

These long-term policies continued to be formulated independently of the real contemporary issue. In speeches throughout the 1883 autumn recess Chamberlain called for a thorough county franchise measure with total resistance to any recalcitrant stand by the Lords, and he publicly challenged Hartington's criticisms of his mobilization of the Federation. Hartington's hostility to a generous measure, particularly for Ireland, and insistence on a simultaneous redistribution Bill were the chief problems of the winter cabinets. Chamberlain recognized his disinclination to ally with intransigent anti-democrats like Goschen and thereby to put himself outside the party consensus—'Why does Hartington think aloud when he thinks one thing and means to do another?'—but was tempted to exploit the opportunities provided by Hartington's bid to consolidate the party moderates and right wing and his periodically threatened resignations, pressing Dilke, a member of the cabinet committee framing the Bill, in January 1884 to 'make Hartington go out on Franchise'. Gladstone, however, sharing Chamberlain's view that the government now desperately needed a new cry and an extended political base, had yet no wish to alienate his conservative wing. He compelled Hartington to accept the principles of a broad scheme by offering sufficient sops on the details to save his face.

The united government front overrode intense Conservative opposition in the Commons, but on 8 July the barrier everyone had forecast was erected: the Lords refused to approve the Bill without an accompanying redistribution measure. Gladstone, anticipating an unleashing of Radical fury and ready to exploit it, was yet intent on keeping it within bounds. He called a party meeting on 10 July to promise a reintroduction of the Bill in an autumn session, but insisted that speeches in the recess be limited to condemnation of the Lords' action and not entail commitments on future action towards them. 'Mend Them or End Them' was, however, added to 'The Peers against the People' in appeals from Liberal platforms, while Chamberlain set out to realize his ambition of a great campaign of 'the masses' against 'the classes', bitterly denouncing the Lords in speeches throughout the country and heading a huge protest march through London. Reproaches arrived from Gladstone, under pressure from Hartington and the Queen, and his notoriety was enhanced by the Aston Riot in mid-October when a meeting in Birmingham addressed by Churchill was broken up violently by a mob.

The franchise agitation was a strange affair. If modern historians of the 1832 and 1867 Reform Acts have increasingly stressed that they were less the product of popular pressure than of initiatives from parliamentary leaders, even more so can it be said of the 1884 Act. There is no evidence of any great popular demand for the Act nor, indeed, of any great reaction; meetings were generally peaceful, and essentially the stage for party activists to harangue already loyal party supporters. Its roots lay in the need of the party leaders to revive public interest in them after four confused, disillusioning years and rally the party faithful; Chamberlain particularly needed to restore his

Radical credentials and produce some means to break through the strait-jacket of Gladstonian Liberalism, while Gladstone himself had every interest in becoming 'The People's William' again to restore the waning popularity of his ministry and reimpose his authority on increasingly discontented subordinates. His speeches in the autumn, though fewer and far more moderate than Chamberlain's, proved singularly effective in doing so. Chamberlain had much of his thunder stolen, while the Aston Riot became a source of acute embarrassment. The Liberal caucus was heavily implicated, and proof that Schnadhorst had subsequently prepared false affidavits was revealed only just late enough for Chamberlain narrowly to overcome a critical vote in the Commons.

His 'unmuzzling' encountered further setbacks. In taking to the platform again, Gladstone was working to counter Chamberlain's plan for a confrontation with the Lords in favour of a compromise over the redistribution issue, and Chamberlain became increasingly agitated during the autumn session by the rumours of inter-party discussions. Negotiations with Salisbury were in fact proceeding, which reached a conclusion in the Arlington Street compact of mid-November. Here Salisbury agreed to ease franchise through the Lords for the promise of immediate introduction of a mutually acceptable redistribution Bill.

This compromise arose partly from the desire of both sides to avoid confrontation, partly through Salisbury's conversion to the idea of a 'democratic' redistribution which the Liberals would have found it hard to dismiss. In outline, it entailed replacing the existing system by one consisting largely of single-member constituencies roughly comparable in size. This proposal was not entirely welcome to Chamberlain and many Liberals. It threatened to wipe out small Liberal county boroughs, to stop the old tactic of putting Whig and Radical candidates in harness—with unpredictable consequences for the strength of the latter—and to undermine the role of local caucuses in allocating votes between different candidates: Dilke claimed that Chamberlain was only won to the final settlement by the allocation of seven seats to Birmingham and hints that the Bill might well prove unacceptable to the Commons. Chamberlain, however, was opposed not merely to the scheme but to any compromise which prevented the 'Peers against the People' election for which he was angling. Parading 'no surrender' from the platform, he had tolerated the discussions only because he believed them doomed to failure and because Dilke had chief responsibility for them on the Liberal side. When Dilke sold the pass to bring off a major political *coup*, Chamberlain was left isolated in a cabinet relieved at the aversion of a constitutional crisis, and had to work hard on Morley and other Radical followers to acquiesce in what he was compelled to claim as Salisbury's capitulation. In reality Salisbury had, on balance, won, by averting a crisis and ultimately providing Conservatism with stronger roots in the rural suburbs and extended county boroughs. Chamberlain, failing to build up the great confrontation, had to return to problems which he had hoped to shunt aside in the great campaign.[33]

Of these, Egypt was the most taxing. To the problems of its financial difficulties had now been added that of the Mahdi's rebellion in its Sudanese dependency. Britain's military withdrawal from Egypt, planned for late 1883, had to be postponed and, when Egyptian garrisons in the Sudan found themselves cut off, the government was forced to take further responsibility. Two decisions were taken early in 1884: the Khedive, newly restored against Chamberlain's wishes, was ordered to abandon the Sudan, and a cabinet committee, including Dilke but not Chamberlain, sent General Gordon with an Egyptian relief force to rescue garrisons in the south. All might have been well but for two things. Further Egyptian military defeats in February effectively isolated Gordon in his base at Khartoum; and Gordon soon stepped beyond his brief, obsessed with the idea of standing up to the Mahdi and restoring order and 'civilization' to the Sudan.

This situation soon began to polarize cabinets on lines similar to those of June 1882. Despite growing public hysteria over Gordon's fate, Gladstone and Granville were intent on Gordon extricating himself without further British involvement. Their optimism was not shared by Chamberlain, Dilke, and Hartington, apprehensive that Gladstone's prevarications would repeat the crisis of June 1882. From February to July, arguments went on over the question of a relief expedition but, with only confusing information at their disposal, the 'jingos' were unable to secure clear majority support. To meet a cen-sure motion in the Commons on 14 February, Gladstone agreed to send extra marines to the Sudanese Red Sea ports and to ask Gordon whether he required extra forces. This secured a Commons majority of forty-nine, but an adverse vote of 100 was registered in the Lords. Later, the slave trade was re-established in the hope of restoring Gordon's authority, though Chamberlain checked a request from Gordon in March to have the slave trader, Zobehr, released from exile to help him. The situation became increasingly confused, and a snap vote in a small house brought a government defeat on 15 March. Though the cabinet in late April decided, by a majority of six to five, on a relief force, Hartington's War Office staff insisted on a large army manœuvre which the Radicals firmly opposed, suspicious that Hartington was angling for reconquest of the Sudan and anxious for a rapid naval advance along the Nile which could quickly relieve Gordon and retire. By its initial decision, the government overcame a censure motion of 13 May with a small majority, but subsequent squabbles allowed Gladstone to impose further delay. Only on 5 August, to head off the resignations of Hartington and Lord Selborne, did he agree to seek a Vote of credit for the War Office's proposed expedition, though this did not check the Radicals' continued opposition—'Hartington is getting his own way about the Nile expedition—and bang go 5 millions,' Chamberlain commented on 12 September. Sir Garnet Wolseley's army soon began its slow crawl up the Nile, and, as the new year was to show, the successive delays portended disaster.

For the government, and for Chamberlain in particular, this problem had been a disastrous intrusion into the chief political event of 1884. His Birmingham supporters were restive at the possibility of a victory for Gordon's clear attempts to commit the government to the Sudan, and he could only fob them off. On 10 March he excused himself to Dr Dale from discussing problems connected with the Red Sea garrisons on the grounds of being too tied up in other business and the Opposition's failure to make the issue a point of attack. Two days before the critical May vote he could write to Bunce that 'the fact is that the "rebels" in the Sudan are the only people who are honestly carrying out the policy of the British Government, and Gordon

himself is the real "False Prophet". All this excitement is got up
to force us into a Protectorate.' While condemning the idea of
a large relief force, he disingenuously omitted to note that
in cabinet he was a leading advocate of immediate military
activity.[34]

In the Commons the situation was even more difficult, and
it was a widely held view throughout the session that Egypt had
put the government's fate in the balance. Since his entry into
Parliament in 1883, Morley had been attempting to build a
strong 'Peace Party' on the backbenches around the Egyptian
question, while Forster and Goschen were threatening a breakaway in favour of direct British responsibility for Egypt and the
Sudan. The Conservatives were set on exploiting the situation,
and Chamberlain had been told that Churchill's express aim
was that 'time ought to be occupied next session in any nonsense so as to throw back the Reform Bill.'[35] Pressing in cabinet
for an expedition was Chamberlain's way of ensuring that
no 'Palmerstonian' cave brought the government down, but at
the same time he was in constant touch with Radicals to prevent
them 'playing the Tory game'. Concentrating their minds on
franchise both furthered his prime aim of passing the Bill, and
deflected attention from his own embarrassment on Egypt—
Morley's weakness was that he was 'incapable of setting aside
minor considerations in the pursuit of a broad general policy'.[36]

Internal Egyptian problems also plagued the government
throughout the year. To deal with its debts Childers had
offered three alternatives in early 1884—continued British
presence until Egypt's finances improved of their own accord;
direct British control and responsibility for her solvency; or
British guarantees for a large foreign loan. With reservations,
the cabinet agreed on 2 April to propose the third to a reconvened international conference. Despite earlier acceptance of
this policy, Chamberlain had now changed his mind, concluding from the parliamentary situation that Childers's proposal could not be carried 'against the Tories and Radicals'.
On 22 March he and Harcourt, throughout discussions the
most earnest advocate of an early evacuation, had indeed
presented a far more radical plan for Britain simply to retire
from the country, liquidate its debts, and abandon all further
responsibility. One further matter to be settled before the con-

ference, due in June, was the length of Britain's stay in Egypt. And though the declared policy was an early withdrawal, pressure from Parliament and the press was growing for direct British control, a policy articulated in cabinet by Hartington. Chamberlain could not accept something 'which means annexation, *English guarantees for the bondholders' debts*, and in the long run war with France',[37] and the cabinet agreed. A compromise was reached that a British presence should be limited to three and a half years—though Gladstone and Dilke pressed for one year, and Hartington and Northbrook for five—with Egypt thereafter to become a neutral area. Chamberlain had suggested carrying this with a cry for Egypt to be the 'Belgium of the East'. Hartington, though accepting the policy, turned his nose up at the phrase.

The most important decision taken was that Britain's guarantee under the Childers plan must be accompanied by reduced repayments of the Egyptian debt—an essentially symbolic gesture to 'snub the bondholders', France's rejection of which broke up the conference in early August. Chamberlain, having accepted the plan reluctantly and threatened resignation were it departed from, now reverted to his former plea for early neutralization of the area and threatening France with a declaration of bankruptcy. Once again the cabinet rebuffed him, this time in favour of a mission under Lord Northbrook to study Egypt's problems on the spot. But Northbrook '"bitched" the whole concern', as Gladstone put it, by reporting in favour of diverting the debt funds to cover administrative costs contrary to international agreement, a British loan of nine millions, and an indefinite occupation. Accepted by the cabinet on 19 November, the proposal was subsequently quashed by Gladstone, like Chamberlain in the minority, and further overtures were made to France on the June scheme.

Chamberlain and Dilke had observed that discussions on the conference always took up two or three hours of cabinet time, 'and [Gordon] five minutes at the fag-end of business'. This was testimony to the issue's complexity, and to the problems of steering between the Scylla of alienating the European powers and the Charybdis of having to present Parliament with a sell-out to France and Egypt's creditors. It also said something about Gladstone, who could occupy his time fiddling with the

financial complexities so dear to his heart and put from his mind
the possibility of a conflagration at Khartoum. But the extended
discussions were not totally unwelcome to Chamberlain. Unable to get his own policy accepted, he foresaw the prospect if a
final decision were taken of either having to acquiesce in a
policy which might antagonize his supporters and possibly
bring down the government, or resigning. Both might be disastrous in the midst of the franchise controversy. As he told
Dilke at one stage: 'We cannot agree to [Northbrook's] plan—
and if we did we should be beaten in the House. We must do all
we can to postpone till after Franchise.' Alongside this essentially negative approach he was, however, also taking more
positive steps in line with the government's general strategy of
drawing Bismarck away from his obstreperous policy of
dividing the 'Concert of Europe' and persuading him to apply
pressure on France. As Chamberlain commented before the
crucial 19 November cabinet, this 'would take time—and if we
could conciliate him, we might do what we like.' Bismarck,
needless to say, was no fool, and had been taking advantage of
his pivotal position to launch a bid for territory in sensitive
colonial areas. The series of *coups* which he brought off at
Britain's expense during the autumn and winter in New
Guinea, East Africa, Cameroons, and South-West Africa provoked a storm of criticism of the government's weakness. Dilke
was particularly annoyed, noting that he had formally annexed
the Cameroons two years before but that nothing had been
done to implement it. 'If the Board of Trade and the Local
Government Board managed their business after the fashion of
the Foreign Office and Colonial Office, you and I would deserve
to be hung,' was Chamberlain's comment. Yet both shared
Gladstone and Granville's view that no British interest was
seriously threatened by German colonization, and that the
important thing was to 'square' Bismarck over Egypt.

More importantly, though, whereas the Colonial and
Foreign Offices were unwilling to give Bismarck a totally free
hand, Chamberlain was actively working for a policy of
appeasement. In early 1885 he was to lament that 'We profess
to approve of their enterprise in general, but we object to every
single application. Where *can* they go and be d . . . d by themselves without our protesting'; but as early as July he had

contacted the German Chancellor's son, Herbert, and praised Germany's help over Egypt while condemning his own Foreign office for 'clumsiness' in its colonial dealings (though he subsequently discovered that Germany herself had been less than straightforward). Unlike other politicians, he was not worried at the threat to Britain's hegemony in South Africa from German expansionism in the area:

For us the whole of South Africa is a burden; if I had had to deal with you I should have said that we would have seen with pleasure Germany establishing herself in Africa . . . I should tell that thorny colony straight out, 'Take care of yourself and declare your independence if you want to'. All we want is Cape Town and the Bay for a coaling station. We can do without the rest; we should be better off.[38]

This opinion represented a blunt, oversimplified, version of what many modern historians have considered the central interest in mid-Victorian imperial policy towards southern Africa.[39] But in 1884 the government took a step in relation to the Transvaal which can be interpreted as a sharp change in attitude towards the hinterland. Since 1881, land-hungry Boer 'freebooters' had spread into the native areas of Zululand, Swaziland, and Bechuanaland. Their presence in the last threatened to link up with Germany's in Angra Pequina, encircling the Cape and spanning routes into the interior. British intervention to avert this was widely called for at home and in the colony, and it might appear at first sight to represent a major development in Chamberlain's attitudes to problems of imperial security that in October 1884 he became a vociferous advocate of military action to drive the Boers back into their ghetto beyond the Vaal.

Expansion by the freebooters had troubled him since the Convention of 1881, reflecting the persistent ambiguity of the British Radical conscience. The strict non-interventionism of Little England attitudes has always combined uneasily with an ascription of responsibility for British governments actively to oppose international injustice and to impose 'civilized' behaviour upon recalcitrant peoples and states. Events in South Africa in 1877–81 had allowed Chamberlain and Dilke to

operate consistently with both attitudes. Through simple opposition to British 'imperialism' they could flirt with the
humanitarian, missionary zeal of the Aborigines Protection
Society in condemning the Zulu War, while supporting the
cause of Boer independence against Frere's annexation: when
Boer settlers took to expropriating land from the natives, the
matter became less simple. And with the cause of the Bechuana
tribes being canvassed by the Revd John McKenzie, promi-
nently supported by Dr Dale and other Nonconformist leaders,
Chamberlain's difficulties were accentuated. His fundamental
views largely reflected the non-interventionism of Kimberley
and his successor as Colonial Secretary after 1882, Lord Derby,
and in September 1882 he told Dale that a risk of antagonizing
the Cape Afrikaners made direct British intervention impossible. Though supporting an unsuccessful demand from
Dilke and Hartington for an expedition in March 1883, he was
a reluctant imperialist; Gladstone easily split the 'forward'
party by inviting him to lead for the government in the Commons, and Dilke, having declined the task, was correspondingly
upset: 'Chmn. will speak in my place. He sided with me in the
Cabinet—but in reality his opinion is with Mr G.' In April
Chamberlain was reinforcing Derby by informing him that,
despite outside pressure, he wanted both Britain and the Cape
to abandon responsibility for the Basuto natives. Yet by
December he was pressing again for an expedition to Bechuanaland—an event perhaps not unrelated to the imminence of a
further McKenzie campaign. That both he and Dilke successfully checked Derby's plan to assume a protectorate over the
Zulus in March 1884 suggests that neither were particularly
keen to stand up to the Boers nor anxious for the natives' welfare
if this entailed permanent British commitments.

Hopes of a settlement were put in the February 1884 London
Convention which extended the Transvaal's internal political
autonomy while delimiting her territorial sovereignty, but the
freebooters came on, and when President Kruger determined
to test the British government's resolution by formally annexing
part of Bechuanaland in September 1884, the time for decision
had come. With a growing public outcry over Germany's
successful colonial gambits, the government had to act, and,
unwilling to fight the German giant, it decided on an expedition

under General Warren against the Boer pygmy which eventually persuaded the settlers to withdraw.

Chamberlain was absent from the 6 October cabinet which took the crucial decision but sent in a paper strongly urging an expedition and worked to build up support for it beforehand. His simple line was that, for parliamentary reasons, and for better or for worse, the government had publicly acknowledged its responsibilities to the natives after the Convention, and Parliament would not tolerate abandoning them now. Like everyone else, he could foresee a possible upset on the question in the autumn franchise session, but there were perhaps further considerations in his mind. Lord Derby's star, in the ascendant when he joined the government after deserting Disraeli in 1878, had gradually waned as his indecision and inability to develop clear lines of policy without Gladstone's guidance became increasingly clear to the cabinet. His decline ran parallel to that of Granville over the Egyptian policy, or lack of one, and both were the subject of wide public criticism. In October 1884, Derby had become a sitting target for those in cabinet discontented with 'Gladstonian' foreign policies—Hartington's 'jingo' wing and the tough-minded Radicals, Dilke and Chamberlain, though over South Africa at least the latter had shown no less uncertainty than Derby. Chamberlain perhaps also had a further point in his mind. Discussing Egypt again with Herbert Bismarck during a visit to the continent in September, he had repeated his earlier conciliatory gestures, noting that 'I perfectly understand that your Government is at present out of humour with us, and I shall try to mend it.' His subsequent comment to Dilke was that '[Herbert Bismarck] does not explain what are the precise things he wants of us, but I begin to think that nothing short of a change in the Colonial Minister will satisfy him.'[40] Derby had requested a Bechuana expedition from the 6 October cabinet, but suggested delay until the reconvened Cape Parliament decided whether to join and assume subsequent responsibility for the area. Chamberlain, taking a front seat on the issue for the first time, made this further temporization the major point of attack, and, together with Hartington, he was making a determined attempt to take responsibility for policy out of Derby's hands.

The possibility of 'shunting' Derby to get a line of policy

acceptable to Germany, and through Germany to France and to Parliament over Egypt, was in January 1885 to become an important aspect of an intended cabinet *coup* planned by Harcourt against the 'Gladstonians'. A 'kite', flown in the *Pall Mall Gazette* by a former Cape minister, F. X. Merriman, after talks with Chamberlain in November 1884, suggests that Chamberlain himself had anticipated this. Chamberlain had apparently given an exaggerated picture of his determination to uphold the 'imperial factor'—i.e. a pro-native policy—in South Africa, and, in criticizing incompetent management at the Colonial Office, Merriman claimed there was a need for men 'who make a business of their work'. He had seen 'only one or two business men in the whole company. Mr Chamberlain, for instance, is a workman. He would push the thing through if he had it in hand.'[41] Just as Morley had been used against Forster in 1882, so now Merriman was being used against Derby. Given his continuing role as government spokesman on South Africa in the Commons, Chamberlain might well have anticipated a lift into the Colonial Office. November, too, was a good time to plan ahead, with the franchise crisis drawing to a close and further rumours in the air of ministerial changes and possibly Gladstone's early retirement.

Such currents of discontent and movements for major political changes were to come to the surface in January, but they meant that the year 1884 ended for Chamberlain on a note of some uncertainty. He could look back over almost five years of office with considerable misgivings. The Reform Bill from which he had hoped in 1880 for a speedy shift in the balance of power within Liberalism had been delayed, and in the interim his own and the government's reputation had been severely compromised by successive problems. Its passage too had added to the damage: Gladstone reasserted his public authority, leaving Chamberlain stranded with the 'no surrender' cry; the Aston Riot was a major embarrassment, coming at a time when several Tories and right wing Liberals had launched a smear campaign against his supposedly ruthless past business practices in Birmingham and his use of the Board of Trade to provide patronage for party workers (a charge from which he was able to defend himself, though it was certainly true that Birmingham municipal appointments were not entirely on the basis of merit). Franchise had also diverted attention from a major issue on which he hoped to make his name as a constructive legislator—the Merchant Shipping Bill.

Based on Samuel Plimsoll's ideas for increasing safety at sea and preventing over-insurance of unseaworthy vessels, this proposal had been held up until 1884 when Schnadhorst could point out that 'There is a good deal of feeling on the matter though it conflicts somewhat with the question of Reform.' Chamberlain found that his argument against weakening the party on Egypt applied equally to shipping. Opposition from shipowners, strongly represented among the Liberals, was furious, and though Chamberlain had been preparing the way with moderate utterances since 1881, he could not persuade the cabinet to make it a matter of principle—despite an offer, though not a threat, of resignation—nor generate wide parliamentary support. Unable to guarantee a Second Reading, he withdrew the Bill in July.

The defeat infuriated him, but he had partly brought it on himself. He refused to co-operate with the shipowners in preparing the Bill except on a formal shipping council which his own officials and insurance underwriters would have dominated, and in speeches at Birmingham in January, and in introducing the Second Reading in the Commons, indicted the shipowners and catalogued extreme cases of over-insurance. He insisted on a wide Bill rather than reform by stages as subsequent governments were to proceed, and set out to fight his opponents rather than conciliate them. Committed by past speeches to a major reform, he appears to have decided to go down with flags flying rather than engage in an extended squabble entailing compromise and interference in the franchise agitation. Practical legislation yielded to the broader aim of enhancing his own popular strength.

This fighting spirit had proved both an asset and a weakness since 1880. Periodically he had forced the cabinet to go against its natural inclinations and respond to left-wing opinion with some well-calculated threat to resign or extravagant public pronouncement. His truculence and suspected disloyalty, however, and sometimes simplistic proposals which betrayed little acknowledgement of general opinion in the parliamentary party, effectively nullified the powers of personal persuasion which he had successfully brought to bear in the state councils of Birmingham. This, in its turn, reinforced earlier prejudices. One was that the quarrelsome Liberals and their leaders could only respond effectively to the new problems they were facing with firm discipline. Gladstone himself was increasingly prone to this view, but from his humble cabinet position Chamberlain was conscious that his own capacity to impose coherence, and to force through the policies he thought necessary, depended on the extent to which he could control parliamentary politics through the extra-parliamentary mechanisms of the platform and the mass party. A second, related, view was expressed in the opinion he delivered in 1885 that he would never again serve in a cabinet on the lines of that of 1880; yet, despite an instinctive temptation in times of crisis to challenge the Liberal coalition with some new political line-up, Chamberlain had shown by his actions a sound aversion to casting himself into the rain-swept terrain beyond the Gladstonian umbrella. Reconciling the aspiration with a disposition towards caution precluded re-adopting the early-1870s idea of a wholly new Radical Party: the task could only be accomplished by sloughing off or beating into submission the conservative prop of the coalition with some dramatic manœuvre in the very near future.

The main thrust of Chamberlain's politics were thus set very much in the same grooves as in 1880. But, as we have observed, the concept of 'social politics' was creeping up on his agenda, partly because of a sense that the time for tackling the old issue of free education was fast approaching, partly because of the housing and agrarian problems brought into prominence during his period of office. There was also his work at the Board of Trade. None of the legislation he tackled was entirely the product of his own inspiration. The 1880 Employer Liability Act, establishing the rights of employees in certain industries to claim against negligence on the part of employers in cases of injury, arose out of a select committee report and private members' Bills which had earlier been adopted by Disraeli's govern-ment. The bankruptcy, patents and cheap trains legislation reflected a broad consensus in business circles on the need for clearing up confusion on these subjects and creating a better infrastructure for commercial progress. His abortive Merchant

Shipping and Railway Rates Bills of 1884 (the latter designed to reduce transport costs for agricultural commodities and industrial goods produced in inland areas like Birmingham, and thereby improve their competitiveness) both arose out of growing pressure in parliament. They all, however, had two things in common—that in one way or another they were protective, 'constructionist' measures which increased the regulative powers of his department over existing rights of property and 'free contract', and that at the same time they were representative of the normal legislative activity in which contemporary governments had grown accustomed to indulge. Beneath the froth of the 'great issues' which shaped party-political debate, the main current of the Victorian state was moving inexorably towards interference and regulation. Two points of relevance for Chamberlain's politics need to be made. One was that in his ministerial capacity Chamberlain showed a particular readiness to mould his measures, and his justification for them, in a distinctly populist manner. The Merchant Shipping Bill, which had as much to offer insurance companies and respectable shippers as sailors in unsafe vessels, symbolized this most clearly: the Railway Rates Bill, designed to increase the competitiveness of domestic producers against foreign imports, was phrased as a conflict between The People and the special interests of railway shareholders, who in this instance for the moment proved victorious. That the welfare of the many needed some sacrifice by the few of their immediate interests was a permanent element in Chamberlain's politics until the late 1890s: his experience in the early 1880s points to the second comment. In the Birmingham mayoralty it had required the mobilization of a powerful, popular 'socialist' ideology to clear away the opposition to necessary improvement schemes by the local authority. In national politics, legislation on comparable 'improvements' was being held up by entrenched interests hiding behind the dominant myths of *laissez-faire* and private property rights. In 1885, Chamberlain's new 'Radical Programme' set out to discard the dead wood of an outmoded conception of government activity, wholly irrelevant to the realities of contemporary political life.

While Chamberlain remained firmly convinced that Liberalism's future was bound up in its capacity to deliver major domestic reforms, there had emerged in the years after 1880 aspects of his character and his approach to certain problems that had earlier been obscure. Irish and colonial difficulties had shown that, rather than possessing any instinctive sympathy for ideas of national self-determination, he was more inclined to pragmatic solutions of practical difficulties in Britain's colonial or imperial relationships. Non-intervention might generally promise to entail lower costs and fewer resulting complications, but not invariably. Nor had he any basic aversion to the use of arms or sweeping legal powers if this was necessary to contain challenges to government policy or authority. 'Legitimate grievances' must be met, but the conscience of the left had to be held in check if there was a need to bring dissidence under control.

In relation to the ministry's colonial troubles, Dilke once observed that his and Chamberlain's difficulties came from holding Radical views on domestic policy with firmly 'patriotic' ones on foreign affairs. What he meant by 'patriotic' was left unclear. Historians of the late nineteenth century have frequently identified contrasting views among imperial policy-makers—between those favouring 'forward' policies, and 'consolidationists': between those wishing to maintain 'informal' influence over dependent countries and extend devolution to the colonies, and those who saw the solution to problems in terms of greater 'Downing Street government': between those whose priority was strengthening the Concert of Europe, and those prepared to risk its unity for more nationally self-interested purposes. In terms of these categories, Chamberlain's behaviour in this period appears less like a coherent policy than a reaction. Related politically to Little England and pacifist opinion, which were effectively out in the cold, and holding down a minor domestic post with no responsibilities for administering foreign policy, he tended to treat overseas problems as an irritating embarrassment rather than a continuing interest. The effect was a form of Little Englandism by default, which periodically erupted in outraged nationalistic enthusiasm for adventures which might, somehow, sort things out. Crudely summarized, his method seemed to be—keep out of things if you can, but if commitments have foolishly been undertaken, and problems arise, take swift action to intervene, retire before the public absorbs what is happening, and inform interested foreign parties that a blooded nose will result from poking it in then or later. Events proved too complex for this line, which found him tied to an indefinite occupation of Egypt, a British protectorate over Bechuanaland which he was anxious to avoid, and almost a reconquest of the Sudan.

Later he made two significant judgements on these years. One was that he grew 'fed up with being kicked all over Europe', the other that the cabinet had dithered and delayed in the face of mounting public criticism, producing a 'policy of drifting which fairly laid the government open to the censure of its opponents'. Chamberlain's temperament inclined him to clear, decisive action and lines of policy, and reacted strongly against submission to what he considered provocative or non-co-operative attitudes: he was 'patriotic' by instinct, rather than carefully thought-out conviction. Gradually this had turned him against Gladstone's proclivity for engineering international and cabinet consensus as he saw its invariable failure to bring success or to maintain public support. The alternatives in terms of his present political position were not easy to formulate. Early in 1885 he described himself as 'steering between Jingoism and peace-at-any-price' in a speech on German colonization, calling it 'awfully difficult work'. But if in the speech he disavowed extreme nationalist reactions to foreign annexations, claiming that 'I do not think that the democracy will have any love for a policy of aggression and intervention . . . I anticipate . . . that you will give no assistance to the party who are clamouring for what they call a strong foreign policy', yet he also showed a growing capacity to manipulate symbols of national and imperial honour. Other nations could not act with impunity without raising 'the old spirit of Englishmen'; and British colonies, 'whose prosperity and welfare are viewed with the liveliest satisfaction by every Englishman', might be sure that 'the English democracy will stand shoulder to shoulder throughout the world to maintain the honour and integrity of the Empire.'[42] By 1885 John Morley was moving towards the view that developing the Midlothian campaign into a consistent programme of anti-imperialism was likely to prove the key to future Liberal progress.[43] The implication of Chamberlain's stand, however, was that if a radicalized Liberalism was to survive as a national party, it could not afford to abandon its Palmerstonian heritage. When Gladstone went for Home Rule in 1886 it was to be on the issues of national and imperial strength that Chamberlain took his stand.

That crisis was also to reveal the true nature of Chamberlain's relations with his leader. So far as the Radical rank and file were concerned, Chamberlain was 'Gladstone's lieutenant', a loyal supporter who occasionally had to push Gladstone in directions he would himself wish to go were he not restrained by the conservatism of his Whig colleagues. Periodically, too, Chamberlain gave the impression that he was on terms of particular intimacy with the Grand Old Man. Neither view had much truth in it. Despite his provincial commercial origins, Gladstone had passed his long career largely in patrician and intellectual circles: Chamberlain's uncultured style and interests were not the material out of which any close personal bond could be created. Moreover, it was a central part of Gladstone's purpose in politics to help the gentlemanly aristocratic and professional cliques which had maintained political control after the 1832 middle-class franchise to survive the working-class ones of 1867 and 1884—crudely, to save the Whigs from their own limitations. Whilst identifying with the aspirations of Radicalism, his aim was to nurse conservative Liberals with moderately progressive measures for fear of finding something worse. He exercised control by personal charisma, over Dissent and Radicalism on the platform, in cabinet through a hand-picked cadre of honourable members of the nobility who could be trusted broadly to follow his lead. Those who failed to fall under the spell were kept at a safe personal distance. Radical spokesmen were tolerated in his circle so long as they kept their place and talked harmless rhetoric—Bright, with his tendency to moralize about international affairs and the laws of free trade economics, struck particularly sympathetic chords, but Forster had soon lost favour when he broke the rules and threatened to become more whiggish than the Whigs.

Chamberlain and Dilke had long since seen through this game—'that inveterate old Tory', Chamberlain had called him not many years before. Yet, though convinced of his own capacity to shrug off Gladstone's humbug, he was still held fascinated by the G. O. M.'s enormous power and ingenuity. Gladstone's very aloofness from his colleagues made his attractions that much stronger when he deigned to lend an ear to his subordinates' opinions, and throughout 1885 Chamberlain's political strategy was to be periodically revised as his leader blew hot and cold in his direction. Chamberlain also believed in his capacity to use Gladstone for his own purposes: in practice, as the Irish and franchise issues in particular had displayed, Gladstone had allowed Chamberlain his head, set him at loggerheads with Hartington, and then blithely assumed a middle ground which isolated the pair and compelled their acquiescence. It was, however, not a tactic which always succeeded. Chamberlain's ambitions for real power, his instability on colonial questions, and the implications of his constructionist views, threatened the basis on which Gladstonian Liberalism operated. This was already exciting Gladstone's suspicions. In 1885 he was to prove his ability, once more, to contain the threat, but in the process destroyed the last of Chamberlain's illusions. When Chamberlain set about openly challenging him on Home Rule, and, moreover, displayed an ability to deploy Gladstonian ingenuity and dissemblance as successfully as the master, but in his own typically blatant and abrasive manner, Gladstone's reservations about his 'lieutenant' turned into open personal hostility.

CHAPTER 5

Diamond Cut Diamond. 1885–1886

Four and a half troubled years of governing had caused perpetual squabbles and intrigues within the Liberal leadership, but its unity and (as had not been the case in the years 1868–74) that of the mass party, had largely been maintained. Ministers were conscious that they had lost popularity, and Chamberlain particularly was worried that not enough had been done to keep its Radical workers and voters in line. Yet throughout 1885 all remained confident that the 'new democracy' would support them against a weak and divided Tory party. Gladstone himself was committed to an early retirement—to the great relief of most of his senior colleagues who were now inclined to throw the blame for the ministry's problems on his head and were increasingly determined to avoid any future cabinet formed on the lines of that of 1880. The Radicals especially were ready to go on the offensive. For Chamberlain the recent Reform Act marked the start of a new era, in which Gladstone's hold over the left and centre would be inherited by himself and Dilke. Hartington's influence among the moderates, and claims as former leader, might prevent their immediate seizure of the highest offices, but together their position in a radicalized House of Commons would ensure that no future government could be formed except on their terms. Chamberlain was anxious to bring his plans to an early fruition before further problems arose to divert attention from the recent propaganda victory over the Conservatives.

Cabinets of early January provided the opportunity. The subjects of discussion were Egypt and German annexations, which perpetuated the previous year's activity of assailing the Gladstonians. Bismarck's annexation of New Guinea had hit the headlines in December and Chamberlain, not liking 'to be cheeked by Bismarck or anyone else', had swung round to Dilke's view that Bismarck 'is making us a laughing stock and must be fought'. The policy of 'showing our teeth' was, despite strong support, as always watered down in cabinet by Gladstone.[1] Over Egypt, too, Chamberlain was more truculent. The August proposals to reduce Egypt's debt had been resubmitted to the Powers in November, but France, believing she had Britain on a string, had as yet refused to reply. Gladstone eventually secured cabinet approval for a stern note demanding her early response, but only after a considerable battle. Most now wanted a swift end to the complications, and Chamberlain later summed up for Harcourt what he believed the only three practical solutions: 'There is Hartington's "Pay and Stay", yours, which is "Pay and Scuttle", and mine, which is "Scuttle and Repudiate".' The last was his old idea to declare Egypt bankrupt, announce Britain's intention to withdraw and resist any further foreign intervention, and only then meet the Powers in conference to discuss future management of the country. Its attractions lay in appealing to both Radical and nationalist opinion in Britain since, as he had said earlier, 'The people will not like . . . a contribution which is really a bribe to buy off foreign powers and which is forced from us.' Harcourt he called a 'Peace at any Price' man for his readiness to pay the bribe, while Harcourt retaliated that Chamberlain was being 'very jingo', wanting 'to "have a go in" at Bismarck and France, by which I suppose he means a European War'.[2] Though this was an unlikely consequence, Chamberlain was indeed naïve in ignoring the fact that any Egyptian policy which did not damage Britain's international relations required 'bribery' of at least one other power. Salisbury later commented that the ministry had achieved its aim of uniting the Concert of Europe—but against Britain: Chamberlain's truculent approach would have exaggerated the trouble.

Gladstone's policy of putting off the evil day satisfied hardly anyone and when, tired and ill, he left the cabinet for three weeks' rest at Hawarden, plots began to erupt. Harcourt took the initiative, sounding out Hartington and Dilke on the possibility of 'shunting' Gladstone and his personal adherents, and reconstructing the government under Hartington with a compromise on Egypt. This suited the Radicals' purpose, but only in part. They had already been discussing the advantages of a cabinet break-down which would either leave a Whig rump to govern, or bring in a weak Conservative ministry, or entail an immediate election. Any of these would free them to strengthen their position in the party. During the cabinets, however, Chamberlain had observed 'a general wish to keep the Government together if possible', and faced the problem that 'I would go out with pleasure, but for this we must have an excuse—either a policy of our own which we can defend which the Cabinet will not accept—or a definite objection to the policy which the Cabinet may adopt, but I cannot find a satisfactory boat to leave the ship in.' Dilke now offered Gladstone's illness as the signal: 'This looks like a bolt on Egypt, which would I fancy drive you and self out at once, as we have gone to the limit of concession to bondholders' ideas.' He also offered 'another rock (a raft if you like to escape a little from the ship)' in Princess Beatrice's wedding dowry, from which residual republican carping Chamberlain fortunately dissuaded him.[3]

He was extremely wary of the Harcourt conspiracy: Gladstone's retirement 'is possible and may be necessary', but he and Dilke had 'to avoid the possible suspicion that we have joined in an intrigue' which 'might ruin us'. He refused to enter any negotiations before Gladstone's definite retirement, and made clear a preference for resignation on his Egyptian proposals over any possible compromise with the 'bribers'. Though he, Dilke, and Trevelyan met on 7 January and agreed that Egypt made a Hartingtonian reconstruction unlikely, manœuvres continued, and Captain O'Shea told Parnell after a conversation with Chamberlain a week later that 'Gladstone says he will retire before the Dissolution. The first men Hartington will send for will be Chamberlain and Dilke', who would demand the right to nominate certain cabinet posts, and impose conditions on future Irish policy. (Dilke had told Harcourt that Chamberlain must be Chancellor, while on 7 January Chamberlain was suggesting Parnell 'or some other Irishman'—O'Shea believed himself—as Irish Secretary.)

Chamberlain himself was determined to take his own line in this uncertain situation, and in three speeches—at Birmingham on 5 and 29 January, and Ipswich on the 14th—he hurled a new factor into the political arena.

Their general line closely followed the pattern which had emerged in *Fortnightly Review* articles since 1883. The 'new democracy', he argued, required new measures, new political methods and a new ideology for Liberalism. Further electoral reforms were advocated, along with the payment of MPs; there should be democratic local government in the counties, and greater equalization of the tax burden through death duties, income tax changes—in 1883 he had suggested a progressive income tax up to 10 per cent on the American model in preference to a wild suggestion from Labouchere for a 50 per cent tax—taxes on the unearned increment of land values, and the 'free breakfast table'. Free education and agrarian reform were, however, placed in the most prominent positions. Policy towards the last was only loosely sketched out, though he was already moving towards Collings's ideas of compulsory purchase powers for local authorities and government loans to create an extensive system of allotments—the later 'Three Acres and a Cow' election cry. It was already beginning to assume the role of a social and political panacea. It would 'replace the labourer on the soil and find employment for him' rather than his being 'driven into the towns to compete with you for work and to lower the rate of wages'. The propertied labourer would acquire an incentive to increasing productivity, thus restoring agricultural prosperity and cutting the price of food to the towns. Compulsory purchase would also be a spearhead for urban slum renewal. The programme would appeal to urban and rural workers and rally the left under Bright's old banners, which in Scotland, Wales, and London at least were already being vigorously waved.

The first speech of the series was couched in his best radical–democratic language—'Jacobin', his opponents called it. He appealed to the rights of the people against the privileges of the few, asking 'what ransom will property pay for the security it enjoys?' The reaction to this was strong, and even Dilke and Morley thought he had gone too far. 'Ransom' he later revised as a doctrine of 'insurance' which the propertied would have to take out against risks of social revolution, but moderates were not appeased, particularly after being told that the party structure was ripe for change: 'The organisation . . . and the programme of the party must be alike enlarged' and 'under the new system you would have the federated association defining and formulating the policy and the programme of the Liberal Party as a whole.' His denial at Ipswich that he was intent upon framing the issues of the next election fell on sceptical ears: adherents in local caucuses were soon mobilizing to propound the new Radical Programme.

The purpose of these speeches is rather unclear. They may have been designed to strengthen his claims in Harcourt's intended *coup*,[4] although Chamberlain had earlier told Dilke that the intrigues were irrelevant to the task of 'stating our views as to the policy which ought to be pursued by any government whether Mr G.'s or Hartington's'. And though his opinions expressed to Dilke and O'Shea implied support for the manœuvres, yet, since his interests lay primarily in gaining his freedom to amass support for the election and its consequences, he can have had little liking for a government constructed by Harcourt and Hartington which would pre-empt the field. Playing 'Jack Cade' again made such a reconstruction that much more difficult.

Edward Hamilton could claim after Ipswich that the speeches had been a 'failure *qua* Chamberlain demonstration', but Gladstone found it easier to believe that 'it is not impossible that there may be a plan or intention to break up the party'.[5] He emerged, refreshed, to impose discipline on the cabinets of 20 and 21 January and secure a re-opening of negotiations on Egypt after a favourable reply from France. Hartington and Northbrook were persuaded to drop their threatened resignations, and Dilke, 'having no orders', joined the Gladstonian majority. Chamberlain was for 'telling the French to go to the devil' but, absent with an abscessed jaw, could not lend his weight to the left–right alignment which might well have broken the government. Egyptian negotiations, subsequently largely shunted out of cabinet hands, ended in an international Egyptian loan and delayed interest repayment on the debt, and Gladstone further strengthened his hand by truckling to the Whigs, who had made a 'dead-set' at Chamberlain over his speeches. He attempted to impose restraint by a censorious letter on 3 February, to which Chamberlain responded with a threat of resignation, unwillingly backed by Dilke, which, he believed, 'would strengthen us in the country'.

Gladstone's reply that a decision on his position should be taken by the cabinet drew a brilliant counter, in effect a manifesto of domestic reform. Since Dilke, now rather enjoying himself running rings round obstreperous MPs in the Seats Bill debates, had warned that 'The object of the Whigs is to force us to war with Mr Gladstone who is strong, and not with Hartington whom we should break', Chamberlain must have been mildly worried by his isolation, but Gladstone himself had no wish to go to war with his left wing and quietly dropped the matter.

News of the fall of Khartoum and the death of General Gordon also required a closing of government ranks after 5 February. The public outcry threw Chamberlain's revival of domestic reform in the shade, and compelled him to accept the cabinet decision to reinforce Sudanese coastal garrisons and press on with Wolseley's campaign. The situation threw him into considerable confusion: 'what can we do? It is equally dangerous [for the expedition] to go or retire.' Confirmation of Gordon's death, he noted, would raise 'a strong party for retirement', but he set himself to work on Morley, leader of this 'party': 'I hate the war . . . but I cannot see that your policy would settle anything . . . We must therefore retake Khartoum even if we leave it again immediately. I am ready to protest and resign rather than commit myself to a permanent occupation or any war of conquest properly so called.'[6] The likelihood of extended military action on the Nile also compelled him to 'reconsider our policy as to hastening the elections', but it did not prevent him from seeking the prime aim of redrawing battle lines in the party. In late February he was working for the withdrawal of Gladstone to leave a 'combination or patriotic' ministry under Hartington, and joined the cabinet majority in pressing for an early resignation after the government's majority fell to fourteen in the 28 February censure motion on the Sudan.

Gladstone had other plans. Determined to retain control of his ministers and anxious to kill the expedition he had approved but loathed, he decided to carry on, and soon found an issue to secure his aims. Russian advances on India, culminating in the Penjdeh incident, provided him with an opportunity to adopt a strongly 'patriotic' stance, restore the government's reputation, and divert attention from the Sudan. His speech on 27

April for a Vote of Credit to finance activity in both India and the Sudan threw the Conservatives into confusion and was accounted by Churchill as having 'done us more damage in the constituencies than any event in Parliament'. Gladstone's abandonment of Gladstonianism caused Chamberlain some trouble. Sections of the left were very restive, Dale warning that 'a great many Liberals' shared his own desire for an immediate negotiated settlement with Russia. Chamberlain was compelled to 'deprecate the Jingo spirit' unleashed by the crisis, and advised the cabinet that 'The time has passed when the Liberal Party can go to war on circumstantial evidence' and it 'would not support the Government on extreme measures'. Yet it was not an issue on which he dared resign. Dale was told that the government's true objectives were not war but negotiation from strength, and was invited to co-operate by showing Russia that 'English opinion is united' against her advances. Gladstone's firm stand worked to the desired end. In early May Russia agreed to arbitration, but by this time 'our impossible campaign' in the Sudan had been downgraded and its retirement was authorized.

Chamberlain's hesitations over the Penjdeh crisis were perhaps also influenced by his simultaneous attention to another matter which he was anxious to turn into a major political issue. Ireland had been placed on the agenda once more by the need to adopt a policy towards renewal of the 1882 Crimes Act. Spencer had been working hard to produce an acceptable package and put forward his suggestions in late March: a curtailed special powers Bill applying nationally and not just to Ireland and, to sugar the pill, either Irish local government reform, a land purchase scheme, or replacement of the Viceroy with an Irish Secretary in the cabinet and a royal residence in Ireland. These ideas were countered by an alternative strategy from Chamberlain.

Coercion was the immediate problem, and Dilke had been told in September 1884 that 'We shall have an awful business over the renewal of the Crimes Act. I wish Spencer could see his way to let it drop, but I imagine there is no hope of this.'[7] An extra factor within a few months was the Radicals' determination on an early election. Everyone now anticipated a Nationalist landslide in Ireland, while the customary loyalty of

Irish voters in Britain to the Liberals was open to severe doubt. In prospect was the danger of Conservatism using a Liberal commitment to coercion to capture Nationalist support, but also the alternative prospect of Radicalism deploying Parnell's following in its future battle to dominate the party. Repeating the Kilmainham formula, or some variant, seemed to Chamberlain to offer considerable advantages, and in November 1884 he had consulted O'Shea over proposals that might appeal to Parnell. O'Shea came up with one on the 27th—renewal of the Crimes Act for only one year, or with considerable amendment, together with democratic local government reforms and 'important accessories'—as yet unspecified—'touching the public Boards in Dublin' (the administrative structure of the Viceroy). Chamberlain responded with an independent move, probably to sound out opinion and bring pressure to bear on Parnell for a closer alignment. On 17 December he wrote to a Radical supporter with Irish connections, W. H. Duignan, a letter which, with approval, was subsequently widely circulated. Though firmly opposing Irish independence, 'sooner than yield on which I would govern Ireland by force to the end of the chapter', he affirmed no objection to Home Rule in principle. Devolution should not come, however, through restoration of an Irish parliament but a more democratic local government system, in particular an 'Irish Board, altogether independent of English Government influence', dealing with education, railways and land, and invested with powers of taxation. How acceptable to public opinion this would be, he did not know, but he offered to cross over to Ireland and speak publicly in its favour.[8]

At the time, this letter backfired. O'Shea later tried to tell Parnell that Chamberlain 'had no intention of flirting with the Irish question behind your back', but Parnell was reasonably annoyed and Chamberlain had to limit further circulation of his letter. Despite this, Parnell was willing to offer his own suggestions, and through O'Shea proposed amendments to the Crimes Act and elaborated on the idea of a Central Board to replace Dublin Castle. County Boards should be created with powers of compulsory purchase and lease of land and, from them and the municipalities, representatives elected to a Central Board with the right to raise rates for a variety of purposes. Parnell, said O'Shea, would be willing to become its chairman. The bodies were to be elective, but special representation for landlords and the failure to include transfer of police control to the Board led Chamberlain to conclude that the scheme was 'more conservative than I expected'.

Parnell indeed appears to have suspected Chamberlain's own scheme, which referred vaguely to legislative powers for the Board and mentioned taxes rather than rates as its source of finance, of being a limited parliament intended to undercut the Home Rule movement, and in letters of 5 and 13 January 1885 asked O'Shea to ensure that Chamberlain realized that agreement on this proposal would not bind the Irish from further demanding their own parliament. O'Shea, however, hoping to secure major political gains from a *rapprochement* of his two patrons, failed to pass on the letters until 1888, when a furious row developed in the Commons because Chamberlain claimed that he had always believed Parnell to be offering the Board as a final solution. It seems unlikely that he did believe this at the time: an extreme Home Rule speech of Parnell on 21 January was certainly intended to make this clear, and later in 1885 he himself was acting on the basis that renovating the Dublin Castle administration and creating a subordinate Irish parliament were two separate questions. Yet, in contrast to Parnell, he appears to have been hoping for a politically significant form of devolution, such as would 'occupy and divide Irish parties, and give them plenty to do in discussion', leaving Irish papers with 'no space for the harangues of Irish patriots in the British House of Commons'.[9]

The details and long-term impact of a Central Board were, however, less important in his calculations than its immediate political role. Though coercion might be passed in 1885, legislation on Irish devolution before the election was out of the question, and the Duignan letter had identified the task as one for 'the first session of a reformed Parliament', a view confirmed in O'Shea's letter to Parnell of 19 January. This meant that its purpose was to bind Irish Nationalism to the Radical leadership for the election, and for intra-Liberal Party battles, both contemporaneous and later. Chamberlain had certainly made this clear in conversation with O'Shea, but O'Shea, seeing Parnell's reticence and not wishing to show Chamberlain the bareness of his cupboard, wrote out a crude statement of this policy for Parnell, sending a copy to Chamberlain in an envelope 'open on two sides'. As presumably anticipated, Chamberlain, fearing repetition of the Kilmainham accusations from this threat of publicity, was compelled to break off negotiations on 19 January and disavow to his friends any intention of an immediate political deal: 'I am very glad to know Parnell's views . . . [and] . . . that we are working on the same lines. [But] experience alone can show if there is any possibility of co-operation between the Irish Party and the English democracy.'[10]

His negotiations were reported to Gladstone and Spencer, among others, and when Spencer produced his own Irish proposals in April, Chamberlain's claim to be party to Parnell's thoughts put him in a strong position to challenge the Viceroy with the alternative of a one-year coercion Bill and a Central Board, which would ease passage of the former and 'place the policy of the Government fairly before the country at the general election'. Spencer at first was mildly favourable, and Chamberlain's position was further strengthened when the Duignan letter finally bore fruit in Ireland. On 22 April the Catholic prelate, Cardinal Manning, approached Dilke to say that the Irish hierarchy knew of the letter and were very favourable. He offered a deal: he would back the scheme if the Radicals could stop the activities of a Foreign Office mission to the Vatican under Lord Errington which was trying to block the appointment of the pro-Nationalist Dr Walsh as Archbishop of Dublin. Chamberlain, after meeting Manning, prepared a detailed draft of his ideas, 'Local Government for Ireland', which combined features from his earlier outline and Parnell's suggestions but ignored the latter's objections to legislative powers which O'Shea had failed to pass on. This was discussed in cabinet on 28 April, but Spencer had now swung round to believing that the Board would be unworkable, and he was backed by Hartington and a majority of the cabinet.

Gladstone again became the crucial figure. Strongly in favour of the scheme despite reservations on details—he particularly wanted devolution of police control with which Chamberlain knew Parnell to be wary of compromising himself—he was anxious for Chamberlain to bring the rest of the cabinet round, and, to avoid an immediate rejection, established a committee to discuss the issue further. Both sides set out to strengthen their hands. Manning had earlier suggested further negotiations with Parnell, and himself had a 'successful' interview with Parnell on 30 April, and a 'more successful' one with the Irish MP, Sexton. Chamberlain himself told O'Shea that he, Dilke, Trevelyan, and the recent cabinet entrant, Shaw Lefevre, were ready to resign if Parnell would commit himself to his January proposals. Parnell was unhappy at having his hand forced by these methods, but O'Shea turned up with an agreement, written in his own hand but purporting to come from Parnell, that, though a one year Crimes Bill would have to be opposed on principle, Parnell would attempt to limit obstruction to it and allow introduction of Chamberlain's scheme.

After considerable lobbying and discussion, the Central Board was rejected by one vote in the cabinet of 9 May. Gladstone commented, in colourful language, that its opponents would soon be regretting their stand, and pronounced it 'dead as mutton'. It was only so, however, if he refused to put up a fight and this, though he worked hard on Hartington in private correspondence and promised Dilke strong backing if he could convert Spencer, he was not prepared to do. The reason was that the issue had assumed wider political importance in a government whose position was now critical. A recent narrow majority in the Seats Bill debate had led to a long discussion on 7 May on the merits of engineering a final defeat: Childers's budget proposals had raised considerable opposition, with Dilke and Chamberlain's objecting to increased beer duties in an election year, and the Chancellor's resignation was repeatedly threatened: Hartington and Selborne had already offered their resignations by the 9 May meeting against a final decision to halt the Sudanese operations. In this situation, Ireland had become the pivotal issue. For the first time in five years Chamberlain was near to acquiring a majority on a policy of his own making which polarized the cabinet very nearly on straight lines of peers against commoners and left and right. If he won and his opponents stayed, he would have effectively dictated party policy for the election and the next government; if they resigned, they would have gone against Gladstone and, Chamberlain believed, majority opinion in the party. If he lost, resignation of the Radicals *en bloc*, uncommitted to coercion and with a big reform project in their hands, would prove a perfect end to the ministry.

Yet, despite his pledge to O'Shea, he did not resign after the adverse decision. Lord Rosebery provided the explanation: 'the key to the situation of the cabinet is Mr G himself. All ministers individually want it to break up and yet none want to break away from the rest disassociated from Mr G. They each want Mr G.'s aegis to be spread over them.'[11] Gladstone, however, was 'bolting' on Ireland. He had written to Chamberlain on 6 May saying that the settlement of franchise and various colonial problems made him a 'free man . . . entitled to claim my release' and that, though favourable to Irish government reforms, he had always 'preserved an entire liberty of action as to the time and circumstances of their application.' His threat of resignation was seriously meant—Mrs Gladstone was soon beginning to pack their belongings at No. 10—but its immediate effect was to stay Chamberlain's hand until he knew in which direction the Prime Minister would jump next. As Gladstone noted, the Radicals held a 'winning position' on the issue which 'by resigning now they will greatly compromise'.[12] Chamberlain, however, was now in the unenviable position of having to deal with Spencer's coercion proposals independently of the Board scheme, and on 10 May warned O'Shea to expect his resignation on them within the week. Though modifying his objections, to appear conciliatory to Gladstone, he was anxious to avoid any commitment which would compromise him with the Nationalists, and set about preventing Spencer from sugaring coercion with any of his remedial proposals, in particular the land purchase scheme which was being strongly canvassed. Stopping this not only made coercion an isolated target, but also kept the Board scheme firmly on the agenda.

The final denouement came when, with only conditional support from Chamberlain, Gladstone announced the early introduction of a two year Crimes Bill to the Commons on 15 May. The absence of remedial measures, which cabinet leaks had led everyone to expect, created consternation, and when Churchill, now translated from the *enfant terrible* of Conservatism into a leading figure by a concordat with Salisbury in 1884, declared against coercion, prospects of a Liberal–Nationalist reconciliation faded. Gladstone's response to the problem was a unilateral announcement of land purchase to accompany coercion. He later claimed that he had understood Chamberlain in a private conversation to be not unfavourable to a one year purchase scheme, but his announcement without prior consultation with anyone was transparently a device to out-manœuvre Radical opposition. But he forgot Dilke. Reinforced by a recent letter from Chamberlain that 'we must go' once the Anglo-Russian negotiations were completed, Dilke was anxious to impose his own will upon a situation increasingly dominated by relations between Gladstone and Chamberlain.[13] On 20 May he resigned in protest at Gladstone's announcement, and forced Chamberlain and Shaw Lefevre, neither of whom were happy at the prospect of Radicals resigning against reform legislation, to go with him. Gladstone himself saved the day, refusing to make a decision on the by now considerable number of farewell letters in his file and calling a further cabinet meeting for 5 June. 'Indiscretions' by Chamberlain by then had made the cabinet division public knowledge, and he prepared his exit with a speech on 3 June calling for the 'widest possible self-government' in Ireland 'consistent with maintaining the unity of the Empire'. Final breakdown became inevitable when a backbench motion was tabled demanding an end to the Dublin Castle administration, and Chamberlain and Dilke, anxious to avoid embarrassment with their resignations still pending, reversed their position on the controversial beer duties. In the Commons vote on this on 9 June, the Nationalists joined the Opposition and sufficient Liberals made themselves absent, after some prompting, to defeat the government by twelve votes. The cabinet breathed a sigh of relief, and agreed unanimously to resign. Its successor, formed by Lord Salisbury after much squabbling on 23 June, was essentially a lame-duck administration. Chamberlain was now free, he told correspondents, to prepare for the election anticipated in November.

These preparations consisted essentially in formulating an election-winning programme which would make him the dominant figure during the campaign and allow him to impose his own terms upon any future Liberal administration. The crucial items in this he and Dilke announced in mid-June: the

counties of the United Kingdom were to have democratic
councils with powers of compulsory purchase for the transfer of
land to tenants and labourers; free education was, finally, to be
put on the immediate agenda; and, in response to growing
nationalist sentiments, largely in Ireland but also in Wales and
Scotland, National Councils were to be established for matters
of local administration and legislation, an advance on the
Central Board scheme for Ireland elaborated upon in the
Fortnightly Review of 1 July. Chamberlain believed that, with
these measures, he would capture the urban voter, popular
movements on the Celtic fringe, and make inroads into the
English rural areas. All sections of the electorate might be
further impressed by a cry on the lines—'We can solve the Irish
Question'.

The opportunity to use it never came. The scheme was only
viable if it captured Irish support, and this proved unforth-
coming. In response to Chamberlain's promise on 9 June that,
if Parnell committed himself to the Board scheme, he would
refuse office in any government which did not accept it, O'Shea
replied that Churchill's recent rejection of coercion might
'satisfy the Boys'. This was confirmed on 28 June: Parnell, said
O'Shea, feared Chamberlain's bid for the Irish vote and was
not prepared to back the Board scheme. Subsequent attacks
upon the Radicals in the Nationalist paper, *United Ireland*,
widened the gap. Nor was the Catholic Church any more
helpful. Manning, averse to public involvement in party controversy, had warned Dilke after 9 May against resignation,
and he and Dr Walsh now refused their support for a speaking
tour which Chamberlain had been planning in Ireland. Like
the Nationalists, they were being wooed by Churchill and the
new Viceroy, Lord Carnarvon, with conciliatory gestures.[14]

Chamberlain made a last bid to shore up his crumbling
relationship with the Nationalists. In a letter of mid-July to
O'Shea for Parnell's eyes, he reviewed the earlier negotiations,
criticized Parnell for what he claimed was his unfaithfulness to
the Radicals, and then raised the political stakes. Nationalist
aspirations, he hoped, might be satisfied by a National Council,
but this was not offered 'as a substitute for Home Rule, as the
demand for a separate parliament . . . is one which may be
treated independently . . . I have not concealed my objections

to such a proposal . . . but . . . [if local government reform failed] no arrangement could possibly bind the Irish people not to pursue their demands further.'[15] In effect, this was a request for a Council to be taken on account, with the hint that Home Rule might be delivered later if necessary. Since Parnell was now *tête à tête* with Carnarvon over Home Rule, he refused the offer, and on 22 July Chamberlain learned that the Irish were intent on holding the political balance after the election. A few days later O'Shea was told that National Councils were no longer on the Radical programme. 'The Irish are gone,' Chamberlain added, but 'I am not certain that I regret it.' '[They] must "stew in their juice" with the Tories until they find out their mistake. Whether the support of the Radicals will be forthcoming is a question. My information . . . satisfies me that further concessions . . . are not at all popular even with our Radical constituents,' he had earlier told Labouchere. Parnell's strategy was mistaken since 'the next election will give a majority to the Liberal party independently of any Irish support'.[16]

The task of formulating a progressive Liberal challenge was encountering other difficulties. Chamberlain saw the value of creating a Radical high command and on 4 July assembled a 'junta' of Dilke, Morley, Trevelyan, and Shaw Lefevre. There were, however, clear differences of viewpoint. Morley's presence Chamberlain had himself questioned on the grounds of his past opposition to government policy and known hostility to 'socialist' land reforms in the election programme. When Parnell put down a motion for 17 July, the latest of a series, demanding an inquiry into the Maamtrasna murders, Trevelyan, loyal to Spencer, refused to join the junta's unsuccessful approach to Gladstone for a reversal of the party's official policy of opposition, and, despite Labouchere's plea to capture the Irish by supporting the motion, Chamberlain and Dilke could only resolve their problems by absenting themselves from the vote. Dilke and Chamberlain had themselves clashed in late June when the former protested at Gladstone's decision to honour Lord Errington for his Vatican services. Dilke was still hoping to create something out of reconciling Manning, but Chamberlain was at the time more interested in keeping Gladstone's support, having heard from Harcourt that

Gladstone would make devolution a prominent issue if he stood in the election: 'On the great issue between us and the Whigs, Mr. Gladstone is on our side, . . . [which] will immensely strengthen our position if we decide to press the matter.'

The decision to drop Ireland from his programme, however, involved a change of attitude on Chamberlain's part to his leader. Gladstone was now no longer an asset but a liability, as he had been in January, and his announcement on the government's fall that he would lead for the rest of the session and then retire must, in late July, have been remembered by Chamberlain with great pleasure. For the first time in almost a decade, the Radicals were 'unmuzzled' and free to drive Liberalism in the direction they desired. Even before Parliament was prorogued on 12 August, Chamberlain set out to seize the initiative with an election campaign never before seen in British politics.

Gladstone had written of his January speeches that they had 'a remote and . . . far-sighted purpose' and that 'there is here a method and system which seems to give the matter a new character'.[17] The autumn campaign indeed displayed a 'method'.[18] Whereas Gladstone's Midlothian addresses, seen at the time as the height of demagogy, had been confined to his own constituency, Chamberlain set out on a national speaking tour through what were likely to be major Liberal voting areas — the North-East in August, Lancashire, Scotland, and London in September, the West Country and South Yorkshire in early October, and thereafter in the Midlands. It was designed to subordinate the peculiarities of political debate in individual constituencies to a universal programme which would mandate any future Liberal ministry. One might expect him to have made great use of the National Federation for his purposes, particularly after persuading Gladstone in mid-July to allow its representatives semi-official status by co-ordinating with the Chief Whip (though Schnadhorst was not included 'because you will frighten the moderates'). Yet he never attempted to seek Federation approval of his policies, nor to use it to dictate to the local parties. The campaign was essentially a personal one, in the style more of a presidential candidate than of a former minor cabinet member, and his superbly rousing speeches were primarily directed at the local rank and file who would then, it was hoped, force their candidates to commit themselves to his programme. Chamberlain could later lament that many county candidates were of Whig background, but console himself that two-thirds had declared themselves for 'three acres and a cow'.

The 'system' in 'The Radical Programme' was not wholly systematic. In his introduction to the pamphlet of that name, published in mid-July and containing a selection of the *Fortnightly Review* articles, Chamberlain announced the appearance of a new Liberal philosophy transcending the old emphasis on individual liberty: 'New concepts of public duty, new developments of social enterprise, new estimates of the natural obligations of the members of the community to one another, have come into view, and demand consideration.' The rich, he declared in public, have responsibilities for care of the poor, and the poor were entitled to a fair share of society's advantages. Poverty 'is a problem which some men would put aside by reference to the eternal laws of supply and demand, to the necessity of freedom of contract, and to the sanctity of every right of property. But . . . these are the convenient cant of selfish wealth.' The new Radicalism sounded 'the death knell of the laissez-faire system . . . the intervention, in other words, of the State on behalf of the weak against the strong, in the interests of labour against capital, of want and misery against cant and ease.' Chamberlain saw himself as tackling 'the social question' with measures his critics called 'socialist', but more perceptive minds recognized that, if the new philosophy was to be spearheaded by free schools, permissive powers of compulsory purchase for local authorities, and minor tax changes, this was thin material with which to upholster claims for a social revolution. When the programme laid as much emphasis on triennial parliaments, reform of the Lords, disestablishment, and other minor changes in the rights of peers, Church and landlord, it was clear that the old Radical programme was being adapted not transcended, and that many of the old causes had to be catered for. Chamberlain was careful to keep his options open: he recommended but did not commit himself to the *Radical Programme*, and in his speeches canvassed any and every issue to which it appeared useful to defer. Yet it did at one level mark an important transformation. Popular Radicalism was inherently faddist and anti-establishment in its orientation,

and Chamberlain shared enough of its heritage, and acknowledged the energy it generated, to respect this. On the other
hand, it had always held only a minority appeal. The 1885
campaign was designed to replicate on a national scale the
formula which had proved so successful in Birmingham during
the 1870s. Radicalism's anti-Church and anti-landlord stance
was to be reformulated in pro-labour terms, and the policies
presented as a practical progressive solution to problems faced
by the community as a whole. Education reforms were divorced
from any sectional interest and presented as a programme of
modernization: taxation and land reforms were offered as ways
of reviving the declining agricultural sector and mitigating the
deep industrial depression of the election year. Around them all
floated those principles of social welfare, a stated determination
to tackle the national disgrace of poverty in the midst of plenty,
which have become the commonplace of progressive politics in
modern Britain.

The 'purpose' which Gladstone noted was clear—to establish
Chamberlain's claims as the man who had won the election for
Liberalism. Gladstone, ill and then recuperating in Norway
until early September, was in no position to impose his usual
restraint, and party agents were soon reporting a stampede of
moderate electors into the Tory camp. It was a fine opportunity for Hartington to reaffirm his claims as next party
leader, and on 29 August he made part of his first campaign
speech a denunciation of Chamberlain's attacks on the rights
of property.

This, if anything, was the turning-point of the election. As
we have suggested earlier, Chamberlain's frequent attempts to
define Liberalism in terms of some unnatural alliance of
Radicals and Whigs were partisan descriptions bearing little
relationship to reality: neither of these tendencies, broad and
amorphous enough as they were in themselves, exhausted
shades of opinion in the party, and the composition of Liberalism, inside and outside Parliament, was far more diverse than
the simple categories of territorial aristocracy and urban industrial bourgeoisie would imply. At the same time, these two
groups provided the two alternative pegs on which the diverse
elements of Britain's main reform party could be hung in the
age of mass democracy. Speculation about their capacity to

continue working in harmony had been around ever since Gladstone brought them together in the 1860s. As the future of Conservatism showed, it was not inevitable that they should clash, nor that ascendant industrialism should triumph over declining agrarianism, if the right banners were waved. In 1885, Chamberlain's campaign placed the question at the top of the agenda for the first time. As he said in October, 'We shall sweep the country with free education and allotments, and the Tories will be smashed and the Whigs extinguished.'

Yet, though secretly launching candidates against isolated right-wing Liberals, Chamberlain had no interest in formalizing the issue during the election itself, well knowing, if only from the contrasted experiences of 1874 and 1880, that divided parties lose votes as a matter of course. Political *coups* were things to work for between elections; and in 1885 the task was to present a post-election *fait accompli*, not generate a disastrous split during the campaign itself. At Hull in early August he had emphasized the need for party unity, and Hartington's chief comment then had been satisfaction at the disappearance of references to Ireland, the one issue which had so far promised to split the leadership.[19] Chamberlain could not, however, ignore the challenge implicit in Hartington's speech, for Hartington was 'up in a balloon, and he perversely ignores the changes in public opinion and the determination of the great majority of the party he proposes to lead.' He himself had to lay down 'a minimum to satisfy the just expectations of the Radical section'.[20] At Warrington on 8 September he retaliated by restating the social question's importance, calling the Whigs generally 'armchair politicians' and Hartington specifically 'Rip Van Winkle'. Hartington was annoyed, but Chamberlain and Harcourt, playing the role of mediator, both saw it as a 'very mild retort'. And by following up in the speech Hartington's denunciation of recent Home Rule declarations by Parnell, he clearly signalled grounds of common agreement and an end to the Radical–Nationalist *entente* against the Whigs. Chamberlain wanted to work with Hartington, he told Harcourt, and 'I do not think he will find me exacting.' The undesirable thing was for Hartington to throw in his lot with intransigent right-wingers like Goschen, who had, Dilke was told, to be made 'impossible for any future cabinet'. Hartington, indeed, gained a rather condescending pat on the back later for publicly spurning Churchill's invitation to join the Conservatives.

In all this, Chamberlain was not renouncing his ambition ultimately to control Liberalism by eliminating 'whiggery'. For the immediate future, however, he was subordinating the idea of a major split to the task of skirmishing for greater Radical influence over Liberalism's traditional élite. This was not quite the view Gladstone chose to adopt on his return from Norway. Convinced after Warrington that the situation was ripe to raise his umbrella once again over the mutually hostile factions, he wrote to Chamberlain, Hartington and Granville, acting leader for the campaign, declaring party unity to be the pre-eminent consideration and asking whether each would support his return to politics. Granville readily accepted, swayed by the Gladstonian assertion that '[Chamberlain's] socialism repels me. Some day mischief will come. The question is, when.'[21] Neither of the two others could afford to refuse outright but both laid down conditions for their entry into any future government—Hartington rejected Irish devolution, Chamberlain insisted on free schools and agrarian reform. Gladstone's reply to both, that election strategy not government policy was the immediate consideration, brought a request from Chamberlain to see the section of Gladstone's manifesto on land reform. This duly arrived, but only after publication of the manifesto, which contained hints at changes in the Lords and relations between Church and state, and four major items: reform of Commons procedure, local government reform, changes in the land laws, and measures to increase voter registration. Free schools were criticized, and compulsory purchase of land ignored. And, despite Gladstone's comment that it was intended to be 'fair' between the Liberal wings, Chamberlain could reasonably describe it to Dilke as a 'slap in the face to us'. Fighting Gladstone, however, was 'not worth the candle' since 'he is squeezable and will probably give way to our views': 'his reign cannot possibly be a long one and it is undesirable to have even the remains of his great influence cast against us.'[22]

On the other hand, he was not prepared to abandon his new-found independence, and wrote to Gladstone that he could not join a government committed only to the manifesto and would require at least the right to a free vote on education, and liberty to implement local government reform with compulsory purchase powers. These demands were modified a few days later in a speech at the Victoria Hall, London, declaring that his membership of a government was conditional on free education, land purchase, and fairer taxation not being specifically excluded from its programme. Granville complained of this 'foolishly spoken' ultimatum, claiming that Chamberlain's head had been turned by the campaign, but Gladstone was right in refusing to consider it a serious challenge—Chamberlain had simply 'gone a little further than he intended'. Believing that a united front had been created for the election, with freedom for the Left to go beyond but 'not to impose their own sense upon all other people', he handed back to Granville responsibility for the campaign.[23]

Chamberlain, indeed, was taking an ambiguous line towards the Gladstonian umbrella. The Victoria Hall statement of 24 September, demanding that items be not specifically excluded from the government's agenda, was a big shift from requiring their inclusion ten days before. Part of the reason lay in Gladstone's reply to his first letter, that, since the 'average opinion of the party ought to be the rule for immediate action', had he been forming a government, 'I should have read the letter with regret.' Chamberlain's response to this warning had been that he was 'quite ready to fall back into the ranks', but he had also shown interest in Gladstone's comment that his thoughts were once more turning on the Irish question.[24] In this lay the possibility of reviving the political relationship of May.

Chamberlain was now having to play his cards carefully. Gladstone's manifesto had been supported by most of the former cabinet, and even by Goschen, leaving him out on a limb with what Goschen was soon to call the 'Unauthorized Programme' of Victoria Hall, and he was under continuous pressure to revise it. Lord Grosvenor, the Chief Whip, wrote that 'you have frightened over shoals of what I call the "floating balance", the men who turn an election. Unless we have unity we shall certainly not win.' Hartington was pressing Gladstone to denounce him for this reason, and Gladstone himself was critical of the 'constructionist' ideology of the 'rampant and

ambitious' modern Radicals, though refusing to break with
them. From the grass roots, too, came worried reports about the
impact of his campaign: in mid-October Chamberlain had to
disavow any desire to use free education against the voluntary
schools. Gladstone's desire to restrain him resulted in a sum-
mons to Hawarden on 7-8 October for their first-ever serious
private discussion, where Chamberlain proved highly accom-
modating, promising to try and prevent free schools coming to
a vote were he in the next government, declaring himself satisfied with the taxation parts of Gladstone's manifesto, and,
according to Gladstone, hinting that he would prove moderate
on land reform. By mid-November he had even publicly stated
that the manifesto might be a workable basis for short-term
Liberal unity.

This gradual move back under the umbrella was an acknowledgement both that his campaign was antagonizing moderate
voters, and that it would be a risky venture openly to challenge
any future government if, as events were tending to suggest,
Gladstone formed it. But he had told Gladstone that far fewer
concessions would be forthcoming were Hartington the next
Prime Minister, a piece of news which elicited from Hartington
the comment that it was premature to think of forming any
government without Gladstone. This Gladstone interpreted as
a situation in which both men wanted his return to assuage
personal misgivings each had about the other—an interpretation convenient for his own political future, but ignoring the
fact that his reassertion of control had blocked any moves by
leaders of the two Liberal wings to find common ground.
Furthermore, he was also passing on an important piece of
information, clearly to Granville, less so to Chamberlain and
Hartington: he would only revise his decision to retire if a 'big
Irish question' arose, to the solution of which he could contribute.[25]

The idea that, if the Liberals wanted him back, they would
also have to put Ireland first on the agenda, was carefully
promoted. Hartington was asked continually to keep an open
mind on devolution, and wrote increasingly agitated replies
insisting that he would tolerate no major concessions to Parnell.
Chamberlain received a clearer message. After nibbling at the
bait set earlier by Gladstone's hint of his growing interest in

Ireland, he had had in reply an interesting query: would he stick to his Victoria Hall conditions if the election returned eighty or ninety Nationalists united on an acceptable scheme for devolution? Chamberlain was sceptical of this event arising, and ambiguous on the main issue: he would be 'bound to strain every nerve' to assist the Government in dealing with it, but was 'not . . . certain that I could not render more help from outside than as a member of the cabinet'.[26] A long discourse from Gladstone on 8 October on Irish affairs produced a comment to Dilke some days later that 'the Irish business is not the first just now'.

This reticence towards Gladstone's advances reflected a perceptive reading of his political style. Just as Gladstone had reunited a divided party around his own leadership by exploiting the great Liberal causes of Irish Disestablishment in 1868 and Bulgaria in 1876, so now he was 'working' Irish questions to gloss over disagreements on domestic reform and 'working' these disagreements to ensure that he alone wrote out the agenda of Liberal progress. It appeared unlikely in September and early October that he would thus be able to change the issue from Chamberlain's repellent 'socialism', but on 18 October Labouchere leaked news of informal soundings Gladstone had been making through his son, Herbert, and Labouchere among the Irish MPs. Their premise was something with which no leading Liberal had as yet dared to flirt— a parliament in Dublin. On 16 November Herbert told Tim Healy that Gladstone was ready to take up Home Rule after the election and produced the outlines of a possible scheme. This information was insufficient to divert Parnell from calling on Irish voters on 21 November to support the Conservatives since Gladstone had made it clear in a speech four days earlier that, though he wanted Ireland to 'speak' in the elections, it was the government's task, not his, to take action—a reticence dictated by his basic inability to win over the leaders of the two Liberal wings.[27]

Chamberlain's reaction to Labouchere's news on 18 October was simple: Gladstone 'seemed to think that a policy for dealing with [Ireland] might be found which would unite us all and which would necessarily throw into the background those minor points of difference about the schools and smallholdings which threaten to drive the Whigs into the arms of the Tories or into retirement.'[28] And when Gladstone confirmed this in a letter of late October, announcing his 'instinct' that Ireland would 'shoulder aside everything else', Chamberlain made his refusal to play the game quite clear. The party, he asserted, would never go beyond National Councils, and it was best to let the Irish 'stew in their juice'. Furthermore, he gave a firm answer to Gladstone's month-old request: unless compulsory land purchase were accepted, 'neither I nor Dilke nor Morley, nor I *think* Lefevre could honestly join any government.'[29]

By the opening of polling on 23 November, nothing had been decided. The party leaders apparently accepted Gladstone's official manifesto, but Chamberlain had made clear that he could not be content with this in practice. Gladstone had shown that he was only interested in dealing with Ireland, but feared to say so publicly because his chief colleagues, though accepting his leadership, rejected the policy going with it. The electorate were being asked to give a mandate for a Liberal ministry whose chief activities promised to be very different from its public pronouncements.

Chamberlain had earlier anticipated a great victory from the elections. Unexpectedly, the county results of December showed that 'the "cow" has done wonders for us', as Labouchere put it. It was fortunate, since the boroughs swung *en bloc* towards Conservatism, and some even of Birmingham's seven seats for a time appeared in jeopardy from a strong attack spearheaded by Churchill's fight against Bright. Gladstone reflected moderate opinion in attributing the setback to four factors in increasing order of importance: advocacy by some Conservatives of fiscal reform in a year of industrial slump; the defection of Irish voters; disestablishment, canvassed by many Liberals and inspiring a 'Defend the Church' campaign from the Tory leaders; and, finally, fear of Chamberlain's proposals.[30]

The implication of his comment was that Chamberlain provided the chief threat to Liberalism's political power, and the result certainly made it hard for Chamberlain to follow through his strategy. His reputation as spokesman of the urban elector had suffered, and the final result of 333 Liberals, 251 Conservatives and 86 Irish Nationalists made nonsense of his prognostication that the party would gain a majority independent of Irish support. It was in a defensive mood that he spoke at Leicester on 3 December blaming the borough results on 'priests, publicans, parsons, Parnellites and protectionists' and disclaiming responsibility since 'this election has been fought upon a manifesto which did not include one point to which the extreme Liberals attach the greatest importance'. Privately, however, he admitted to Harcourt the failure of his campaign and his uncertainty about what the voters really wanted,[31] while Grosvenor's assessment on 12 December that the new Commons contained well over 200 Hartington supporters to 100 Chamberlainites, represented, if accurate, an unfavourable balance for seeking to gain control.

Two pieces of advice reached Chamberlain in early December. From Reginald Brett, Hartington's former secretary, came the view 'I am afraid that you are not strong enough yet to do without the moderate Liberals. Nor is it perhaps desirable that our party should be cut of one pattern.' Accepting defeat gracefully was, however, not Chamberlain's style: as he told Labouchere, 'I was forced to speak yesterday at Leicester and you will see I had a dig at the Whigs. I will drive the knife in on the 17th.' Labouchere's own view was to use Gladstone's flirtation with Ireland to take over the party: 'Would it not be wise to use the G.O.M. to settle this issue and get it out of the way. If he agrees with Parnell, he will not agree long with his Whig friends.'[32] Humbly acquiescing again in Gladstone's leadership so soon after his unilateral declaration of limited independence was equally unappealing, particularly when there was an alternative line available. 'The G.O.M. is very anxious to come in again,' he told Labouchere on 7 December (not entirely accurately—Gladstone was at the time angling for a Parnell–Tory agreement on Home Rule which the Liberals could support). 'I am not, and I think we must sit on his Irish proposals.' Chamberlain's new plan was to restructure the party in opposition, as he had tried after 1874: 'I should like [the Conservatives] to be in for a couple of years before we try again, and then I should go for the Church,' he had told Dilke on 29 December. A meeting of the 'junta' on 5 December agreed to the strategy, though rejecting the disestablishment weapon. That Chamberlain had even considered using it is testimony to the fineness of the line separating 'new' and 'old'

Radicalism. Its likely political effectiveness was also open to question. Since a large number of Liberals had committed themselves to it in the election, it would undoubtedly have proved a potent issue, just as it had after 1874, with which to tax whiggery; and in October Granville had suggested to Gladstone that Chamberlain might be intent on using disendowment to finance free education—certainly a plan Chamberlain had favoured in 1874, and one which might now avert the hostility expressed in the election by ratepayers to further subsidies of education. On balance, however, disestablishment had so far proved counter-productive: Dilke had abandoned it in Chelsea, as had Shaw Lefevre in a vain attempt to avoid defeat in Reading, while Chamberlain himself, after a first enthusiasm, early in the campaign had become very elusive.[33]

Whatever the issue that ultimately might be used, Chamberlain was convinced, so he told Morley, that remaining in opposition was far preferable to entering a government based on Gladstone's manifesto. With the Irish balance in the Commons and Gladstone's new interest, the manifesto was in reality no longer the issue. What keeping the Unauthorized Programme on the agenda now meant was keeping a big Irish programme off it—not an easy task. Until Parliament met in mid-January, the party was scattered, recuperating from its electoral exhaustion. Gladstone was confining his soundings to select moderate Whigs, and Chamberlain's only *entrée* into the circle was through the untrustworthy Labouchere's contacts with Herbert Gladstone. Until Gladstone's intentions were clarified, it was dangerous for Chamberlain to take any public stand on Irish matters. Conservative politicians, too, were preparing to manipulate the situation for party advantage. There had already developed between Chamberlain and Churchill, despite differences of background and temperament, and the clash over Birmingham politics, a deep mutual regard: both were intent on driving the 'old guard' from their respective parties, and were prepared not only to exploit the others existence as an argument in their own party for more radical methods, but even, at least in appearance, to work out tactics to their mutual advantage. Labouchere again provided an intermediary, and on 3 December had told Chamberlain that Churchill was preparing to break with the Nationalists and unite Whigs and Tories against a Parnell–Radical *rapprochement*. Precisely because he feared the consequences of this, Chamberlain retorted that it would 'be the making of the Radical party' and that Churchill should 'leave us to deal with the Whigs and not force us to unite the party against the Tories'. Staying Churchill's hand was also high among Salisbury's priorities, wary as he was of being ousted in a realignment of the political centre, and he was insisting on quiescence to allow Gladstone time to blunder.[34]

In this uncertain environment, Radical strategy could only be promoted by the crude means of the platform. On 12 December Dilke publicly advocated allowing the Conservative government to tackle a list of reforms which Salisbury had announced at Newport during the campaign. This was a direct snub to those who wanted to deal with Ireland, and a hint at cross-bench co-operation to isolate the Nationalists. Chamberlain and Lefevre later claimed that Dilke had gone further than the agreed policy (though Chamberlain did defend it to Morley immediately afterwards) when it became clear that two key Liberal groups had been antagonized—those who saw Conservatism as the devil, and those who regarded Chamberlain in the same light. Recognizing that both Gladstone and Ireland were to be 'shunted' by this strategy, Herbert Gladstone and Wemyss Reid, editor of the *Leeds Mercury*, and an admirer and later biographer of the recently deceased Forster, countered by releasing to the press on 16 December the outlines of a Home Rule scheme prepared with Nationalist help, stating that Gladstone was ready to form a government to implement some such measure.

The 'Hawarden Kite' threw the political world into turmoil. Gladstone declared it a speculation on his views, not an expression of them, hoping to avert any Liberal polarization. But Herbert's action had proved successful in removing the initiative from Chamberlain and the Radical Programme in favour of Gladstone and Home Rule. Chamberlain was in consternation, worried that 'a large number, perhaps the majority, of Liberals will support *any* scheme of Mr Gladstone's', and hence convinced that 'we must not commit ourselves against it yet: . . . we must let the situation shape itself before we finally decide.'[35]

When the situation did finally 'shape itself', Chamberlain was to be found firmly against the Home Rule Bill which Gladstone prepared in 1886. The reasons are by no means clear, and are further obscured by Chamberlain's own tendency to extreme inconsistency in his comments. The stand which he publicly adopted is summed up by an early biographer, N. M. Marris, and remains the conventional interpretation: 'Mr Chamberlain's attitude . . . was governed by his belief that Home Rule . . . ultimately entailed the separation of Ireland from England, and the disintegration of the Empire.'[36] His claim was to be inspired by a desire for a unified and cohesive British Empire, while Home Rule was tantamount to, or would entail, disintegration of that Empire at its very heart.

The plausibility of this claim is enhanced by Chamberlain's subsequent career, but not by his earlier one. Whereas he had frequently supported extensive devolution to Ireland, he had never shown the slightest interest in, or support for, imperial unification. During December 1885 he also made it clear that his objections to the 'separation of Ireland' were far fewer than to some sort of half-way house. 'I would rather let Ireland go altogether than accept the responsibility of a nominal union,' he wrote to Gladstone. To the 'Kite' scheme 'I would infinitely prefer separation'; and of an amended version published by Labouchere on 27 December he commented, 'It is ridiculous, and separation at once is infinitely preferable.'

During the 1886 debates Chamberlain came to accept the principle of a devolved legislature in Dublin, and to centre his opposition to Gladstone's proposals on their failure to ensure sufficient 'imperial safeguards'. Two issues assumed considerable importance. One was that the draft Bill gave customs and excise—and hence the power of fiscal independence—to the Irish legislature and Chamberlain, it has often been suggested, feared the prospect of tariff barriers arising against British goods at a time of commercial depression when he was beginning to consider ways of opening up, not restricting, intra-imperial trade.[37] Certainly this was a consideration which weighed with many British exporters, and in Protestant Ulster the threat of its export-based industrial structure being moulded to the demands of the economically-backward, rural,

Catholic, south of the island was the major issue. How far Chamberlain himself was affected is more uncertain. As yet the question of 'economic imperialism' was not something he had come seriously to consider, and the inevitability of a protectionist Ireland was not assured. Some, like Parnell, had ideas of developing Ireland behind tariff walls, but for many of the lawyers, tradesmen and farmers who formed the backbone of Irish nationalism the British trade was far too important a source of their livelihood for protection to be undertaken lightly. Moreover, the relevant section in Gladstone's Bill was omitted before being presented to Parliament, which should have abated Chamberlain's opposition, even if he feared the long-term consequences of Irish internal self-government on this point. As we shall see, precisely the reverse happened.

The second matter was to be Chamberlain's prime target in the Bill—the exclusion of Irish representation from Westminster. Representation, he claimed, was 'a symbol of the effective union of the three kingdoms'. On 9 April 1886 he offered the Commons a major alternative to Irish devolution— a federal structure for the whole United Kingdom, reflecting, he said, the growing desire for federation of the whole Empire: 'The retention of the Irish representatives is clearly the *pierre de touche*. If they go, separation must follow—if they remain, Federation is possible', he told Dilke on 3 May 1886. Three days later, however, he was noting that 'retention . . . is only with me the flag that covers other objects', and that he wanted 'the whole Bill recast and brought back to the National Councils proposals'[38]—and this less than a month after informing the Commons that 'those National Councils I, for one, am not likely to put forward again'. As he had earlier told Labouchere, 'The difficulties of any plan are almost insurmountable, but the worst of all plans would be one which kept the Irishmen at Westminster while they had their own parliament in Dublin.'[39] It is no wonder that Gladstone later asserted that he would never again work with Chamberlain and his 'fluctuating schemes'.

The view that Chamberlain resisted Home Rule on grounds of imperial unification is altogether implausible. This is not to say that there was no continuity between his basic perspective on Home Rule and his later espousal of imperial federation. In 1886 he told Arthur Balfour that *his* Radicalism at least demanded a strong imperial parliament, a view reflecting the Birmingham experience that, where there was 'work to be done', political authority had to be clear and decisive. Chamberlain was never happy with arrangements which, like Home Rule, threatened to create overlapping, ambiguous, allegiances, or, like the structure of Empire he later inherited, rested on informal co-operation between independent authorities rather than formalized legal powers. This did not entail any intrinsic tendency towards state centralization. Like Gladstone and others he had over the previous years presented speeches and memoranda advocating forms of parliamentary devolution, so that an extended local government system could cater for questions of purely local or regional concern, relieve Westminster of trivial matters which consumed its time and energy, and provide it with better opportunities to concentrate on the important issues of the day.[40] Greater efficiency at the centre and more democracy in the localities was a prime objective. The National Councils scheme, entailing bodies indirectly elected from reformed county and borough councils with responsibilities over matters which presently fell primarily within the ambit of the Local Government Board and a number of other government Boards and Commissions was perhaps the furthest that such principles could be pushed. Federation was an altogether different matter, of course. In Chamberlain's correspondence of December 1885, and an article published anonymously in February 1886, we can find grounds for doubting his seriousness in advocating it. The message coming through was that the constitutional upheaval involved placed federation in the realms of Utopia rather than real politics. Even so, it did have the attractions of logical coherence. To put Ireland in a unique position of internal legislative autonomy raised serious questions of fairness to the rest of the Kingdom and, in the absence of any basic constitutional document, left the precise relationship between Westminster and Dublin open to interpretation. Federation at least provided a mechanism for equal treatment of all parts of the Union, and clarity on the separation of powers.

Chamberlain's instincts in this respect, combined with the weakness we have observed earlier of his sympathy for ideas of national self-determination, were antipathetic to the terms in which Gladstone and others appeared to be approaching Home Rule in 1885. Though the cry of 'Justice for Ireland' was always waiting in the wings, no senior Liberal had considered Irish legislation as anything other than a means of weakening the challenge of nationalism to preserve British rule. Even Chamberlain, always the most ready to flirt with the Nationalist Party, did so primarily as the best tactic to further the remedial legislation, and to enhance the political strength, of the Radicals. Gladstone in 1885 might see himself as developing the tradition, hoping that a 'union of hearts' would replace coercion as Britain's method of maintaining peace in Ireland: to Chamberlain, Ireland's vote in 1885 and the sorry experience he had undergone trying to make Parnell stick to agreed principles of devolution suggested that a Dublin parliament would not take the wind out of nationalism's sails, but provide a focal point of Irish nationhood and an instrument for extracting further powers of self-government out of Westminster.

In the existing parliamentary context, with strong possibilities of a right-wing Liberal revolt, it would also throw any Home Rule ministry into apparent collusion with Parnell on the central principle for which his party had been fighting. And this was Chamberlain's central consideration. Though he had serious objections to the idea of Home Rule, this does not provide a sufficient explanation of his decision to oppose it—so too did Dilke, Lord Rosebery and many others who ultimately clung to Gladstone's banner. Whatever Chamberlain's views on what in principle was the thing to do, he rarely moved without an incentive provided by the balance of political forces in his immediate environment. Gladstone had brought the issue forward in the context of a complex party-political situation, and Chamberlain was not alone in defining his position in terms of it. As the inimitable Churchill commented, 'Joe is right to walk warily. If the G.O.M. goes a-mucker, it may be a good thing for everybody.'[41]

Chamberlain had refused to discuss Irish policies before the 'Kite' because he was determined to keep out anything which cut across the issues on which he had fought for power in the election. His first comments on the 'Kite' reflected a continuing preoccupation with the results of that election. He argued, quite simply, that Liberalism's majority position, eroded in

1885, would be destroyed completely if the 'magnificent lunatic', as Dilke once described Gladstone, was left free to turn
Home Rule into Liberalism's new cause.

The state of public and parliamentary opinion towards the
cause was unknown, but it could reasonably be guessed at.
Many Liberals were anxious to recoup lost Irish votes, some had
a conscience about delivering 'Justice to Ireland', and many
shared Schnadhorst's view that 'I do not think there is any love
for the Irish about but I am sure there is an eager desire if
possible to get Ireland out of the way.'[42] Legislating with
belligerent Nationalists holding the Commons balance appeared a horrifying prospect, and offering the choice 'Home
Rule or Coercion' to a party which had experienced five years
of disaster with the latter was likely to appeal. On the other side
lay deep hostility to further appeasement of forces which had
produced such disruption in and out of Parliament: solidarity
which could be mobilized with Ulster Protestantism: long-
standing 'no-popery' and anti-Irish feelings in many parts of
Britain, particularly Lancashire; and, not least, pure un-
adulterated nationalist identity with the unity of the Kingdom.
To many middle-class voters, Home Rule would appear a final
irresponsible Liberal swing to the left after condoning attacks
on private property and the Church. It was not clear that there
would be compensating gains. Schnadhorst had warned
Chamberlain two years before, without respecting his own
advice in 1886, that 'the cry of "Justice for Ireland" would not
awaken enthusiasm in the English constituencies . . . [W]e
cannot win the election of '85 as we did that of '68 on the cry of
"Justice for Ireland" *by itself* . . . [S]ide by side with the claims
of Ireland must be put the claims of England and Scotland.'
Chamberlain had taken this to heart in 1885 and, even without
the Irish dimension, failed. Despite the favourable county
results, Schnadhorst's earlier comments might still apply: 'The
labourers will vote for the party which they think will better
their conditions—[the land question] is a matter with them not
of sentiment but of bread and cheese.'[43] What bread and cheese
did Home Rule have to offer them? And would even those
voters who had remained loyal in the recalcitrant boroughs
forgive a party which dropped all concern for their problems to
appease the apparently insatiable Irish?

In the battle of slogans, Home Rulers were likely to be out-stripped. Churchill's 'Ulster will fight and Ulster will be right' was a new entry, but seemed like having a good run for its money: 'Home Rule is Rome rule' was always a good bet: 'The Union must be preserved', imported by Bright to support the North during the American Civil War, could be revitalized, and it certainly impressed Bright himself, who always referred to the Nationalists as a 'rebel party'.

Favourite, however, was 'The Empire in Danger', and those who backed it received a good return. Gladstone might claim that his Bill was compatible with 'the integrity of the Empire', but 'imperial integrity', like 'parliamentary sovereignty' in British debates during the 1970s over the Common Market, was a notoriously ambiguous concept. This ambiguity was its strongest attraction as a slogan for opponents of Home Rule. It was clear to Chamberlain that this was what Churchill and the Conservatives would employ to improve their fortunes, as he told Dilke after the 'Kite':

Why the d . . . d could Gladstone not wait till Parnell had broken with the Tories? . . . [I]f they are wise they will throw everything else aside and go for 'The Empire in Danger', dissolving at the earliest possible opportunity. The Liberals would be divided and distracted and I think we shall be beaten into a cocked hat.

His comment illustrates three things. One is that Chamberlain's subsequent stand on the imperial unity issue reflected, not a unique appreciation of Home Rule's dangers, but his adhesion to the cry that defined all opposition to the Bill. A second was that his immediate objection was not simply to Home Rule, but to taking initiatives in the direction of the Nationalists rather than waiting for them to come cap in hand having failed with the government. Thirdly, it makes his overriding fears about the electoral implications of Home Rule quite plain.

The prospect of a Conservative dissolution was to be averted, but an election seemed inevitable, were Gladstone to go ahead. If he formed a Home Rule ministry, the Commons might rebel, entailing a dissolution or a Conservative successor which would certainly go to the country. If Home Rule passed the Commons, the Lords would reject it, and an election on 'The Peers against the People' might have little impact when the only 'People' affected would be the Irish. Liberal divisions were inevitable. Chamberlain was not opposed to ditching the Whigs, but in later years observed that 'I should not have broken up the party, I should have strengthened the party by dropping the Whigs, and I should have carried not one but two or three unauthorised programmes.' In the case of Home Rule,

the fear is that anything like a bargain with the Irish would be resented by the English and Scotch workmen and that a Tory–Whig coalition appealing to their prejudices against a Radical–Parnellite alliance would carry all before them . . . English opinion is set strongly against Home Rule, and the Radical Party might be permanently (i.e. for our time) discredited by a concession on this point.[44]

Liberalism's future lay in a long-term leftward shift, not in a sudden lurch around a minority cause. Labouchere's advice of early December had to be rejected in favour of Brett's, which, of all things, involved fighting Gladstone's influence over the Radicals in order to keep the Whigs within the party.

In the uncertain post-Kite situation, however, Chamberlain could warn Gladstone and Radical followers privately that Home Rule would be disastrous, but not as yet go into public opposition to his leader; and a speech in Birmingham on 17 December, intended to 'drive the knife' into the Whigs, became a cautious calculation on the political balance which finally came down in favour of ejecting the government. This abandonment of agreed tactics infuriated Dilke, but was inevitable, and it was the first jab in a prolonged fencing match among the Liberals. Hartington publicly rejected Home Rule on 21 December, embarrassing Gladstone and offering his leadership of the right-wing reaction, and Morley countered demanding a Home Rule ministry, alreading balking at Chamberlain's lead: Harcourt was 'raving against the "Old Man and the Old Cause"', and angling for a Hartington–Chamberlain compact to stop Gladstone.

Dishing Gladstone was not going to be an easy task for Chamberlain. In late December Dilke made a speech emphasizing National Councils as the only possibility for Ireland, but with the divorce scandal which was ultimately to ruin his career now in train,[45] Dilke's word carried decreasing weight. Chamberlain was pandering to Morley's anti-militarism by claiming that Home Rule would create a hostile, independent Ireland, imposing increased armaments on Britain, but Morley, like Labouchere, was resisting his entreaties. The Radical junta was now a dead letter. Nor was a junta of the 'strong men' of the ex-cabinet capable of offering an alternative. On 25 December Harcourt wrote to Granville asking for a leadership meeting, as a means of 'bringing Gladstone to book', but was rebuffed. Instead, at Chamberlain's suggestion, Hartington, Harcourt, Dilke, and he met on 1 January. They threatened to call a party meeting unless Gladstone disavowed Home Rule, but Gladstone had in letters to Chamberlain and Hartington been refusing to commit himself to any definite plans, and in the absence of these a party meeting was absurd. Gladstone simply wrote refusing to meet the chief dissidents except individually after his arrival in London for the meeting of Parliament on the 12th. 'It is evident that he proposes to "nobble" us in detail,' was Chamberlain's rueful comment.

He was, however, already preparing to be 'nobbled'. On 1 January Hartington seemed willing to follow Dilke's public advice and go for the Central Board, but found that he could no longer carry Chamberlain on this. The problem which had dogged Chamberlain since 1882 was re-emerging: prepared for Hartington's succession on the right terms, he could not afford to accept it in opposition to Gladstone. Harcourt had earlier observed that he wanted Hartington to oust Gladstone but 'will not promise to support [him] afterwards', for, as Chamberlain told Dilke, 'the Whigs are our greatest enemy and we must not join them if we can help it.' In early January he was having to move closer towards Home Rule by recommending a Dublin parliament with Ireland placed in a restricted protected status. Granville's comment was that 'I do not see the bridge over which even the Prince of Opportunists can pass. But while we are certainly not the people to cross it, . . . it would be a mistake to barricade it against his passage.'[46]

Gladstone indeed was still hoping that most of his former colleagues could be drawn across the bridge. He was working on moderate Whigs to isolate Hartington, and at his private meetings in early January refused to make any commitments on future policy which would allow further polarization. The situation was moving in his favour. On 20 December he had made a last desperate plea through Arthur Balfour, Salisbury's nephew and one of Churchill's Fourth Party men, for cross-bench co-operation on Ireland, but the resignation of Lord Carnarvon in mid-January signified the end of this possibility. Parnell had reaffirmed his support for the Tories on the 9th, but his future clearly lay with Gladstone. The Conservatives themselves were in some confusion. Churchill, having pressed for legislation which would attract the Whigs and thereby, he hoped, keep the government in office with himself in a pivotal position, was now opposing coercion, introduction of which, as Chamberlain observed to him, would entail the ministry's rejection on some side issue. Chamberlain also warned against a dissolution, ostensibly since it would throw Liberalism united into Gladstone's arms. Despite hoping for the government's continued survival, he was also preparing contingency plans for Gladstone's accession which did not involve Liberal commitments on Ireland. On 21 January a shadow cabinet meeting discussed his plan for an amendment to the Address from Collings on the lines of 'Three acres and a cow'. Gladstone agreed to a three line whip on the vote, and, through O'Shea, Chamberlain asked Parnell for Irish backing. When the government finally decided to risk the toss and give notice of the introduction of coercion, its fate was sealed. On 27 January, on Collings's motion, it was defeated by 79 votes, though Hartington took 18 Liberal MPs into the Tory lobby and 76 abstained. Chamberlain had pinned the party to agrarian reform, but in circumstances which made it totally irrelevant.

Gladstone replaced Salisbury and faced the task of forming his government. For his chief colleagues the question of whether to participate or not involved fine calculation. Gladstone had managed to avoid committing either himself or most of the party on Home Rule, and approached the most reticent candidates for office with a shrewd memorandum in which the ministry's tasks were stated as being to 'examine whether it is or is not practicable to comply with the desire of [Irish MPs]' for a Dublin parliament. Anticipating that Gladstone would fail and they would reap the benefits, Hartington and many Whigs declined even this open-ended invitation, but neither Harcourt nor Chamberlain was willing, as yet, to risk outright resistance.

Both took their decision to join reluctantly. Attempting to impose conditions on Irish policy, they were bluntly advised not to prejudge an open inquiry. Gladstone held the whip-hand in allocating offices, though he had some difficulty in filling them, and the plum jobs were directed away from Chamberlain. He was offered the Admiralty, a graveyard for any Radical, aspired to the Treasury, and asked for the Colonial Office. His claim to a post which, if not amongst the most powerful state offices, carried a prestigious title and a higher salary rate, received from Gladstone, according to Chamberlain, the disparaging response, 'Oh! A Secretary of State!' This insensitivity to Chamberlain's *amour propre* extended even further when Gladstone selected the Under-Secretaryship later offered to Jesse Collings as one meriting a cut in salary for the sake of government economy. Chamberlain himself eventually accepted what was virtually a demotion to the Local Government Board, and there was little cheer to be gained when he viewed the rest of the cabinet. Dilke was excluded because of the divorce case. Morley was included, but promoted over his head as Irish Secretary, and designated as Gladstone's instrument for dividing the Radicals: Chamberlain paled visibly when he heard the news. The Whig representation—Spencer, Ripon, Kimberley, Granville, Childers—were to rock the boat, but would never leave it since only Gladstone would by now have seriously considered them for high office; Campbell-Bannerman and Mundella were firm Gladstone men, though Trevelyan remained attached to Chamberlain—the last of the junta; and Harcourt, however opposed to Gladstone and Home Rule, was not going to abandon his promotion to the Exchequer without very good cause.

So far Chamberlain had consistently followed his own advice after the 'Kite' of 'wait and see', muttering practical objections to Home Rule in speeches, and participating in anti-Gladstonian cabals, but not risking total opposition. He was in a cabinet which largely shared his own reticence about Home Rule, and which was only a Home Rule ministry because those who refused office did so refusing even to discuss the policy. There was a chance yet that Gladstone might give up his impossible task, leaving Chamberlain in a powerful position as a Gladstonian who yet shared Hartington's reservations and could thus rally all sections of the party. He also soon found that, though neglecting him after the election, Gladstone was now paying more attention and within a few days of forming his government in early February requesting his views on Ireland.

Chamberlain's answer reflected a line which he had been developing over the previous fortnight. When seeking Parnell's aid in defeating the Tory government, he had also asked whether Irish support would be forthcoming for local government reform and land purchase schemes, with Home Rule delayed to a time when opinion had been better prepared. This was a plan on which the Liberals might have united—at the time, indeed, Hartington was hinting at his readiness to take even wider devolution—but it would make Gladstone redundant, and Parnell, believing he could get Home Rule from Gladstone, declined. When Chamberlain passed this suggestion, together with a detailed land purchase scheme, on to Gladstone, it was placed on the shelf to collect dust. Part of Chamberlain's intentions in this can perhaps be gathered from a *Fortnightly Review* article of 1 February written anonymously before the government's fall.[48] In it he rejected as impracticable all schemes of political reform in Ireland and instead suggested inviting Parnell or, if he refused, some other Irish politician to enter government and frame a land purchase measure. Refusal should be met by publication of the correspondence and an appeal to the electorate. His thesis was that 'if there were no agrarian discontent in Ireland, the desire for Home Rule might be safely gratified, but in this case it is almost certain that the desire would not exist'; and if the Liberals went to Ireland, denouncing Nationalist sacrifice of the tenants for Home Rule, the Irish MPs 'would have some difficulty in justifying themselves to their constituents.'

Fragmenting the Irish phalanx in this way was a bold but rational plan to pacify Ireland without breaking the Liberals: with Gladstone intent on holding the initiative, it was out of the question. Instead Chamberlain resorted to the more tortuous manœuvre of supporting O'Shea's candidacy for the Galway by-election after his rejection by the Nationalists for refusing their ticket in 1885. Parnell declined to oppose because of his liaison with Mrs O'Shea, creating a rift with some of his followers who then put up their own candidate. A major row ensued. But Chamberlain had neglected to note that, for the first time, Parnell was king in Ireland, not *primus inter pares*, and when, on 9 February, he turned on the rebels, resistance collapsed and O'Shea gained his seat.

Gladstone had determined on ensuring Parnell's support and Chamberlain's stratagems held no appeal. He was left for a month to plan a futile measure of local government reform while Gladstone and his close allies made plans for Ireland. The parliamentary party was soon setting down to the work of a legislative programme of minor reforms, satisfying to the left but giving him no credit for their inspiration. He might have been hoping that Gladstone would decide on the sensible course of going slow on Ireland, and, though on 7 March Harcourt claimed to have an abbreviated draft Home Rule Bill, Gladstone did in fact approach the issue gingerly. On 13 March he presented the cabinet with a Land Purchase proposal involving £120m loans from taxation to be repaid over twenty years on the basis of existing land values. At a time of falling land prices, it constituted, as Gladstone intended and Chamberlain pointed out, a massive bribe to the Irish landlords which many were later inclined to accept. As it happened Chamberlain's own scheme presented to Gladstone in mid-February had also been generous (which later caused him some embarrassment when Herbert Gladstone leaked the details), and he did not push his objections to Gladstone's measure on these grounds. Instead, he demanded an outline of the prepared Home Rule Bill, without which, he claimed, he could not evaluate the security of the proposed loan. Gladstone was unwillingly forced to concede this, Chamberlain objected, threatened to withdraw, and two days later sent in his resignation on the grounds that massive credit was being used, not to solidify Anglo-Irish relations, but to prepare for an independent parliament which would be an insufficient guarantee of repayment. Trevelyan sided with him, but Gladstone persuaded both to stay until they had heard the details of his Home Rule measure.

The next cabinet was delayed until 26 March. In the mean-time Gladstone, Spencer, Morley and Granville worked on possible compromises with Chamberlain's earlier paper on land, and Harcourt attempted negotiations on Home Rule. All Chamberlain could suggest was a federal plan on American lines—hardly helpful when he had several times rejected it as utopian.[49]

Chamberlain's vigorous reaction had been unexpected, and Gladstone opened the 26 March cabinet with a conciliatory gesture to avert a polarization of his cabinet. He suggested proceeding with a Home Rule resolution to the Commons, with details to be presented later. To be committed in this way was not on Chamberlain's agenda, and he retaliated with a direct demand for answers to four questions on the prepared scheme: Would Irish representation at Westminster cease? Would the Dublin parliament have control over taxation, customs and excise? Would the Irish executive make appoint-ments to the law courts? Would any residual powers go to the Dublin rather than Westminster parliament? The answer to each was: Yes; at which he and Trevelyan collected their papers and left. 'Nothing in this whole affair gave me greater satisfaction than Chamberlain's resignation,' Gladstone later commented. His leading opponent in cabinet had gone out on an issue with Radicalism confused and divided. Liberalism would have a Radical programme, but the *coup* planned by its leaders since August was now dead.

Why did Chamberlain take this gamble? That he thought Home Rule inexpedient is not a full reason, since so did half the cabinet who did not resign. By now, indeed, he and others on what was soon to be called the 'Unionist' side were less than fully confident that the electorate would reject Home Rule Liberalism. He was also aware that 'The immediate result [of fighting Gladstone] will be considerable unpopularity and temporary estrangement from the Radical party,' and soon found that this applied even in Birmingham. Most of the city's leading families and all but one of its MPs—Henry Broadhurst, the prominent trade-union leader imported to enhance the credibility of Chamberlain's pro-labour appeal in 1885—had strong reservations about Gladstone's Home Rule strategy, but Schnadhorst, key organizer of the caucus, was setting out to turn the local party and the Federation against him, in part out of resentment at Chamberlain's past refusal to consider him for any more prestigious position.

Chamberlain could have remained in the cabinet, allying with Harcourt to delay, modify, or perhaps even hold up indefinitely the Home Rule Bill. The succession to Gladstone might then possibly have been his. But he was impatient. The leading contenders for power were all intent on establishing their claims in the impending crisis, and Chamberlain saw that his earlier actions had lost him any possible role as Gladstone's right-hand man. To stay on through long, tortuous manœuvres would allow Gladstone to strengthen his hold on the party while still leaving open the possibility that his Whig opponents would win the day. On balance, declaring publicly his opposition to Gladstone seemed the best tactic. Whether Gladstone won, lost, or gave up the struggle, the shattered Liberal leadership would eventually have to resolve itself on some line or other, and, from his independent position, Chamberlain would be in a far stronger position to dictate his own terms for participation in any new party structure. 'I think I shall win this fight,' he told Dilke in May, 'and shall in the long run have an increase of public influence.'

The task after resigning was to present himself as leader of a strong left-wing threat to the ministry, thereby forcing Gladstone to abandon or emasculate his scheme and hence acknowledge his political importance. Much to his annoyance, the number of Radical backbenchers ready to back their dislike of Home Rule with action was far smaller than he expected. Furthermore, a difficult game had to be played. Open collaboration with the right-wing opposition would ruin his Radical credentials, and on 6 April he wrote to Bunce denying rumours of negotiations. On his own, however, he could do little, and if the Tories and Hartington decided to ignore him, he would be isolated totally. While trying to convince the government that it could do nothing about Home Rule without him, he had also, therefore, to convince other Unionists that they could only defeat it with him. Judicious release of cabinet secrets to Churchill had paved the way for Unionist co-operation, and at a dinner on 22 April Chamberlain convinced Balfour at least that it was upon him that the future of Home Rule would depend.[50] He, Hartington, Churchill, and Salisbury were later successfully to co-ordinate tactics, despite great personal suspicion, and Chamberlain's advice was frequently the most important influence on their strategies—though Hartington ignored it, at considerable cost to his Liberal reputation, by agreeing to a joint meeting with Salisbury at the Opera House on 14 April.

After Chamberlain's resignation, Gladstone had gone ahead fast with his plans for Ireland and on 8 April presented his first measure to the Commons. Abandoning his former caution he had decided to promote Home Rule before land purchase, a move with the additional boon of embarrassing Chamberlain who had resigned primarily on the latter. In replying to Gladstone's great speech introducing the Bill, he intended to review the conditions on which he had entered government and refer to the 15 March resignation letter, having obtained, so he thought, the Queen's permission through Gladstone. But Gladstone tricked him. He interrupted his speech of 9 April four times to protest, inaccurately, that royal permission extended only to the measure before the House and not to the Land Bill yet to be introduced. Whether Chamberlain anticipated this or not—he had been warned beforehand by Churchill and a careful reading of Gladstone's letters would have revealed ambiguities—the event delighted the Irish, but did not detract from Chamberlain's belief that his speech had been a great success, at least in displaying Gladstone's unfair treatment of him.

It was in fact masterfully constructed. Morley had told him that concessions were to be made to one of his objections: to guarantee repayments under the Land Bill, and avert an independent, possibly protectionist, tariff policy in Ireland, customs and excise were now to be levied by the Imperial Parliament. Clause 24 of the Bill excluding Irish representation now assumed even greater importance. Chamberlain levelled his basic objection that representation was necessary to symbolize the unity of the Kingdom and the subordination of any Dublin parliament, but added that the absence of Irish MPs from the body levying revenue contravened the oldest of Radical principles, 'No Taxation without Representation'. Without representation, there could be no permanent solution;

Irish politicians would constantly complain of exploitation by the English Treasury, and movements would arise to break the last imperial links. Chamberlain also took up in his speech Churchill's flirtation with the Ulster Protestants, a useful weapon in appealing to Dissenting followers, and tied together all his objections by abandoning the National Councils scheme and advocating plans for a United Kingdom federation. Scotland, Wales, and Ulster, as well as Dublin, were each to have legislatures within a union framework, thereby reconciling the principles of democratic devolution, the protection of minorities, and sovereignty of the Imperial Parliament.

For non-recipients of his private correspondence in recent weeks, this was a bolt from the blue. Churchill and Hartington had urged him simply to oppose the Bill and not fool around with alternatives unacceptable to other Unionists, but, having established an *entente* with the right wing, Chamberlain's concern was now to find his strongest position. He would accept Home Rule, reinterpret it under a scheme broad enough to validate his Radical credentials and divert suspicions of a united anti-Gladstonian cave, thereby stabbing Gladstone's Bill in the back.

His objections had struck home at the weak spots in the Bill, and when Gladstone next spoke he shrewdly responded to them: Clause 24, he suggested, might be 'reserved for further consideration', as would safeguards for the Ulster minority, while other objections should be left for debate in the Committee stage of the Bill. The Land Bill, introduced on 15 April, also showed modifications, in particular conceding Chamberlain's protest at the size of the proposed loan. Now Chamberlain raised another charge. The new figure, he argued, was far too low to cover the cost of purchase, and the proposal to draw repayments of the loan from Irish excise duties imposed by the British exchequer was complicated, an admission of distrust in the new parliament, and would still provide a lever for separatist agitators. After Gladstone's concessions, however, his speech was in a conciliatory mood, declaring that amendment of Clause 24, which he had earlier called the 'key to the whole situation', would make all other safeguards in the Bill unnecessary.

The issue of Clause 24 was complex, and Chamberlain had

good grounds for claiming that Gladstone had given insufficient attention to its problems. But he played it up essentially for propaganda purposes. Apart from its symbolic value, Irish representation also appeared one thing that Gladstone could not yield. It had been included in the early schemes of Labouchere, Healy and Herbert Gladstone, and Parnell himself wanted it. But Granville, Harcourt, and Morley were all insistent on removal, or severe curtailment, of the Irish MPs, and for most Liberals the one thing to be said for Home Rule was the shunting of disruptive discussions of Irish affairs from the Commons. For Chamberlain, Clause 24 had the same virtues as Clause 25 of the 1870 Education Act—it could be claimed as a minor issue on which the government was being unreasonably pig-headed, and a major issue of principle affecting the whole nature of the Bill: Nationalists might be expected to balk when he claimed that concession on this issue would ensure that 'except in name . . . it would be difficult to see very much difference between the proposal and the proposal of national councils . . . or a single national council'.[51]

With his views stated to the Commons, Chamberlain next had to guarantee his position in Birmingham. Having already postponed a meeting of the '2000' until the Bills were introduced, he now wanted to address it on 21 April against Schnadhorst's desire for further delay. The speech was carefully constructed, declaring uncompromising opposition to the Land Bill, but asserting that amendment of Clause 24 and satisfactory guarantees for the Ulster minority would allow him to vote for Home Rule. With Bunce in control of the Management Committee, and a strong speech from Dale supporting his reservations, Chamberlain defeated Schnadhorst's attempt to prevent a vote and gained approval for the principle of 'Home Rule, yes: exclusion of the Irish, no'[52]

With Birmingham temporarily secure, Chamberlain set to work on the task of strengthening his parliamentary position. Most Liberals were anxious to rebuild party unity, and negotiations between government and dissidents were the order of the day. But as Churchill summarized the position: 'Gladstone is pretending to make up to Joe in order to pass his Bill; and Joe is pretending to make up to Gladstone in order to throw out his Bill. Diamond cut diamond.'[53] Labouchere was the intermediary—a perfect choice for such dishonest brokerage—and the basis of negotiations was a hint thrown out in Gladstone's earlier speech, that if the Second Reading were carried, the Bill would be open to amendment in Committee. Chamberlain emphasized that he wanted a restructuring of Clause 24, and minor amendments on imperial taxation and the over-representation of landed interests in the new legislature, to vote for the Second Reading: the assurances, however, had to be given in advance and made public. Labouchere's advice to wait for the Committee stage was rejected outright: 'I know enough of parliamentary tactics to be sure that . . . we shall get nothing, but be beaten in every division'. The compromise of a free vote in Committee was likewise brushed aside. Chamberlain knew his chief weapon was a threat to the Second Reading, and was not ready to disarm without good cause.

Though Harcourt warned that 'You and I know Gladstone well enough to be quite aware that the notion of your dictating to him publicly terms of surrender is quite out of the question', Chamberlain's stand could rightly be described by Labouchere as this 'sic volo, sic jubeo style', and by Morley as a 'five-barrelled ultimatum'. Though unwilling to lose face by giving way, the government could not dismiss such threats. Shaw Lefevre had recently fought Forster's old seat at Bradford and lost half the Liberal majority, despite Irish support, largely because of the Land Bill, it was thought: and in late April, after MPs had faced their constituents during the Easter recess, Chamberlain could threaten the government with a hundred Liberals opposed to Home Rule, of whom fifty would support the Second Reading if Clause 24 were amended. Gloom pervaded the Home Rule camp. A manifesto from Gladstone on 1 May aggressively supported Home Rule with a cry of 'the masses against the classes', but also publicly abandoned the Land Bill and declared a vote for the Second Reading to be a vote simply for the principle, not the clauses, of the Bill. There were also private concessions. Labouchere observed that major revisions of Clause 24 would cause a cabinet split but offered Chamberlain three alternatives: an open vote in Committee on the clause; amendment to exclude the Irish for three years, and their automatic return unless further legislation were passed—Morley's suggestion; or the elimination of Clause 24 entirely.[54]

The last major concession attracted Chamberlain, though he feared that exclusion at this stage would not preclude its re-introduction in Committee. It also undercut his major weapon against the Bill. His response was to demand a statement that, if the Bill passed its Second Reading, it would be then withdrawn for drastic overhaul. This was tantamount to Gladstone's suggestion on 26 March for a Home Rule resolution, but Labouchere noted that the government now had gone too far to accept it. It gave consideration to a further compromise but, as Chamberlain had anticipated, became bogged down in the implications that Irish representation would have for other clauses in the Bill. Gladstone himself appears to have given the mediators little help. Labouchere, the Chancellor, Herschell, and the Chief Whip, Arnold Morley, were left to conduct negotiations designed largely to keep his worried cabinet intact.

Chamberlain, too, was making compromise difficult. To Morley's fair comment that he was trying to make the cabinet go down on its knees, he retorted in a letter read out in cabinet that Morley had changed his captain but was still a 'powder monkey': Harcourt was told that 'I do not want a compromise . . . but I am compelled to make advances to satisfy the anxiety of my friends'—which showed that yielding on Clause 24 would not be a final solution: in a letter to Labouchere for the cabinet he claimed that 'I doubt if, even with my assistance, the second reading can be carried'—which eliminated any reason for conceding his objections.[55] The most drastic rebuff came on the eve of Gladstone's introduction of the Second Reading on 10 May. On Saturday 8 May, the day on which Labouchere had told him there would be an important cabinet, Chamberlain published in the press his decision to vote against the Bill unless Clause 24 were altered, but added that the Bill was founded on incorrect principles and needed reconstruction along federal lines; and, when Labouchere told him of concessions agreed in cabinet, he followed up this slap in the face with a series of telegrams declaring the 'surrender' to be 'complete'. News of these soon became public and Gladstone was compelled to deny any intention of major reconstruction.

It was still unclear, however, what he would say on 10 May,

and Chamberlain had prepared his tactics with other Unionist leaders. If major concessions on Clause 24 were offered, he would announce the need for amendments to other clauses—'if the Bill gets into committee it will go to pieces on one of these rocks'—and 'I shall make it clear that the concession does not satisfy me except as a step towards the complete recast of the Bill.'[56]

This proved unnecessary. Gladstone produced one of his famous 'porridge' speeches, the substance of which escaped even acute observers. Concessions were made—the Irish MPs might sit in Westminster for certain, particularly taxation, debates—but the tone was hostile, and any changes, it appeared, would be conditional on Irish approval. Parnell, that is, not Chamberlain, was the man the government was concerned to accommodate. The speech upset those Liberals who had worked for compromise, but it had the advantage from Gladstone's viewpoint of building up further tension. On 5 May Chamberlain had lost a vote in the Federation central committee,[57] a grave setback though one allowing him to persuade Bunce and others into resigning and moving further into his camp, but Gladstone was heartened into believing that further delay would swing opinion in his favour.

The speech, too, was a perfect opportunity for Chamberlain to discredit Gladstone and his intermediaries, and on 12 May he called a meeting of fifty-two opponents of the Bill which declared unanimously against further private negotiations and in favour of rejecting the Bill without substantial changes. Two days later he and thirty-two followers attended a Hartington gathering of sixty-four. For the first time, hard-line opposition to the Bill could be assessed. The joint meeting was necessary, Chamberlain argued defensively to his brother, Arthur, anticipating objections from Birmingham, in order to display the opposition's cohesion since he no longer expected further concessions.

In Parliament, he was becoming the linchpin of the opposition. The Conservatives wisely left the running to Liberal defectors, and among these Chamberlain's marginal group of 'sympathetic critics' held the Bill's fate in their hands. His position, however, was still difficult. The conciliatory gestures might impress Birmingham and wavering MPs, but the mass party, fearing an impending split, was little affected. Herbert Gladstone claimed that he would never get a hearing outside Birmingham, and Labouchere that his name was met at meetings with stony silence. His position in Parliament was also insecure. Close Radical supporters were few: the dissidents who failed to attend the 14 May meeting were likely to turn tail at the first opportunity, and those who went were in many cases moderates using Chamberlain's name, as he knew, to protect themselves from their constituency parties. Private negotiations continued throughout May over the strategy of dropping the Bill after its Second Reading, to reintroduce it in a modified form during the autumn, but little changed until Gladstone summoned a party meeting for 27 May which Chamberlain refused to attend, though many supporters did. Their resolution was severely shaken by Gladstone's offer to 'reconstruct' Clause 24 in a wholly new Bill if the Second Reading were carried.

Chamberlain's latest demand had been publicly accepted and he was only saved from a humiliating acquiescence with the help of his allies. On the 28th Churchill and Sir Michael Hicks Beach launched a clever debating attack which forced Gladstone to reassert his point of the previous day in a manner which made the likely 'reconstruction' of his Bill appear minimal. Chamberlain called a meeting to rally his still-shaken followers on 31 May, at which he was able to advise only a policy of abstention on the Second Reading. Three factors, however, allowed him to get what he wanted. One was the attendance of many Hartington men to swell his depleted ranks; the second was a letter from Bright, requested and read out selectively by Chamberlain, advising abstention but observing his own decision to vote against, which set a good example for many MPs to face their constituents; the third was an announcement that Conservatives would not stand against Liberal Unionists in the event of an election—the repetition of an offer made to a Hartington meeting two days earlier. With this reinforcement, Chamberlain was able to obtain the support of forty-six MPs against the Bill.[58]

His position restored, he could afford to speak for the first time during the Second Reading debates on 1 June. Here he rejected voting for the Bill, despite Gladstone's pledge of subsequent withdrawal, as tantamount to a commitment of support for the later measure, and insisted on its substitution by a Resolution. Once more, having been conceded his chief demand, he shifted ground while continuing to accuse Gladstone of intransigence. And, despite last minute manœuvres, the political balance laid down on 31 May was reflected in the final vote on 9 June. The Bill was defeated by thirty votes, ninety-three Liberals joining the Opposition. After a brief cabinet discussion Gladstone dissolved Parliament as he had been threatening for some weeks, the Liberals' first step into a political wilderness which was to last for twenty years.

Explanations of this disaster have been many and varied. J. L. Hammond once implied[59] that Gladstone in effect killed his own Bill by refusing concessions or making them with a bad grace—a view Chamberlain himself was inclined to publicize. But Home Rule did not fail solely through such tactical and personal deficiencies.

Gladstone's correspondence of late 1885 shows that three worries dominated his thoughts: the challenge of Irish Nationalism, the increasingly ungenerous narrow-mindedness of many Whigs, and the 'rampant ambition' of the truculent Radical leaders. These problems became inextricably entwined in his mind as posing an extended threat to the fabric of British political life and its development along lines of moderate and peaceful progress. He became determined in the final years of his career to present a radical solution—a solution whose essential element consisted in a *concordat* with Parnellite Nationalism to put Hartington and Chamberlain in their traditional roles subordinate to his personal interpretation of Liberalism. It was an egocentric, authoritarian, conception of the party, though one with which his colleagues were familiar. For the first time, however, Hartington and Chamberlain, himself an egocentric authoritarian, had decided that they could afford to pick up the gauntlet. Neither was inherently as inflexible as Gladstone, or the other, at times liked to make out. In relation to Ireland, virtually every leading politician after the 1885 election accepted that changes would have to be made in the province, and the question of reform was more a matter of degree than of principle. All—including Gladstone before the Kite forced his hand—recognized the dangers in taking any initiative before some degree of political consensus had emerged. Only Gladstone had the courage, or, as it turned out, foolhardiness, to think that a viable government could be formed with concessions to Ireland as the core, and not merely a part, of its programme. The impossibility of the task had been clearly established by April 1886; and once Gladstone had succeeded in forcing Hartington to concede the principle of devolution, and in compelling Chamberlain and Hartington to work closely together, if only against him, the statesman-like course would have been to retire and leave his natural successors to work out the future along lines he had laid down.

Carrying on with, rather than initiating, Home Rule, heading a cabinet of the 'second eleven' and opposed by his best ex-ministers was Gladstone's prime contribution to the Liberal split. It reflected a determination pure and simple to crush those, particularly Chamberlain, who had dared to challenge him and, in a rising spiral of hostility, increased their own determination to bring him to his knees. The sort of concessions and compromises which had kept the Liberal leadership in harness for two decades, and which backbench MPs continued to urge over Home Rule, were not possible once Gladstone decided to slough off his conservative wing and undermine the leading spokesman of the left. The parliamentary skirmishing of spring 1886, even had it succeeded in getting Home Rule through its Second Reading, would still have made only a marginal difference to the outcome of a winner-take-all contest which would not be decided, everyone recognized, for some time after the implications of the inevitable election had been worked out.

In the event, none of the Liberal leaders secured their aims from Home Rule (and among the Conservatives perhaps only Salisbury, though at a higher cost than he anticipated). It proved to offer insecure foundations for a new Gladstonian Liberalism, and the stigma attached to devolution as a result of the circumstances in which it was adopted in 1886 certainly delayed its extension to Ireland far longer than was necessary. In this respect, Chamberlain's advice of December—to wait for Parnell to break with the Conservatives and force him in his isolation to accept a prolonged programme of reform from a more broadly-based Liberal government—was perhaps a more practical suggestion. If Gladstone's plans came unstuck, so too did those of Hartington and his followers, whose moderate, centrist, position gradually turned under the impact of the struggle into a defensive conservatism. Chamberlain's intentions simply vanished into thin air. He soon found that his marginal position as a critical Home Ruler, intended to be the pivot around which the re-formation of a Liberal coalition would be undertaken, was wholly untenable. Through political skill he won every battle, but victory in the campaign eluded him. Whether his loss ultimately benefited Liberalism, as Gladstone believed, is uncertain. It has often been claimed that Gladstone persistently underestimated Chamberlain's abilities, the strength and significance of his 'constructionist' policies, and that personal misunderstandings exacerbated political disagreements unnecessarily. There is some truth in this. Though Gladstone was right in believing that Chamberlain's strength was often exaggerated, not least by Chamberlain himself, growing personal dislike blinded him to the fact that, if treated with respect, Chamberlain could prove an amenable and co-operative colleague: when ignored or put on the defensive, as after December 1885, his reactions could be unpredictable and dangerous. Furthermore, Gladstone failed to appreciate that Chamberlain's ideological synthesis of Radicalism and 'constructionist' policies had an important role to play for the future: certainly after 1908, the last Liberal government found it the most useful counter to the challenge of Labour and Tory radicalism. Gladstone, however, appreciated something which Chamberlain failed fully to grasp in 1885: the mid-Victorian Liberal electoral coalition largely survived by underplaying the politics of economic self-interest, and once Chamberlain inscribed them on the Liberal banner in 1885, the basis of that coalition was severely shaken. Gladstone's mistake was to believe that it could be restored by transcending social issues with the moral crusade of 'Justice for Ireland'. Chamberlain had long before observed that cries of 'Bread for the Starving' had a far stronger mass appeal than those of 'Education for the Ignorant', and in the 1890s showed that Gladstonian moral politics stood little chance against a new party appealing to the economic self-interest of a disparate popular electorate.

New party lines were not, however, drawn by the vote of

June 1886, nor by the election beginning on 1 July, significant though the results were in raising Conservative representation from 249 to 316 seats, cutting the Gladstonians down to 191 with 85 for their Nationalist allies, and leaving Liberal Unionists holding the balance with 78. Many Liberal dissidents survived largely due to Conservative neutrality, but, as in the Home Rule debates, their independence was jealously guarded. Hartington had founded his own Liberal Unionist Committee in April though Chamberlain, wary of antagonizing Radical supporters, declined to join until after the vote, meantime arranging for his brother Arthur to form a National Radical Union, whose vice-chairmen would be the forty-six rebels of 31 May. Its programme, representing once more a shift of ground, was the old National Councils scheme. From this position he issued an election address on 11 June attacking Gladstone's Bill and officially launched the Union at a Birmingham meeting on the 18th.

In the election Chamberlain's candidates carried Birmingham's seven seats despite Gladstonian opposition in two and the concession of one candidacy to a Conservative follower of Churchill, but his early prediction that the working-class elector would not take Home Rule proved largely false. Only in Birmingham itself, Ulster, and some areas of Lancashire and of London, which had unexpectedly inclined towards the Tories in 1885, did significant blocs of working-class Unionists emerge. Over the country as a whole, though Schnadhorst's optimistic view that Home Rule would carry the day proved absurd, the imbalance of votes between the two sides was far less drastic than that of seats in the Commons. Chamberlain had several times predicted that abstentions would determine the electoral result, and, helped by the large number of uncontested seats, so it proved. As one writer has observed, 'Unionist hegemony was ushered in by default rather than by conversion'.[60] In the long run the significance of the election perhaps lay primarily in exaggerating the slow trend in British politics towards an electoral polarization on class lines—a trend with important implications for the behaviour of all the leading contemporary politicians, but for none more than Chamberlain's. For Gladstone had carried 'the masses' and aligned Chamberlain with 'the classes', ejecting him thereby from leadership of 'the party

of progress'. The active elements in Chamberlain's Radical
Unionism consisted primarily of sections of middle-class Nonconformity, whose main stem lay rooted still in Gladstonian
Liberalism. How it would fare grafted insecurely and, Chamberlain hoped, temporarily on to what he had always considered sterile conservative forces committed to the defence of
traditional religious and social privileges, was a question he had
yet to think of posing, let alone answering.

CHAPTER 6

In the Wilderness. 1886–1892

Few were willing to predict the outcome of the four-party system which had emerged from the 1886 election. Churchill acquired a strong position as Chancellor in Salisbury's new government, but Conservatism remained insecure so long as he harboured hopes of greater influence still by using Liberal dissidents to lever the 'old guard' out of their positions in the party. The Irish party, too, had its problems, and only Parnell seemed able to unite Catholic interests, agrarian reformers, constitutional and revolutionary nationalists. For Liberalism the difficulties were even greater. Home Rule provided a new Gladstonian umbrella, but under it warring factions thrived and Harcourt did not merely reflect his own reticence in claiming that '9 people out of 10 think Ireland a bore, and would gladly turn to something else.'[1] Liberal Unionism was an even more ramshackle affair. It retained the party machinery in some constituencies: in others ejected Unionists formed small committees of local notables: elsewhere, in particular Birmingham, the two sides remained uneasily together. Nor was there parliamentary unity. Gladstone claimed that many Whigs had long wished to abandon ship, and Home Rule simply provided a convenient life raft. Though this applied to very few—most disliked Tory reactionaries and electioneers as much as the gyrations of the Radicals and Gladstone himself—Hartington reflected their general ambiguity in saying that he would not unite Liberalism under Home Rule, but refusing to work towards any form of compromise. He was widely believed to be looking for a Unionist coalition, and to be restrained only by reticence among some of his allies.

Chamberlain was the prime problem. Hartington must have felt himself fated: having resisted Chamberlain's attempted *coup* in 1885, he now found him playing a pivotal role in the new Unionist grouping. Though on the most optimistic calculations Chamberlain's personal following was only a dozen MPs, his influence among the rank and file, and his role as a symbol that Unionism was not simply a force of right-wing reaction, made his position strong. Salisbury's Commons majority depended on Liberal Unionist votes, and these Hartington could deliver: but Hartington felt that he depended on Chamberlain, and, as Churchill and Arthur Balfour had been arguing, the government might be better advised to deal directly with the Radical rather than the 'slippery Whigs' if the Unionist alliance was to be maintained.[2]

Chamberlain's own plans for the future were very different: 'Of course I shall be Premier, there is nothing more certain, and . . . I will *rebuild* the fortress. I will *re*form the Party, so rudely torn asunder by Mr Gladstone . . . We shall not have Home Rule, we shall have improved Government in Ireland, there shall be great Reforms throughout Great Britain and Ireland.'[3] Nothing could be done, however, until Gladstone's control over the Liberals was removed, either by death, retirement, or his ejection as a political liability. Sir Henry James, Hartington's adviser, and Collings were both informed in July that 'it is no use issuing manifestos or anything else' before then, since 'we must "lie low" until the inevitable disappearance of the G.O.M.' This perfectly reasonable calculation was unfortunately to be upset by Gladstone's health and determination; by the time of his retirement in 1894, the chances of reunion had long passed.

The success of Chamberlain's short-term holding operation depended upon two things. One was that Hartington should retain a clear division between Liberal Unionism and the Conservatives to prevent supporters being tempted back into the Liberal fold and leaving Chamberlain himself stranded. After the election Salisbury pressed Hartington to form a coalition government, although without much enthusiasm, and in return for Hartington's refusal on the grounds that he could not carry his left wing with him, Chamberlain acknowledged the Whig as his leader and merged his group into a single Liberal Unionist parliamentary party. The second was that the government itself should avoid 'playing the fool', as he put it to

Dilke, and alienating its Liberal allies. The parliamentary situation was now comparable to the one he and Churchill had both angled for in December 1885, though the united Radical phalanx had gone, and Chamberlain could now publicly announce that he would support the government from the opposition benches so long as its policies were not objectionable to Radical opinion, hoping, he told Dilke, that 'Randolph will give me all I want.' Churchill's Dartford speech in October, approved by Salisbury, promised a policy of peace, retrenchment and reform—just what was needed. It remained unclear whether the cabinet would accept its practical implications. Two issues created friction. Both parties had committed themselves to county government reform in 1885, but Chamberlain and Churchill wanted a wide democratic measure, while Salisbury, his party still dominated by the Tory squirearchy, was hostile. Further, Churchill proposed a budget with minor tax redistribution, increased local government grants and reduced defence expenditure. Chamberlain saw it in advance and declared it one he would himself have wished to introduce, but by December the cabinet was engaged in a major row, with the service departments strongly opposed to defence cuts. Though Balfour believed that 'we cannot turn Radical even to preserve the Tory party',[4] neither he nor Salisbury could see a way to break the *impasse* faced with Churchill's backbench support and the threat of Chamberlain's defection. Churchill himself broke it. Miscalculating disastrously, he resigned on 23 December over the War Office estimates and Salisbury, suspecting Churchill's weak position on this, unexpectedly accepted.

Chamberlain's plans were thrown awry. Whether Salisbury could afford to dispense with his truculent but popular Chancellor was unclear, the main danger lying in prospects of a Churchill–Liberal Unionist centre coalition. Salisbury again offered to serve in a Hartington ministry, an option for which Chamberlain expressed approval since it would leave him free to manœuvre with Churchill outside the coalition, although this threat to party unity may also have been designed to prevent Hartington's absorption by the Tories. A further problem was that cabinet leaks from Churchill had already led him to fear 'that we are in for a prolonged period of reaction', and this now appeared likely to come about. Intent on keeping his options open, he immediately used a speech in Birmingham to sound out the possibility of a negotiated peace with the Gladstonians. Harcourt and others took up the hint, which resulted in two months of abortive discussion in the new year between himself, Trevelyan, Morley, Harcourt, and Herschell at the Round Table Conference.

Agreement on Chamberlain's new proposals to the conference for land purchase and federated provincial assemblies on Canadian lines appeared at one stage a possibility, but Gladstone's insistence that reunion required commitment to the principle of Home Rule and the concurrence of Hartington convinced Chamberlain, quite rightly, that Gladstone was interested in the appearance of possible reconciliation, not the reality. As Dilke was informed, the conference soon became a sham, each side skirmishing to convince Liberal opinion that it was the other's intransigence which hindered reunion. On 26 February Chamberlain forced the issue with a letter to *The Baptist* newspaper condemning Home Rule as an obstacle to other, more important, domestic reforms, which provoked the Liberals into ending discussions. He had yielded much in the negotiations, whether seriously or tactically, but was not prepared to lose face by returning to the fold on terms which Gladstone could claim a victory for his Home Rule stand and in what would be, inevitably, a subordinate position.

Salisbury's own problems over Churchill were solved by Hartington's offer of Goschen for the Exchequer. A Liberal Unionist financial expert and the leading right-wing critic of Gladstone's 1880 ministry, he was a perfect choice, though Churchill's budget and county government reform were the price paid. But Chamberlain's difficulties over these were far outweighed by Irish problems. Under the impact of economic depression and political disillusion, the province was reverting to disorder. Parnell presented a Bill in the short 1886 autumn session to reduce judicial rents, which Chamberlain suggested the government counter with a major land purchase scheme. Rejection of this plan compelled him to open the first crack in the Unionist alliance by abstaining on Parnell's motion while Hartington voted for the government. When the National League subsequently launched upon Ireland its Plan of Campaign for unilateral rent cuts, a situation reminiscent of the early 1880s soon resulted, which the government determined to meet by extending the old Gladstonian policy, preparing a fierce coercion Bill and minor land reforms. Chamberlain protested at the former, but he had implicitly accepted Gladstone's dichotomy of 'Home Rule or Coercion' and in March 1887 announced general support for the government measure while working hard in Committee to limit its terms. This caused severe problems in Birmingham, where on 5 April the '2000', for the first time, voted against the stand he had taken. Even Collings and Powell Williams, the two local MPs closest to him, were very uneasy, and only Bright's support and the much-publicized *Times'* articles, 'Parnellism and Crime', linking Nationalist leaders directly with various outrages of the early 1880s, prevented open rebellion. Chamberlain needed a major land reform to satisfy his supporters.

Arthur Balfour was now Irish Secretary. Despite appearances to the contrary, Balfour had already established by the gunboat diplomacy he had employed as Scottish Secretary against crofter risings in the Western Isles that his dilettante exterior concealed a firm and purposeful approach to politics. His toughness in Ireland and parliamentary skill soon made him the most powerful figure after Salisbury. But when he presented an advance copy of his first major measure on land, Chamberlain was furious: 'I am sure that I shall not be able to keep my section of the Liberal Unionists in heart on such thin porridge . . . The Gladstonians are preparing for a great campaign in the country on Coercion, and they will carry many with them.'[5] The government, convinced that minor extensions of Gladstone's Acts were the most that its party would take, announced that no amendments to the Bill would be accepted.

To meet this situation, Chamberlain began to run a new hare. On 11 June he wrote to his son, Austen, that he was looking 'to the possibility of a strong Central Party which may be master of the situation after Mr Gladstone goes', and three days later told a Birmingham meeting that the country's pressing problems could be solved only 'at the hands of a national party which should exclude only the extreme sections of the party of reaction . . . and the party of anarchy'. He and Churchill, now strongly antagonistic to his former colleagues, were by this time working closely together, with ideas of carving out under Hartington's aegis a coalition of Tory Democrats, Liberal Unionists, and perhaps discontented Gladstonians like Harcourt. Though in many respects a logical implication of plans considered by all the participants since December 1885, the prospect was no nearer implementation. Rumours were circulating in July that Salisbury would retire in favour of a Hartington ministry more capable of handling the parliamentary disruption created by Irish legislation, but Hartington, the key man in the enterprise, ostentatiously stood aloof from all the plots. He was now much happier backing Salisbury than providing a figurehead for any realignment dominated by his supposed allies.

Though Chamberlain's call for a new party fell on stony ground, it served a useful tactical role in the immediate crisis, for he could not oppose the Land Bill without disrupting the Unionist alliance, nor support it without alienating Radical followers. The Centre Party proposal, coupled with threats to launch independent candidates in by-elections, served to exert maximum pressure on the government to make concessions while convincing Birmingham of his divergence from its policy. This limited aim was indeed achieved. Birmingham held firm, while Salisbury was forced to impose on a Tory party meeting the most important of Chamberlain's amendments—a reduction of judicial rents, Parnell's demand of the previous autumn on which Chamberlain himself had abstained.

The tactic failed, however, to meet an equally grave crisis in August, when the government decided, without consultation, to proscribe the National League. Chamberlain again sounded out the possibility of Liberal reunion and again his objections were passed on through Hartington to Salisbury. The first received short shrift—Gladstone knew he had Chamberlain on the run; and this time the government would not yield. Warning Hartington in desperation that they were being squeezed out between the policies of coercion and Home Rule, he insisted that they launch an independent programme based on the provincial assemblies scheme he had developed at the Round Table. Both Hartington and Churchill replied that this would be unacceptable to their followers, and, in the absence of a united policy, the embryo party split three ways over Gladstone's motion on 26 August censuring proscription. Bright, Hartington, and Churchill led a majority into the government lobby, a number absented themselves, and Chamberlain and five supporters voted with Gladstone.

The political situation plunged him into a mood of deep depression. He was isolated in Parliament; Birmingham was growing openly rebellious; Trevelyan's defection after the Round Table marked the beginning of Radical Unionist disintegration, and further embarrassment was created by Gladstone's blatant disavowal of any commitment to the details of his Home Rule Bill. By-election results showed a strong movement of opinion away from Unionism. Chamberlain had found that time and tide wait for no man; the holding operation of June 1886 was being swept aside. 'I am at my wit's end', he told Hartington, 'to know how to treat the situation in public and what to say to prevent the disappearance of our followers in the country.' He had, he told Collings prior to a visit to Ulster, 'an uncomfortable feeling that I have five [speeches] to make and nothing that I wish to say . . . To my mind [the situation] gets more and more hopeless'.[6]

Fortunately Salisbury stepped in to save him from immediate embarrassment, worried that he might desert the alliance or attempt to shore up his position by running amok with new schemes. Chamberlain had already on 20 August attempted to impress his followers by identifying the recent passing of Collings's minor Allotments Act as an example of Tory Radicalism, and Salisbury had no desire to be the butt of this sort of charge. On 28 August he offered Chamberlain a temporary appointment in Washington to represent Canada in a fishing dispute with the United States. This tough nut would either make him or break him: in either case it would dispose of him until the political climate cooled down.

Three important events occurred during the visit to North America between October 1887 and March 1888. One bears upon his developing imperial ideas, discussed in the next chapter. Equally important was the success of his diplomatic mission. The treaty formulated by Chamberlain and his aides was ultimately rejected in the American Congress, but a subsidiary agreement, reached in anticipation of this contingency, successfully governed fishing relations between the countries for many years. The third event was that, like so many of his contemporaries, he took his pick of the choice American marriage market.

The wedding to Mary Endicott, daughter of the American Secretary of War and of good New England Puritan stock, was delayed until the presidential election of November 1888 had been completed. It took place after a short, secret engagement and a dramatic dash, incognito, by Chamberlain to Washington. He was now fifty-two, she twenty-five, and a contemporary of the children of his first marriage, Beatrice and Austen, born in 1862 and 1863 respectively. (Among the children of his second marriage, Neville was now nineteen, Ida, Hilda and Ethel in their mid- and early teens.) Though apparently incongruous, this family set-up appears in practice to have worked successfully: unquestioned obedience to the father was a central element in the Chamberlain household, and Mary's pleasant open personality soon won over the children. Chamberlain, indeed, claimed that she had brought them far closer to him than ever before, and her arrival certainly marked a new phase in the family's development. Austen, having survived the rigours of Rugby and Cambridge as son of the English Robespierre, was being groomed in his father's *cabinet* for an early political career. He eventually won a seat in 1892, when Gladstone's generous welcome in the House produced almost the only public display of personal emotion from Chamberlain that his contemporaries were ever to see. Neville was regarded as likely to prove more promising in business than in politics, though he blotted his copybook somewhat as manager of a West Indian sisal plantation in which Chamberlain's diversified investments took a tumble in the early 1890s.

The maturity of a new generation of the Chamberlain dynasty had coincided with Joe's own emergence from the gloomy reserve brought on by the death of his first wives. Neither Beatrice nor his sister and housekeeper, Clara, were able to provide either the female companionship Chamberlain needed, nor the skills as a hostess which his expanding social circle in the early 1880s required. The advent of Mary Endicott had, indeed, displaced one particular candidate for a place at Chamberlain's side. In 1883 he had met Beatrice Potter, the young, attractive, headstrong daughter of a moderate Liberal MP, whose interest in social philosophy and science were to lead her from a youthful infatuation with the individualistic economic Darwinism of Herbert Spencer to the state socialism of her eventual husband, Sidney Webb. Between 1883 and 1887, she and Chamberlain had indulged in a spasmodic flirtation fraught with mutual misunderstanding and clashes of personality. Chamberlain appears to have taken the initiative in seeking a socially acceptable partner, and to have maintained a real liking for her lively personality and conversation. But, as Miss Potter fell increasingly under the spell of his 'gloom and seriousness', his political ardour and the charismatic sway he exercised in both the meeting hall and the drawing room, he retreated emotionally, not just from the implications of her *laissez-faire* philosophy, but also from her assertive independence of mind and unpredictable responses as she sought to cope with her growing hopeless passion. As he early explained to her, Chamberlain womenfolk were entitled to hold their own views, but not to tax *him* with them should they contradict his own—let alone to allow them to introduce emotional complications into his life. Though, according to Beatrice, he once proposed marriage and was rejected, the 'enigmatical relationship', as she once called it, was doomed from the start through his inability to unbend emotionally and respond on equal terms to her. Miss Endicott was much more in his line—sympathetic, supportive, decorative (as Beatrice, being told of Mary's lovely skin and pleasant eyes, superbly commented, 'Not much behind it'), accomplished in polite society, and utterly loyal.

The acquisition of a new fiancée and the success of his diplomatic mission in the winter of 1887–8 had a major effect upon Chamberlain. They restored his spirits, provided new political opportunities, and gave him confidence in his capacity to set off on a different track. Birmingham supporters played their part by arranging delegations and public meetings to welcome him home from America, while the council made him a freeman of the city; the government boosted this with a state dinner in his honour and the Unionist press turned his mission into a triumph. Politicians were anticipating a new departure: Reginald Brett told him that the Whigs were using coercion to 'crawl back into the old grooves. Even now they are alarmed lest you should have returned from America with some new plan or suggestion which would disturb the situation.'[7] Chamberlain did indeed have a new plan, but one on balance welcome to the Whigs. During his absence the unstable structure of Liberalism in Birmingham had collapsed. Following the '2000' vote of April 1887 Schnadhorst launched a campaign in the local party which had by March 1888 produced Gladstonian majorities on the divisional committees. Birmingham Conservatives shrewdly set out to exploit this by threatening to abandon the 'neutrality' pact of June 1886 unless Radical Unionism gave active support to their local candidates. And since Schnadhorst, with victory in sight, was in no mood for compromise, Chamberlain faced a decisive choice—either a journey to Canossa on Home Rule to regain control of his organization, or secession into a new political movement; and the latter meant conceding Conservative demands if his followers were not to be squeezed out or seduced by Schnadhorst's promise of electoral security.

Too much had already been staked for anything other than the second course of action to be practicable policy. On 15 April Chamberlain told the Radical Union executive that Schnadhorst's 'packing' of committees meant that the local Association was no longer representative of Birmingham opinion, and six weeks later held the inaugural meeting of a Birmingham Liberal Unionist Association. Structured on the same democratic lines as its predecessor to fight local and parliamentary elections, it received a new Irish programme. Drafted by himself and Bunce, and eventually backed by Hartington, the 'Unionist Policy for Ireland' contained three items—a broad land purchase scheme, public works for the poorer areas, and a system of provincial councils. Though little except critical attention greeted it in the parliamentary arena, its main function was to rationalize the declaration of independence in Birmingham. Chamberlain urgently needed a Radical Irish programme as a cover for the fact that the first task of his new organization was to be the ultimately successful support of a Conservative candidate in a May municipal election. 'The difficulty', he told Miss Endicott, 'is to get the rank and file to vote for a "Tory" . . . The issue is doubtful at present and we are risking a great deal by thus burning our boats and throwing in our lot with the Conservatives.'[8]

In May 1888 Chamberlain did indeed burn his boats. Liberal reunion, always a possibility beforehand, became highly improbable given increasing electoral interdependence with the Conservatives. And the face of Birmingham politics was irretrievably transformed. The old coalition of press, pulpit, plutocrats and People which had secured a single-party monopoly was broken. Whereas in the late 1870s all but one of the city councillors had been nominees of the Liberal machine, by 1891 there were but 24 Liberals to 29 Liberal Unionists and 19 Conservatives. Harris and Schnadhorst who had invented and run the caucus parted company with the bulk of Birmingham's leading industrial families who followed Chamberlain on his new course—Dr Dale was representative of many who had provided its moral and ideological enthusiasm and retired from the front line in the climate of bitter internecine warfare which followed the split. Chamberlain's new movement was but a pale shadow of the old. The original caucus had been created for eminently practical purposes—to ensure after 1867 that the Liberal elector in a three-member parliamentary constituency cast his two votes in the most efficient manner possible, and after 1871 to cope with the complexities of the cumulative voting system for the School Board; beyond this, though, its democratic ideology and structure had provided a channel for reformist causes to make their opinions felt, a mechanism for welding them together in a broad progressive coalition, and an environment in which the Chamberlainite oligarchy which assumed control was required to maintain a permanent dialogue with the grass roots. The new Liberal Unionist party was basically a personal machine built around a one-man programme with the sole aim of perpetuating control by the Chamberlain–Kenrick clan and their friends over the council and in the parliamentary divisions The formal structure of its organization replicated that of the old machine: in reality, decision-making was even more concentrated in the hands of Birmingham's social notables. Overseeing its operations, and later representing Chamberlain in the national Liberal Unionist organization, was Chamberlain's closest political intimate, J. Powell Williams, the city MP who had proved his worth as a parliamentary organizer during the Home Rule debates.

Undoubtedly the new party had a strong popular base. It is hard to define with precision the lines of political cleavage within Birmingham's electorate, but it seems clear that Liberal Unionism successfully tapped changing views within the middle and working classes of the city as well as producing a strong personal vote for its dominant personality. Although not undisputed, there is evidence that, even before 1888, the basis of Birmingham's traditional Liberal monopoly was under challenge. Disillusion among the professional middle classes and sections of the working class hit by economic uncertainties in the early 1880s has lost many urban seats to Conservatism in Britain, and Churchill's vigorous campaign in 1885 proved that even Birmingham was not immune, the challenge being contained largely because the Corporation had been able under the Redistribution Act to obtain a gerrymandered allocation of wards in the seven constituencies to ensure Liberal majorities in each.[9] Locally, the Conservatives had a valuable weapon: by the 1880s the optimistic glow of Municipal Socialism had dimmed considerably, Birmingham's councillors were more complacent, and, as the Corporation sought to cope with the financial consequences of its earlier expensive projects in a period of commercial downturn, the Liberal monopoly was an obvious scapegoat for all local grievances.

The city, too, was changing. Increasing costs of local raw materials, the decline of iron relative to steel as a widely used material, changing tastes, and the difficulty of generating sufficient capital for modernization from the small commercial enterprises, meant growing problems for Birmingham's traditional craft workshops in an age of intensified competition. Long-standing allegiances to Liberal principles were being shaken, and, in the intimate environment of the workshop, the influence of employers upon their workers to support more conservative parties could be significant. Elsewhere, many firms were following the Nettlefold example towards consolidation and large-scale production, and on the outskirts of the city new heavy engineering and machine-tool factories were being established which ultimately transformed Birmingham's industrial character into its modern aspect. These changes to the old sociological basis of Liberalism were accentuated by growth of the new white-collar class, and the decline

of geographical cohesion as industry and housing spread out-
wards beyond the city boundaries.[10]

None of these social changes meant that Liberalism would
inevitably be superseded, but they did provide popular anti-
Liberal parties with the opportunity to expand their foothold
in sections of the electorate. What was unique in Britain about
the Birmingham experience and later that of the West Midlands
as a whole, was that the initiative was seized and held by the
nationally tiny Liberal Unionists. Even in its homeland its
electoral strength was by no means great. In a crucial by-
election in Central Birmingham during 1889, the Liberal
Unionist candidate gained 5,621 votes to the Gladstonian
Liberal's 2,561, compared with the result in 1885 of 4,989 for
John Bright and 4,216 for Churchill. Assuming a broadly
similar electorate, and that the decline in turnout affected both
candidates equally—two not entirely legitimate assumptions—
we can suggest that something like two-thirds of Albert Bright's
vote in 1889 came from former Tory voters, a third from
Liberal defectors. If Chamberlain's party offered local Tories
the marginal votes needed to gain council seats, and an established cadre of local leaders with the status and expertise to
provide them with credibility, its own basis was solidly rooted
in a Conservative electorate.

At the level of national politics, Chamberlain remained
systematically ambiguous about the nature of the new party
structure within which he was beginning to operate. Many of
his followers needed convincing that Liberal Unionism was a
viable independent force, whose eventual objective was Liberal
reunion. Yet in 1887 he had been talking of a 'Centre Party' in
which Churchill's radical Tories had a significant part to play,
and Churchill was the man Birmingham Conservatism looked
to as its leader and inspiration. In the reorientation of 1888,
part of the price Chamberlain paid for an electoral alliance
with the local party was a promise that, when Bright's increasing ill-health compelled his retirement, Churchill would
have Liberal Unionist backing to stand in the vacant constituency. Yet Chamberlain had little real interest in such an
arrangement. Churchill posed potentially strong competition
to his plans for regaining control in Birmingham, and his
strength on the Tory backbenches compromised Chamberlain's

claim to be the man who, by his pivotal parliamentary position, was alone capable of drawing the government away from reactionary politics. His future promised to lie in dealing directly with the Tory leaders rather than their erratic critic. Conversely, Churchill's interests lay increasingly in weakening the Liberal Unionists to make himself the key figure on the government's left wing, with the result that between 1887 and 1889 he and Chamberlain engaged in a series of public squabbles, Chamberlain claiming that Churchill's open hostility to the ministry threatened the Unionist alliance, Churchill retaliating that he would not 'enter into competition for the smiles of Hatfield'. The relationship finally terminated in April 1889 when, on Bright's death, Chamberlain reneged on his earlier promise and asked Balfour to force Churchill's rejection of the candidacy Birmingham's Conservatives were demanding. Since the government's best strategy lay in aiding the weak Liberal Unionists at the expense of their menacing ex-colleague, Balfour was more than ready to oblige. He eventually succeeded in the task, and Chamberlain repaid the debt by denouncing a new programme of Churchill's as a 'crazy-quilt'. Even in 1888, however, he had been introducing ambiguities into the 'Centre Party' concept, by declaring that the party division lay no longer between Liberal and Tory, but Unionist and Parnellite, and 'a National Party has at last been brought into existence'. Conservative government, was the implication, was proving Churchillian in spirit without any need for Churchill himself.

There were other factors which reinforced Chamberlain's need for closer relations with the government. Salisbury wished to dispose of his grossly inadequate Home Secretary, Henry Matthews, whom Churchill had foisted on to a Birmingham seat in 1886, and Chamberlain had to petition strongly to prevent him being removed by means that would have entailed an election in one of the more insecure constituencies of his stronghold. The two Birmingham parties continued to squabble, and Salisbury and Hartington were required in 1890 to present an agreement covering their respective local representation and reaffirming the national policy of 1886 that seats should be fought by candidates of the incumbent party.

Internal Liberal Unionist changes in 1889 also had their

effect. To avert the prospect of Chamberlain's reorganized local party intruding, as it had after 1874, into their oligarchic committees elsewhere, the Whigs persuaded him to merge his Radical Union into the central Liberal Unionist Association, while accepting the creation of a West Midlands association covering the counties of Warwick, Worcester, and Stafford in which Chamberlain could exercise a free hand. For Chamberlain, this meant working in the area with strong Conservative local parties whose allegiance generally lay with Salisbury rather than Churchill. Inevitable conflicts again required intervention by the Tory leadership: Balfour had to be called in to impose Austen on East Worcestershire in 1892 against local opposition to his support for disestablishment.

A further major development was that, very reluctantly, the government gradually accepted Chamberlain's interpretation of the political situation. His claim that Liberal Unionist voters, particularly Nonconformists, remained 'loyal to the Union' only because they had their own independent candidates seemed confirmed in a Central Office report of 1889, a conclusion which entailed maintaining the artificial over-representation of Liberal Unionist MPs. It is testimony to Chamberlain's powers of persuasion that, largely unquestioningly, the government also accepted that Liberal Unionism needed Radical legislation to retain its support. Chamberlain's own brilliantly successful election results while campaigning with Radical policies offered ample confirmation. Albert Bright's success in the 1889 by-election, and Schnadhorst's failure to make any inroads in Birmingham council elections, foreshadowed the 1892 general election results, when Unionism produced massive majorities in the contested constituencies. More than that, the whole West Midlands duchy went against the national swing to Liberalism, five gains and two losses providing Unionism with 30 out of 39 constituencies. Contrasted with the defeat of Hartington's moderate successor in Rossendale on his elevation to Duke of Devonshire in 1891, the message seemed plain. The cartoonist 'Spy' grasped the situation in 1890 when he captioned his sketch of Chamberlain 'His influence accumulates though his party decays'. Radical Unionism comprised little more than the six Birmingham MPs: Liberal Unionism as a whole was on the wane, living off

Salisbury's credit, without cohesion or an independent political stand. Chamberlain was rising above this. To his talents on the platform he was adding considerable skill as a parliamentary tactician and debater ('He never spoke like this for us,' was Gladstone's comment), and his star rose as the government increasingly accepted his views on legislation.

The county government reform Bill of 1888 had been of major importance in this respect. Though Chamberlain was not consulted over the measure, Salisbury wrote that 'We have acceded to your views . . . to a great extent . . . [O]ur people will be very discontented at the absence of nomination from the councils: and I look forward to considerable trouble'.[11] The exclusion of Ireland, the absence of democratic parish and district councils—integral parts of his and Dilke's earlier schemes—and the eventual withdrawal of licensing clauses were objections that Chamberlain levelled, to no avail: but the provision of a wide democratic measure was probably the single most effective argument that he could present to his followers in the reorientation of April 1888: 'The Tory party', he told them, 'is not what it was.' Twelve months later, after further legislation, he declared himself 'willing to admit that this government does not go far enough for me: but then I never knew a government that did.' The stand he took was that of sympathetic critic, with a commitment not simply to keep the government in power *faute de mieux*, but to work for Unionism's overall success so long as his supporters could be appeased. On these terms, the government was prepared, as much as it could, to grant his requests. In Ireland Balfour extended existing legislation on land purchase in 1888 and 1891, laying down the programme of 'killing Home Rule by kindness' which was ultimately to transform the vast majority of Irish tenants into owner-occupiers; and he instituted relief, land congestion and development programmes of a significant nature. In return for Chamberlain's support on coercion, he also took up several of his suggestions for its moderation in practice. Wide democratic local government, however, the Tories could not accept, and a limited measure in 1892 had, as Chamberlain prophesied, to be withdrawn. On domestic reform he felt confident enough by 1889 to moderate the argument he had levelled against Home Rule since 1886, that it was holding up progressive measures throughout the United Kingdom. He appealed to the government to follow up its successful county government measure with free schools and agrarian reform, aid to secondary education, Scottish local government reform and parish councils, crofter legislation, and reform of the Employer Liability Act. Scotland received democratic councils in 1889, and the inclusion of free education provisions paved the way for their extension to the rest of the country in 1891. The move was partly based on the argument Chamberlain had been presenting for some time that the declining voluntary schools could only be helped without raising severe sectarian conflicts by universal free education, and partly due to economic prosperity after 1887 and Goschen's ingenuity at the Exchequer. Goschen was also able to extend funds to secondary education. After Collings's study of the failure of the 1887 Act to redistribute land, he and Chamberlain pressed for the 1892 Small Holdings Act, though it failed to contain all the compulsory purchase powers they desired. The Scottish crofters received further help, though a Bill Chamberlain had prepared was unacceptable to the government. Employer Liability amendment was attempted in 1890, but opposition in the Lords forced its withdrawal. Only democratic parish councils were consistently refused.

These measures, however restricted, provided a powerful rationalization of Chamberlain's anomalous position as a left-wing Liberal keeping a right-wing Tory Prime Minister in office, and they further persuaded him that he might be able to find a permanent home in the Unionist coalition. His standing with the government increased as he continued to deliver the goods, particularly on Ireland, still the key political issue. In 1887 and 1889 he toured Scotland, and in 1887 Ulster, with the message that practical reforms were being sacrificed to the Utopian goal of Home Rule, and that Liberal opposition to coercion constituted implicit approval of anarchy and disorder. More important were his private attacks on Parnell to discredit the Gladstonian cause. The Times's 'Parnellism and Crime' articles eventually led in 1888 to the government establishing a commission on the disorders of the early 1880s. Though it reported in 1890 that many charges of Nationalist collusion in lawbreaking were justified, it fell flat after a letter, printed in

The Times and purporting to have been written by Parnell in approval of the Phoenix Park murders, had been proved a forgery. This caused Chamberlain's stock with the government to fall significantly. It was he, convinced by O'Shea that the letter was genuine, who had been largely responsible for persuading the government to appoint the commission. The government's initial response to Parnell's request for a select committee had been that his proper recourse lay in a private action against *The Times*, but the prospect of creating immense political capital from a public inquiry had proved too tempting. Parnell always believed that ultimate responsibility for the forgery lay with O'Shea rather than Richard Pigott, a newspaperman who fled the country when exposed as the writer of the letter and who was later revealed as a double-agent in the complex world of Irish underground politics. In this respect, it is singularly odd that Chamberlain should have received soon after the revelation early in 1889 a letter from O'Shea holidaying in Madrid that he had 'by chance' caught sight of Pigott there but a few hours before Pigott committed suicide.[12]

The disaster of the commission had one beneficial consequence—that of enabling Balfour to persuade his colleagues of the need for greater concessions in Ireland. It was overshadowed completely in the following year when O'Shea successfully sued his wife for divorce in an uncontested case which cited Parnell as co-respondent and ultimately destroyed his career. Most historians would now agree that O'Shea's change of heart towards an affair that he had not only condoned but also benefited from politically for years was rooted in political rather than private motives. As he noted to Chamberlain, 'He who smashes Parnell smashes Parnellism.' After consulting Chamberlain, he at one point offered Balfour the chance to make political capital out of the case. Balfour claimed to have refused, but certainly one Tory was of the belief that O'Shea had fortunately been 'kept to his guns', reflecting deep government involvement in the case.[13] Chamberlain's papers contain comments from O'Shea noting the high legal costs of the case and the pressure he was under to drop the matter for a large 'consideration'. Countering the Parnellite offers was perhaps practical help that Unionists might have offered. (Chamberlain's own finances became very shaky soon afterwards, though largely through the collapse of investments in South America and the West Indies.)

The increasingly close links between him and the Conservative leaders reached their high point in January 1891 when Salisbury joined him on the platform at the first joint meeting of the Birmingham Unionist parties, and Chamberlain announced that 'now I neither look for nor desire reunion' of the Liberals. Inability to reach agreement on Home Rule was the root cause of this situation, but it was reinforced by the fact that, with growing clarity, Chamberlain came to see that he had no important role in the Liberal Party to return to. He had campaigned as former leader of the left to turn Radical Gladstonians against Gladstone himself on the grounds that Home Rule was holding up all their cherished reforms. This should have proved appealing at a time when the Federation, freed from the restraining influence of defecting moderates, had approved wide reform programmes. But Chamberlain had underestimated the Radicals' capacity to incorporate Home Rule into their canon of beliefs, and Gladstone's capacity to persuade them that the satisfaction of other demands was conditional on the prior satisfaction of Ireland's: claiming to be a Radical while rejecting Gladstone's spiritual guidance seemed to the left mere hypocrisy. Chamberlain failed to predict how virulent would be the hostility to him. His reasons for aligning with the Tories were ignored by an idealistic Radicalism which so believed in its enemy's satanic qualities that it could not but conceive of the temporary expedient as a moral betrayal. 'Our Joe' soon acquired the new name 'Judas', and former latent suspicion of his machiavellianism was turned into a general character assassination. Chamberlain's response that it was they, not he, who had been the turncoats in 1886 merely redoubled the assault and reinforced his role as the scapegoat for parliamentary and electoral failure. Such treatment, and systematic exclusion of his followers from the old reform organizations, contrasted sharply with the deference with which Balfour and the Conservatives treated him. He became increasingly unwilling, he said as early as 1887, to reunite 'with a party—or faction—controlled by Labouchere, Lawson, Conybeare and Co.' The Liberal left he denounced in 1889 as 'New Radicals', truckling to the prejudices of the 'People with a capital P', 'who have never shown the slightest constructive capacity—who are in short the Nihilists of English politics.' Active Nonconformity he condemned in 1890 as 'more fanatical, more bitter, more selfish and more unscrupulous than I have ever known the champions of the Church to be.'

His denunciations of his former allies reflect no change of overall policy or philosophy on his part, but rather personal resentment, as well as the political calculation that he had to compete for the Liberal rank and file while convincing the government that Radicalism offered a set of sane, practical measures. It was not Radical policies he opposed, so he claimed, but the Radicals' methods: and the growing competition after 1886 between different Liberal groups to impose their pet issues upon the leadership amply supported his claim that the grand old coalition was now simply a factious agglomeration. 'Mr Gladstone has not only divided his party—he has demoralised it, and it is no longer Home Rule which separates us,' he told Dale in 1890.[14]

Yet to be a Radical, and particularly one whose support still came largely from Nonconformists, on the left wing of a Conservative-dominated alliance was no easy task. Free education had only been possible by its extension to the voluntary schools, and Chamberlain had eventually ducked the issue by absenting himself in 1891 from the vote on this clause. Over disestablishment he trod a wary path. In 1886–7 he was telling supporters both that it was the one issue on which Liberalism could reunite, and that it was an issue which 'may be postponed for the present'. After informing Balfour in 1892 that he would only support disestablishment motions when they had no chance of being carried, he eventually voted for the Liberals' Welsh Disestablishment Bill in 1895, after three years negotiating to develop his own scheme and pressing it on Balfour as a worthwhile reform which would help Welsh Liberal Unionism (a political force whose importance was hardly obvious). In 1894 he managed to avoid supporting Liberal temperance proposals on the grounds that they failed to include a right to compensation, but abandoned Unionism on Harcourt's redistributive budget and, after failing to reach a compromise between government and opposition, on the Parish Councils Bill. Taxed with the Liberals' call for 'One man, one vote', his evasive reply, rooted in Salisbury's refusal to accept any suggestions for electoral reform, was that they should first set about modifying the over-representation of Ireland.

In the 1892 election Chamberlain could claim that the 1885 Unauthorized Programme had been passed by the Conservatives; but asserting this was a way of covering up the fact that much on the old Radical agenda had still to be implemented. When he stood side by side with Salisbury in Birmingham in January 1891, he was already anxious to ditch the rest. From his new position he simply could not compete in this area with the Liberal left, and, having committed himself to the Unionist alliance quite simply because there was nowhere else to go after 1888, he found himself tied to the apron strings of the old Radical enemies—Churchmen, landlords, plutocrats, aristocrats, and publicans. By 1891 he was desperately on the hunt for something new to do in his newly adopted political role.

CHAPTER 7

Proud To Be Called a Unionist? 1892–1895

Within a few months of one another in 1886 the two most dynamic politicians of their generation had been flung from the front rank of politics. Chamberlain and Churchill were victim to their respective leaders' justified belief that neither would stop at deposing the men and principles traditionally guiding their parties and constantly redrawing the lines of party warfare in order to secure personal and electoral success. Speaking perhaps for Salisbury as well as himself in 1887, Gladstone claimed not to fear future legislation, but 'the men of the future—personalities of the stamp of Randolph Churchill and Chamberlain'.[1]

Randolph's future, as it happened, lay behind him. His erratic temperament was reinforced by bitterness over his fall, and the syphilis which made his final years so tragic. In 1887 he and Chamberlain had been likened to rogue elephants careering round the political arena, but Chamberlain had cut his losses, built a new regional political base, and taken a consistent line in adapting himself to the requirements of Hartington and Salisbury to regain his power. Churchill closed off every line of escape by attacking in turn Conservative, Liberal Unionist, and Liberal leaders, failing in a bid to recapture the Nationalists, losing the confidence of his Tory Democrats, and squandering his grass-root resources. He was an isolated backbencher when, on 25 May 1892, Salisbury called the first joint meeting of the Unionist leadership. It marked Chamberlain's successful escape from isolation. Though unwilling before 1894 to announce that 'I am, and shall be in the future, proud to call myself a Unionist and be satisfied with that title alone', and despite Salisbury's ruefully admiring comment in 1895 that he

had been sitting on the fence for nine years, he was now en-
sconced among the leadership of a new, permanent, political
party. With Hartington's transference to the Lords in 1891 he
became Liberal Unionist leader in the Commons, though,
conscious of his ambiguous position, insisting on a full party
meeting to approve the appointment and permit his right to a
free vote on disestablishment. In the same year Balfour became
Leader of the Commons on the death of W. H. Smith. As
Salisbury's nephew and one-time member of the 'Fourth
Party', Balfour had become adept at mediating between the
Conservative left and right wings, and after 1886 had effectively supplanted Churchill in the crucial role of link-man
between the cabinet and Chamberlain. Now he and Chamberlain provided a powerful duumvirate in the Commons, ready
to lead the new party through the next decade.

At the May 1892 meeting, however, Chamberlain found
himself in his customary position as a minority of one. On the
question of timing the next election, his strong preference was
for the autumn, but Salisbury, though likewise inclined, deferred to the insistence of Devonshire and the Tory agents upon
an early dissolution. The July results perhaps confirm Chamberlain's idea of allowing more time for the Liberal tide to ebb:
273 Liberals were returned to 268 Conservatives, with eighty-
one Nationalists to a Liberal Unionist rump of forty-seven.
Salisbury may not have been displeased. He felt far safer facing
a weak Liberal ministry ('Too small! Too small!' was Gladstone's comment on his majority) and using the Lords to block
'dangerous' legislation than forming a further minority, or
coalition, government with the need to square a still far too
independent Chamberlain. Liberalism's legislative failures—
'jam yesterday and jam tomorrow, but never jam today', as
Chamberlain derided its domestic record—and the crushing
electoral defeat of 1895 appeared to confirm his comment to
Dilke in 1892, which merely reiterated the point he had made
in 1885: 'My prediction is that, unless the Gladstonians give up
the idea of a separate Parliament for Ireland . . . they will not
obtain power—though they may obtain office—for this
generation.'[2] But the prophecy that Liberalism would be isolated on the imperial question and ruined as an effective
agency of domestic reform was one which he had been forced to

make largely self-fulfilling in the struggle to guarantee his own political future.

His claim in 1892 that the Unauthorized Programme had been implemented was meant to suggest that the old 'stupid party' had become converted to a new 'party of progress', and this largely by his own efforts. At best the claim was an exaggeration: free schools had come, but Goschen had done little in the way of transferring the burden of taxation from the poor to the rich, and the mild agrarian reforms and local government changes had, except perhaps in Wales, only marginally undermined the old rural élites. But if Unionism was an unpromising vehicle for Radical progress, it was important for Chamberlain, as the 1892 election approached, that it should be 'progressive'. Birmingham would not forgive any major betrayal of the old spirit, for, as he told Balfour in 1891, 'you cannot . . . keep Radicals in the sound faith of unionism by tickling them with whiggery. I would undertake to lose Birmingham in twelve months by modelling myself on the articles of the *Times* in the speeches of Lord Hartington.'[3] Furthermore, a new 'Unauthorized Programme' was vital in providing him with a significant role in the Unionist alliance. A place would always be found for him in any future government, but it was bound to be a subsidiary one unless he could create the necessary bargaining power. The leverage provided earlier by his claim to represent the marginally significant Radical and Nonconformist Liberal defectors grew increasingly implausible, and he had to construct a new line of argument. The answer to his problem was to be found in the view he had presented in 1882: 'The Whigs as a party are played out, and the next great fight will be between the Tory democrats and the democratic Radicals.'[4] Flung from leadership of the latter, he set out to adopt that of the former as Churchill's star gradually waned. But, though Churchill had often angled opportunistically for Liberal defectors with Liberal measures, this tactic was no longer possible: ex-Liberals hoping to work with Tories were better advised to ditch their Liberalism and draw on autochthonous traditions in the Tory party.

The appropriate philosophy had been expounded by Disraeli at the Crystal Palace in 1872, when he had accused Liberalism of designing radical changes in the structure of

British politics and society and neglecting the welfare and the grievances of the working class. Tory social reform had been offered as the counter to Liberal destruction.

That there was working-class discontent needing attention was even more obvious in 1891 than in 1872. The housing and land agitations of the early 1880s had been succeeded by demonstrations over unemployment and falling wages, followed by increasing trade-union membership, the creation of 'general' unions, an import of socialist ideas and personalities into their organizations, and hesitant steps towards an independent Labour party. The 'Labour problem' was acknowledged by Salisbury's appointment of a Royal Commission in 1891, and many 'young Liberals' were angling to strengthen themselves with pro-labour programmes, as Chamberlain himself had in 1873. In the late 1880s, Chamberlain was slow to join the band-wagon, but he did so eventually with a major speech at Portsmouth on 2 April 1891. The 'Labour Question' he here declared to be the prime task facing any constructive statesman, and the solution was to be found in an extension of state responsibility for the welfare of society's underprivileged through a programme of social reform. This attention to 'social' issues, anticipated in 1885, was now, however, to be divorced entirely from the philosophy of Radicalism with its inherent hostility to the interests supporting Unionism, and to be backed by the claim, made by Chamberlain in a *Nineteenth Century* article, 'The Labour Question', of November 1892, that 'in social questions the Tories have almost always been more progressive than the Liberals'.

If applied to recent years this was a gross exaggeration: though Salisbury's government had passed protective factory, shipping, and mines legislation, Gladstone's 1880 and 1886 ministries had equally taken minor but important steps in this direction. At the time though, like Disraeli's bid, it was a promising counter to Liberal policies. Parnell's downfall and the approaching election were to compel Gladstone to approve the Federation's Newcastle Programme of 1891—a culmination of his gradual deference to his strengthened Radical wing after 1886. Chamberlain derided Newcastle as a 'pudding-stone' programme, a conglomerate of pressure group interests, and it allowed him to widen the division he had raised in 1885 between 'negative' Liberalism and 'constructive' Radicalism, subsequently pressed against the 'Nihilists of English politics', into a clear split between outdated Liberal demands for structural changes in society and progressive Unionist measures of social welfare. It also reflected his general view that the best form of defence is attack, for he was politically committed to all the key Newcastle principles—Welsh and Scottish disestablishment, temperance and land reform, parish and district councils, electoral reform, Employer Liability amendment, and even, in part, Home Rule. As Balfour told Salisbury after the 1892 election, Chamberlain was anxious for a Unionist synthesis, but, fearing that the Liberals would 'introduce Bills to the principle of which he is pledged, while the Conservatives oppose them', he needed the Tories to counter with a social reform programme, which he was ready to frame on Conservative lines.[5]

It was a moot point whether the Conservatives were interested. Salisbury himself had spoken publicly of his government's favourable record on social reform, but the only cause he had ever seriously promoted was that of working-class housing in 1883–4, in his own bid to don Disraeli's mantle, and at a time when the English upper classes set out almost universally to parade their social conscience. Chamberlain, as always, believed that vague phrases were not enough: programmes of practical measures were needed, both to appeal to the electorate, and to twist the arm of party leaderships. At Portsmouth he had offered free education and smallholdings, extended factory, public health, and sanitary dwellings legislation, and the radical suggestions of old age pensions—a proven vote-winner in the Aston by-election of March 1891—and industrial accident insurance. The first three of these were implemented during the last year of Conservative government, but for the general election Chamberlain was preparing other items—industrial arbitration courts, shorter working hours, financial aid for house purchase and improvements, as well as pensions and accident insurance—and attempting through Balfour to gain official Conservative backing. Salisbury's response to his speech early in the 1892 campaign pronouncing the completion of the Unauthorized Programme did not bode well: 'If you say that the Tories have given in on all the points on which you differed from them in 1885—you give them an uncomfortable feeling that they have deserted their colours and changed their coats.'[6] He had no wish as yet for Chamberlain to kick over the traces and publicize his leading role in a new party of reform, and, though not precluded from pushing his programme, Chamberlain was sufficiently wary of opening a breach to fall back into the ranks and build his campaign around the Unionist theme of raising the Home Rule bogey and stirring up the Ulster protestants.

Though informing a friend in the wake of the election that 'the future is blank to me politically', Chamberlain was to make good use of the three years of Liberal government. The introduction of Gladstone's Home Rule Bill in 1893 allowed him to allay the qualms which many Unionists still had about his sympathy for Nationalist aspirations. He and Balfour worked in close harness to co-ordinate opposition strategy and devised ingenious tactics to embarrass the Liberals; he reversed his position on Irish representation, now partially accepted by Gladstone, and his provincial councils scheme was quietly relegated to the sidelines. Taking a prominent part in debate and turning it into a personal duel between himself and Gladstone, Chamberlain became the hero of the Tory backbenches. The demise of Home Rule was already guaranteed when the Lords came to deliver their death-blow in September.

But this, and Rosebery's subsequent replacement of Gladstone as Prime Minister in 1894, created an interesting situation. Unionism had now lost the rationale for its existence, and, though its leaders could feel certain that negative opposition to Home Rule was a fairly safe stand to take, a negative attitude to other reforms was, as Salisbury's ministry had acknowledged, a dangerous game to play. In the period of uncertainty after 1893, they were more than ready to listen to anyone who might propose a strategy which would be, as Chamberlain put it in a subsequent bid to capture Salisbury's ear, 'attractive as well as safe'.

After the false start in the 1892 election Chamberlain had opened a new campaign with the *Nineteenth Century* article of November. The prop on which he hung his proposals was the advent to Parliament of several working class MPs, among them independents like Keir Hardie, and the theme can be summed up in his comment to Dilke, who saw the event as of major significance: their influence, he said, was 'immensely exaggerated. A political leader having genuine sympathy with the working classes and a practical proposal could afford to set them aside.'[7] His suggestion was in effect for Unionism to steal the 'Labour Programme': the miners' eight-hour day, arbitration boards for industrial disputes, amendment to conspiracy and Employer Liability laws, payment of MPs, and old age pensions were declared fit subjects for legislation by established politicians.

The points to which he attached most importance, not surprisingly since they symbolized major departures from existing principles, were pensions and accident insurance, on both of which he spent considerable time in formulating his own policies. His interest in the latter was sparked by the demand from both Labour and business for amendment to his Employer Liability Act of 1880. Employers disliked being taken to court after industrial accidents to face unpredictable awards and legal costs, while trade unionists wanted an end to the defence often used in court of 'common employment' (under which workers were claimed to have consented to the risks of a job by accepting it initially), and to the right taken up by many employers to 'contract out' of the Act by subsidizing contributions to workers' Friendly Society insurance schemes. This second, they claimed, undermined the role of the unions and removed pressure from employers to improve safety precautions. Amendments to the Act had been long attempted, but always defeated—the last time in 1890—by the opposition of unions, employers, or the powerful Friendly Societies.

Chamberlain's proposal, adopted from Sir John Gorst, onetime Tory Democrat and party organizer, who in turn had taken it from Bismarck's anti-Socialist welfare legislation in Germany, was to break the *impasse* by laying down a new principle. Compensation for accidents should no longer derive from the proven liability of employers, but from a general social duty to assist 'the wounded soldiers of industry'. Statutory contributions should be exacted from both sides of industry and paid into Friendly Society accounts, with the government bolstering the fund from general taxation, to cover the costs of compensation.

Presented to Balfour in January 1892 as 'undoubtably the fairest plan' (and one on which it would be 'extremely desirable to present . . . as part of the Programme on which we shall go to the country'), it had secured considerable support. But organized Labour was not interested, and in deference to its demands the Liberal government brought forward in 1893 a Bill to end contracting out and the claim of common employment. Chamberlain was wary of opposing Labour demands outright, though he eventually rejected the ban on contracting out as strengthening trade unions to the detriment of industrial peace and undermining the industrial co-operation created by existing voluntary insurance schemes. He persuaded Balfour to arrange a joint abstention of the Unionist parties in the Commons vote, and Salisbury to undermine the Bill by passing destructive amendments on this point in the Lords. The government withdrew its measure, adding fuel to the fire that it was building against the Lords, but also allowing Chamberlain to crow that 'jam today' was something the Liberals could not offer. He also had something else to crow about. The Conservatives shared his reticence about opposing organized Labour head-on, and, despite likely costs to the Exchequer, recognized that Chamberlain's scheme offered to outflank it among working-class voters while appealing to the financial interests of Friendly Societies and business, which preferred standard insurance contributions to involvement with the courts. Salisbury publicly adopted the scheme in 1893 as an alternative to the Liberal Bill, and when the Unionist government came to deal with the issue in 1897 there was crossbench agreement that legislation along these lines was alone possible.[8]

The second major strand to Chamberlain's bow—pensions— fared less well. Brought forward at a time of growing discontent with the Poor Law system, particularly after Charles Booth's dramatic revelations of conditions among the aged poor, Chamberlain's proposals were for voluntary contributions from the worker to be paid into a Friendly Society account with the government matching the sum out of general taxation. Interest on the funds he calculated, would allow payment of a five shilling a week pension over the age of sixty-five, or to a man's widow if he died beforehand, and cover the administrative costs. (He modified the details of this during the next decade, though the basic principles remained.) Though every contemporary who considered pension proposals had Germany's system in mind, Chamberlain himself, after initial uncertainty, rejected the compulsory scheme operating there as unacceptable to the British working class. He also rejected Charles Booth's own suggestion, soon adopted by Labour, for a non-contributory government-financed scheme which, with its enormous costs and 'socialist' implications, placed it out of court for Unionist politicians. Chamberlain offered a middle way in the debate over poverty, which would remove the stigma of pauperization from one important section of the 'deserving poor' while offering an incentive to thrift and 'self-help'.

But, though too conservative for Labour, it was far too radical for other important groups. Business had little to gain from it; its costs to the taxpayer, though yet incalculable, promised to be huge; and the Friendly Societies saw the spectre of government surveillance of their operations looming on the horizon. Chamberlain canvassed the scheme as a member of a parliamentary committee set up in 1891, and on a showpiece Commission established by the Liberal government comparable to that on housing a decade before. Jesse Collings was allocated the task of putting up working-class witnesses to speak in its favour. But though Chamberlain was successful in winning Charles Booth for his minority report, a majority on the Commission bowed to conservative forces and came out essentially in favour of the *status quo*. His propagation of the cause during the 1895 election was muted after advising Salisbury that 'it would be prudent to leave the matter for further discussion before an attempt is made to deal with it by legislation'.[9]

There is no reason for thinking of Chamberlain's view, that his interest in the labour question arose from a 'genuine sympathy with the working classes', as an act of self-deception. Though it was no more than his duty as Birmingham's first citizen to dole out continually to the endless local charities and relief agencies which, with his unsuccessful investments, gradually whittled away the fortune made from Nettlefold's patent, his political stance on domestic questions continued to be structured in a pro-labour direction. Yet his adoption of social reform in the 1890s does require deeper analysis. We have already identified the party political context which provided an immediate incentive for seizing on the issue; further comment needs to be made on the ideological framework within which it was bedded. One such has been proffered in Peter Fraser's biography:[10] in the 1890s, the 'threat of social war and crippling internal disunity transformed Chamberlain the aggressive Radical into Chamberlain the defensive Unionist'. Social reform was a conservative, Bismarckian, bid to maintain the social order against challenges from below, and pitched in essentially conservative terms.

Of course, the stabilization of social and political relationships under European and American capitalism is what policies of social reform, as opposed to social democracy, have always been about, whatever regime or party has set out to apply them. Historical interest lies in identifying the differing pace of reform at which different agencies have proceeded, how its costs were allocated throughout different sections of society, and the distinct rhetorics employed to mobilize political forces required to implement the necessary programmes. In Chamberlain's case, it is undoubtedly true that his social perspective was undergoing change in the 1890s. Not only was he no longer overtly challenging England's traditional establishment, whatever his private views on its inherent decadence might have been, but his personal response to his Radical and Socialist critics betrayed a growing snobbery as 'Society' offered him a place—his unpublished satirical play on contemporary politics (*The Game of Politics*) written in these years is as interesting for its expression of social contempt for his political opponents as for its hostility to their aims and methods. He was adopting the classic method by which an *arriviste* lays his own claims to be a 'gentleman'—the denunciation of 'ungentlemanly' qualities in others. To the aspirations of new leaders among the working class he was increasingly unsympathetic—he no longer saw any great need for their class spokesmen to participate in the legislature, he rejected all 'socialist' and 'collectivist' ideas going beyond municipal socialism, and had nice things to say only about old trade-union leaders like Henry Broadhurst, now rather isolated in the Trade Union Congress.

His new conservatism was given full expression when, exploiting the post-Home Rule vacuum, he launched a campaign from Birmingham in January 1894 around the issues of social cohesion and the unification of right-wing politics. He was 'proud' to be called a Unionist, 'believing it is a wider and nobler title than that either of Conservative or Liberal, since it includes them both—since it includes all men who are determined to maintain an undivided Empire, and who are ready to promote the welfare and the union, not of one class, but of all classes of the community.' '[P]erpetual constitutional experiments' should be abandoned and a 'national party' created to tackle the immediate problems of poverty, the distribution of wealth and relations between Capital and Labour.[11] Social reform was the new 'insurance' which would protect property and avert political revolution.

The conservative role of Chamberlain's statements to Parliament and to his party followers was clear. Just as in 1885 Conservatives and right-wing Liberals had set out to turn middle-class voters against a radicalized Liberal Party by exploiting fears of 'ransom', so now Chamberlain was aiming to define social stability and cohesion as the salient political issues—a philosophy which might finally override his supporters' sympathy for the old Liberal causes and turn their passive acquiescence in a Tory leadership into active engagement in an effective right-wing coalition.

This slide towards a more conservative stance had, however, a rather different character from the one which Devonshire, with Salisbury's encouragement, was promoting among the bulk of Liberal Unionism. Chamberlain's price was his adventurous social reform programme. Here, parallels between the precedents set by Bismarck in Germany, with his plans to dissolve the power of Labour, and Chamberlain's perspective can mislead. The latter would have little sympathy for the anti-democratic philosophy of a powerful organic state ruled by Prince, Junkers, and bureaucracy. His justification for state action was invariably couched in terms of the old Utilitarian principle of 'the greatest happiness of the greatest number'. Socialism and Labourism he conceived not as serious alternatives to contemporary capitalism but as defensive reactions to economic and social insecurity, dooming them to sterility as constructive approaches. The worst way of dealing with popular grievances was the equally defensive posture favoured by men like Salisbury and Devonshire. Birmingham electoral politics defined both Chamberlain's own conception of the world and the method to avert political polarization on class lines. Here there was a 'natural' alliance between the 'progressive' commercial classes and the toiling masses, forged and maintained by populist ideologies and policies, and capable of beating Gladstonianism on its home ground of the provincial urban constituencies. Constructing this alliance on a national scale was the essence of Chamberlainite politics in the early nineties, a far more important task for him than reconciling former Radicals to the traditional agencies of privilege. It did not appear to strike him that social reform had a special capacity to create electoral success in the West Midlands. Here the traditional weakness of its trade-union structure might not only produce a middle class more responsive to labour, but also a working class more inclined to rely upon the generosity of employers or, in Chamberlain's new programme, the state, than upon the welfare benefits which, elsewhere, union membership might provide. Whatever the peculiarities of the case, Peter Fraser's comment quoted earlier requires amendment: it was not so much the threat of social war which turned Chamberlain from Radicalism to Unionism, but that Chamberlain the pragmatic, populist Radical, driven into Unionism by the demands of political survival, exploited the bogey of social war to create a national party moulded in the progressive image of Birmingham's classless politics.

When he launched his new campaign in 1894 he had already begun to attract a considerable body of 'Tory Democracy' opinion. Balfour, as usual, was ready to give him his head, but pinning Salisbury's abstract utterances down to practical policies was the key task. Here the Liberal agitation brewing against the Lords in 1894 promised to be useful. Salisbury had already adopted Chamberlain's advice in January to amend the Employer Liability Bill and pass the Parish Councils Act, though rejecting a further suggestion to deflect the Liberal attack by a commitment to departures from the hereditary principle in the Lords. On 29 October he received a long paper in which Chamberlain advised countering charges that the Lords was a reactionary body by its introduction of a major reform programme, allowing the working class at the next

election to 'choose, with their eyes open, between political
revolution and social reform'. The programme had been
announced by Chamberlain a fortnight earlier in Birmingham.
It proposed arbitration courts, shorter hours for shop assistants,
labour exchanges, an anti-immigration Bill, Artisan Dwellings
amendments, facilities for house-buying loans and cheap railway travel for workers, accident insurance, more secondary
schools for rural areas, and the old Gothenburg temperance
scheme. As always, Chamberlain had selected from issues being
currently canvassed those he thought likely to have maximum
political impact. Labour exchanges promised to be popular in
a year of high unemployment, though he had rejected similar
proposals in 1886; accident insurance and home loans were
conspicuous Liberal failures; London Unionists in particular,
regrouping largely under Chamberlain's inspiration in a fight
against the left-wing Progressive Party's control of the County
Council,[12] were exploiting working-class fears over poor East
European Jewish immigrants competing for employment;
Gothenburg was revived to counter Harcourt's attempt to turn
his Local Veto Bill into a major Liberal cause.

It seemed a good programme, and Salisbury approved of
everything except limiting shop opening hours and Gothenburg
—shopkeepers and publicans were too sensitive and volatile to
be affronted. But in his carefully worded comments, he
gradually pruned the rest to be left only with housing improvement and arbitration courts, both having crossbench support,
as items for immediate action. More importantly, he rejected
the manifest ploy to gain official Unionist approval. Precipitous
adoption of the programme by the Lords would, he said, lead
the 'interests' behind the party to rebel; it would also commit
a future Unionist ministry in advance, and 'It is needless to say
that this is a wholly unexampled proceeding.' Chamberlain
could do nothing but accept this deflating response, while
warning that a Unionist government without a programme
would soon encounter serious problems with the electorate and
its own rank and file.[13]

Salisbury's genius, it has been said, was of the negative
kind.[13a] Pessimistic by nature, he saw his political role as that of
stifling change and absorbing reform pressures to preserve the
great traditional institutions of British society. Chamberlain had

appealed to this sentiment, emphasizing protection of the Lords by a programme which was 'attractive as well as safe' and did only what was necessary: accident insurance, he argued, need not apply to domestic servants since 'they are not voters, and have no organisation', while details of the proposals did not matter at the moment since 'they will constitute a demonstration and will in all probability never be discussed in detail.' Failure to make headway with Salisbury, however, put Chamberlain on another tack. Devonshire now became the target, and here a quite different set of arguments was important. The electors, Chamberlain told him, were not interested in the Lords at all, but 'in social questions and the problems connected with the agitation of the Labour Party', and the danger was that Liberalism would attempt to revitalize itself by succumbing to Socialist demands as they had earlier done to the Radical pressure groups. (The year 1893 had seen the formation of the ILP and radical motions to the TUC, which 'amount to universal confiscation in order to create a collectivist state', Chamberlain told the Duke.) Social reform from the Unionists was the only possible counter.[14] Less perceptive a reader of the political situation than Salisbury, and ready to believe anything of the Liberals, Devonshire might well have fallen for the lurid arguments which Chamberlain was parading before Unionism's middle-class supporters. Equally effective was a further message Chamberlain sent through Sir Henry James, in which he warned that, though Liberal Unionists might get office in any future government, they would have to fight for important places: and, unless social reform were accepted, 'my personal inclinations would lead me to stay outside in an independent capacity'. The logic of this was clear: unless Devonshire identified himself with the programme, there would be no united front against Salisbury in any future haggling over offices.

Devonshire took the hint, and along with James and Balfour was to be heard recommending social reform from party platforms in the following months. The time for decision came three days after the Liberal government fell on 21 June 1895. A meeting of the Unionist leaders agreed to form a coalition ministry and dissolve Parliament. Backed by Devonshire, however, Chamberlain presented an ultimatum: he could not join the ministry without agreement on overall policy. Salisbury bowed to the threat: 'general lines had already been stated in [Liberal Unionist] speeches and particularly in [Chamberlain's], and though details were necessarily left open there was no difference as to principle', Chamberlain reported him as saying. An Unauthorized Programme was for the first time authorized, and confirmed by Salisbury's first speech as Prime Minister, and the success was reinforced by considerable over-representation of Liberal Unionists in the new government. The subsequent election, producing a Unionist majority of 152 and a decimated Liberal front bench, seemed to set the stage for one of the great modern reform ministries.

That reality belied appearances was marked by Chamberlain's new post. On 24 June he rejected offers of both the Home Office and the Exchequer and insisted on taking the Colonial Office to further a policy of imperial unification. We shall see below the significance he attached to imperial questions, but perhaps the real reason why he rejected a domestic post lies elsewhere.

For some time Salisbury and many Conservatives had been anticipating Chamberlain's membership of a coalition government with dread. They had observed his growing influence among backbenchers and local parties, the appeal of his 'democratic Tory' principles, and his electoral successes. His restlessness and sensitivity to popular feeling almost guaranteed that at some future date the Unionists would come to blows over domestic reform, and Salisbury's wise concession in June 1895 was designed largely to put off the evil day.[15] He had accepted the principle of social reform, but timing and the 'details' were significantly left open. Chamberlain himself had no illusions about Unionist reform intentions; the party leaders he had described earlier as 'weak in constructive statesmanship', asking 'Why should I ruin myself . . . only to be a subordinate member of a Cabinet with whose general policy I am not in hearty sympathy?'[16] He was determined not to ruin himself. Holding an important domestic post, he would have his capacity to deliver reform put to the test for the first time, and, in a cabinet whose basic instincts were for the quiet life, there were two possible consequences—loss of reputation through enforced inactivity, or a revival of intra-party warfare from disruptive policy initiatives. By now he was weary of fighting for his political life and constantly putting himself out on a limb. Earlier in the year, indeed, he had gone into one of his deep depressive moods and seriously considered retirement when his reputation was subjected to severe criticism. An intra-Unionist squabble at Leamington, which he settled with a high-handed threat to resign unless Balfour and Devonshire imposed discipline on the local Conservatives, had been used by sections of the Tory party and press—the 'old guard', some whose career prospects had waned as those of the Liberal Unionists waxed, and young 'High Tories' who suspected the *parvenu* businessman's infiltration of 'their' party—to revive his past record of disruption and sow suspicions about his future conduct. Salisbury and Balfour publicly expressed their confidence in him against the recalcitrants, but Chamberlain must clearly have seen that, despite his past efforts for Unionism, he still had far to go in gaining the party's confidence. There was one obvious solution—gradually to bow out of domestic issues, hoping that Salisbury would keep his promises, and ease himself into the minor, non-controversial, post at the Colonies. Here, he had said many years ago, there was 'work to be done'—work which, acknowledging that his political role over the past few years had now become exhausted, he could do untrammelled by past commitments with the prospect of creating for himself a wholly new reputation.

The press was surprised at this outcome, but Chamberlain's association with the rising spirit of imperialism had grown in the period of political isolation. A few years later he was to make an observation that Disraeli had been right: in modern politics, social reform and imperialism had to go hand in hand. The logic seems plausible. No democratic nation could expect its people voluntarily to shoulder the burdens of Empire without allowing its benefits to percolate down to the masses: conversely, winning over the economically advantaged and politically powerful to the idea of treating the masses generously could be achieved by showing how the surge for imperial unity and greatness demanded a healthy and contented populace at home. In both the international and domestic arenas, the random interconnections of competitive private interests and aspirations needed to be moulded by the state for the higher objectives of national cohesion and strength. Chamberlain was not alone among late-Victorian imperialists in exploiting this two-way relationship extensively—Lord Rosebery and Alfred Milner were among the distinguished company—but it was a relationship he had developed slowly.

In 1901 Rosebery was to claim that the Liberal Home Rule split had been 'far more on what I call foreign and imperial questions . . . than on the Irish question.' While he was attempting to exorcize the ghost of Little Englandism from the Liberals, this pronouncement was convenient but untrue—Salisbury more accurately noted that Ireland 'awakened the slumbering genius of English imperialism'. Though Disraeli's bid to press an adventurous foreign policy against Gladstonian internationalism had come to grief in 1880, public opinion had gradually taken his views to heart as Gladstone's ministry unwillingly succumbed to the logic of imperial security requirements in an age of international big-power competition. Home Rule was only tangentially related to foreign and imperial issues: Unionist claims that it entailed disintegration at the imperial centre and hence serious consequences for relations with the periphery were sheer hyperbole. Yet it confirmed fears of Gladstonian tendencies to 'unpatriotic' policies in times of crisis; and with the departure of the 'Palmerstonians' in 1886, and subsequent ascendancy of Harcourt and Morley, diatribing against the 'Empire of swagger', Unionists could exploit nationalist feelings and tar Liberalism with a Little England brush which Rosebery and other, despite strenuous efforts, had problems in diverting.[17]

Chamberlain's experience before 1886 had awakened him to the view that Liberalism had to be 'patriotic' or it was lost, but his delicate political position restrained any public excesses, with the difficulty observed in 1885 of 'steering between Jingoism and Peace-at-any-price'. In late 1886 he was pressing Churchill to prevent the government 'playing the fool' with a Disraelian policy during a resurrected Balkan crisis, and later warning Austen not to 'prosecute your Jingo inclinations'. But by 1892 he could give Dilke this advice: 'Be as Radical as you like, be a Home Ruler if you must, but be a little Jingo if you can.'[18]

The 'jingoism' he urged on Dilke and was increasingly to

practise himself had no necessary connection with his unexpected declaration in 1886 that he wanted a federated
United Kingdom as the first step to complete federation of the
Empire (and Dilke himself favoured a 'forward' foreign policy,
stronger national defences, and 'special relations' with America
and the colonies, but believed imperial federation to be
utopian). Yet the two went, to some extent, hand-in-hand,
largely among politicians without direct ministerial responsibility—the Imperial Federation League, founded in 1884 by
Rosebery and Forster, was partly designed to generate support
at home and in the 'white' colonies for expansionist ventures
safeguarding British colonial interests. With increasing international tensions, and the extension of Britain's world responsibilities as it sought to safeguard its interests, the New
World of America and the self-governing colonies came to be
seen as important economic, military, and political resources to
counter-balance the Old World powers, with imperial unification as Britain's ultimate destiny as a world power.

This was to be Chamberlain's position in 1903, but after 1886
he set himself the more prosaic task of escaping his Little
England past. The Home Rule crisis had seen him parading the
virtues of Empire, but a new spirit entered his public statements
in the winter of 1887–8 during his American visit. At the
Toronto Chamber of Commerce he said of imperial federation,
'If it is a dream . . . it is a grand idea . . . Let us do all in our
power to promote it. True democracy does not consist in the
dismemberment and disintegration of the Empire, but rather
in the knitting together of kindred races for similar objects.'
He complemented this with advocacy of a concept familiar in
Dilke's writings, but which he himself had only once before
publicly articulated (on the visit to Birmingham in 1877 of
General Grant)—the 'invisible bonds' linking Britain, Canada,
and America in a 'Greater Britain . . . infallibly destined to be
the predominant force in the future history and civilisation of
the world'. On his return to England, as well as in other North
American speeches, these themes were given wide prominence.

Promoting them at this juncture could serve two immediate
purposes. One was integrally related to his prime task of
settling the fisheries dispute. By stressing the imperial link he
could allay Canadian suspicions while compromising their

interests in the negotiations—significantly enough, during his first Canadian public interview he had hedged when asked for his views on federation—and by talk of a 'Greater Britain' hope to moderate American intransigence (though polyethnic America did not fully take to his ideological fancy). The second purpose was to project himself in Britain as a statesman. Desperate to recoup the political losses of 1887, he returned home promoting himself as successful arbitrator in a major international dispute, whose horizons had expanded beyond English domestic squabbles. Advocating imperial unification at a Devonshire Club dinner attended by leaders of all parties, he emphasized his decision to speak on a national issue, more important than mere partisan disputes—a theme in line with his call to Birmingham for a 'National Party' to deal with problems at home and abroad untainted by Gladstonian sectionalism and old-fashioned Toryism. The imperial stand was reinforced by a 'jingo' utterance in May 1888 on South Africa when he stood alongside the Revd McKenzie at the London Chamber of Commerce to denounce a new phase of Boer expansionism. Repeating the now standard arguments of the interventionists he called for Britain to fulfil her responsibilities to protect the natives, preserve peace in the area, and safeguard her interest in open lines of commerce to the African interior: 'the abandonment of these duties would be as fatal to our national prosperity as it would be discreditable to our character and national honour.' Earlier warnings he had given against intervention were now brushed aside, as was the story told to Herbert Bismarck that Britain's sole interest lay in the Cape naval base. British paramountcy in South Africa was now declared the key issue, and government policy, formerly that of 'shirking', should now be one of asserting power despite Afrikaner reticence and the risks of foreign objections.

The reversal of all Chamberlain had stood for publicly in the decade before 1886 proceeded rapidly after 1888. He invited Lord Wolseley to Birmingham in 1889 and called for closer imperial defence links and a more efficient volunteer force in England. Later in the year he went out to Egypt and, primed with information from British administrators and Egyptian collaborators, returned to tell Birmingham that direct investigation of the wonders being wrought by British government there had compelled him to 'change his mind' on the issue of retention. Balancing this with well-publicized minor criticisms of the regime, he drew many waverers from their hankering after an early withdrawal, and by 1892 could tell Balfour of his hope that the Liberals would raise Egypt on the Address, since it would 'force their leaders to show their hands'.

Pushing a strong patriotic and imperial line on the domestic stage was primarily designed by Chamberlain to identify the Liberals as fundamentally out of line with public opinion and the realities of world affairs—the logical consequence of his discontent with Gladstonian internationalism before 1886, and the 1886 split itself. It was also designed to draw his followers towards mainstream Unionist opinion and commend himself to its leaders, and on occasions he tried to show his usefulness to Salisbury in international negotiations through his contacts with Herbert Bismarck and Clemenceau. Of particular importance, though, were the arguments which he deployed in his 1888 speeches and which, though subsequently muted, later emerged as a key item in his imperial ideology. By 1895, his 'imperialism' had traversed a wide field, covering colonial expansion, increased control of dependent territories, unity of 'Greater Britain' or the 'Anglo-Saxon race', concern for natives, and closer economic, military and political relations (which had priority was unclear) with the self-governing colonies. For what he declared his prime aim, imperial federation, 'I have never seen my way to any practical scheme'. 'Imperialism' was a phrase in search of a policy. But the most important rationale he presented for it in 1888 was an economic one. Commenting at McKenzie's London meeting on the recent economic depression and high unemployment, he had asked rhetorically: 'Is there any man in his senses who believes that the crowded population of these islands could exist for a single day if we were to cut adrift from us the great dependencies which now look to us for protection and assistance, and which are the natural markets for our trade?' In a more positive vein at the Devonshire Club he had claimed that 'Experience teaches us that trade follows the flag, and even in commercial questions sentiment is a powerful influence on the question of profit and loss . . . We have to watch for opportunities to strengthen the ties between our colonies and ourselves.'

This appeal represented Chamberlain's decision to exploit the imperial issue in the context of the 'Great Depression'—the phenomenon of greater cyclical activity around a slower growth rate which characterized the late-Victorian economy.[19] It was not the first time that he had acknowledged this problem. The 1879 depression he had argued to be a product of Disraeli's expensive and disruptive imperialism, condemning in passing Sir Michael Hicks Beach's suggestion to expand exports to colonial Africa as a 'gigantic joke'![20] Agrarian reform he had later justified as a means to ease unemployment in the towns and restore rural prosperity, though this argument largely reinforced Radical hostility to "unearned" rents and land concentration. He had also urged Rosebery, Foreign Secretary in 1886, to give government backing for loans to build railways in China, and, on a visit to Turkey, advised a modernization programme based around railway development. Both suggestions were perhaps designed to contribute to long-term stability in these areas, but it is perhaps no coincidence that the Midlands were a major supplier of staple items in railway construction.

Other politicians, in the meantime, had been devoting more attention to the matter. Many Conservatives had involved themselves with the Fair Trade League founded in 1881 to secure revisions of Britain's traditional free trade policies, and Churchill, having found that ' "Fair Trade" and "taxing the foreigner" went down like butter' with his audiences at the time, persuaded Salisbury to establish a Commission on trade in 1885 and spearheaded a campaign on the issue in the election. Chamberlain appears to have been somewhat unsound on free trade. Farrer, his chief Board of Trade official, later said that he had some difficulty persuading his chief of the merits of free trade arguments, and in an 1881 cabinet Chamberlain had surprised colleagues by advocating retaliatory tariffs during European trade negotiations. But in 1880 he had condemned a campaign for retaliatory duties on sugar, with some justification, as an 'artificial agitation' with 'so little foundation of real grievance', and in the Commons and during the 1885 election rigidly upheld free trade principles.

The political difficulties this produced, however, were very great. Sensitive as a former businessman in a business community to Chamber of Commerce opinion, he found it moving towards fair trade views. We have already noted the difficulties Birmingham industry was undergoing. Leading members of the Fair Trade League came from the city, and its Chamber of Commerce had argued for an imperial customs union to the trade Commission. Churchill's candidacy in the 1885 election, when he had run close behind Bright, showed up Chamberlain's problem: 'Fair Trade; you have no notion of what a hold it has upon the artisans. It almost beat Broadhurst. I had to neglect my division to fight Fair Trade in his; and it took me all I knew to get him in.' In 1887 the local Chamber of Commerce and Conservative Association both explicitly committed themselves to fair trade policies, as did the Conservative Union conference of October, though Salisbury, worried that this would embarrass his Liberal Unionist allies, particularly his new Chancellor, Goschen, subsequently quashed the decision. Public opinion was irresistibly drawing Chamberlain to consider Britain's commercial and industrial problems, and before his North American visit he had asked Salisbury to include within his terms of reference negotiations on 'commercial relations between Canada and America'. Observations there confirmed reports that Britain's important Canadian market was under threat from vociferous calls for a North American commercial union to overcome high American tariff barriers.

His speeches in 1888 identified him with a body of local and national opinion which was looking for ways to tackle the economic difficulties. As one writer has noted,[21] it represented particularly his usual tendency to see the world through the eyes of Birmingham's electorate, but it should be noted that this tendency had now been strongly reinforced. Flung by Home Rule out of his role as principal lead in a national Radical chorus, he had to play on the more restricted stage of the industrial Midlands. With its business community worried about trade, and many Radical supporters removed by Schnadhorst and replaced by a Conservative prop devoted to fiscal reform, it was advantageous to declare a new political interest. But not for many years did he consider tariff reform a viable option, given the Liberal free-trade backbone of his party. He refused to attend the local Chamber of Commerce after its vote, and condemned the Conservative Union motion, since 'the English people were firmly wedded to free trade and would never be persuaded to return to the small loaf'.[22] A Canadian politician reported him in 1890 as favouring preferential tariff relations with the colonies, but determined to keep this private: 'In the present condition of opinion in England it would never do.' A brief hint at fiscal reform from Salisbury in the 1892 election he called an 'unfortunate allusion' which had 'cost us a dozen seats in the counties'.[23]

Most fair traders, save agriculturalists yearning for pre-1846 days, saw the answer to Britain's economic problems not in protecting the home market, but in expanding exports in the face of growing foreign and colonial protection. Some intended tariffs as a retaliatory instrument in trade negotiations—others hoped to use imperial ties to reduce colonial tariffs, or to create a great 'common market' on the lines of the German Zollverein. Chamberlain's association of the commercial and imperial questions in 1888 did not lead him to accept the two chief proposals available for achieving the latter: complete intra-imperial free trade he rightly observed to be unacceptable to the colonists, and reciprocal preferential tariffs he claimed would bring insufficient gains to compensate Britain for higher import prices and foreign retaliation. Closer imperial links were rather to be sought, he said at the Devonshire Club, in a 'union for defence'.

What this meant, and how it would improve trade, were left unclear; but his emphasis on it here, and in later speeches, suggests that commercial problems were not the sole reason for his attention to imperial unification. If economic difficulties had taxed him most electorally in 1885, in government between 1880 and 1885 it had been the ideological and financial problems of imperial defence which had been his major headache. He had discovered that important strands of British public opinion wanted to 'stand up to the foreigner', but that the country was historically devoted to government economy and anti-militarism which put her commitments far beyond available resources. Salisbury bemoaned in 1886 that the problem of conducting foreign policies was 'to be always making bricks without straw', and Chamberlain himself as late as 1887 observed that Britain's weakness entailed 'a much stricter policy of non-intervention than in the past'.[24] Responsibility for local protection of the 'white' colonies proved a major burden—a 'millstone' around Britain's neck, Disraeli had long ago called it—which was the chief reason for nineteenth-century British governments seeking to devolve the burden by creating strong self-governing colonies, a programme symbolized most recently by Gladstone's approach to Empire, and to South Africa in particular. The newer alternative being canvassed, however, was for the colonies to devote resources to a more integrated imperial defence system. This was the programme advocated by founders of the Imperial Federation League in a year which had seen colonial troops accompanying Wolseley's expedition to Khartoum. It was the premise also of a proposal put by the South African politician Jan Hofmeyr to the first Colonial Conference in 1887, contemporaneous with the imperial flag-waving of the Queen's Jubilee, for an imperial tariff to raise revenue for imperial defence.

Chamberlain, having originally been identified with the devolutionist viewpoint, was moving in the late 1880s towards this position: a way had to be found to promote 'jingoistic' policies which he believed domestic and international politics required without imposing an intolerable burden upon the British budget. Imperial consolidation was not designed primarily to promote trade with the self-governing colonies but to provide extra resources for pulling Britain's chestnuts out of the fire in those unpartitioned areas of Africa and Asia for which the European powers were now engaged in almost continual competition. In terms of future economic benefits to Britain, Chamberlain's thoughts were focused more on the 'new' Empire than on the old. This became clear during the Liberal ministry after 1892. Economic downturn, following hard upon panic over prohibitive tariff rises in America in 1890, provided an opportune climate for public discussion upon the question of empire and trade; deep divisions between the Foreign Secretary, Lord Rosebery, and many of his cabinet colleagues on defence and foreign policy were open to easy exploitation by Unionist 'jingos', while Rosebery himself, intent on showing that Liberalism could prove even more 'patriotic' than Unionism, began to raise the temperature of the discussion. In this respect the parliamentary debates on Uganda in 1893 were of major importance in the development of Chamberlain's views. Rosebery was anxious after the collapse of the British East Africa Company to pre-empt a German take-over by annexing the Uganda area and thereby providing a launching pad for eventual reconquest of the Sudan. To win the support of his reticent colleagues and Liberal backbenchers, he formulated a powerful, if largely spurious, argument: Uganda was at present economically worthless, but Britain had to 'peg out claims for posterity', prevent the imposition of a German tariff and the intrusion of German commerce, and use the railway which would place troops transported from the coast on the Sudanese border to develop a thriving hinterland market for economic exchange with Britain.

The Unionists gave full support to this programme, and Chamberlain in particular argued the case for 'pegging out claims' in considerable detail. He also took the opportunity to broaden his justification of empire. So far he had spoken almost entirely in terms of consolidating and exploiting existing imperial links. He now began condemning the Liberals' 'dilatory' policy-making, claiming that 'I, and those who agree with me, also have a policy, and I believe in the expansion of the Empire.' In the series of speeches which he delivered throughout 1894 to advocate his domestic programme, the policy of deliberately annexing as yet unclaimed territories, particularly in Africa, was presented as a complementary theme. The break with his own former, and Britain's traditional, policy of limiting imperial responsibilities was justified largely on the economic grounds that 'if it were not for the gigantic foreign trade which has been created by this policy of expansion, . . . we could [not] subsist in this country in any kind of way.' This grossly exaggerated claim would appeal to specific trades with an interest in opening up new territory—not least in the Midlands, the centre of Britain's metal and weaponry industries—and was pitched to the wider audience as a solution to contemporary unemployment, an alternative, as he had said earlier in his *Nineteenth Century* article, to Labour demands for government legislation providing public works projects (a reversal of the principle he had accepted in 1886).

If expansionism was one theme he had developed out of Rosebery's ideological appeal, there was another which soon appeared. 'It is not enough,' he started telling audiences in 1895, 'to occupy certain great spaces of the world's surface unless you make the best of them— . . . We are the landlords of a great estate: it is the duty of a landlord to develop his estate. . . . [M]any of these possessions are still almost unexplored, entirely undeveloped. What would a great landlord do . . .? If he had the money he would expend some of it at any rate upon improving the property, in making communications, in making outlets for the products of his lands.'

Politicians well-advanced in their careers but facing an uncertain future must perhaps often be inclined to look to their early successes as a pattern for further ones. In 1895 Chamberlain was searching for a role in the forthcoming, unpromising, Unionist government. He had sown his wild oats and reaped ten years in the wilderness, and was anxious to establish himself as a constructive statesman by activities which minimized political risks. The Colonial Office seemed to offer this opportunity with a set of self-imposed tasks which he felt eminently capable of undertaking. Furthering closer imperial links, his ostensible reason for taking the post, was a long-term venture: but 'pegging out claims' through imperial expansion and the development of 'undeveloped estates' had gone down well in 1893 with Parliament, the Chambers of Commerce and the public at large. Seeing in the 'third world' territories, as A. P. Thornton has noted,[25] 'another great slum-ridden Birmingham', ripe for improvement and modernization on lines laid down by the imperial administrations of India and Egypt, Chamberlain could see himself for many years to come with useful work to do which was 'attractive as well as safe'.

CHAPTER 8

A Radical Turned Patriot. 1895–1900

In the 1895 election Unionism had offered a formidable united front against Liberal disharmony. A broad coalition spanned the right and centre of British politics. Salisbury, its leader, stood as guarantor of the privileges of the Establishment—Devonshire as symbol of moderate respectability—Chamberlain was both guardian of the commercial interests of the middle class and the governing classes' white hope for extending the party's popular base and appeasing working-class discontent. The classic Liberal trinity of Peace, Retrenchment, Reform was a specific now successfully peddled by Unionist politicians, and the nation's strength and honour, its constitutional stability and social unity, seemed as safe in their hands as ever they did in Palmerston's. The new government contained the best political talents of the country. With Salisbury at the Foreign Office and Hicks Beach at the Treasury, international and financial affairs appeared in solid, experienced hands. Balfour's capacity to conduct efficient business in the House was long since established. From the Liberal Unionists came sources of strength unknown to recent Conservative administrations. Grossly over-represented in the government, several (among them Collings, Powell Williams, and the new Lord Selborne, Salisbury's son-in-law appointed Chamberlain's under-secretary) gained minor offices, though the cabinet posts were not wholly commensurate with their aptitudes and experience. Sir Henry, now Lord, James was denied the Woolsack he coveted and made do with the Duchy of Lancaster; Devonshire, Lord President of the Council with responsibility for education, had been offered the Foreign Office but declined, facing the prospect of a constantly interfering Prime Minister; the ex-Viceroy, Lansdowne, found his diplomatic talents severely under-used at the War Office; and Goschen, shying away from having financial unorthodoxy imposed upon him at the Treasury, went to the Admiralty. The Liberal Unionists carried big guns, but Salisbury's dominance over the Tory cabinet majority was, in the initial stages of the ministry at least, sufficient to ward off any ambitions they might have harboured.

Chamberlain himself, adapting to the low-status Colonial Office, was soon to prove, as in the 1880 cabinet, the ringleader of cabals to take the conduct of government policy out of the hands of his superiors. Domestic reform still seemed the central bone of contention. 'Vote for the Unionist and Social Reform' was a prominent slogan in 1895, though, as Balfour's secretary, J. S. Sandars, was later to observe,[1] the election had been fought primarily on a negative campaign against Liberalism. In 1895 Chamberlain rejected Devonshire's suggestion to amalgamate the two party organizations, ostensibly because of residual reluctance at the grass roots of their own party, but conscious, as always, of his need for an independent power-base in the event of political disharmony.

In the cabinet of 1895 he was undoubtedly better received on personal terms than in that of 1880: he had, after all, established himself as a 'gentleman' as well as a political convenience. Even so, only Balfour appears to have struck any response in Chamberlain's emotions comparable to that which had once bound him to Dilke and permeated the love–hate relationship with Churchill. There was a mutual respect for the toughness, realism, and hard logic which identified their respective political styles, and mutual recognition of the warmth of feeling which lay suppressed beneath their public *personae*. Balfour's sceptical but radical mind had, so far at least, complemented Chamberlain's rationalistic earnestness in providing Unionism with the progressive stance they believed was needed to govern in the modern world. Balfour, too, had gradually brought Salisbury round to recognize that Chamberlain's temperament responded well to personal cultivation, and social relations were well-established between Hatfield and Highbury. Yet there was no symbiosis between these two self-sufficient personalities. The abrasive intellectual High-Toryism which had characterized the younger Cecil had mellowed into a more benign, if still reserved and supercilious, temperament, more adept at responding pragmatically to the anathema of Chamberlainite politics. Yet there was an immoveable barrier which divided two men each convinced that they possessed the distinct legitimate qualifications of birth and achievement for governing Britain. Increasingly, Salisbury's politics were becoming built around the task of restricting Chamberlain's mobility of action, a task fraught with difficulties as not only the 'slippery Whig', Devonshire, but many leading Tories and even Balfour began to lose confidence in Salisbury's capacity to cope with contemporary problems. For his part, Chamberlain had learned that persuasion, not force, would have to be his method of approach towards Unionist disagreements, particularly since the government no longer needed Liberal Unionism for its majority in the Commons; but Salisbury was the chief obstacle to his ambitions for the ministry, and for Salisbury's personal and political style he could summon up none of the admiration that, even in the worst days of their relationship, he had been able to extend towards Gladstone's enormous power and energy.

Among Chamberlain's objectives, the first was to make something of his new office. The Colonial Office was to remain no longer a backwater, but become the linchpin of the government's political objectives. Having been induced to take up responsibility for the Empire, he became intent on making Unionism the party, not so much of domestic, as of imperial, reform, with clearly defined tasks—colonial development, and imperial integration, with federation as the ultimate goal, however much this might still appear, he admitted, a 'vain and empty dream'. Despite its aristocratic bias, Unionism was also to offer a business administration, with imperial economics as its focus. All state offices, foreign, military and domestic, were ultimately geared to commercial affairs, he told an audience in 1896, and the best government was that which contributed most to expanding trade by finding new markets, developing old ones, and retaining a fair share in existing ones.

The task to which he had given prominence most recently was developing undeveloped estates. But development needed money, and of this he had no ready supply. He could have tried blackmailing Salisbury for it in June as the price for taking the Colonial Office,[2] though this might have meant an empty place at the Exchequer. Immediate steps were therefore taken to find sources of supply outside the normal parliamentary grant, so tightly controlled by both the Treasury and the House. His first suggestion, on which six months of discussion were wasted, was to reserve interest payments on the Suez Canal shares to the Exchequer for the sole use of colonial development projects, but the support of Salisbury and Balfour was gradually undermined by Hicks Beach's refusal to countenance any such indirect imposition on the British taxpayer. Failing in this, Chamberlain presented a more ambitious scheme—to raise loans at low interest rates with government backing, invest them in the colonies at marginally higher rates, and use the difference for imperial defence, communications or the subsidy of colonial exchequers. This sort of funding might go down well in improving Birmingham, but Beach balked at the British Exchequer backing the dubious, high-risk projects associated with the colonies (a fact of life to which Chamberlain's earlier disastrous venture into West Indian sisal production testified). Again the plan was scrapped, and Chamberlain found himself over the next few years skirmishing for every penny with what Salisbury called the 'Gladstonian garrison at the Treasury', whose chief permanent official was the archetypical Gladstonian, Edward Hamilton, a man endemically suspicious of 'giving the Secretary of State [for the Colonies] a blank cheque'.[3]

In this respect the West Indies were to prove Chamberlain's greatest problem over the years. The area's single-crop economy was in difficulties, and European tariffs and bounties to domestic sugar-beet production had brought its old sugar industry to ruin and, a more important fact in Westminster, its administrations near to bankruptcy. Chamberlain persuaded the Treasury to bale out Dominica with a £15,000 grant in 1895, but had his plan for a £100,000 loan to develop harbour and communication facilities rejected. An increase of European bounties in 1896 induced him to appoint a Commission to study the problem on the spot. He had already prepared a grand scheme of grants to the tune of £200,000 and loans over five years for £120,000 to provide the islands with a modern infrastructure, more efficient sugar production and diversification of exports, and warned a Liberal Commission member that the alternative, in a case of 'imperative necessity', was counter-vailing duties against the Europeans. The Commission's depressing report in 1897 was accompanied by a majority proposal for extensive financial aid, but Chamberlain brought before the cabinet in November a minority recommendation to impose countervailing duties. Beach's determined opposi-tion, on free trade grounds and fear of the domestic impact of sugar price increases ('I would sooner see the West Indies ruined than the Unionist Party'),[4] swayed the cabinet contrary to his own expectations, but, victorious over Chamberlain's shrewdly deployed advance guard, he was now on weak ground to resist the Commission's majority proposals. Under threat of Chamberlain's resignation, he had to disgorge large sums to cover administrative deficits in the West Indies, and later pro-jects for increasing agricultural production and transportation.

Problems still remained. The Jamaican government had to be rescued in 1899, and further aid culminated in 1902 with a quarter-million pound loan for the area. Chamberlain, how-ever, was now pushing hard the tariff threat which he had earlier skilfully used against the Commission and the cabinet. Curzon, the Indian Viceroy, was persuaded to insert a thin end of the wedge by tariff protection of Mauritian sugar, and the issue was gradually pressed to a point where Lansdowne, then Foreign Secretary and representative at the Brussels negotiations on sugar, took an unapproved initiative in 1902. Threatening to give preferential rates to West Indian sugar on recently imposed war tariffs, he forced his European counter-parts into agreeing to dismantle their bounty systems. Even Beach had by this stage accepted preference as a bad alterna-tive to pouring funds into an apparently bottomless pit. The agreement, and Chamberlain's schemes undertaken earlier, did much to improve the West Indies, although endemic prob-lems have persisted throughout the whole of this century.

There were other major problems which Chamberlain tackled in this general field. He helped establish the School of Tropical Medicine to fight malaria, the heaviest of the white man's African burdens; he secured Treasury loans for irriga-tion and communications in Cyprus; in West Africa he pressed on railway construction into the interior.[5] In 1899 he steered through an important Act to give British backing for dominion government loans. In addition he attempted to ensure that colonial exploitation was efficiently conducted. George Goldie had his Niger Company charter removed because Chamberlain believed him intent on quick returns from a commercial monopoly rather than on long-term development. Salisbury opposed this, much preferring old-fashioned 'informal' imperialism to direct British responsibility, and Chamberlain was himself sufficiently a child of his age to look for development primarily through private business ventures rather than direct government activity. He had told the Commons that government assistance would be forthcoming for promising schemes, and there were several successful partnerships—shipping in the West Indies was expanded through state subsidies to the Elder Dempster shipping line, for instance. But there were grand failures as well. Lipton's tea concern would not invest in the West Indies without impossibly large government underwriting, and Cecil Rhodes's plan for government credit for his 'Cape to Cairo' railway was accepted unenthusiastically by Chamberlain and rejected by Beach.

Chamberlain privately condemned selfish capitalists who wanted government protection for their activities but would do nothing even marginally affecting their profit margins in return, but he had to face the fact that British shareholders generally saw economic imperialism in terms of immediate profits, not long-term imperial growth rates. Chamberlain's vision was largely a personal one, and, operating as he was through a colonial service largely insensitive to the notion of promoting investment and trade opportunities, he could count on few of his agents to help bring the vision to realization. At home he faced Beach's determination to resist financial heterodoxy and colleagues indifferent to his enthusiasms for grubby projects in faraway backwaters. (Mrs Asquith once caught Salisbury in an ironic mood: 'I heard [Chamberlain] at Grosvenor House. Let me see ... what was he speaking about? ... (reflectively) Australian washerwomen? I think ... or some such thing.')[6] The plan to turn his Office into a major department of state was firmly controlled by a slow expansion of staff, and one official later noted that 'in 1896 the work fell into arrears from which it has never recovered.' Westminster politics could not accommodate the enlightened despotism which had 'improved' Birmingham in three years, and there was little enough change in the imperial slums after eight years to justify comparable boasting.

Chamberlain's problems were further complicated by the fact that a colonial development programme could not be pursued *in vacuo*. A rational allocation of resources to secure maximum long-run benefits was subsumed in the short-term expedients of rescuing declining areas like the West Indies. Development also merged with the prime task of keeping areas safely under British control. West African development was dominated by the task of keeping out the French: attempts to modernize Sierra Leone through taxes on the natives caused uprisings which cost more to quell than the intended revenue. Above all, Chamberlain faced the task of ensuring that the vast mineral wealth being unearthed in South Africa was used to strengthen, not undermine, imperial influence in the area.[7]

He had entered the Colonial Office knowing, like his colleagues, that a crisis here was in the making. For years successive governments had aimed to create a united South Africa capable, like Canada, New Zealand, and the nascent Australian Federation, of standing on its own feet while acting as an agent of British policy in the region. Domestic political attitudes, ranging from ultra-imperialists to extreme Radicals, differed, however, over the extent to which Britain should actively further federation and control the unified colony. The chief problem lay with the Transvaal. Vast funds from its mines, particularly after major discoveries in the late 1880s, were contributing to rapid economic development in South Africa. But there were constraints. Kruger's regime rested on support from the conservative Boer farmers whose use of native labour was believed to restrict flows to the mines and whose resistance to change blocked the creation of a modern political infrastructure. The Uitlanders—foreign, largely British, capitalists and skilled mine-workers on the Rand—had economic restrictions imposed by government control of the railways and dynamite monopoly, and were denied equal civil and political rights with the native Boers. Taxation financed government hangers-on and corruption rather than further modernization. London generally shared the frustration of commercial interests, both British and Afrikaner, in South Africa, and grew increasingly worried that any federation would be dominated by a wealthy and largely hostile Transvaal, particularly when Germany began angling for influence in Pretoria. But, hesitant about reviving the political problems of 1877–84, British governments had taken few steps actively to intervene in the Republic, and largely followed a policy of geographical and diplomatic containment. More aggressive spirits were discontented. Cecil Rhodes, Rand magnate and Cape premier, was determined on bringing the Republic into a British South Africa, and British politicians, though suspicious of his personal ambition, vulgar financial dealings, and close political relations with the Cape Afrikaner Bond Party, began to see in him the prime agency against Kruger. His South Africa Company was given land north of the Transvaal for mineral exploitation to counterbalance, it was hoped, the Republic's wealth, but by the mid-1890s it was clear that immediate benefits were unlikely and that the operation was adversely affecting the Company's financial position. Rhodes began to turn his attention to the Transvaal itself, with the object of undermining Kruger's power by mobilizing the Uitlanders around their economic and political grievances.

When Chamberlain assumed office, a violent clash in Johannesburg seemed on the cards. Two alternative imperial strategies were available to him. One, formulated by the former High Commissioner, Sir Henry Loch, was actively to encourage the Uitlanders' demands, ensure a presence in the area of British troops, and take advantage of any uprising to assert 'the imperial factor' in the future political evolution of the Transvaal. This, Rosebery and Lord Ripon, Chamberlain's predecessor, had eschewed: though ready to intervene and mediate between the contending parties in any confrontation, they would not encourage it. To maintain the traditional policy in South Africa, they had early in 1895 replaced Loch by Sir Hercules Robinson.

That Chamberlain had successfully applied pressure upon the Conservative government in the late 1880s to end Robinson's earlier period as High Commissioner because of his responsiveness to Afrikaner and colonial opinion was an indication that he would take a different line from Ripon. Chamberlain had long since discarded his old non-interventionist views.

In 1888, when Dilke sadly observed that he had become strongly 'anti-Boer', he had privately stated his new approach: 'I am inclined to advocate a bold policy, fully recognizing Imperial responsibilities and duty, but then I intend that it should be the policy of the Imperial and not of the Cape Government, and should be carried out by officials taking their instructions from the former.'[8] Specific objections to the Transvaal government's policies were reinforced by such wider views on the question of self-determination: 'I warn [the advocates of independence] that the day of small kingdoms has passed away,' he told a Scottish audience in 1889, a view he was now applying generally to world affairs. Colonial competition between the great powers, he had come to believe, made earlier policies of 'informal' imperial influence totally unviable, and Britain had rapidly to consolidate control over her existing spheres of influence. This view of Empire, grander and more determined than that of most previous Colonial Secretaries, made him eager to advance a solution to the South African problem. There was, perhaps, a further factor. In his restless pursuit of political influence and prestige, he was, early in the life of the new Unionist ministry, angling for something which would prove, as he is reported to have later called the Boer War, 'a feather in his cap'.[9]

In this context, things were set in train for tacit connivance at Rhodes's plan to bring down the Kruger regime. By its very nature the enterprise was based on dubious premises from the British point of view: designed to enhance direct British control of the area, it depended upon being able to use successfully a man like Rhodes, deeply opposed to 'Downing Street government' and favouring greater colonial autonomy, who had once contributed financially to the Irish Nationalist cause. Given, however, the persistent problem of rousing support in Britain for direct intervention and the danger of alienating opinion in Cape and Natal colonies, Chamberlain had little option but to try exploiting the Cape premier's ambitions for his own ends. In November 1895 he transferred to Rhodes's Company part of the Bechuanaland Protectorate adjacent to the Transvaal for the building of a railway northwards—a genuine objective, but one with the prime immediate aim of providing a base at Pitsani for Company police to be grouped ready for moving to

Johannesburg in the event of an Uitlander revolution, now being actively encouraged through Rhodes's fellow mine-owners. The Randlords themselves were already in a truculent mood after an earlier diplomatic crisis in which Kruger had closed transport routes with the Cape and Chamberlain had secured their reopening.

Despite later disavowing full knowledge of Rhodes's intended *coup*—'I did not want to know too much,' he once commented[10] —Chamberlain was well aware of the plans being made, and in late 1895 recognized that the sudden development of diplomatic problems with Russia and America risked creating complications. In mid-December he warned Rhodes that the Uitlander revolt 'should come *at once* or be postponed for a year or two at least'. Unwisely, he hinted at a clear preference for the former, and was soon disappointed to learn that the nerve of the Rand capitalists had broken: 'The Transvaal business is going to fizzle out,' he told Salisbury on 29 December. Belatedly recognizing the possibility of events moving beyond his control, he dispatched a telegram warning that any attempt to instigate rebellion from outside the Transvaal would be wholly unacceptable. It arrived too late. Believing that the imperial government would provide *ex post* legitimation, Dr Jameson led his Company police from Pitsani in an unauthorized invasion of the Republic. Johannesburg, however, failed to respond: his force was surrounded and compelled to surrender.[11]

Identification with the unprovoked invasion of a self-governing state could do Chamberlain nothing but harm. 'If this succeeds,' he told his wife, 'it will ruin me. I am going up to London to crush it.' He immediately disavowed the Raid and compelled Rhodes, who was inclined to take advantage of action he had not authorized, to do the same. This did much to restore the situation. But the ensuing outcry was considerable. In Britain, critics of Empire were outraged at the Raid, and began to hint at conspiracy originating in the Colonial Office; ultra-imperialists and the extensive network of the South Africa Company were furious with Chamberlain's 'betrayal' of the heroic Jameson; among his colleagues and knowledgeable Liberals, suspicions were raised at his competence in letting the affair slip beyond his control.[12] It soon promised to turn into the most serious threat yet to his career. As always, Chamberlain proved to be at his most ruthless and ingenious with his back to the wall.

An immediate diplomatic consequence of the Raid offered the first opportunity to save his credibility. In November Salisbury had rebuffed the latest attempt by Germany to be recognized as an interested party in British South Africa, but, seeing a useful opening, on 3 January the Kaiser sent a telegram of support for Kruger's resistance to aggression. Roundly condemned by British ministers, the telegram allowed Chamberlain to divert attention from the central issue by successfully pressing Salisbury to send extra ships to the area, less as a serious defence against possible German intervention than as an ' "Act of Vigour" . . . required to soothe the wounded vanity of the nation. It does not matter which of our numerous foes we defy, but we ought to defy someone.'[13] Two weeks later he delivered a speech in a statesmanlike vein, praising the virtues of 'patriotism' while condemning the incontinence of extreme 'jingoism', and expatiating on the dangers of Britain's 'Splendid Isolation' among the world powers, which required greater exploitation of the imperial link to ensure national security. This, and a powerful defence to the Commons of his limited involvement in the Raid, did much to restore his damaged reputation.[14]

In South Africa itself, however, Britain's policy was in ruins. Kruger's position had been strengthened, and Afrikaners in the Cape had been alienated. Chamberlain yielded to pressure and agreed that Jameson would be brought to trial on his release from the Transvaal. Rhodes was compelled to resign the Cape premiership, and the Company's police force was disbanded, though demands for withdrawal of its charter were rejected. The prospects of gaining any significant political capital from the fiasco were lost. Sir Hercules Robinson travelled to Pretoria, but infuriated Chamberlain by agreeing to disarmament of the Uitlanders and failing to secure guarantees for internal reform in the Republic. Chamberlain's own initiatives failed. His plan for a 'great coup' in getting Kruger to London for discussions was rejected in Pretoria—a scheme of 'Home Rule for the Rand', which would create a threatening *imperium in imperio* within the Transvaal, fell flat, partly because, with his

growing proclivity for 'open diplomacy', Chamberlain announced the scheme in London before officially delivering it to
South Africa.

At home the government was eventually compelled to concede a parliamentary inquiry into the Raid, and the full glare
of publicity was directed between February and July 1897 at
what, it soon became clear, was an unedifying story. Chamberlain had to fight tooth and nail to prevent its report from im-
plicating him in planning the operation. It was a superb, if
disgraceful, exercise in political survival. He was himself a
leading member of a committee part of whose ostensible task
was investigating his own, and his department's, role in the
affair. The leading Liberal members, Harcourt and Sydney
Buxton, were dissuaded from probing too deeply for fear of
weakening Britain's authority in South Africa—diplomatic
contretemps with the Transvaal in August 1896 and April 1897
here helped to create the necessary climate. Their hostility to
Rhodes was also played upon to divert their attention outside
the Colonial Office. Chamberlain's main defence, that, while
aware of the tensions in Johannesburg, he knew nothing of the
Raid itself, was disingenuous: since no one but Jameson had
foreknowledge of his sudden decision to go in, the issue of
Chamberlain's foreknowledge of a co-ordinated plan to unseat
Kruger by revolution and invasion was befogged. This justification, however, faced problems: there were in existence telegrams from Rhodes's London agents retailing conversations
with the Colonial Secretary prior to the Raid which effectively
undermined his case. The story of the fate of these telegrams is
a saga in itself: suffice it to say that the inquiry's attempt to
retrieve a number of the more incriminating were unsuccessful,
and copies Chamberlain had himself made were not offered for
public inspection. Manœuvring in this way, of course, severely
compromised him with the South Africa Company, eager to
pass the buck in its own battle for survival, but Chamberlain
ultimately defused this danger as successfully as he did that
from the inquiry. Threats were levelled against the charter and
blandishments to its leading officials delivered—Harcourt was
furious that, in his speech accepting the inquiry report,
Chamberlain backtracked on its open condemnation of Rhodes
by describing him as a man of honour who had made a 'gigantic

mistake' in pursuit of a patriotic ideal. Making scapegoats of various minor Company and government officials allowed the chief protagonists to evade their responsibility for the affair.[15]

The consequence for British policy towards South Africa of the Raid and its effects was a retreat to the earlier methods of containment rather than intervention. Rhodes was *hors de combat*, the Uitlanders returning from political to financial pre-occupations, and Cape politics were in a state of uncertainty. Chamberlain was in no position to pre-empt Kruger's rapid rearmament of his people. However, his protests at breaches of the Conventions in August 1896 and April 1897 were, despite Salisbury's reticence, accompanied by a reinforcement of military strength in South Africa in a successful display of that 'brinkmanship' which was to become his definitive style in foreign affairs. They showed that his nerve had not been broken by the Jameson fiasco and, reinforced by the flood of diplomatic exchanges published in Blue Books to blacken the name of the Republic's illiberal regime, provided effective propaganda: they did little to bring the Transvaal closer towards a South African federation. And there were two consequences of the events of the years 1895–7 for Chamberlain's approach to the later crisis of 1899. On the one hand, the compromising of his reputation dictated a much more hesitant and circumspect handling of the policy of aggression when readopted in 1899: on the other, the success of his diplomatic confrontations in 1896–7 engraved far too deeply on his mind the view he had expressed to Salisbury that 'if [the Boers] see we are in earnest, I believe they will give way, as they have always done.'[16]

After 1895 and the failure of his South African policy, Chamberlain's attention had begun to move elsewhere. His 'Splendid Isolation' speech of January 1896, designed primarily as a smokescreen for the Raid, had aroused widespread comment on Britain's international position, and foreshadowed an initiative later in the year. The speech had emphasized imperial unification as a solution to problems of 'isolation', and in two speeches of March and June Chamberlain related this to commercial issues. His public declarations since taking office had clearly identified him as the leading spokesman for commercial interests, and a circular of November 1895 to colonial governors requesting information on the state of

British exports to colonial markets had been given wide publicity. (It perhaps also confirms the Canadian premier, Sir
Wilfrid Laurier's, later comment that Chamberlain was a
'Little Englander in his imperialism'—only as an afterthought
were questions on problems of colonial exports to Britain
added.) Worries at the Treasury that Chamberlain's attention
to commercial questions were drawing him towards an un-
healthy interest in tariffs were confirmed by the two 1896
speeches.[17] In them he offered his first detailed proposal for
imperial unification, built around the notion of an imperial
Zollverein on the German model—an old Fair Trade League
scheme. The plan he recommended was for Britain and the
colonies to be free to impose tariffs against the outside world,
so long as all were remitted in full to other members of the
Empire. Though entailing Britain's abandonment of strict free
trade, Chamberlain advocated the plan on free trade grounds:
eliminating colonial tariff barriers would 'be the greatest advance that free trade has ever made since it was first advocated
by Mr Cobden', the benefits to British exports more than compensating for increased import prices and possible foreign
retaliation.

According to his wife, Chamberlain had had this scheme in
mind for years (though he had publicly rejected it as impracticable in 1888), but the reasons for his initiative at this point are
unclear—it certainly did not originate in the as yet unreceived
results of his commercial circular. In part it was the follow-up
to a move from his predecessor, Lord Ripon. Under pressure
at a colonial conference in Ottawa during 1894 for Britain to
allow greater colonial tariff flexibility and imperial preference
relations, Ripon had responded by advocating intra-imperial
free trade. This, however, had been designed to engineer a
stalemate. The Liberal government, pressed to consider tariff
relations by the Imperial Federation League (which then broke
up because of its failure), had determined to steer clear of this
controversial issue, and Ripon's suggestion in 1894 was designed to throw colonial governments on the defensive with the
one tariff scheme advantageous to Britain which the colonists,
concerned to protect their infant industries, could not accept.[18]

Chamberlain perhaps hoped by his publicity to create a
climate more favourable for consideration of the plan at the

colonial conference which was anticipated, following the 1887 precedent, for the Queen's 1897 Jubilee. Conditions in Britain at least seemed suitable for a good reception. The Zollverein was explicitly recommended in the context of the panic over 'isolation': 'What is the greatest of our common obligations?' Chamberlain asked. 'It is imperial defence. What is the greatest of our common interests? It is imperial trade.' Defence depended on ways and means, and made questions of imperial finance and trade all-important: 'The Empire *is* commerce,' he stressed. Further, 1896 had been a year of commercial scares, culminating in the success of the popular pamphlet *Made in Germany*, which reflected unease over foreign competition and the 'dumping' of German products at below-market prices. Chamberlain himself disavowed hysteria on the question in a November speech, arguing that German producers were unfortunately better than British competitors at catering for the market, but, as in 1888, his speeches reflected a concern to direct protectionist impulses in Britain into more constructive channels.

The Zollverein proposal, however, fell flat. Chamberlain had little technical equipment with which to counter criticisms from free-trade economists and Liberal politicians; British industry was moving into boom conditions; colonial governments wrote the scheme off, as they had in 1894, as an absurdity. By December Chamberlain was noting his pessimism about useful discussions at the 1897 colonial conference, and was soon arranging merely an informal gathering of colonial premiers for the Jubilee. By April, however, events had made a full-scale meeting seem beneficial. In 1896 Wilfrid Laurier's Liberal Party had come to power in Britain's largest and wealthiest colony, Canada, on a platform of greater protection and closer American links at the expense of the British connection. In office, however, it set about giving a preference to British imports of one-eighth, raised to one-third after a year, on its new tariffs.

Hopes in London of further developments at the conference proved premature. Chamberlain favourably impressed the premiers by his attention to their opinions and problems and by showing that his horizons were not totally restricted to those of the British Treasury and Foreign Office, but his proposals for a Zollverein and a representative imperial council were coolly received, the latter foundering on problems of delegated authority. Britain had one concession to colonial wishes—renunciation of the 'most favoured nation' clauses of commercial treaties with Germany and Belgium which extended colonial tariff preferences to them—but it was her demands on the colonies, especially for contributions to imperial naval defence, which dominated the proceedings. On this the South African and Australian colonies made offers, financially small but ideologically significant, but Canada, it emerged, was using her fairly costless tariff concessions as a way of deflecting pressure on this front. Chamberlain obtained a commitment to more regular conference meetings, but, overall, it appeared that everyone favoured closer imperial relations only so long as major sacrifices of money and political autonomy were not required. Chamberlain's disappointment was tempered only by his earlier more realistic anticipation of limited success.[19]

By mid-1897 Chamberlain had placed his stamp upon the Colonial Office and advanced some way towards publicly defining the government's key concern as being the state of the Empire. But no ambitious plans had been launched on the cabinet as in the years after 1880. There had been rows over imperial finances and politically more important ones over the 1896 Education Bill (see p. 258); his 1895 commercial circular had been mildly resented by the Board of Trade in whose province strictly it belonged; the Zollverein speech was delivered without cabinet approval, but few colleagues had objections to what was in effect testing the wind with a proposal for which most had some sympathy. Indeed, in the aftermath of the Jameson Raid, the Colonial Secretary had been in a rather more subdued mood than when he had made his grandiose electoral promises in mid-1895.

   Relationships in cabinet, however, took a new turn in 1897. A deteriorating international situation threatened to raise problems comparable to those which disrupted the ministry of 1880. Before long the government was caught up in disagreements between those like Salisbury intent on maintaining the existing balance of international power and a system of multilateral negotiation and agreement, and a radical cabinet group intent on more aggressive policies. Not without significance, perhaps, the core of this radical group comprized Chamberlain, Devonshire, Goschen, and the Liberal appendages of Unionism who had balked most at Gladstonianism in the 1880s and now formed the bulk of the talent in an otherwise average cabinet. The disagreements struck at the basis of Salisbury's conduct of government and not merely his authority as Foreign Secretary. The principle on which he had run his earlier ministries had largely been that of leaving ministers free to run their departments with minimal supervision. In 1895 there had been a tacit understanding that, if Salisbury did not openly obstruct the formulation of domestic reform policies—and even here Devonshire and Chamberlain had in 1898 to force the implementation of Irish local government reforms left over from 1892—then harmony would prevail and ministers would be left on a long leash. Chamberlain in particular was free to play around at the Colonial Office, and Salisbury expected a restoration of his autocratic control over international affairs to rescue them from the brash handling of his predecessors, Rosebery and Sir Edward Grey. The hope that it might be 'business as usual' proved illusory.

The government had taken office at a time of high tension.[20] Britain confronted France over territory in Siam and West Africa; Germany was angling for a share of hegemony in South Africa; Russia had been offered new opportunities for expansion in the Near East due to massacres of Armenian Christians within the Ottoman Empire and a subsequent Turkish–Greek war; President Cleveland of America caused acute embarrassment by threatening high-handed action in Britain's conflict with Venezuela over the boundaries of British Guiana. But the period of 'splendid isolation' in January 1896 had given way to more relaxed days. Negotiations were completed over Siam, and opened on West Africa. The Kaiser was firmly but delicately warned off South Africa. Paradoxically, those who later emerged as Salisbury's leading 'jingo' critics overrode the tough line he wished to take over the two other issues. Salisbury was forced to build an international concordat against Russian influence in the Near East when his cabinet rejected the Disraelian tactic of sending out a British fleet, and he was soon despairing of protecting Turkey's integrity. Towards what he saw as the troublesome American ex-colonists with grandiose ideas, Chamberlain and younger cabinet members enforced a conciliatory line and the opening of negotiations which, in 1899, ended in a favourable arbitration for Britain. Chamberlain in fact attempted to link these two problems. He was anxious for closer relations with America, partly from sympathetic attachment based on marriage ties and an old Radical hankering after the 'classless' democracy which America symbolized in Britain, but largely from a sense that America's rapidly growing power could be harnessed to aid Britain's overseas commitments. During negotiations over Venezuela he attempted to draw Anglophile American politicians towards joint action on behalf of Turkey's maltreated Christians, though without significantly denting the Republic's matured isolationism.

Salisbury's difficulties with his cabinet began to grow apace when he clashed directly with Chamberlain over the latter's departmental responsibility for West Africa. In mid-1896 France retired from the conference discussing the long-standing scramble between French and British traders for concessions and territory in the hinterland, protesting against Britain's recent decision to undertake a reconquest of the Sudan. Chamberlain had long seen West Africa as a politically sensitive issue, and in 1885 warned a cabinet that the Chambers of Commerce would never forgive a government which neglected the Niger trade.[21] Now at the Colonial Office, he had to bear the brunt of any criticism, and in a speech at Birmingham in November 1896 undertook to resist territorial expansion by any nation which, unlike Britain, attempted 'to secure the monopoly for its own products by preferential and artificial methods': 'Under these circumstances, I say it is a matter of life and death to us that we should not be forestalled in these markets of the future to which we may have learned to look for the extension of our trade and even for the subsistence of our people.'

This was not Salisbury's way of looking at the world. Evaluating foreign affairs from an essentially Eurocentric viewpoint, he saw the scramble for colonies largely in terms of its impact upon the continental balance of power, Britain's prestige in Europe, and the protection of key strategic routes and outposts.

Anxious to minimize the growing conflict with France over North-East Africa, he wanted an early settlement of the West African difficulty. Chamberlain warned him against the pursuit of a conciliatory policy, arguing in June 1897 that 'if we do not show that we will not be trifled with, we shall finally be driven to war, with the disadvantage of having surrendered much that is valuable', but his reservations failed to prevent Salisbury reopening negotiations with an intimation that Britain was ready to prove amenable. Chamberlain soon withdrew his initial acquiescence. French activity in the region during the negotiations left him worried at the prospect of a *fait accompli*, with Britain having lost much valuable territory, and anxious for a correspondingly aggressive military policy. The problem here was that British forces could not be spared for what Salisbury and Lansdowne considered a minor issue, while George Goldie, fighting Chamberlain's attempt since early 1896 to 'expropriate him, lock, stock and barrel',[22] was unwilling to make the Niger Company's police force available. By the autumn of 1897, Chamberlain had therefore decided to take matters into his own hands. He approved the formation of a force of native troops under Lord Lugard to pursue his own clearly stated policy: 'We ought', he told his Under-Secretary, Lord Selborne, '—even at the risk of war—to keep the hinterland for the Gold Coast, Lagos and the Niger territories,'[23] and on 1 December was protesting strongly at the Foreign Office's willingness in the negotiations to yield French enclaves on the Niger threatening trade routes inland. Though not opposed to settling on reasonable terms, he was convinced that 'the French only propose to abandon doubtful claims in exchange for the surrender by us of undoubted rights.'[24] Salisbury's desire to settle, strengthened by apprehensions that the French government would create a warlike climate to divert attention from the Dreyfus affair, was matched by growing bitterness in Chamberlain: 'I thought [Salisbury] was entirely with us,' he told Selborne, 'and now he is prepared to give away everything and get nothing. I am more than sorry to differ from him, but I cannot stand it.'[25] At a critical stage of the negotiations in January 1898, he brought their disagreements to cabinet, and gained a victory. A majority of his colleagues, as well as the Commons, warmly welcomed an aggressive stand against France and the West African Frontier Force which was ready by March to pursue it.

The outcome was a series of confrontations with French forces at key points in the Niger region. The danger of miscalculations risking open war was recognized and avoided, and a solution was reached at the Commission in a feverish climate. A final hitch occurred over French claims for the township of Ilo on the Niger's lower reaches, which Salisbury was inclined to yield until Chamberlain, threatening 'I have gone to the extreme limit to which . . . I am entitled to go', offered minor compensation in the Gold Coast, while advising that, if the negotiations collapsed, Britain should simply seize French territory and reopen the whole issue. Salisbury and the French negotiators backed down, and agreement was reached on 14 June 1898.

The tensions which had arisen between Chamberlain and Salisbury during these eighteen months marked a changed climate in the ministry. The former had become increasingly restless with the Foreign Office's whole conduct of international affairs. It was partly a disagreement over perspectives. As colonial minister, Chamberlain looked at the issue from his departmental viewpoint rather than in an overall diplomatic context, and he had an interpretation of the future economic value of colonial expansion alien to the minds of Salisbury and his advisers. Differences arose also from the contrast between the patrician disdain with which Salisbury and his officials tended to view the transient enthusiasms of public opinion, and Chamberlain's growing sensitivity to 'jingo' press and backbench opinion. He was beginning to present, and to regard, himself as the 'strong man' of the cabinet, and Salisbury as the representative of an outdated Gladstonian proclivity for international consensus and conciliation. Late in 1898 he was to describe him as a 'peace at any price' man, applying the label he had formerly pinned on Bright, Morley, and Harcourt, and acknowledging Salisbury's growing horror of war and anxiety for peaceful diplomatic settlements.[26] There was also a further difference between them—that of temperament. Salisbury's assured, sophisticated grasp of international diplomacy was never fully appreciated by a man who had acquired political power through truculence, the exposition of clear, well-publicized, programmes, and the delivery of brash demands on his superiors. As G. M. Young once noted of Chamberlain's old opponent, Roebuck: 'Nothing is so bloody-minded as a Radical turned patriot.'[27] Chamberlain himself was all too ready to see in the necessary resolution of international disagreements the basis of 'appeasement'.

Throughout 1898 his martial mood grew, and at the same time he came face to face with the problem which continually preoccupied Salisbury: it was not an easy task to build the bricks of a foreign policy without straw. In the China crisis of 1898, consciousness of this began to dawn, and, in fighting to uphold the tottering Chinese Empire, he set out to forge a new solution to the problem of Britain's extended overseas interests.

Defeat by Japan in 1895 and Russia's eastwards consolidation on her borders posed a major threat to China's integrity, and with it Britain's extensive political and economic influence.[28] The Empire's riches and political weakness were a vacuum into which expansionist powers were more than willing to be drawn and when the volatile Germany, ostensibly retaliating for the massacre of missionaries, seized the port of Kiao-chau late in 1897, a major crisis had been created. Within weeks a Russian fleet sailed into Port Arthur, compelling British ships to withdraw and inflaming nationalistic opinion at home. The move posed little threat to Britain's strategic interests, but it promised to be an important weapon for Russia to bully Peking into giving preference in the international competition for trade and financial concessions, and perhaps ultimately into accepting territorial expropriation. For Britain, the prime task was preserving the *status quo* and thereby her existing advantageous position. Balfour declared early in 1898 that 'Our interests in China are not territorial; they are commercial', which involved opposition to any partition and retention of the 'open-door' for trade and investment.

Britain's capacity to do this was the subject of considerable scepticism from Salisbury, who warned Chamberlain that perhaps the only course available was the seizure of territory compensating for Port Arthur: 'It will not be useful, and will be expensive; but as a matter of pure sentiment, we shall have to do it.' Chamberlain initially concurred, suggesting approaches to Japan for help, but his ideas began to change as

Salisbury turned towards attempting to achieve his prime aims by negotiation with Russia, on the grounds that 'It is the best chance of an equilibrium of Europe.' His desire for negotiations, based on a plan for a 'partition of preponderance' without formal territorial dissection in the unstable empires of both China and Turkey, reflected in particular his view that Britain's disagreements with France in Africa made it impossible simultaneously to resist Russia, France's partner in the European Dual Alliance, in China.

Though his discussions ground to an unsatisfactory halt in February 1898, Salisbury's strategy was already under fire at home. Chamberlain had been warning of the unpopularity of the policy, and by February Unionist backbenchers were up in arms at the failure to 'stand up' to Russia. He, Balfour, and Hicks Beach favoured a stronger line and in January delivered truculent speeches to fortify Salisbury and warn Russia against assuming that expansionist designs would be meekly tolerated. The 'hawks' in the cabinet further contained the old Palmerstonians, Goschen and Devonshire, the former sensitive to financial opinion in the City, the latter to fears in Lancashire, where his family had extensive interests, about a threat to the Far Eastern cotton trade. Chamberlain's own responsiveness to views among the business community was reinforced by his worries over growing government unpopularity: 'If you [read all the papers] I think you would agree with me that grave trouble is impending upon the Government if we do not adopt a more decided attitude in regard to China,' he told Balfour in early February.[29] The China crisis, furthermore, was a chance to undermine Salisbury's overall control of foreign policy to which on so many other grounds he was increasingly opposed. Salisbury's disappearance in early February on one of his periodic visits to southern France for health reasons provided the first of several opportunities to challenge his policies. Chamberlain contacted Balfour on 3 February with a radical alternative to Salisbury's approach on China—that of co-ordinating with Germany and America for joint enforcement of Russia's commitment to the 'open-door' and, were this refused, her ousting from Port Arthur. Speedy action, he argued, was needed to appease Parliament, though it might prove 'too strong for the cabinet'. Chamberlain's intended partners in the

enterprise were an obvious choice. As in the Near East, he was
hoping to call Britain's 'Anglo-Saxon' fellows to her aid, while
Germany, as well as having interests in China, was the pillar
of the Triple Alliance with Austria and Italy against France
and Russia. But America, in imminent collision with the Spanish Empire in the Pacific and Caribbean, had little desire as
yet for involvement in China, and the idea Chamberlain had
earlier suggested of using Japan against Russia proved unsuccessful. Germany became of major importance, but there
were difficulties. Her seizure of Kiao-chau had been partly
influenced by Salisbury's refusal in late 1897 to concede territory in Samoa (which Chamberlain, though resisting concessions in West Africa, had been ready to yield in return for
New Guinea). He was now determined to overcome the two
countries' differences, and in mid-March the financier,
Alfred Rothschild, held a dinner at which Chamberlain,
Devonshire, and Sir Henry Chaplin, President of the Local
Government Board, met the Anglophile German diplomat
Baron Eckardstein and arranged a meeting between Chamberlain, Balfour, and Hatzfeldt, the German ambassador. In
the meantime, events advanced. News of Russian successes
in acquiring leases from Peking compelled a cabinet on
25 March to implement the long-considered plan of seizing
Wei-hai-wei, a harbour facing Port Arthur but of symbolic
rather than commercial or naval value. Only Chamberlain
dissented, convinced now that in this way of appeasing public
opinion lay the path to the partition he feared. He was insistent
that only a combination of powers hostile to Russia could save
the situation.

Balfour succumbed to his arguments and contacted Hatzfeldt in advance of the arranged meeting to impress upon him
the need for an understanding. Hatzfeldt was suitably cool,
welcoming closer relations but observing also Chamberlain's
role in blocking German claims on Togoland and Samoa—a
role Salisbury had studiously cultivated to reinforce his own
objections. Balfour promised to modify this, and four days later
Chamberlain met the ambassador. He immediately sidestepped
the Togoland issue, declaring Britain's foe in West Africa to be
France, not Germany, and followed this hint at a common hostility to Germany's European enemy by identifying their

further common interests in China. The 'isolation', which two years before he had called 'splendid', he now pronounced untenable. Hatzfeldt then interpreted him as suggesting Britain's adhesion to the Triple Alliance as an alternative, though Chamberlain's own version was narrower: 'an alliance might be established by Treaty or Arrangement between Germany and Great Britain for a term of years. That this should be of a defensive character based upon a mutual understanding as to policy in China and elsewhere.'[30] From the standpoint of the Foreign Office these different interpretations were less significant than the basic suggestion of a major departure from traditional principles of non-alignment. Yet they reflected the divergent premises of the participants. Chamberlain wanted backing in China and other colonial areas—Hatzfeldt, reflecting opinion in the German Chancellery, was more interested in a realignment of European relations.

The divergences were more sharply defined at a further meeting some days later. Hatzfeldt presented Salisbury's case —that Britain's best tactic was to conciliate Russia in China, separate her from France, and stand up to France in Africa. Responding to this test of his seriousness, Chamberlain claimed, somewhat at variance with his actions at the time, that Britain's interests in West Africa were minimal compared with those threatened by Russia in China, and he offered what he considered tempting bait—acceptance of Russia's existing position, but joint Anglo-German protection over the remainder of China, with Germany free to expand inland from her concession area on the central coast and allowed to raise funds from the Peking government for an army, leaving Britain with a free hand in the south. If Russia contested either power's claims, here or elsewhere, each would come to the other's aid under a defensive pact. Hatzfeldt, looking for the diplomatic *coup* of Britain's adhesion to the Triple Alliance, was less than candid in his report of these terms to the German Chancellery —not surprisingly: the plans involved Germany standing as a buffer between Russia and British control over the rich pickings of southern China.

Chamberlain's bid for a colonial realignment was checked. Despite his hint at a general colonial settlement, from which Germany hoped to gain much, he made clear that China was his top priority, and, unfortunately, Germany was not un-happy with events here which diverted Russia's attention from Central Europe. An alliance with Britain was not unwelcome, but it would have to be firm and on Germany's terms at a time when anti-British feeling at home offered a useful means to justify her naval programme. Chamberlain was proving am-biguous over the Triple Alliance, however, and the Chancellery was unwilling to 'pull Britain's chestnuts out of the fire' in China until the pressures of isolation had greatly increased her difficulties.

There were conflicting views on the German side towards these discussions—even more on the British. Chamberlain had told Hatzfeldt that his suggestions were purely personal ones (though the cabinet was informed), aware of hostility at the Foreign Office towards an innovatory and precarious, though in many respects logical line—that, if Russia was a threat in China and France in Africa, losses could be minimized by a full settlement with their natural enemy. Salisbury's comment on this came from his resting place in France on 9 April: 'France certainly acts as if she meant to drive us into a German alli-ance: which I look to with dismay, for Germany will blackmail us heavily.' Chamberlain was underestimating these costs, particularly ones which Salisbury feared most—the consolida-tion of two armed camps across Europe which might one day commit Britain to a European war against her wishes and interests.

Chamberlain's initiative, though as yet not sufficiently well advanced to offer an acceptable alternative to Salisbury's line, was providing a rallying point for discontent in cabinet. As acting Prime Minister, however, Balfour was taking care to en-sure that political differences did not get out of hand by treading an ambiguous path. On 5 April, the day before the Easter recess, he hinted to an anxious Commons at the possi-bility of Anglo-German co-operation since their interests 're-quire them to join an alliance' to ensure that 'China shall not fall prey to any exclusive interest', and he had encouraged Chamberlain's activities. But in a long letter to Salisbury re-counting the negotiations, he dissociated himself from the alliance enthusiasts—'a very motley cast'—and on the same day as his Commons speech observed to Hatzfeldt that he shared German scepticism about an immediate agreement. Chamberlain's growing enthusiasm was a case, he said, of 'more haste, less speed'.[31]

The pace was indeed slackening. Chamberlain's hopes had revived in late April after a direct initiative to the Kaiser from Eckardstein, but at a meeting with Hatzfeldt on 25 April the ambassador suggested delaying any final settlement until Britain had reached prior understandings with the Triple Alliance partners Austria and Italy. Chamberlain responded belligerently that China and Germany, not Italy and Austria, were the issues, and warned that a rebuff would entail Britain settling with France and Russia, a far more costly affair for Germany in the long run.

Salisbury's return from France put a temporary halt to his subordinates' initiatives, but he was in a difficult position. Chamberlain had increased his influence significantly during the premier's absence, and, on reporting his discussions, made clear his intention of pursuing the question further: 'Recent experience seems to show that we are powerless to resist the ultimate control of China by Russia, and that we are at a great disadvantage in negotiating with France, as long as we retain our present isolation, and I think that the country would support us in a Treaty with Germany providing for reciprocal defence.'[32] Salisbury agreed that 'a closer relation with Germany would be very desirable; but can we get it?'; and he then proceeded to rebuff German colonial demands on the grounds that 'you ask too much for your friendship.'

With the China affair being widely interpreted as a débâcle, however, Salisbury, under strong public criticism, was determined to retaliate and restore his authority. On 4 May he delivered a speech to a Primrose League meeting which became immediately notorious for its use of the current phraseology of social Darwinism. He argued that the world was composed of 'living and dying nations', in which old powers—by implication China, Turkey, Portugal, and Spain, at the time in the throes of her disastrous colonial war with America—were doomed to extinction at the hands of nations more fitted to survive. The further implication for China at least was that its disintegration was part of an inevitable evolution, certainly not cause for panic or a major rearrangement of world affairs. He

extended his implicit criticism of Chamberlain's views by stressing that Britain's imperial security was best guaranteed by
international co-operation, not by sectional alliances. Chamberlain, not prepared to see his new initiative nipped in the
bud, retaliated at Birmingham on 13 May by publicly reaffirming the importance of territorial integrity and commercial
freedom in China. On Salisbury's hope to reach an accommodation with Russia he had one comment, 'Who sups with
the devil must have a long spoon', and he delivered the first
public declaration of his new proposals: 'If the policy of
isolation . . . is to be maintained . . . then the future of the
Chinese Empire may be, and probably will be, hereafter decided without reference to our wishes and in defiance of our
interests . . . [W]e must not reject the idea of an alliance with
those powers whose interests are most nearly approximate to
our own.' Germany was not explicitly mentioned, but
America's entry in force into the Pacific was warmly welcomed
as a future support; and, countering Darwinism with contemporary racial ideas, he advocated an 'Anglo-Saxon Alliance',
an informal relationship based on 'bonds of amity with our
kinsmen'.

Elsewhere in the speech he spoke of the need for more open
diplomacy, but the success of his call to take international
politics from the hands of diplomats, among whom his influence was limited, on to the platform where he was strong, did
not bode well. German leaders were amused and annoyed at
the crude appeal for help—Russia furious at the insult—
America too preoccupied to respond. Asquith led Liberals in
derision of 'touting for allies in the highways and by ways of
Europe', the diplomatic class condemned a 'lamentable dissertation on the high principles of policy from one not primarily responsible for their execution'.[33] Chamberlain had
forcefully, though unconvincingly, to deny in the Commons
any major disagreement with Salisbury, but he had achieved
by his speech two significant gains: the traditional policy of
diplomatic non-alignment had been publicly questioned at the
highest level; and he had personally identified himself to
the press and the Unionist rank and file as the chief inspiration
for a new, aggressive, and imaginative alternative to Salisbury's flaccid acquiescence in the unfolding of inevitable,

but for Britain disadvantageous, world events.

For the moment at least, however, Salisbury regained some control, and events in South Africa were soon to enable him further to deflect Chamberlain's enthusiasm for a new line. In Portugese East Africa the port of Lourenço Marques on Delagoa Bay offered the Transvaal's last links with the outside world through non-British territory, providing a route for the weapons with which Kruger was arming his loyal supporters. Delagoa was, said Chamberlain in 1896, 'the key to the situation in South Africa—and it is to us of supreme importance.' In 1897 a chance arose to gain control of the Bay and the railway inland when Portugal, in grave financial problems, appealed for a British loan. Salisbury and Chamberlain, despite Beach's reservations, jumped at the chance, but found Portuguese councils deeply divided and Germany anxious to complicate Britain's position by applying strong pressure in Lisbon. Chamberlain advocated a tough line and argued in a cabinet of April 1898 that, if Portugal went back on the deal, Britain should 'not treat her treachery with indifference'. He persuaded Salisbury to overawe Portugal with the dispatch of warships to Delagoa, but the result was counterproductive. Discussions temporarily ceased, and it was not until June that agreement was reached for joint Anglo-Portuguese control of the Delagoa harbour and railway complex in return for an £8m British loan. Germany, backed now by France, blocked the arrangement, and in mid-June delivered a set of colonial demands for her neutrality in the affair.[34]

Four days later Chamberlain assembled four ministers, Goschen, Henry Chaplin, Selborne, and Lord George Hamilton, to meet Lascelles, the ambassador to Berlin. His aim was to persuade Lascelles to go behind the back of Count von Bülow, the German Foreign Secretary, and appeal directly to the Kaiser for Anglo-German co-operation, having been informed by Eckardstein, not entirely accurately, that Wilhelm was more favourable than his ministers to an *entente*. By now Chamberlain was angling for agreement over a wider area—he privately worked out a draft treaty for an Anglo-German defensive alliance against a two-power attack in Europe, hoping, presumably, that this would minimize the colonial concessions entailed in any settlement. The bait was again tempting, but Lascelles had been impressed by Chamberlain's insensitivity to German suspicions of Britain's reliability in the event of a European war and to the problem of her isolation between two hostile powers. And he found the Kaiser more interested in immediate colonial acquisitions than long-term possibilities.

Though Lascelles's soundings came to nothing, Chamberlain and Salisbury had again crossed swords in cabinet. The Prime Minister unsuccessfully argued the traditional policy of rejecting German claims for a say in South African affairs against Chamberlain's insistence that control of Delagoa had to be acquired and that, as he put it some days later, the world situation called for a general colonial settlement with Germany. Forced to open Anglo-German negotiations, Salisbury, however, shrewdly employed them to embarrass the cabinet pro-Germans. He had once said of Chamberlain that he 'hated to give anything away', and, while presenting a conciliatory appearance himself, exploited this widely-believed image of Chamberlain to slow down the negotiations and whittle away Germany's colonial claims. Simultaneously, he worked on Chamberlain to convince him of Germany's greed and obstreperousness. By the time that he retired to France for his autumn health visit, allowing Balfour and Chamberlain to overcome outstanding differences and reach a speedy settlement on 30 August, the seeds of suspicion had been well-nurtured, and Chamberlain was extremely unhappy about the whole affair: 'The only advantage to us is the assurance of Germany's abstention from further interference in Delagoa Bay and the Transvaal—in other words, we pay Blackmail to Germany to induce her not to interfere where she has no right to interfere. Well! it is worth while to play Blackmail sometimes.'[35] The price for German neutrality, however, was high—joint Anglo-German control of the Delagoa complex if Portugal sacrificed it for financial aid, and secret clauses for partition of the Portuguese empire if it collapsed (clauses which 'perfidious Albion' partly neutralized in a later treaty with Portugal guaranteeing her territorial integrity). Chamberlain's disillusionment was represented in his view that the price paid would have been reasonable as part of a general settlement but 'the whole tone of the negotiations shows that Germany feels no particular gratitude to us . . . [and] we are likely to find [her] as unreasonable in the future as [she has] been in the past.'[36]

If Salisbury's conduct of these negotiations had weakened prospects of an Anglo-German *entente*, his handling of the Fashoda crisis in the autumn and winter considerably restored his overall authority. Kitchener's Nile expedition finally avenged the death of Gordon in September 1898 by defeating Sudanese forces at Omdurman, recapturing Khartoum and thereby making Britain master of North-East Africa—with the inevitable consequence of reviving France's old jealousies. The force she had earlier sent under Captain Marchand had positioned itself at Fashoda, contesting British supremacy in the upper Nile, and France demanded major concessions for its removal. No one on the British side was inclined to yield, particularly with Rosebery's followers among the Liberals standing firm on Sir Edward Grey's doctrine of British supremacy in the area, though differences of emphasis emerged in the government. Salisbury's aim was to give France an opportunity to withdraw from the confrontation with the smallest possible loss of face: Chamberlain led a group which in effect was requiring at least a public display of France's humiliation, and he was instrumental in securing a provocative mobilization of the fleet to which France likewise responded.

In the tense confrontation, the government managed to exploit nationalist feeling aroused by Omdurman to force France into an unfavourable settlement early in 1899, and Salisbury's strategy of keeping open conciliatory lines of communication paid off against Chamberlain's policy of unyielding confrontation.

Salisbury, indeed, was convinced from Chamberlain's manner in cabinet and on the platform that he was intent on deliberately engineering war with France. It was an impression Chamberlain himself conveyed. In October he told Eckardstein that, once Britain's military preparations were completed in the new year, the government would 'present our bill to France', and, 'should she refuse, *then war*'. He was tired of French colonial intrusions: 'The time has come when England and France have to settle all their differences once and for ever . . . The English nation is in a mood where she will fight rather than give in a single iota. [The latter] would mean the upset of the present government.'[37]

His reading of contemporary public opinion can be doubted —the jingoistic upsurge of Fashoda was short-lived and in part artificially engineered with Liberal Imperialist assistance— and his stand reflected more a desire to gain a major *coup* on the colonial front after the previous few years of ambiguous diplomatic success. Beyond this, an *impasse* in Anglo-French relations would mark the collapse of Salisbury's policy of preserving a balanced European Concert, and perhaps removal of the main check to Chamberlain's own colonial policies. One of Chamberlain's growing band of admirers had spelled out the implications of this in March: 'If there is to be a war, you will have to run it', since 'Everyone looks to you just now as the man who is standing up for England.'[38] Chamberlain's physical resemblance, long-since noted, to the younger Pitt did not mitigate his confidence in his ability to act as a great war leader.

Salisbury, however, kept sure control over events. Combining hawk-like noises in Britain with dove-like ones to France, he was able to produce 'peace with honour' out of Fashoda, while simultaneously dealing with France's Russian ally to arrange by April 1899 a 'partition of preponderance' in China. Chamberlain had already recognized the Prime Minister's regained ascendancy over foreign affairs, as well as his own exaggeration of public opinion towards Fashoda, in a speech at Wakefield in December 1898. Closer Anglo-German relations were strongly advocated, but he called for a *rapprochement* rather than any formal departure from isolation, stressed the value of a settlement with Russia over China, the preservation of peace with France, and a broadening of the base of international co-operation.

Chamberlain's attention to the wider international scene declined somewhat after the Fashoda incident. South Africa once more began to dominate his thoughts as a further, this time the final, Transvaal crisis came to a head. 1897–8 had not been good years for Britain. Kruger had not only been able to strengthen his military position, he had also successfully fended off threats to his political ascendancy from more liberal elements in the Republic, a severe blow to British hopes. But a new element had been brought into the situation. Early in 1897 Sir Alfred Milner had been appointed as successor to the highly unsatisfactory Robinson. Drawn from his permanent post at the Treasury, rather to Beach's annoyance, Milner's reputation was as a skilful administrator, a strong personality, and a high-minded devotee of Empire. An advocate of national recon-struction and crypto-Bismarckian state socialism to further efficiency and social harmony in Britain, he was a favourite with imperially-minded Liberals of the Rosebery faction, whose identification with social reform and a strong foreign policy offered the clearest challenge to Chamberlain's own stance in domestic politics.

From his appointment Milner had adopted a more energetic approach than his predecessor, fastidiously collecting and pub-licizing the ills of Transvaal society and busily constructing a loyal army of officials and agents in South Africa committed against the Kruger regime. And by the winter of 1897–8 he had reached pessimistic conclusions on the Transvaal problem. He increasingly despaired of an internal evolution favourable to British interests, and began advocating tougher action by the imperial government: 'Looking at the question from a purely South African point of view, I should be inclined to work up to a crisis, not indeed by looking about for causes of complaint, or making a fuss about trifles, but by steadily and inflexibly pressing for the redress of substantial wrongs and injustices.'[39] In London this was not popular. Selborne had warned that, given difficulties with Russia and France, the 'South African piece' was 'off the board here just at present'. Chamberlain himself added that, with the need to restore British credibility and conciliate the Cape Afrikaners after Jameson's Raid, it was better to carry on taking issue only over clear breaches of the Conventions and hoping for Kruger's retirement or ejec-tion. At the same time, he took care to keep his options open by making clear that he was not opposed in principle to a confron-tation: if Kruger took advantage of Britain's international diffi-culties to go for complete independence, it 'would give us an opportunity to settle the South African question once for all.'[40]

Occupied during 1898 with the Delagoa question, Milner was content to follow Colonial Office advice, but in November he returned to England on leave determined to press the case for a stronger line. The mood in London appeared to have changed little. Writing to Salisbury after their meeting, Chamberlain observed that Kruger's rumoured attempt to raise a loan in England should be resisted unless concessions of political rights to the Uitlanders were made, and that attempts should be made to propagate his 'Home Rule for the Rand' plan. But his general line was to 'keep peace with Kruger unless he were very outrageous'.[41] Milner, though his views remained unchanged, acknowledged that 'it is no use forcing them upon others at this stage,' but he did gain the impression that if he managed, as he put it, to 'advance matters', Colonial Office backing would be forthcoming.[42] Chamberlain's fingers were still sore from the burns of 1896, but he was ready to use the lull in the international situation to back Milner if an overwhelming case were to be presented.

The acquisition of such a case was aided by two factors early in 1899. One was prospective renewal of the Transvaal government's dynamite monopoly concession, over which Milner persuaded Chamberlain to send a long dispatch on 13 January to Sir William Butler, acting High Commissioner in Milner's absence, condemning this long-standing grievance of the Rand mineowners. More important was to be the killing in Johannesburg in December of an Uitlander, Thomas Edgar, by a Transvaal policeman. The South Africa League, founded after Jameson's Raid to agitate for absorption of the Republic, took up the issue in a campaign against the unpopular Boer police, and petitioned Butler for help in redressing the grievance and securing major reforms. Butler, a man with little time for the idealistic, aggressive imperialism with which he believed Chamberlain, Rhodes and Milner cloaked the low selfishness of the Rand capitalists, refused to forward it to London, much to Milner's chagrin. But the issue soon escalated. A League-organized meeting in the Transvaal was broken up, organizers of the petition were summonsed and only released on high bail, and in February Edgar's killer was acquitted. Uitlander activists, backed by Milner on his return, began to prepare a further petition.

March saw two further developments. On the 20th Chamberlain addressed the Commons on South African affairs. As yet he was unable to comment officially on the petition still to be finalized, and he rejected calls for intervention in the Transvaal's internal affairs over recent events. But he also warned Kruger to implement domestic reforms promised in the wake of Jameson but not yet undertaken. Kruger initiated the second set of events. Having already attempted to appease the Randlords by financial concessions which would protect the dynamite monopoly, he now responded to the Edgar problem by promising greater Uitlander representation in the Volksraad. Milner claimed both initiatives a sham, and neither proved helpful to Kruger. Negotiations over the dynamite concession collapsed in late March, the mineowners stiffened by Chamberlain's Commons speech and hints that their interests would be better furthered under British rather than Boer rule, and they now swung their support behind the franchise reform movement. On 24 March, the second Uitlander petition was signed, sealed and dispatched to London.[43]

Events were rapidly overtaking the old policy of 'pinprick' objections to breaches of the Conventions. The issue was being channelled into the single line of internal electoral reform which, though a dubious British concern under the 1884 Convention, constituted a powerful moral weapon against Kruger's regime and, if successful, the most useful way of weakening Boer control of the Transvaal state. On receiving the petition, however, Chamberlain had to present the cabinet with a dilemma: 'If we ignore altogether the prayer of the petitioners it is certain that British influence in South Africa will be severely shaken. If we send an ultimatum to Kruger, it is possible, and, in my opinion, probable, that we shall get an offensive reply, and we shall then have to go to war, or to accept a humiliating check.'[44]

The petition indeed constituted a test of British, and Chamberlain's own, credibility. For four years he had been publicizing objections to Kruger's regime and reaffirming his predecessors' claim of British legal entitlements to 'suzerainty' over the Transvaal—a right guaranteed in the preamble to the 1881 Convention which Britain claimed still applied, though it had in fact been deliberately omitted in 1884 to appease the Boers. Britain's refusal to back its claims with action would thus be a major victory to Kruger. Could, however, the risk of war be considered? For, though British forces in South Africa had been reinforced in 1897, they were wholly inadequate for a rapid and successful campaign, while Afrikaner opinion in the Cape, and the majority of English Liberals, would be quick to oppose anything looking like a war of aggression. Since the 1870s, successive British governments had found South Africa an embarrassment in domestic politics, and Salisbury's was convinced that a vigorous policy could only be pursued now with considerable cross-bench support. Furthermore, as Milner later pointed out to Greene, the British agent in Pretoria: 'British Govt. is slow to move. Public opinion has been quite averted from S. Africa and is only gradually regaining interest in that subject'—a piece of information which Chamberlain was continually impressing upon Milner. Parliament and the press were, indeed, heaving a welcome sigh of relief after the alarms of 1898, and Milner could be told in June by Fleetwood Wilson, a bellicose Under-Secretary at the War Office, that 'it is the same apathy everywhere . . . The *Times* and all the newspapers swear by you, but when it comes to *backing* you they all talk of time and patience'.[45]

It was therefore with considerable hesitation that, on 2 May, the cabinet considered the Uitlander petition. Sensitive to its mood, Chamberlain proposed steering a middle way between ignoring the petition and delivering an ultimatum with a dispatch 'intended as a protest and still more as an appeal to public opinion', avoiding threats 'which would commit us to ulterior action', but recounting in strong language Kruger's unkept reform promises of 1896. Even this was unpopular, Balfour, among the leading sceptics, noting it as a turning-point which might entail war. Chamberlain was compelled to ask for a decision to be delayed until Milner's views on the subject had been received.

The complex relations between Milner and Chamberlain at this point began to have an impact on events. Milner had long believed that Kruger would never willingly reform his nation, that his promises to do so could not be trusted, and that ultimately war would have to decide Britain's claims to paramountcy in South Africa. His actions in the coming crisis were essentially designed to engineer a confrontation which would force the British government into decisive action to break the diplomatic *impasse*.[46] Chamberlain, too, has often been con-

sidered as holding these views, but, as always with such important events in his career, his aims and motives are very unclear. There are grounds for believing that he did not anticipate
a war. In 1897 he had stated his confidence that the Transvaal
would fall peaceably into a South African federation,[47] and
Wilson could write to Milner from the War Office in mid-June
1899 that 'You will know Chamberlain's mind, I do not, but
he is freely credited with a resolve not to fight. He knows that
a Government which goes to war loses the next election as a
matter of course . . . and that "peace with honour" pays with
the elector.'[48] This is certainly consistent with views Chamberlain had long ago delivered on war and democratic politics,
and also with his comment to Salisbury in 1897 that the Boers
always yielded to determined pressure. At points in the coming
crisis, too, he showed a readiness, not shared by Milner, to take
concessions from Kruger as major diplomatic victories providing 'peace with honour'. But one should not ignore Chamberlain's inclination to play things by ear in complex situations.
He did not share Salisbury's deep abhorrence of war, and the
impression emerging from his papers is that winning the diplomatic battle with Kruger was of overriding importance compared with the means necessary to do it. Confident that it paid
to 'be a little Jingo if you can', he was intent on taking a strong
line in South Africa, and dominating his strategy was the idea
of developing policies compatible with this which were capable
of forging a consensus of opinion among Milner's administrators, the Unionist leadership, and broad centre-right opinion
among the Opposition.

Consistency in these circumstances was not easy to develop.
He faced cabinet colleagues reticent about risking war and a
Liberal leadership deeply suspicious of his intentions, while
many Unionists and Liberal imperialists put their prime trust
in Milner's aggressive stance. Milner had been sent out deliberately to reverse his predecessor's appeasement policy, and
had then been allowed to build a wide reputation in England
and a monopoly of communications from South Africa to the
Colonial Office. As George Wyndham, then an Under-Secretary, told him in May, though with some exaggeration: 'Even
if [the cabinet] wished, they *dare* not reject or modify any

advice which you tender.' He had influential supporters spoiling for a fight, and the threat of resignation if Chamberlain could not get the cabinet to take his line.

Chamberlain and Milner remained loyal to each other throughout these years. But Chamberlain distrusted his High Commissioner's capacity for tactful handling of the situation, and his lack of contact with English, as opposed to South African, opinion. Yet he was prepared to use Milner's influence to the full. On 28 April he had called for his opinions on the situation in South Africa, making clear that he wanted a strong line to use on the cabinet and that 'your discretion as to what you can wisely and advantageously write for the purpose indicated is unfettered.' The reply was described by Chamberlain as 'stiff, and, if published, make either an ultimatum or Milner's recall necessary.' It reiterated the need for Transvaal franchise reform, described the Uitlanders as 'helots' in the Republic, raised the spectre of a Transvaal intent on driving British influence into the sea, and claimed that 'The case for intervention is overwhelming.'

Faced with this, a reconvened cabinet of 10 May caved in and accepted the draft dispatch Chamberlain had prepared earlier. Its immediate use was, however, pre-empted. Cape Afrikaners, worried about the escalating crisis and influenced by hints from Kruger, were advocating a dialogue between the contending parties, which Milner, though considering it a 'good stroke of business' by Kruger, suggested adopting. The cabinet grasped eagerly at this postponement, as did Chamberlain, though he was soon regretting it: 'I would have preferred to get our statement of the case published before the proposal for interview. If the present negotiations continue or a Conference is arranged [Milner] will have to withhold the [draft despatch] otherwise Kruger might withdraw on the pretext that the tone is hostile.'[49]

A conference was finally arranged at Bloemfontein from 31 May to 5 June between Kruger, Milner, and their assistants. The contents of the 10 May dispatch, privately but not officially communicated to Kruger, formed the basis of discussion. Chamberlain had defined Milner's two basic tasks. One was to concentrate on franchise or, if it appeared feasible, 'Home Rule for the Rand'. The second was that 'In view of the momentous consequences of an actual break with the Transvaal, public opinion will expect us to make every effort to avoid it, and will not appreciate technical objections or points of etiquette.'

Chamberlain was already worried about Milner's letters betraying 'the existence of somewhat strained feelings—whereas coolness and sweet reasonableness are more than ever necessary', and Milner proved as hard to control as had Jameson earlier. Chamberlain, like Milner, was intent on 'working' the conference to display Kruger's intransigence, but Milner, rather more an administrator than a diplomat, having decided that the conference was a sham, was determined that nothing should be allowed to obscure the divisions. He rejected Chamberlain's advice to invite the Cape premier, Schreiner, who might mediate in the confrontation, and presented Britain's demands: increased Uitlander representation in the Volksraad, a five-year retrospective residence qualification for the franchise, and a Bill embodying these provisions to be passed in the current Volksraad session. Kruger responded with the offer of fewer seats, a complicated 'sliding scale' seven-year residence qualification, and no commitment on the last point. This offer meant that negotiation not confrontation was the order of the day, and Chamberlain telegraphed warning that 'It is of the utmost importance to put the President . . . clearly in the wrong' before any break were contemplated. The message arrived too late. Having received an unfavourable reply to his demands, Milner abandoned the conference—a major diplomatic error as he later admitted.

Britain now had to prepare her line in the absence of any clear advance plans or publicity for her case. Chamberlain was ready with an ultimatum should it be needed which he delivered to Milner on 7 June, widening the specific franchise demand to one for the 'repeal of all legislation passed since the Convention of 1884, restrictive of the rights and privileges enjoyed by the aliens when the Convention was arranged'. Public opinion both in England and South Africa was, however, clearly not prepared for it, and as a prelude on 14 June a new Blue Book was published containing the 'Helot' despatch and Chamberlain's 10 May draft.

This attempt to recoup some of the support lost by Milner's

premature withdrawal proved disappointing. Afrikaner opinion was hostile to Milner's comments—in England, critics noted that there had been considerable room for manœuvre at the conference. Chamberlain commented that 'opinion in the House of Commons is fluid, and, on the whole, I think, bad.'[50] Furthermore, Kruger strengthened his hand by introducing his own proposals to the Volksraad. Chamberlain had to advise Milner, despite warnings from Selborne of Milner's possible resignation and the risk of a Uitlander collapse as in 1895, that a showdown was just not possible. He presented Milner's request for extra troops to the cabinet, but, as Salisbury noted to the Queen in early July, the cabinet was in a pacific mood and 'this country, as well as the cabinet, excepting perhaps Mr Chamberlain, were against a war.'[51] The request was rejected on 15 July. But even Chamberlain was hedging his bets. On 26 June he delivered a tough speech insisting on major reforms in the Transvaal, but deliberately declined to take full responsibility for Milner's extreme views: 'I am abused . . . because I published his despatch which was sent to me for publication. What would have been said if I had withheld it?'

July found the two once more very much out of step. Under pressure from the Bond Party, Kruger amended his proposed Bill to give a seven-year retrospective franchise. Many Uitlanders were anxious to accept, and Chamberlain took it as a major concession, telegraphing Milner that no *casus belli* could now be raised, and welcoming it in the Commons as Kruger 'having accepted the principle for which [the government] have contended'. With Selborne's backing, however, Milner subsequently persuaded him to use the concession for further demands. The cabinet was persuaded to request a joint Anglo-Transvaal inquiry into the new Bill's implications and operations, and thereafter a new conference to settle outstanding grievances.

This was a deliberately provocative move. Kruger's acquiescence would constitute his formal recognition of Britain's rights in internal Transvaal matters—refusal would excite suspicions of the seriousness of his intentions, and perhaps allow Britain the opportunity to appoint a unilateral, and highly partial, inquiry. The demand, telegraphed off in late July, was backed up by speeches in Parliament from both Chamberlain and Salisbury on the 28th, which presented a united government front determined upon 'securing justice to all the inhabitants of the [Transvaal]'. There was considerable support for this shrewd manœuvre, presented by Chamberlain at least in moderate tones. But it raised further problems with Milner, partly over the response if Kruger declined the proposal, partly over a new Transvaal initiative.

In mid-August, the Republic's State Attorney, Jan Smuts, approached Greene, the British Agent in Pretoria, offering to accept Milner's Bloemfontein demands if the joint inquiry were not pressed. Milner's objections to both the terms and the channels of communication were in marked contrast to Chamberlain's hope that it might be the basis of a settlement. His optimism began to waver with the later presentation of three demands only hinted at in Greene's personal negotiations —Britain's promise not to intervene further in internal Transvaal matters; abandonment of her suzerainty claims; and the settlement of future disagreements by arbitration. Milner feared that Chamberlain would accept this and himself advised total rejection, but the latter's response was more complex. He noted on 24 August that 'we cannot go on negotiating for ever and we must try to bring matters to a head' since 'I dread above all the continual whittling away of differences until we have no *casus belli* left'; yet 'The next step in military preparations is so important and so costly that I hesitate to incur the expense . . . so long as there seems a fair chance of a satisfactory settlement.'[52] To resolve this complexity he adopted a two-pronged manœuvre. At a meeting of his Birmingham party on 26 August he launched an attack on Kruger, who 'dribbles out reforms like water from a squeezed sponge . . . The issues of peace and war are in [his] hands . . . The sands are running down the glass . . . The knot must be loosened . . . or else we shall have to find other ways of untying it.' The mixed metaphors contained a clear purpose: the tone made settlement around an anodyne compromise very difficult, while Kruger was being delivered an unofficial ultimatum which could be claimed as a great diplomatic victory if he gave way.

The official response was formal delivery of his July dispatch demanding a joint inquiry on franchise, and a message welcoming Smuts's proposals. On the three Transvaal conditions, however, he agreed to discuss arbitration at the proposed conference, gently dismissed the Transvaal's claim to sovereign independence, and expressed the hope that future British interference would not prove necessary. This unprovocative dispatch did, however, have a sting in the tail: without a speedy reply, Britain would withdraw her acceptance of the Smuts offer.

In England this strategy was not entirely well received. Many Liberals condemned his speech as deliberately inflammatory—which it was—and Beach criticized the dispatch to Salisbury, complaining particularly that no cabinet had been called to consider so important a decision. Salisbury was later to admit the mistake, complaining of Milner and 'his jingo supporters', who had put the government in a corner: 'And therefore I see before us the necessity for considerable military effort—and all for people whom we despise, and for territory which will bring no profit and no power to England.'[53]

The 28 August dispatch indeed proved a catalyst. Milner had been pressing for an ultimatum in the event of its rejection, though Chamberlain's intention was to continue applying pressure by the appointment of a unilateral franchise inquiry. But the Transvaal's response—withdrawing the Smuts offer, retreating to the seven-year franchise proposal, and only criticizing, not rejecting outright, an inquiry—heightened the tension. Chamberlain's comment on the reply was that

it is clearly dilatory. It is possible . . . that [the Boers have] determined on war, and desire a few weeks further preparation; but it is more probable that they seek delay in the hope either of divisions of council in this country or of a diversion on the part of the Uitlanders . . . If the reply now sent had come in the early stage of the negotiations I should have been inclined to treat it as the basis for further discussion. But it is the last of a series of communications . . . all of them vague, inconclusive and unsatisfactory . . .[54]

Chamberlain, still it appears believing that the Boers would not resist Britain's demands by force, again faced a dilemma: continuing negotiations would entwine Britain further in the diplomatic net of the 'slim' Boer politicians, increasing the political uncertainty which was damaging business and commerce in South Africa, complicating Britain's foreign relations, and risking an interpretation as a sign of weakness. An ultimatum would, however, be overreacting to Kruger's reply.

On 8 September he again took a middle course with a dispatch declaring the reply unacceptable, stipulating the Smuts offer as the now minimum concession, and insisting on an inquiry and a further conference to consider the issues of arbitration and other grievances. To the inclusion of 'ultra-arbitration' questions Salisbury and Beach objected, but were overriden by Chamberlain's insistence that upholding British authority made 'an advance in our claims imperative if the S.A.R. still continue their recalcitrant attitude'. But the punch was added at the end of the dispatch. An immediate reply was demanded, and an unsatisfactory response would lead Britain to seek a solution by other means. This solution was implied by the approved transfer of 10,000 troops from India to Natal.

Lack of a clear-cut case had delayed Britain's final demand, but two other factors had also contributed. The government was wary of confronting a full mobilization of 40,000 Boers with the limited forces yet available. Milner's oft-repeated demands for troops had been rebuffed by a cabinet wary of provoking a Boer rising. A further complication was the War Office's retreat from earlier claims that a mobilization in England could be rapidly undertaken, to talking, in mid-August, of a timespan of three to four months. Chamberlain was suitably annoyed, but even so remained less than fully sensitive to the military problem:

My own opinion is, as it has always been, that both Milner and the military authorities greatly exaggerate the risks and dangers of this campaign. I have never believed that the Boers would take the offensive at this stage—nor do I fear a British reverse if they do . . . When all the reinforcements are landed . . . we shall be quite a match for the Boers . . . There is one advantage in delay which is that such a volunteer army as the Boers' is apt to melt away if they are kept dallying without serious work to do.[55]

This was gross irresponsibility, explicable only by Chamberlain's extrapolation from the balmy days of the Warren expedition to very different circumstances.

A second reason was the hope that Kruger would still see sense, under pressure as he was from Cape Afrikaners and English Liberals who, though critical of the government's bellicose moves, were calling for him to make concessions to avert war. Once again his government hedged. In reply to the 8 September dispatch it accepted a joint inquiry, but on the seven- rather than the five-year franchise. Salisbury was for further delay, but Chamberlain insisted on his calling a cabinet for 22 September and mobilizing an Army Corps in England. Instead of an ultimatum, however—advised against by Milner, worried still about the military situation—an 'interim dispatch' was returned, reviewing Britain's claims with increased emphasis on its 'suzerainty' and the Republic's failure to fulfil pledges under the Conventions. The ultimatum was finally drawn up seven days later while awaiting a reply, with its demands widened to cover Uitlander rights, the guarantee of civil liberties, an arbitration tribunal, 'most-favoured-nation' commercial rights for Britain, arms reductions, and an end to further arms imports. It was further agreed to recall Parliament for 17 October to vote supplies.

Once again Milner advised delay in sending it, with beneficial results. Aware that its only chance of military success would come from taking the initiative, the Transvaal government on 9 October—the very day on which Chamberlain's final ultimatum was approved—demanded the withdrawal of British troops from her borders and a halt to reinforcements. Overjoyed at this outcome, Chamberlain rejected the demand. On 12 October the Orange Free State threw in its lot with the Republic, and pre-emptive military strikes were launched by the Boers into Natal and Bechuanaland.

When the jingoistic hysteria and imperial fervour it aroused had subsided, the Boer War proved to be an ominous entry into the twentieth century for Britain. It was to reveal grave weaknesses in her military machine and state apparatus; it brought into the limelight domestic social conditions which undermined any remaining complacent belief in the health, happiness and instinctive patriotism of the British working class; and it displayed the tenuous diplomatic position which Britain held in international affairs. Like America's Vietnam War in the

1960s, the Boer War exposed the pretensions and vulnerability of a rich and mighty Empire proclaiming liberal and democratic principles when faced with a shrewd and determined people intent on their independence, and in the first decade of the new century it instigated a radical rethinking among politicians of the tasks which modern government would have to undertake.

Over the origins of a tiny war in a far-away country which had so important an impact there is still considerable disagreement. Many socialist and left-wing Liberal critics have seen it as one waged for the rich Rand capitalists. If conceived as an illustration of the political power of Capital, this view is sadly defective: most mineowners certainly wished to dispose of Kruger's regime, but most also anticipated, correctly, the financial costs which war and internal strife would bring them. They as frequently found themselves the objects of pressure from imperial administrators and politicians as the reverse. More conventional historians consider Britain's strategic and military interests in the Cape, threatened by a hostile Afrikaner nationalism, as the significant factor, though both Chamberlain and Milner rejected this at the time as the key issue. Certainly it was not a war on behalf of 'justice for the Uitlanders' —their grievances were but important pawns in a much bigger game. 'British prestige' was a further factor: Salisbury's cabinet was dragged, often kicking and screaming, into confrontation because Milner and Chamberlain had engineered positions entailing considerable loss of face if Kruger were allowed his way. The influence of War Office staff and military men seeking, as always, to justify their existence was an additional, though minor, contribution.

It is worth distinguishing between the issues at stake in the war and the reasons for the outbreak of hostilities, though, as we shall see, complete separation is impossible. There was widespread agreement in Britain that the Transvaal's integration into a united, British, South Africa would serve Britain's interests. While the Republic's virtual autonomy was upheld by Boer nationalist aspirations, it constituted, at the very least, a thorn in Britain's flesh, and, at most, a potential threat to peaceful economic and political development under British auspices in South Africa. Some historians might suggest that

Britain's interest in the Republic's future derived from strategic factors, but it seems difficult to deny that local economic issues lay at the root. Apart from wildlife only three significant entities existed beyond the Vaal—the natives, the mines, and the Boers. By at latest the 1890s the first issue had virtually been absorbed in the second—protecting natives from the Boers meant 'civilizing' them into the work ethic of the mines. The outstanding problem was: for whose benefit was mineral exploitation and the commerce arising from it primarily to be developed? Salisbury's view that the Transvaal would bring 'no profit and no power to England' was simply bad bookkeeping.

Yet involvement in what Austen Chamberlain later admitted to be a war of aggression was not a necessary consequence. Salisbury himself reflected a common view that the game was not worth the candle: persistence with earlier 'containment' policies, early disappearance of an ageing Kruger, impending numerical ascendancy of the Uitlanders and pressures from liberal Cape Afrikaners would eventually reconcile the Boers to British rule, or at least lead to open internal conflict in which Britain could intervene with little cost and total justification.

In explaining why war came about, the contributions of Chamberlain, Milner, their acolytes, and pressure on government policy from Rosebery's Liberal followers have to be considered. Unlike Salisbury and most of the Foreign Office who were rooted in the mid-century liberal tradition of foreign policy, these men came to think about world affairs only after 1880, and their limited experience had led them to the belief that events significant for the future lay in the colonial world, not in the European heartland. From a variety of motives—idealism, patriotism, economic interest or political ambition—they had cast themselves as leaders of a movement for imperial unification to strengthen Britain's economic and military position ready for twentieth-century problems. They also believed, or at least were constantly asserting in public, that this movement was at a crisis point where, as Chamberlain put it in 1896, 'opportunities once let slip might never recur'. The closer their attention was directed to problems on the periphery of Empire, the greater was their sense of urgency—a chain of bellicosity ran from Salisbury through Chamberlain to Milner. And within the Empire they saw two great problems: the serious risk of Canada's integration into the American market, which was a major influence on Chamberlain's actions over the tariff question; and the Transvaal, a pinprick exaggerated into a symbol of the great test facing Britain—whether she had the determination to consolidate her far-flung possessions, or whether she would lose them through neglect, weakness of will, or incompetence. When Chamberlain came later to call the Boer War a war not simply to uphold Britain's immediate interests in South Africa but to preserve the Empire, he was not just indulging in the natural hyperbole of wartime rhetoric, but articulating a prime element in the ideology of contemporary imperialists. For South Africa, it meant that, whereas former British governments had invariably searched for excuses to avoid direct intervention, leaving it to the Cape and Natal governments to maintain Britain's hegemony in the region, that of 1895 was positively on the hunt for excuses to get further involved.

Though Chamberlain's conception of what was at stake in South Africa entailed a consistently aggressive policy towards the Boers, it is not entirely accurate to call the war, as did contemporary Radicals, 'Chamberlain's War'. Three things contributed.

Milner himself recognized that Kruger's followers saw the issue to be survival for their whole culture and way of life, for which their developed nationalist feelings would probably lead them to fight. Chamberlain, however, as his earlier approach to Ireland had perhaps demonstrated, could be singularly insensitive to nationalist sentiments other than British ones: even up to the last minute he was expecting Kruger to bow to an inevitable loss of power rather than take on a hopeless war. He greatly miscalculated.

The second factor was that Chamberlain and his colleagues had led Kruger to believe that the odds were not entirely against them. They could hope for a failure of Britain's nerve as in 1881, particularly if early successes came their way; and British forces in South Africa were wholly insufficient to overawe the Transvaal or impose rapid defeat—the military strategy, indeed, was to 'hold the ring' at key defensive points until adequate reinforcements had arrived for a counter-attack. With the risk of occasioning a premature Boer rising or being branded the aggressor as in 1895, Chamberlain had refused to press hard for reinforcements before he could carry overwhelming support in the cabinet and Parliament. Engineering a diplomatic crisis without the force to back it up or to bully the opposition into a peaceful settlement was a second mistake.

The third factor was depending on Milner, who did much to avoid any peaceful outcome. At Bloemfontein he deliberately checked any possibility of a favourable compromise, and during the summer of 1899 successfully set out to persuade Chamberlain that Kruger was bluffing, that Cape Afrikaners would force concessions, that the continuing uncertainty affecting commerce and mining production must come to a speedy end, and that an agreement acceptable to Kruger would prove disastrous for Britain's interests and honour. By 8 September Chamberlain had to present the cabinet with the view that 'What is now at stake is the position of Great Britain in South Africa and with it the estimate formed of our power and influence in our colonies throughout the world.' Milner had ensured that everyone—himself, Chamberlain, and the government—would lose face if Kruger were not brought to heel.

Chamberlain's own conduct of affairs during 1899 was not of the highest calibre. Certainly he was in a difficult position mediating between the doves in cabinet and the hawks who monopolized his sources of information from the diplomatic front in South Africa. Yet it was precisely the fact that he lacked a strategy of his own which created this position, along with the misapprehensions he occasionally displayed of the military situation and Kruger and Milner's intentions. Throughout the year he swung often erratically between willingness to reach diplomatic agreement with the Transvaal and eagerness to deliver ultimatums which would entail open confrontation. In the face of Milner's single-mindedness, and with the memory of the Jameson fiasco constantly to remind him of the price of failure, Chamberlain never displayed that firm grasp of the issue which would have been needed to steer Britain away from war.

His uncertainty and inconsistencies had, however, assisted

the central task of creating propaganda necessary to ensure that war was undertaken with maximum political support. It won over opinion in the colonies, gained fervent Unionist and Liberal Imperialist backing, and ensured an unenthusiastically patriotic stance from the new Liberal leader, Campbell-Bannerman, and the Liberal centre. Anti-war, pro-Boer opinion was isolated. In Cape Colony Afrikanerdom was split, a minority instigating an abortive rebellion, the majority declining to side with their ethnic compatriots to the north and acquiescing in the martial law imposed in 1900. With regard to the British population, Jameson's Raid had ultimately served Chamberlain's purposes. Like most settler populations, those in the Cape and Natal jealously protected their autonomy from imperial control except when they needed bailing out of trouble. In the short term Jameson had discredited a 'patriotic' line: in the long run he had induced Kruger to organize powerful military forces which increasingly seemed to threaten the primacy of the British South African people. For once, imperial troops and Downing Street government promised them deliverance not enslavement. Frequently, their main criticism of Chamberlain had been his failure to take bolder and tougher action: in Britain, this was Chamberlain's trump card. During the debate on war financing he could claim that 'From the first day I came into office I hoped for peace; I strove for peace . . . In our endeavour to maintain peace we have shown the utmost conciliation.' Few Liberals believed him, but no one of importance would contradict him. His two-and-three-quarter hour speech was acclaimed a masterful apologia, and a critical amendment was dismissed by 362 votes to 135, double the government's paper majority.

Throughout the war Chamberlain remained active behind the scenes, critical, like many others, of inadequate organization at the War Office and incompetent generalship in the early days which led to the major defeats of 'Black Week' in December and the isolation of Ladysmith, Mafeking, and Kimberley. A stream of demands and recommendations left his desk. More important, however, was his role as the government's most powerful speaker. Military defeats led Liberals to attack the government in early 1900 and criticize Chamberlain's responsibility for the war. On both sides of the House there were ideas afloat for a national government under Rose-bery. But in two major debates of January and February, Chamberlain powerfully defended his own and the government's reputation. And, by June, with Lords Roberts and Kitchener commanding the South African force, the tide had turned completely: the beleaguered towns were relieved, the Orange Free State and Pretoria taken, the Boers' largest field force knocked out, and Kruger and his chief supporters were heading into exile. All that was left was what appeared to be a wholly unimportant set of guerrilla forces.

The approach to war had raised one complication which related to Chamberlain's wider concern with international affairs. Britain's great fear was that entanglement in South Africa might lead the European Powers to combine and make irresistible demands upon her, and the advent of war in fact brought widespread hostile comment on the continent. Britain's agreement with Germany in late 1898 was designed to forestall this, but tension in Samoa, an island under joint Anglo-American-German condominium, introduced new instability. With the advent in late summer 1899 of the Transvaal crisis, Britain needed some gesture of German neutrality, and the Kaiser's planned visit in November was being seen in this light. On 18 September, however, Salisbury noted Germany's apparent intention to use the crisis for colonial gains. Chamberlain, backed by Devonshire, maintained the 1898 line: he would 'make no objection' if 'you think it necessary or desirable to pay the price for the Emperor's support'. Salisbury did not, and Chamberlain was compelled to go behind his back to advance the negotiations which Salisbury was deliberately extending. Chamberlain's plan, for Britain's withdrawal from Samoa in return for concessions in Tonga, the Solomons and West Africa, eventually became a basis for settlement a few days before the Kaiser's visit.

With this, and Salisbury's absence from formal celebrations on the visit due to his wife's death, Chamberlain saw an opportunity to revive his proposals for closer Anglo-German co-operation. In conversations with Wilhelm he suggested coordination over Germany's recently planned Baghdad railway and partition of the disintegrating territory of Morocco, and revived with Bülow the notion of a 'general understanding' in

China, where trouble was again brewing. The Empire's now inevitable collapse under Russian pressure, he claimed, needed joint activity by the two powers and America. Bülow appeared favourable to the general line, though not an immediate settlement, asking Chamberlain to improve Germany's relations with America, strained during the Spanish War.

In response, Chamberlain spoke out at Leicester on the day after the Kaiser's departure. He called for a strengthening of the 'union—the alliance, if you please—the understanding' between Britain and America now that Venezuelan difficulties had been resolved, and claimed that in Europe 'The natural alliance is between ourselves and the great German Empire.' There was here the possibility of 'a new Triple Alliance between the Teutonic race and the two great branches of the Anglo-Saxon race', who shared so much of their culture in common, and who could be 'a still more potent influence in the future of the world'.

Chamberlain, as before, fell into the common racial rhetoric of his day, but if he exaggerated the prospects for this alliance —or, perhaps better, 'special relationship' since he thought mutual understanding more important than treaties—it was less, as some writers have argued, because he was impressed by the elegance of his racial analogies, than that he let his conception of what was desirable run away with his sense of the practical. In England, press comment from *The Times* downwards derided the pronouncement at a time of hostile public opinion in Germany, while the German chancellery was again embarrassed. Bülow ignored Chamberlain's call and spoke out for closer German relations with other powers. Chamberlain was annoyed at the snub, but it was one his own unskilful diplomacy had brought on his head.

Assessing Chamberlain's contribution to British politics in the years after 1895 is not easy. The focus in this chapter had been on his involvement in international and imperial affairs, but Parliament and the press devoted, as always, more time and space to domestic issues than these, and Chamberlain's speeches, again as always, were carefully balanced to cover contemporary debate in both arenas. But his decision in 1895 to cease concentrating on domestic affairs and attempt to define overseas ones as the vital issue of the day had proved amply justified. His public standing and political influence had vastly increased. Events had assisted him in this: the domestic scene remained fairly quiet, and the economy healthy while colonial tensions grew. His populist style proved as successful in creating an atmosphere of crisis and generating mass support when transferred from Radical demagogy to 'open diplomacy'. The jingoism and imperial fervour excited by the Boer War was not his creation alone, but he had made himself the acknowledged leader of those who wanted to educate public opinion for an uncompromising imperial policy.

Though fruitful in terms of personal popularity, his new interests had been less so in practical effect. It is perhaps an exaggeration to claim that his only success in the sphere of progressive imperial improvement was the replacement of gas by electric lighting in the Colonial Office, but not a great one. Colonial politicians found a minister for the first time prepared to treat their claims with serious consideration and lend a sympathetic ear to their problems, and there was certainly a heightened awareness that imperial unification was a viable, and perhaps inevitable, process; but transferring it into practice had not advanced significantly.

He had certainly been effective in imposing a tougher line on Salisbury's conduct of foreign affairs, though here again it had needed men of similar views and corresponding authority like Devonshire, Goschen, Lansdowne and the more ambiguous Balfour to carry the day. Increasingly, however, it had been he who took the lead in laying down alternative long-term strategies in terms of which resistance to Salisbury's control could be defined. In foreign as well as domestic politics, Salisbury's genius was of the negative kind. Conscious of Britain's limited resources, of the difficulties under a democratic constitution of raising large defence estimates, stimulating and maintaining opinion for a strong policy, and committing the country to permanent alliances, he refused to be optimistic about imperial benefits, directed a healthy scepticism at the blandishments of Germany and other suitors, and was a master of ingenious techniques to block 'utopian' ideas from amateurs like Chamberlain, and of diplomatic inventions to preserve British interests and prestige at cut-price rates. For him, the tide of history could be restrained but not diverted from its course, and he was often to quote against himself the response of a Chinese official refused British help: 'I understand—we rule over two great Empires in decline, you and I.' It was Chamberlain's claim that the threatened degeneration of Britain's world-wide commercial and, through her naval forces, military hegemony could be checked—that the imperial link could be reforged and strengthened, and ties with America and Germany developed to create a new world in which Britain's interests were safeguarded. Though offering a strong ideological counter to Salisbury's pessimistic defence of traditional policies, telling against it was a clear absence of success. Persuading the colonies, let alone America and Germany, to subsume their differences in a common front had not proceeded far, and in 1900 it was still Salisbury's cautious, Eurocentric isolationism which held the field.[56]

CHAPTER 9

Old Shibboleths and a New Panacea. 1900–1906

Liberalism, while benefiting since 1895 from the customary mid-term swing of the electoral pendulum, had wholly failed to exploit it to effect. Existing divisions had been accentuated by the predominance of international questions. Rosebery and Harcourt had thrown up the leadership in turn, and Morley was sulking in his tent. Uneasy control was exercised by Campbell-Bannerman in the Commons and Spencer in the Lords, relics of centrist Gladstonianism. The Radicals were flagged on by an ageing Labouchere in ineffective and out-moded opposition to Chamberlain's strident imperialism—Rosebery's clan, bidding for the leadership, did little but echo Unionist ideology. War hysteria shattered the uneasy coalition. A censure motion of January 1900 gained no more support than that of October 1899, and in a division of July 1900 the party split three ways, with Campbell-Bannerman adopting the humiliating line of walking out with the smallest third. Though Liberal Imperialist backing for the war stirred demands for a national coalition in the darkest days, Unionist leaders neither wanted nor needed any repetition of 1886. Roseberyite moral support was useful, but Chamberlain was not alone in wishing to rebuff any political challenge from this quarter, and in the 1900 election set out to dish the 'Lib. Imps.' as Laboucheres in disguise with the cry 'Every vote given against the Government is a vote given to the Boers.'

Roberts's military victories provided an opportune climate for Unionism to exploit the upsurge of popular jingoism for electoral benefit, but Chamberlain's desire for a June Khaki election was frustrated by other international tensions and he had to wait for formal annexation of the Transvaal in early September 1900 before a further pretext for dissolution came along. The war may not have been 'Chamberlain's War', as many claimed, but the election was certainly his election. In a whirlwind campaign he set out to make South Africa the sole issue for decision. The election was designed to be a personal vote of confidence in himself, justifying his past policies, delivering him with a mandate for reconstruction in South Africa, and providing an accretion of popular authority which would make him an irresistible force in the next government. The Liberals were to be dished completely by the insinuation of pro-Boer sympathies (Chamberlain 'played it down low to the "man in the street" ', noted Beatrice Webb), and few Liberals counter-attacked effectively. Only Lloyd George did so, launching a campaign against the hard-faced men round Chamberlain who had done well out of the war by their business and financial dealings, which led to his violent ejection from a Birmingham meeting in 1901. 'The more the Empire expands, the more the Chamberlains contract', was a telling comment, if not on Chamberlain himself, at least on his relations and Unionist business circles in Birmingham, and had earlier put him on the defensive in Commons debates.

The predictable electoral result was still impressive. Twelve by-elections had been lost since 1895, and the 1900 turnout was low, partly for technical reasons, but perhaps also warning that strident imperialism did not have the deep popular sympathies which Chamberlain attributed to it. Yet, with a gain of three seats, Unionism had done what no other party had for a generation—it had won two successive elections, a phenomenon puzzling many like Salisbury who took the 'swing of the pendulum' as a basic law of democratic politics. Attributed largely to Chamberlain and his policies, the result gave him the sought-for authority among Unionism's rank and file. Yet it was still insufficient to dislodge the control of Salisbury and the 'Hotel Cecil'.[1] Through age and illness, Salisbury yielded the Foreign Office to Lansdowne, but he was determined to soldier on, and persuaded Beach to do likewise, in large measure to counter Chamberlain's influence. There were minor ministerial changes, with Selborne taking Goschen's place at the Admiralty, thus compensating slightly for Chaplin's removal from the radical group on international affairs. But it was an uninspiring cabinet to present to the new century. Three quarters had been in cabinets before 1887, a half before 1885, and a quarter were relics of the 1870s. As Balfour was to lament in 1902, there was little talent elsewhere to replace them.

With its largely artificial majority and tired leaders, the government was soon to stumble. Though in early 1902 Liberalism was still split three ways on the guerrilla war raging in South Africa, its wings were finding new issues to exploit. Campbell-Bannerman sought to undo the moral cloak of imperialism with an attack on the 'methods of barbarism' of farm-burnings and concentration camps used by British forces to deprive the guerrillas of refuge and civilian support, compelling Chamberlain and Milner to intervene with the military to reform camp conditions. Rosebery in an imaginative performance at Chesterfield in December 1901 called for a Liberal 'clean slate' with the removal of Little Englandism and Home Rule. Exploiting publicity over the poor physical condition of army recruits and War Office incompetence, he advocated a programme of 'national efficiency'—'administrative, parliamentary, commercial, educational, physical, moral, naval and military fitness'—which could alone live up to the demands of Empire. Independent Labour activity, arising out of the Taff Vale decision and the formation in 1900 of the Labour Representation Committee, was soon to affect the soft underbelly of Unionism's limited attention to domestic matters.

Yet in 1900 Chamberlain could feel optimistic. With a popular ascendancy comparable to that of Gladstone twenty years before, he had a new seven-year lease of power to implement the policies he had initiated in the last decade, to impose his stamp on Britain's domestic and international evolution with great constructive changes. Now in his sixty-fifth year, he had a last chance to play his trump cards; and it soon became clear that, unlike Randolph Churchill with Ulster, he had drawn the Two and not the Ace. Social reform was checked; colonial development became a lost cause; the German alliance collapsed; a gradual and painless unification of the Empire was stultified. Soon, the Opposition began to counter-attack, and his own colleagues to respond with blind disregard for agreed conventions. As always in such circumstances, Chamberlain's instincts were to overturn the table and start a new game with fresh rules and higher stakes. The tariff reform cry of 1903 was a not unpredictable response to three years of political frustration.

When compared with Chamberlain's programme in 1895, the Unionist domestic record in 1905 does not appear totally deficient. House-purchase facilities were extended; an Aliens Act was finally passed in 1905, as were limited provisions for labour exchanges; factory legislation and industrial arbitration boards were extended. With the Jameson inquiry hanging over him, Chamberlain (after considerable pressure) had persuaded the cabinet to go ahead in 1897 with accident compensation, and he steered it through a wide range of attacks in the Commons. Agricultural labourers, seamen, and domestic servants were excluded (though later covered in 1900), which was the major point of Liberal attack and Chamberlain failed to secure restrictions on contracting out. But though the measure was to be largely superseded by Lloyd George's radical scheme of 1911, it marked a major step forward. Salisbury pronounced during the debates that 'Mr Chamberlain is the spokesman of our party' on social questions, which J. L. Garvin interpreted as a sign of Chamberlain's authority.[2] It was much more a way of passing the buck, shifting responsibility for the government's failure to proceed more rapidly from his own shoulders. On the symbolic pensions issue it was clear that Unionism was still 'lacking in constructive statesmanship'. Chamberlain announced in an optimistic vein in 1896 the establishment of a Treasury Committee under Lord Rothschild to consider pensions, but this soon became an instrument to shelve the issue. Its report pronounced every scheme considered either too expensive or unacceptable to the Friendly Societies. New Zealand's introduction of pensions in 1898 and discontent with the failure of Rothschild inspired a vociferous campaign in 1899, but even Chamberlain was now wary of taking the issue up again and tried to avert an Opposition amendment to the Address since 'This would be awkward for many of our men.' Increased pressure in Parliament, as well as in Birmingham, finally produced a select committee under Henry Chaplin, the last man to favour drastic change, which reported in July 1900 for a five shilling per week pension to those over sixty-five, paid out of poor rates and Exchequer grants. Though non-contributory, the scheme imposed stringent tests of past thrift and present need for entitlement, and effectively represented a minor extension of the old poor-law relief system. Chamberlain objected, to no avail, against the government's commitment to so limited a measure, but the expense of war precluded further debate or action.

In 1901, with the prospect of a return to peacetime conditions, Chamberlain delivered several speeches hinting at his revived interest in the issue, and at Birmingham in January 1902 called for agreement between Labour and the Friendly Societies on a practical scheme. The T.U.C. Committee's response, demanding a non-contributory scheme, he instantly dismissed as unhelpful and thereafter dropped the whole issue.[3]

He certainly continued to see pensions as a valuable measure, but equally certainly recognized the problems it posed for Unionist politicians—the apparent Utopianism of Labour plans, resistance of Friendly Societies, and scepticism among businessmen and taxpayers. The mood among these last groups had also changed significantly from the early 1890s. Reforms appealed when Labour was being singularly truculent and the Unionists were in opposition: successful counter-attacks subsequently by employers minimized Labour's apparent threat, and many Conservatives, among them Stanley Baldwin, were later to lament the ungenerous, self-centred mood of Unionist backbenchers in the 1900 Parliament.

Chamberlain's failure to push the pensions issue reflected an appreciation of the difficulties of appealing to his party on it, but also the general drift of his interests since 1895. Philanthropists and intellectuals had throughout the 1890s been re-evaluating the causes of poverty and possible responses, but Chamberlain had largely ignored questions that might once have been grist to his electoral mill. Social reform in general, and pensions in particular, no longer had the same role to play in a grand programmatic strategy for modernizing the old 'stupid party' when he was absorbed in the election-winning imperial issues on which he could carry all strands of Unionism.[4]

Pressing for pensions after 1900 would certainly have split the leadership, and largely against him. Beach had made this clear in a circular of late 1901. The economic boom after 1895, which had supported expenditure on accident insurance, educational and other grants, imperial and defence projects, had tapered off: the war had compelled considerable extra rises in taxation. Taxes, Beach argued, were reaching the limit of what was politically and financially viable. And, though his Gladstonian mutterings of general economy were largely ignored, his explicit selection of pensions and other non-war expenditures as items which had to be deferred or reduced threatened a major confrontation if Chamberlain took to domestic reform once again.[5]

His circular also explicitly criticized rising Colonial Office estimates, and thereby challenged Chamberlain's second interest—undeveloped estates. The attractions of this programme had in fact declined significantly, and Chamberlain's public references to it were now infrequent. Costs reduced its popularity—its share of the estimates had almost quadrupled since 1895, though only to just under one million—and it had degenerated, as indeed it began in Uganda, into rescuing lame ducks like the West Indies. The war, too, took its toll, with railway development in West Africa being held back. In 1902 the last West Indian grant was extracted, to be succeeded by the most expensive project Beach had yet been asked to support—South African reconstruction.

Chamberlain's third aim had been to end Britain's policy of non-alignment. Despite Bülow's rebuff in 1899, he was still eager for an Anglo-American-German understanding, and 'At the right time and opportunity, he would follow the Leicester speech by other speeches in the same sense.'[6] In the year 1900–1, at a time when the Boer War had created a common European hostility to Britain, his formula was again to be put to the test. On Germany's initiative an international force had been mobilized to protect legations in Peking from the Boxer rebels, but embarrassment for Germany seemed inevitable when Russia subsequently threatened withdrawal from the enterprise. Salisbury, though indecisive, was reticent about pulling Germany's chestnuts out of the fire until Goschen and Chamberlain insisted on action to widen the disagreement between Russia and Germany. In October 1900 agreement was reached on an economic partition of China. In line with Chamberlain's earlier suggestions, Britain was to be dominant in the Yangtse with Germany acting as a buffer against Russia in Shantung, but with both committed to an 'open-door' policy in the whole country 'so far as they can exercise influence'. This 'Delphic formula', as Julian Amery calls it,[7] was tested when Russia applied pressure in Peking for control over Manchuria. Chamberlain, with Devonshire's help, began again angling through Eckardstein for joint Anglo-German resistance, claiming that Britain would soon have to make a definitive choice between the Dual and Triple Alliances, and, in the face of German reticence to interpret the 1900 agreement as committing her to oppose Russia's ambitions in north China, again offered a deal over Morocco and promised to open more formal dealings once Salisbury had gone off for his customary rest in the summer of 1901.

The situation, however, had become critical by May. Lansdowne had already prepared terms of a possible colonial arrangement with Germany, though appalled at the price Britain might have to pay. A cabinet committee was appointed to consider seriously for the first time whether anything was to be gained by translating the informal soundings which had been taking place into official negotiations. Its conclusion was negative. An expected rebuff was delivered in a long memorandum from Salisbury, arguing that isolation was 'a danger in whose existence we have no historical reason for believing', but the very existence of the committee was itself testimony to Salisbury's waning control, and the key objections were presented by the pro-Germans themselves. Chamberlain declared an immediate settlement impossible, since Germany was insisting on the test question of Britain's readiness to join the Triple Alliance. With the tension generated by the Boer War, however, closer relations would have to come gradually through the prior settlement of China and other colonial disputes, on which Germany was still proving unco-operative.[8]

This effectively marked the collapse of his plans for a new world system to defend British interests in the unpartitioned colonial world. He was soon turning towards settlements elsewhere, pressing in late 1901 for a complete understanding with Japan (though Lansdowne's Anglo-Japanese agreement of 1902 was more limited in scope), and taking private soundings of France in 1902, which the Foreign Office was soon to adopt with a vengeance and bring to the *entente cordiale* of 1904. For Chamberlain these were poor substitutes. In the rapid economic and imperial expansion of America and Germany he had seen massive support for resistance to Britain's natural competitors for the apparently rich and easy pickings of Africa and the Middle and Far East. For the 'Teutonic' and 'Anglo-Saxon' nations to clash would be suicide; together they could shunt France and Russia aside and carve up the world between them.

Most modern commentators have tended to follow contemporary Foreign Office opinion on this. It is suggested that Germany's insistence on exploiting Britain's embarrassment for short-term advantage made any long-term understanding impossible, while British interests essentially required playing the traditional role of non-aligned guardian of the European balance of power against German national aspirations. The first view has considerable validity. Chamberlain here found himself caught in a cleft stick; the more enthusiastically he pressed for German co-operation, the more Germany saw signs of British weakness to be further exploited and the less she felt able to commit herself for fear of antagonizing the Dual Alliance prematurely. The second view is more dubious. Germany was to pay heavily for overestimating her own strength with the setback of 1918 and the partition of 1945, but the military alignments of 1914 and 1940 proved suicidal for Britain's economic and imperial hegemony. Despite Salisbury's scepticism, and the protests of Radicals before and after the First World War, it was to become increasingly difficult to see how non-alignment and the defence of vital British interests could be made compatible. Given the choice of possible partners, and the international context in which initiatives were made, Chamberlain's pro-German policies, however unsatisfactory, were not so outrageous as they appear at first sight.[9]

The collapse of the Anglo-German *entente* proposal had a significant impact on Chamberlain's ideas. It constituted a major tributary to a confluence of events early in 1902 which hastened his progress towards tariff reform. On 25 October 1901 he delivered a speech lamenting German reticence and, as an aside, defending Britain's South Africa policy by comparing it favourably with 'methods of barbarism' used by other European powers in past wars. It was interpreted as a slight on German actions in the 1870 war against France, and provoked strong reactions there which led Lansdowne formally to cut off the alliance negotiations in mid-December. A public rebuke from von Bülow on 8 January 1902 allowed Chamberlain to change mounts and ride the tide of anti-German opinion which the Boer War had engendered and which formerly he had tried to assuage. On 11 and 13 January he ostentatiously delivered rebukes, which led *The Times* to comment that 'Mr Chamberlain is at this moment the most popular and trusted man in England.'

He had already been in the process of a reorientation when, on 6 January, he addressed the West Birmingham Relief Fund as its President to deliver his appeal for 'sensible' pensions proposals. This unlikely venue was also used to announce a new direction with the decline of his hopes in Germany: 'We are the most hated nation of the world, and also the most loved . . . We have the feeling, unfortunately, that we have to count upon ourselves alone, and I say therefore, it is the duty of British statesmen . . . to count upon themselves alone . . . I say alone, yes, in splendid isolation, surrounded by our kinsfolk.' By criticizing the German reaction to his 'methods of barbarism' speech, he provoked Bülow's response two days later: by exploiting the theme of isolation, he again conjured up the issue of relations with the colonies as he had after the Kruger telegram in 1896. Imperial integration was once more being pushed to a high point on the agenda and on 23 January he telegraphed invitations to the colonial premiers for a further conference during the investiture of Edward VII to discuss the 'political relations between the "Mother Country" and the colonies, imperial defence, commercial relations of the Empire, and other matters of general interest.' With Germany unwilling to help arrest the challenge to Britain's world-wide interests, Chamberlain was now falling back on the imperial resources over which Britain had more direct influence, and which would be absolutely vital for survival if 'isolation' was to remain for the indefinite future.

Since the disappointment of the 1897 conference, he had made few moves in this direction. Steering through the Australian Federation Bill in 1900, an event which, with the federation of South Africa, he had often declared the precondition for imperial federation, he rejected suggestions in the debate for colonial representation in the imperial parliament as unacceptable to colonial opinion. At the same time he put a damper on his Zollverein scheme: 'I have not proposed that: I have merely stated that that alone seems to me to be a proposal which might be seriously considered', though certainly not in the immediate future. Military relations during the Boer War appeared to offer promise, and since mid-1899 Chamberlain had pressed for official colonial contributions of troops. All colonial premiers gave willingly, save Laurier who did not want to alienate French-Canadian opinion and suggested a volunteer force. But as Chamberlain minuted in October: 'We do not intend to accept any offer from volunteers. We do not want the men' (on which grounds offers from the West Indies were rejected: this was to be a 'white man's war'), and 'the whole point of the offer would be lost unless it were endorsed by the Government of the Colony'.[10] In March 1900 he used these contributions to make private soundings in the colonies for an imperial military council, beginning with joint participation in the eventual settlement of South Africa. But Australia failed to reply and Laurier's was deflating. Chamberlain had clearly not expected much, and noted that Laurier's comments could be used 'to answer Lord Rosebery or anyone else who may think that the time has come for some great movement in the direction of Federation'. Both he and Salisbury publicly warned during the year against precipitous attempts at unification: 'The movement is one which must come from our colonies and must not be unduly pressed upon them by us.' The break with Germany had turned him against his own advice; and this was reinforced by news of an independent initiative from Laurier in December 1901 involving a conference without British participation to discuss closer colonial links.

The final factor which contributed to Chamberlain's change of direction in 1902 lay in internal Unionist politics. Salisbury had hung on long enough to see the diplomatic radicals reach the end of the cul-de-sac he had predicted, and his early retirement was being widely rumoured during the winter of 1901–2. Balfour was his obvious successor, but the balance of power and even the membership of the new cabinet was unclear. Given their past relationship, Chamberlain could expect even greater influence than under Salisbury. But, by giving public notice that imperial unification was now the key contemporary issue, he was effectively laying down a programme for any future cabinet and reasserting the primary role of his own office. This was to prove important in view of the threatening issue emerging from subterranean depths—the problems of education and Nonconformity. In the winter of 1901 discussions were in progress over Devonshire's bid to provide a complete recast of the country's educational system, and, with the problems it posed for Chamberlain, he cannot have been averse to forcing the imperial question and deflecting attention from this embarrassment.

Education and Empire were, in fact, to proceed hand-in-hand throughout 1902. Devonshire's proposals, ultimately inspired by his permanent secretary, Robert Morant, were to exploit problems raised by the Cockerton judgement of 1901, declaring School Board establishment of secondary education *ultra vires*, in order to transfer, both secondary and primary schools from the Boards to the now democratic local authorities. A patchwork system was to be replaced by one capable of running on far more efficient lines. Nonconformist dislike of having their School Board bastions abolished was likely to be exacerbated by the more dangerous suggestion of dealing with declining voluntary school funds by putting them under local authority control, providing them with rate-aid, and hence overturning the Cowper–Temple compromise on unsectarian education. This full scheme had been proposed as early as 1895, but Chamberlain, fearing strong Liberal opposition and the alienation of his Nonconformist supporters, had combined with Salisbury, who aimed to uphold the voluntary school principle, and managed to remove this second aspect. The consequence was that the 1896 Bill encountered strong opposition from Unionists wanting support for the Church schools as well as from Nonconformists and had to be withdrawn.

Morant and Devonshire, assisted by Balfour, were determined not to make the same mistake in 1901.[11] 'Throwing the Church on the rates' they saw as the only way to amass support for their rationalization measure. Chamberlain and Salisbury again checked it in December 1901, but faced strong pressure for funds from Unionist backbenchers. War financing had hit the government grants which had kept many voluntary schools afloat for years, and Chamberlain's initial suggestion, to deal solely with the secondary education question and wait for the war's termination to release further funds, was clearly unsatisfactory. He therefore soon accepted an earlier suggestion from Morant to keep the full proposal but introduce the principle of 'local option' on rate-aid to denominational schools. This undermined the whole idea of rationalization, but promised to be the only way of appeasing Nonconformity.

After extensive, and acrimonious, discussions the Bill was finally introduced in this form and passed its second reading in May 1902 by 402 to 165. On the 16th of the month Chamberlain spoke on it to his Birmingham party, facing sullen Nonconformist discontent but relatively confident that, if tactfully handled, it would not erupt into open hostility. He was confident for another reason. The major part of his speech was devoted to changing the issue and giving Birmingham something much more important to think about than religion, which was its business interests. With more circumspection than in 1896, he hinted again at necessary changes in imperial fiscal relations.

The opportunity for this move had come with Hicks Beach's April budget, in which increases in direct taxation necessitated by the war had been balanced by revenue tariffs on corn, grain, meal, and flour. The corn tax was unpopular, and Chamberlain had warned his agent to be ready with appeals for national sacrifice to counter cries of 'Grinding the Poor' which it would raise. It took on a new dimension, however, when agricultural spokesmen, imperialists, and colonial politicians noted its protectionist possibilities, and the opportunity it offered for preference to the colonies. Campbell-Bannerman denounced it as the thin end of a protectionist wedge, and Balfour had forcefully to deny any relationship with the forthcoming Colonial Conference. What would happen at the conference, Chamberlain did not know but he was certainly not going to allow options on its policy discussions to be closed. The Birmingham speech was designed to guarantee his freedom in pursuing the new imperial initiative.

Without explicitly referring to the corn tariff, he made it quite clear in his address that Britain faced an urgent need to think seriously about the economic and budgetary principles which had formerly guided her actions. He referred again to the diplomatic isolation, and to the threatening economic expansion of other powers:

The political jealousy of which I have spoken, the commercial rivalry more serious than anything we have yet had, the pressure of hostile tariffs, the pressure of bounties, the pressure of subsidies, it is all becoming more weighty . . . [T]he intention is to shut out this country . . . from all profitable trade . . . and . . . to enable those foreign states to undersell us in British markets . . . At the present moment, the Empire is being attacked on all sides, and, in our isolation, we must look to ourselves.

Imperial integration was vital, since 'the days are for great Empires, not for little states'; and new responses to the challenge of the modern world should not be limited by adherence to 'old shibboleths'.

Liberals denounced this implicit attack on free trade principles, and Unionist 'fair traders', particularly agriculturalists whose voices had been increasingly heard in recent years, welcomed it as a major harbinger of change.[12] It also made an impact on the cabinet. Beach reiterated the view that the corn tariff was purely for revenue, but stated publicly that greater free trade within the Empire might be worth some departure from universal free trade. Options were thus kept open for the colonial conference which met from late June to early August, 1902.

In his opening remarks to it Chamberlain reiterated his 1900 public statement that suggestions for closer relations should come from the colonies themselves, and throughout the early meetings he generally played the role of impartial chairman, expositor of official British views, and occasional examiner of proposals from round the table. His only serious initiative, prompted by pressure from the service departments, was to revive the 1900 plan for an imperial council, with at first advisory and then executive and legislative functions, primarily related to defence policy and conditional on increased military and financial contributions from the colonies to Britain's imperial burdens. Unenthusiastically proposed, it was promptly ignored. Few colonies save South Africa saw immediate advantages from the proposal, and Chamberlain had told Selborne earlier that the colonies would only seriously consider moves on this front after British economic concessions: while Beach held out against tariff preference, little success could be hoped for.[13]

In the midst of the conference three important events occurred which gave a new edge to the discussions. In early July Chamberlain was travelling down The Mall in a cab when one of the decorations, erected for the Coronation celebrations, fell. The horse shied, a strap in the cab broke, and a heavy metal-framed window dropped on Chamberlain, severely cutting his head and forcing him to lay up in hospital for two weeks. This was followed two days later, on 9 July, by the vote on the 'local option' clause of the Education Bill in a Committee session which was proving long and disruptive. Balfour announced in this debate, after strong Tory backbench pressure, that he would allow a free vote on the clause, and that his own sympathies were with the amendment to delete it. The clause was excised. On the following morning Chamberlain received a letter in hospital from Salisbury announcing his decision to resign.

There is no evidence that these three events were related, but it seems implausible that they were not. Balfour could not have taken his own step without a major confrontation unless Chamberlain had been indisposed; and, though Chamberlain had earlier made it clear that he would willingly accept Balfour's accession,[14] the accident offered a perfect opportunity for a change of Prime Minister when Chamberlain's claims could not be put forward with any great force. Salisbury, too, though the recent end to the Boer War was a factor in his decision, must have seen that there was the danger of a major row over Education, and that, as Prime Minister, Balfour would be in a far stronger position to deal with it. Balfour immediately contacted Chamberlain to ensure his support, and Chamberlain sent a message to a party meeting welcoming Balfour's appointment. It must have been a bitter pill, however, for a man who had, five days earlier, quite literally been betrayed.

Balfour consulted Chamberlain over some of his new appointments, and sugared the pill by bringing his son, Austen, into the cabinet as Postmaster General. But Chamberlain was in no physical or mental state to participate fully in building the new ministry. The only condition he imposed was that he remain Colonial Secretary, and be given the freedom to visit some of the colonies in turn—a move which was to have important consequences later in the year. Balfour had shown by his role in the education controversy that, though anxious, as always, to mediate by dextrous manœuvres between various factions in the party and cabinet, he was not going to be Chamberlain's tool. Instead, he was intent on keeping in line with the solid body of Tory opinion, and was studiously backing Devonshire's claims on one of the few issues on which the Liberal Unionist leaders had disagreed in recent years. The Balfour regime was going to be a monarchy, not a duumvirate dominated by Chamberlain's mass appeal. Though Lord George Hamilton later claimed that Balfour's involvement in education subsequently allowed Chamberlain to dominate the new cabinet, education was the main issue of the day, and on this Chamberlain was isolated. Yet the reconstructed ministry also offered Chamberlain a new opening. Beach, a main prop of Salisbury's resistance to Chamberlain's ambitions, had insisted finally on retiring, and his successor at the Treasury was to be C. T. Ritchie, a prickly, forceful, character, who had constructed the local government Bill in 1888, had done good work earlier at the Board of Trade, and who had once been a firm advocate of fair trade policies. If they proved likely to advance colonial integration, fiscal changes now appeared an open possibility.

Chamberlain returned to discussions at the colonial conference to find that this indeed seemed the only promising line of advance. Laurier had brought with him a number of skilled advisers who were soon presenting a strong case for Britain offering preferential tariffs, and, though Chamberlain had opened the meetings with his old idea of imperial free trade, this was soon shunted aside. Without cabinet authorization, he plunged into detailed discussions on the possibilities of reciprocal imperial tariff relations. And, despite the desire of other colonial premiers and British Board of Trade officials that the conference should restrict itself to a general statement favouring preference, he and the Canadians successfully pressed for more detailed official analysis once the conference was ended. There was, however, one serious problem. The Canadians stated, with support from the other colonies, that further preference on British goods could be given only by raising tariffs further against foreign imports, not by reducing existing ones to Britain. This clashed with Britain's traditional doctrine on the issue, and particularly with Beach's recent statement of the cabinet view that only moves towards imperial free trade would justify a change in Britain's fiscal policy. Chamberlain was not put off: 'It is not, with me, primarily a question of money sacrifice; it is primarily a question of the unity of the Empire, and I am firmly convinced that unity cannot be effectually secured in the future unless we can improve and extend our intercommercial relations.' It was not a matter for 'accurate balance sheets', and 'we need not look too closely into the exact benefits we have obtained.'[15] After the events of the previous six months, Chamberlain was now ready to cast caution to the winds for the sake of any advance on the imperial front.

Isolation, foreign trade competition, and overextended military commitments were problems which had in recent years been extensively debated by ministers, officials, and journalists, and Chamberlain's statement to the colonial premiers that closer imperial relations must be cultivated despite short-term costs to Britain reflected a growing consensus of opinion. As yet, however, there had been little serious assessment of the level of costs that might be tolerable. Chamberlain still had to tackle the preference question at cabinet level and, though preparing for this by accepting a final resolution at the conference urging Britain to consider colonial rebates on existing and future tariffs, could not commit the government to acting on it. Canada made sure he had a strong weapon. Facing pressure at home for higher overall protective tariffs, Laurier observed that without rapid action from Britain his country would soon have to take an independent line.

Armed with this, Chamberlain for the first time brought proposals to the cabinet, using as his spearhead the idea, largely symbolic though important economically for Canada, to rebate the corn tax on colonial produce. Unexpectedly, Ritchie asked for a month's delay until mid-November to consider the question, and returned with a classic Treasury disquisition on free trade. Securing the uncertain benefits of colonial concessions, he argued, would involve a protectionist spiral in Britain, raise import bills, and generate foreign tariff retaliation. On these grounds, a corn tax rebate, however innocuous in itself, should be rejected as a thin end of the wedge. He was supported in this view by the Scottish Secretary, Lord Balfour of Burleigh, but Chamberlain's argument that the vital colonial link would be threatened without early concessions carried most of the cabinet and Ritchie was forced to accede to the general principle of preferential tariffs. He secured, however, an important concession to his position as Chancellor: a final decision on the corn tax would be delayed until he had seen whether he needed revenue from it in his next budget.[16]

On the verge of leaving the country, Chamberlain was later quoted by his wife as saying: 'Ritchie has been overruled on the Corn Tax. Now I can leave for South Africa with an easy conscience.' Yet, despite this major success in cabinet, his optimism was not so great the late autumn of 1902. Ritchie was clearly manœuvring to frustrate his plans, and Chamberlain advised the Canadian Finance Minister to frame his next budget on the assumption that the corn tax would disappear, though with contingency plans to alter his tariff levels if a rebate were given.

More depressing was the wider political scene. By-election results had begun to show a major swing to the Liberals, now uniting rapidly round the education issue, even in Tory strongholds. Party agents assigned responsibility to the corn tax's unpopularity, though Chamberlain, for obvious reasons, discounted it as merely an additional weapon being used by the chief threat—active Nonconformist opposition to the Education Bill. In open revolt after the July amendment, and infuriated by further changes introduced to deflect Anglican and Catholic pressure, Dissent was launching a powerful campaign in the country and detaching many Liberal Unionists: 'I told you that your Education Bill would ruin your own party,' Chamberlain told Devonshire. 'It has done so. Our best friends are leaving us by the scores and hundreds and they will not come back . . . D—n the Bill!'[17] Devonshire, however, was unresponsive to Chamberlain's problems, which were accentuated when, on 30 September, his Birmingham party passed a motion hostile to the government's Bill. He called a further meeting on 9 October to reassert his authority, asked for his supporters' detailed objections to the Bill, promised to see whether changes were possible, but then promptly ignored their demands. He could do no other. Throughout August and September Balfour and Devonshire had been bombarded with a series of increasingly agitated letters warning of the political risks and urging modifications to appease Nonconformist malcontents, but, recognizing that Chamberlain was isolated in the party on the issue, they saw their prime task to be that of averting threats from Anglican ultras led by Lord Hugh Cecil and Winston Churchill, in open rebellion in the Commons to establish claims to the ministerial appointments which they believed had been unjustly denied them in the July reshuffle. Balfour helped Chamberlain slightly with a speech condemning extremists of all hues, but effectively left him to sort out his own troubles, and even demanded his public support for a closure on the long-drawn-out Committee proceedings.

By October Chamberlain was plunged into one of his old depressions, and his letters showed clear signs of irritation and despair. As in the winters of 1881 and 1882 he saw the government failing to provide an adequate response to growing unpopularity; as in 1887 he could see his political base disintegrating; and as in 1887 and 1895 he was under strong personal attack, now accused of being 'Judas' to his oldest allies in politics. Other Unionist leaders could not help him as in the past—they were now the main cause of his problems. But if his difficulties were similar to those of 1887, he had also already prepared a comparable solution. Dissatisfied with his role in British politics, he was set on becoming an imperial statesman. Balfour in July had agreed to let him visit the dominions in turn, and Chamberlain was intent on exploiting the opportunity this provided. Many invitations had come from the colonies requesting his presence, but he had picked on the unsolved problems of the South African peace as the arena in which his capacities could be given most prominence. In November 1902 he abandoned the government to its fate and set sail for South Africa.

The guerrilla war of 1900–2 had been brought to a conclusion

at Vereeniging in May, when Britain, appalled by the military
and financial costs of the war, agreed to a negotiated peace on
Chamberlain's prime condition that the Boer generals accept
annexation of their country. In 1900 he had laid down the
principles of future policy: British supremacy to be guaranteed,
but with equality of treatment of British and Afrikaner subjects;
an early return to self-government in the Republics but within
a federation which, if necessary by subsidized immigration,
British settlers should be in the majority in the Cape, Natal,
Rhodesia, and the Transvaal.[18]

The central objective he laid down was that of reconciliation
with Afrikaner opinion. This created problems with Milner.
Milner had continually opposed a negotiated peace, believing
that only unconditional surrender would destroy Boer nationalist aspirations, and had successfully sabotaged negotiations in
1901. He had also proposed the offensive measures of moving
the Transvaal capital from Pretoria and banning Afrikaans as
an official language. In 1902 he colluded with Cape 'loyalists' to
impose direct rule on the Cape rather than risk Premier Sprigg's
government becoming reliant on Bond support if the prorogued
parliament were reconvened. Chamberlain had only managed
to override him by mobilizing opinion at the Colonial Conference, exploiting discontent among Milner's Liberal supporters,
and threatening Sprigg with further direct rule if the reconvened parliament failed to approve war indemnities and confirm sentences imposed by military courts on the Cape 'rebels'.

In some respects Milner's approach, now and later, appeared the more logical implication of the imperial perspective
he shared with Chamberlain. This was to make South Africa
and the other colonies far more responsive to the priorities of
the imperial government and to create far greater unity and
homogeneity within the Empire. Chamberlain's idea for reconciliation in South Africa not only entailed tolerating
cultural diversity but, given past history, was more likely to
lead to colonial opinion unifying around opposition to Downing
Street government than Milner's method of divide and rule
from the High Commissioner's office. Time would tell whether
liberal or authoritarian imperialism would produce the desired
long-term goal.

The immediate problem in South Africa, however, was an

economic one. Normal economic life had to be restored quickly to the war-shattered areas, and Britain's aim of creating an efficient infrastructure for maximum exploitation of the mines had to be furthered. Chamberlain's hope that British–Afrikaner co-operation could achieve it invariably yielded to Milner's methods of autocratic planning through his 'Kindergarten' of bright young administrators and close co-operation with loyalist politicians, the model set by Cromer's administration of Egypt. Reconstruction was also a political problem for Chamberlain at home. From the British point of view, the success of Chamberlain's mission to South Africa was primarily going to be determined with reference to his success in limiting costs to the hard-pressed British Exchequer.

In August 1901 Chamberlain obtained £6½m from Beach to finance post-war measures, but he had to accept in principle a report produced earlier in the year for the Transvaal itself to support most of the costs of reconstruction. A ten per cent tax was imposed on profits from the mines, and in August 1902 Chamberlain expressed the hope of raising a further £100m contribution.

Discussions opened after his arrival in South Africa soon proved this to be utopian. The mineowners were, naturally, hostile, and could legitimately claim that the war had damaged plant and dispersed native labour to an extent which made great financial impositions out of the question—particularly when Chamberlain overrode, for domestic political reasons, Milner's request to import unskilled labour from outside the subcontinent. Milner had paved the way, however, for agreement to be reached on a £30m contribution from the mines, and Chamberlain successfully telegraphed London for this to be matched by a British loan based on the Transvaal government's assets with the mineowners guaranteeing the first year repayment. War compensation also promised to be a major cost to Britain, and here Chamberlain, soon after landing in Natal, played superbly on the colonists' patriotism to induce its government into dropping a £1m claim. After discussions with Milner, however, he agreed that establishing Britain's credibility in the Transvaal required a major gesture, and London again had to agree to a telegraphed request for £4m.

Chamberlain's arguable success on the financial front was

matched by that on the political. Accepting that local self-government in the defeated Republics was as yet not possible, he helped plan a legislative council with nominees of Milner's government, capital, labour, and the burghers on which Boer guerrilla leaders eventually agreed to serve. A council was also established to control the police and allocate investment loans, the basis, it was hoped, for a federation of the two Boer Republics. The sullen Boer farmers, however, were hardly willing to look kindly on these examples of British control, and Chamberlain set out on a month-long trek over the veldt to win allegiance for their new governors. This ambitious enterprise, though successful in rallying support from some Boer leaders, was not entirely helped by Chamberlain's status as originator of the war and his inability to give promises for the future on self-government. Sometimes he tried to convince that the war had been 'inevitable', at others that it was 'brought about by a misunderstanding'; at times claiming that the two ethnic groups had common interests in co-operation, he called at others, Gladstone-like, for a 'union of hearts'.

Reconciliation was also the task he set himself on reaching the Cape in February 1903. War had polarized political conflict between the Bond and loyalist Progressive parties, which in long, tortuous manoeuvres Chamberlain tried to allay. He succeeded in acquiring certain gestures of 'loyalty' from the Bond and persuaded the Progressives to accept an amnesty for Cape 'rebels'—thereby drawing the Moderate Party from the Bond, which, with the disenfranchisement of many 'rebels', allowed the Progressives to take office under Jameson's premiership after the 1904 elections—but ethnic politics continued to dominate South Africa.

Milner believed that Chamberlain had been duped into far too many concessions to anti-British elements on his visit—though Chamberlain always ostentatiously resisted pressure for major revisions of the peace treaty—but his definition of British policy as one of economic progress and political reconciliation provided a solid foundation for defence of Britain's interests in the area. In the immediate future bad harvests and low output from the mines made life in the old Republics hard, and it took a change of government at home to bring about a return to self-rule and federation. On one issue, of major significance for the future, Chamberlain and his successors, in pursuing a policy which for Edwardian days seemed progressive, abandoned earlier enlightened policies: economic development required a large, disciplined work-force and reconciliation demanded a loose rein on internal colonial affairs. The price for a British South Africa was abandonment of imperial responsibility for the black population and their increasing subjection to a coalition of the two white ethnic groups.[19]

If Chamberlain's visit in 1902 had a significant, though arguable, impact on South Africa, its effect in Britain was far more obvious. Whether intended or not, it turned into a gigantic personal promotion campaign. The political and financial negotiations, announcements of successful conclusions, the veldt trek and innumerable speeches were all given prominence in the British press. On his return he met with great acclaim, and Birmingham Unionists who had led the 1902 revolt were among an enthusiastic reception committee. Liberals were less than happy, Campbell-Bannerman observing that 'Evidently Joe will return in triumph, and it will not be easy to be decently appreciative.'[20]

Chamberlain's position contrasted sharply with the waning popularity of his house-bound colleagues: 'You will find the Government *much weaker* than when you left,' he was told in March.[21] 'The by-elections have gone badly and over 30 of our men are in a state of mutiny'—a reference to the Tory 'Young Turks', who had found a new target in Brodrick's unwieldy and expensive army reform scheme. Furthermore, absence had not made Chamberlain's heart any the fonder. He returned, Balfour later noted, 'rather ill, rather irritable, and very tired': he 'hated the political situation' (giving an unrestrained piece of his mind to colleagues whose actions displeased him), and 'unconscious to himself, he was perhaps influenced by the notion that his councils had not all the weight which his public position justified.'[22]

To be more accurate than Balfour was ready to admit, Chamberlain received a slap in the face from the cabinet. Ritchie had decided to use the escape clause of the November agreement to prepare a budget cutting income tax and scrapping the corn tax, threatening resignation were it rejected. Despite Austen's plea to call the bluff, Balfour effectively left the cabinet with a free choice on the issue after Chamberlain's return and on 31 March the budget was approved. Chamberlain took on the unpleasant task of disillusioning colonial leaders with a series of truculent letters defending the decision by attacking colonial parochialism and selfishness.

Strong opposition in cabinet secured Chamberlain the right to reopen the tariff preference issue later, but he took no steps to mobilize support nor did he threaten his own resignation against removal of the corn tax. This inactivity he was later to justify as determined by the budget's proximity and the cabinet's general sympathy to his overall policy. In reality, Ritchie had outwitted him. His motives in challenging Chamberlain are unclear, though the influence of his new permanent officials may have tempered his former fair-trade views. More important, perhaps, were the corn tax's un-popularity and a desire to make a great show with his first budget. Perhaps, too, just as one of the 'Young Turks' had recently been heard talking of 'pulling Joe down a peg or two', a man like Ritchie, gruff, sensitive and unexciting but of high ministerial ability, might well have seen his popular budget cuts as making up for the years his career had been held back by the Liberal Unionist advent to Toryism and Chamberlain's ascendancy. Chamberlain, having so far failed to popularize his preference ideas, was in a weak position to fight Ritchie's package of tax cuts at a time of growing business depression, war-weariness and, for the first time for a quarter-century, general inflationary pressure. Moreover, Balfour was sitting on the fence, wary of losing a new Chancellor and perhaps feeling his way gingerly in his new office, but also certainly not averse to having subordinates check Chamberlain's overbearing influence.

The logic of Chamberlain's thinking since the late 1880s had led him to favour major changes in fiscal policy and imperial relations. Until now, however, he had approached the matter cautiously, aware of the complexity of the issues involved and the problems of implementation. There seemed little to be gained, as the Zollverein speeches had shown, by dramatic moves. But in 1903 he had come up against Ritchie's barrier to gradual advance at a critical juncture. In itself, this pointed to

the need for drastic action—Ritchie would, in some way, ultimately have to be brought to book. Yet Ritchie's resistance and
cabinet cowardice in the face of it raised wider issues: was
Unionism, as presently constituted under its existing leadership, able to see the real contemporary problems and grasp at
the nettle? Its 'reactionary' deference to Anglican interests,
muddled handling of defence and imperial problems, and
timidity towards social issues suggested to Chamberlain that it
was not. He also believed that the voters were saying this
through the by-elections. This assessment both reflected and
was reflected in his own political position. Many commentators
have seen tariff reform as Chamberlain's response to his difficulties over education in 1902, and this certainly contributed
to his actions in the autumn. More generally, however, by
April 1903 he was finding that, one by one, his options on the
policies with which he was most closely identified were being
closed off. And, ever since 1872, it had been his characteristic
style in circumstances of government unpopularity and personal inability to influence cabinet policy to find some way of
flexing his political muscle and breaking out of the *cul-de-sac*
into which the existing structure of political power and debate
had driven him. The situation was now ripe for another classic
initiative. It was being widely anticipated, and Campbell-
Bannerman had advised his colleagues to lie low and await the
response to the South African triumph.

Chamberlain himself lay low for two months, assessing the
political climate, but his depression soon lifted. During the
Easter recess his wife noted that people were 'all impressed by
the difference in the tone of his mind. They find him much
more inclined to take a vigorous view of things and with a
return to his old habit of *ideas*.' Tackling a long-term realignment of party relations was what Chamberlainite politics was
all about, and bound to revive his interest. In mid-April he
contacted his agent, Vince, to explain that the electoral situation showed the government to be exhausted and in need of a
new programme, which he was thinking of offering with an
exposition of fair trade views attached to a strong imperialist
appeal. Approval was forthcoming, and on 15 May Chamberlain delivered to his local party a speech which Leopold Amery
was to call 'a challenge to free trade as direct and provocative

as the theses which Luther nailed to the church door at Wittenberg.'

The speech began with now-customary appeals to the 'imperial spirit', calls for firmer foundations to avert imperial disintegration, and praise of colonial war contributions. Britain had to respond, and she had also to find a way of protecting colonies who aided her against hostile foreign actions like Germany's commercial retaliation against Canadian produce after 1897. Upon this he based scepticism of the 'interpretation of Free Trade which is current amongst a certain limited section' that 'our only duty is to buy in the cheapest market without regard to where we can sell.' Identifying 'free trade' with 'free imports' prevented Britain helping colonies against third parties, and meant that 'we cannot make any difference between those who treat us well and those who treat us badly'. 'I am perfectly clear that I am not a Protectionist,' but a world had emerged 'that was never contemplated by any of those whom we regard as the authors of Free Trade.' Britain had a choice—either to uphold principles held 'by a small remnant of Little Englanders of the Manchester School' and reject preferential treatment of the colonies, or not to be 'bound by any purely technical definition', and instead, 'recover our freedom, resume the power of negotiation, and, if necessary, retaliation' when British or colonial interests were threatened. The question had now to be openly discussed, and 'whether [a general election] is near or distant, I think our opponents may, perhaps, find that the issues which they propose to raise are not the issues on which we shall take the opinion of the country.'

Public reaction to the speech was immediate and strong, though Chamberlain later claimed that it had surprised him. The speech had, however, been well-constructed to present a radical popular appeal while remaining, despite Leo Amery's comment, ambiguous on the practical implications. Furthermore, though clearly delivering a challenge to Treasury policies in a situation where knowledge of ministerial disagreements over the corn tax was widespread, Chamberlain took care to remain within broad official guidelines. The cabinet has agreed on 12 May that Balfour would on the 15th rebuff a deputation of Unionist backbenchers supporting the corn tax, and argue that its revival could only come when 'associated with some great change in our fiscal system'. Chamberlain had said that he would speak in the same vein at Birmingham, and this, in principle, he had done. But the contrast with Balfour's deflating comments was marked. Even more striking was the contrast with Ritchie's comments while announcing repeal of the tax on 23 April, when he had gone out of his way to condemn arguments used by Beach and others to justify its imposition and took a swipe at Chamberlain by claiming that it 'lends itself very readily to misinterpretation'. Ritchie had also, however, rejected use of the tax 'unless there is some radical change in our economic circumstances or it is connected with some boon much desired by the working classes', another opening like Balfour's which gave Chamberlain an opportunity to develop his line. In Commons debates on 22 and 28 May Lloyd George exploited Ritchie's comment to taunt Chamberlain with his failures over pensions, to which bait Chamberlain suitably rose by suggesting tariff revenues as a possible source of funds. Further, he 'made members opposite a present' of the fact that fiscal reform would entail food tariffs, though contributing to employment and higher wages, helping the farmer and preventing 'dumping' by foreign manufacturers.

Balfour was visibly annoyed by these remarks, which showed that Chamberlain, though not openly challenging government policy, was exploiting items in it vaguely hinting at hypothetical contingencies to engineer a stampede of the party and sectional economic interests behind an aggressive campaign against the Chancellor. Nor was he, as in his 1902 speech, talking of negotiations with the colonies to work out reciprocal tariff arrangements, but of a unilateral upheaval of Britain's whole fiscal structure. Furthermore, tariff reform was no longer simply being sounded out, as in 1896 and 1902, but translated from a general aspiration into the chief item on a party election agenda.

Like Gladstonian Home Rule, Chamberlain's proposals entailed defining a future role for his party around a single great issue; and contemporaries could see, as Randolph Churchill had said of Gladstone, that if the Grand Old Man went a-mucker it might be a good thing for everyone. Rising Liberals like Lloyd George were straining to challenge Chamberlain on a great old Liberal cause, though Campbell-Bannerman, as shrewd as Salisbury in his heyday, advised lying low to let Unionist splits widen. Ritchie had put Chamberlain with his back to the wall and saw he faced the choice of fading into obscurity or fighting to win a notable personal victory. In the cabinet Lord Londonderry, Lord Balfour of Burleigh, and Lord George Hamilton swung behind him. Outside it, Beach was roused to defend once more the principles of sound finance and limited government he had upheld against Chamberlain for seven years. Churchill and the Cecil connection shrewdly perceived that Chamberlain's plans threatened to transform the old landed Anglican Tory party into what they described as a 'secular, materialistic' (i.e. middle-class, business) party in which their ancestry would no longer be at a premium, whereas bringing Chamberlain down would open up a pathway to the top. In the Commons they were busy organizing an opposition group. An important new element was the growing reticence of senior Liberal Unionists—Devonshire, Lansdowne, and Lord James. Chamberlain complained that Devonshire had given no previous indication of his opposition when he attempted to stop Powell Williams circulating the 15 May speech through the party machinery, and warned that the Birmingham section would have to extend its propaganda independently. James's views in part reflected his annoyance at being forcibly retired from the government in 1902, but Devonshire's position was more complicated. Though long an advocate of imperial federation, he also symbolized the great Whig tradition with its long-standing free trade tradition and suspicion of the politics of popular enthusiasm into which Chamberlain was once more threatening to plunge the party. Devonshire cloaked a shrewd mind with a studiously cultivated nonchalance towards the conduct of affairs, and he could perhaps recognize that Chamberlain's bid challenged Balfour's authority, and that the Prime Minister would soon be on the look-out for a strong man to lean on in order to resist it. Devonshire set out to be the man who, by his reluctant opposition to Chamberlain, could hold a pivotal role in the coming conflict.

Balfour's own personal views are virtually impossible to determine clearly. Concerned to strengthen imperial defences, and sharing Salisbury's secret view that free trade severely hampered Britain's international negotiating position, he later observed that events over the previous decade had made discussion of the tariff reform question inevitable: 'Chamberlain's action has precipitated the crisis, has made it more acute and more dangerous, but it could not, I think, in any case have been long postponed.'[23] But Chamberlain had presented a political, as much as an intellectual, challenge and Balfour had to treat it as such. With protectionists, fair traders, and imperial idealists in full cry on Chamberlain's bandwagon, his prime responsibility as Salisbury's heir was to retain full control over Unionism's divergent factions. Chamberlain, the most dynamic and popular of his subordinates, could not be openly disavowed, though he might be used, as Gladstone had earlier used him over franchise and Ireland, to draw the party towards desirable reforms without assuming overall control. His immediate response in the Commons after Chamberlain's speech was to prove his guide throughout the ensuing maelstrom. Defending the spirit of the speech, and Chamberlain's right to independent utterance, he laid major emphasis on the importance of retaliatory tariffs in strengthening Britain's bargaining position. Reconstructing Britain's fiscal policy to solidify the Empire he declared a matter needing more careful calculation: 'The thing is worth getting if you can get it without paying too heavily for it'.

This was a shift of emphasis of major proportions. For retaliation, Chamberlain later said, 'I would never have taken off my coat.' As I have tried to show in earlier sections of this book, Chamberlain was always less impressed by the economic benefits to Britain of tariff changes within the Empire than he was by the long-term advantages of greater imperial military and political co-operation to counter the expansion of other world powers. The new programme, of course, was built around the promise of better economic prospects for the British producer and consumer; but, as Chamberlain had earlier made clear to Milner during private conversations in South Africa, the ultimate economic vision was that of a great unified imperial market, perhaps in the long run autarkic, which would minimize Britain's reliance upon trade with unstable or potentially hostile countries elsewhere in the world. The policy of opening up foreign markets with retaliatory tariff threats was an item essentially tacked on to gain mass support in the domestic political arena. Paradoxically, fair-traders had so far invariably regarded imperial preference as a marginal change which would encounter the least political opposition while being capable of extension for much wider protectionist purposes. Now that Chamberlain had raised it as part of a grander plan, preference became the extremist policy, and retaliation, which Chamberlain rightly observed might lead far more rapidly to the insular protection his opponents feared, became the moderate policy—one whose vagueness and apparent costlessness to the consumer threatened to compromise the imperial aspect of tariff reform.

Balfour had one further response to Chamberlain's declarations. He told the Commons that 'this question is not a question that this House will have to decide this session or next session or the session after.' In a bid to keep his present government together, he was shunting action over fiscal changes off on to the next one.

The Whitsun recess averted immediate trouble over Chamberlain's speech, but a stormy cabinet meeting was held on 10 June at which he threatened resignation in the face of strong criticism. Balfour, determined to retain control, did so by the device Gladstone had used in February 1886. There was to be an open inquiry into fiscal reform—one, in practice, conducted solely by Balfour on information provided by his brother, Gerald, at the Board of Trade. In the interim, cabinet members were to preserve public silence, though Ritchie might offer comments in the Commons when announcing the inquiry.

Chamberlain was loath to abandon the initiative. He made it clear that he would spread propaganda through the Birmingham machine, and effectively broke the truce in a speech of 26 June by criticizing dogmatic adhesion to free trade. In the Commons, 130 supporters of fiscal reform met on 24 June, though, in the uncertain climate, they could only give support to the inquiry, while sixty MPs formed a Free Food League on 13 July. This rapid polarization was not entirely to Chamberlain's advantage. The danger was emerging of a counter-productive party split like that of 1886, whereas the aim of the May speech, like those he had delivered on franchise in 1883 and 1884, had almost certainly been to rally grass-roots opinion and overwhelm conservative resistance to him in cabinet. He was not well prepared for an extended battle. As even close supporters critically observed, he had launched an attack against a bastion of British policy of fifty years standing, the principles of which had been honed to a fine edge by economists and government officials, and he was armed with little detailed analysis save of journalistic and partisan pamphlets and the arguments of a few Canadian civil servants. He had formed no cadre of followers, and no clear policy except the unpopular suggestion of food taxes. And even by the 26 June speech he was on the defensive, abandoning the plan to use tariff revenues for social reforms as a long-term venture and advocating applying them to reduce war tariffs on tea, coffee, sugar, and perhaps tobacco. The great reform was reducing to a redistribution of indirect taxation, and the 'free breakfast table' cry of the 1860s was being mobilized to counter the 'small loaf' cry of the 1840s.

His propaganda machine, however, was extending. A Tariff Reform League was founded on 21 July of prominent business men and political notables guided by the driving force of the economic historian Professor Hewins, and supported by leading journalists like J. L. Garvin. This was not intended to replace his own Tariff Reform Committee, recently set up in Birmingham under Vince, since 'I cannot depend entirely upon the League, and I must have my own organization, entirely under control'.[24] Chamberlain had slipped the catch on a Pandora's box, to release a hoard of fanatics, ambitious intriguers, frustrated intellectuals, and special economic interests which would be difficult to organize for a single line of attack. The national press was also turning in his favour—Lord Northcliffe's *Daily Mail*, first of the modern mass-circulation dailies, came round in the late autumn[25]—and funds rolled in to support what became the most powerful propaganda machine that British peacetime history has seen.

The prime target at which it was directed for the moment was the Unionist leadership. If this could be won, Chamberlain believed he could confront the Liberal reaction with a united force, since 'The party tie is with most men the strongest of all'. Free fooders were coming under pressure from their constituency organizations, but the significant figures were still those like Devonshire, whom Chamberlain and Balfour were both

urging throughout July to commit himself to some form of
fiscal reform. The latter, it became clear, was beginning to play
a double game: while working on a way of keeping Chamberlain in harness, he was building support elsewhere for his own
programme. On 30 July he sent Devonshire, the first cabinet
member to see it, his *Notes on Insular Free Trade*, a draft study
of Britain's trade position. It came with recommendations for
an agreed government policy of 'fiscal freedom', involving retaliatory tariff threats against high-tariff competitors. No
reference was made, however, to any policy of preferential
tariffs, and Chamberlain was reported as having dropped an
earlier suggestion for a general protective tariff.

Devonshire appeared not dissatisfied. But at cabinets on 11
and 13 August, to which Balfour offered his *Notes* for approval
and publication as well as policy recommendations contained
in a 'blue paper', he had shifted his ground. There were two
reasons. Balfour's suggested policy was fiscal freedom, with
conditions that tariffs imposed should be neither protective nor
raise the cost of living to the average working man, but with the
additional suggestion for discussions with the colonies on preference. The second resulted from the first. Chamberlain accepted
Balfour's paper—and therefore Devonshire rejected it. This
was not simply because of the general departure from free
trade, to which Ritchie, Hamilton, and Lord Balfour objected,
but of the policy implications. Under it, he claimed, the government would be led on the downward path to the perdition of
protection, and 'the whole policy sketched out by Mr. Chamberlain' could be advocated. The implication was clear. For
Devonshire to be satisfied, Balfour had to produce something
explicitly disavowing Chamberlain which would force him
either to eat humble pie or to leave the government.

Balfour still hoped to keep his cabinet together. He postponed
a final decision for a month, rejecting Ritchie's request for
further delay since Chamberlain was straining at the leash and
threatening to 'consult the constituencies' in the autumn, and
Balfour himself needed a settlement to face a Conservative
Union conference in October. In the meantime, it became
clear that Devonshire was gaining ground. Bombarded by appeals from Chamberlain, Ritchie, and Balfour, he had made
himself the key man in the cabinet. For the moment he was

prepared to work closest with Ritchie, responding to blandishments from the other two with the Chancellor's request for
more detailed statements of Balfour's policy (a request rebuffed as 'premature') and claiming that he owed commitments
to the free traders—a statement of misplaced loyalty calling
forth a strong broadside from Balfour. Yet he also showed himself conciliatory, suggesting that Balfour draft broad outlines of
a policy which could be presented as parliamentary resolutions
and limit freedom of expression among ministers during the
autumn.[26] Essentially flying by the seat of his pants, Balfour
promised to see what could be done. He framed a series of vague
resolutions advocating fiscal reform for retaliatory and revenue
purposes, so long as this did not involve duties on raw materials
and cost of living increases. But, determined still to appease
Chamberlain, he emphasized the practicability of preference,
and allowed his brother to forward a plan Chamberlain had
devised in July for tariffs on meat, fruit, and dairy produce
rather than corn, with reduced tea, coffee, cocoa and sugar
duties. Devonshire rejected the drafts he received on 7 September: his position was hardening, he said, against any
compromise leaving Chamberlain free to advocate his full
programme.

Chamberlain's difficulties were mounting. While holding
the initiative in the country, and apparently possessing Balfour's blessing, he was yet losing ground in the cabinet. The
trend of Balfour's thinking was clearly towards preserving the
political balance intact and maintaining control by pandering
to Devonshire's recalcitrance. For this reason, Chamberlain's
own attempts to sway the Duke soon became half-hearted, and
at one point even deliberately provocative by making favourable references to Sweden's protectionist policies. If Devonshire
was ready to compromise, Chamberlain was weak—if he was
intransigent, Balfour might have to abandon him to keep
Chamberlain, who would then have the whip-hand. One
alternative, which Harcourt thought possible, was for
Chamberlain to 'put so much water in his wine as to induce the
Duke to stay for the present and . . . have some dilatory
declaration to the effect that opinion is not now ripe for any
action.'[27] This, for reasons given later, Chamberlain was unwilling to adopt. But there was, however, one outside danger to

be considered. Chamberlain had observed earlier to Lord Minto, Canadian Governor-General, that retaliation was a popular policy 'and might be carried immediately if it stood by itself'. Continued intransigence from Chamberlain might decide Balfour to repeat the blow his uncle had delivered at Randolph Churchill in 1886; his dismissal, followed by consolidation of a Balfour–Devonshire cabinet committed to retaliation with strident appeals for party unity to defend them againt their critics, would be a bold, dangerous, but possibly successful strategy.

On 1 September there took place the funeral of the old Lord Salisbury. It was appropriate that at his interment his successors should have pronounced the last rites over the party he had created and so often predicted that Chamberlain would destroy. Chamberlain made Balfour the offer of his resignation, though under conditions that might minimize the costs to himself and mitigate the rift in the party. It was confirmed in a letter from Birmingham on the 9th after receipt of Balfour's draft resolutions, and proposed that

if you cut out the preference part of our scheme you might keep the Duke and possibly the other recalcitrants in the Cabinet for a moderate policy of Retaliation . . . My own opinion is that . . . it would ultimately be extended and would include the preference that I desire; but it may be wise to bow to the storm and in the first instance jettison the most unpopular part of the programme. Of course if this were done I must leave the government, but I should do so gladly and without the slightest trace of bitterness.

He and Balfour discussed the matter for an hour before the 14 September cabinet on fiscal reform, Chamberlain offering to try and persuade his followers, including Austen, to stay on.

The events of this meeting were later variously interpreted by its different participants. On one thing everyone agreed— Balfour curtly dismissed memoranda from Ritchie and Lord Balfour rejecting any departure from free trade. He was going for fiscal reform, and presenting them with a choice between their principles and their offices. He then set to work on Devonshire, dropping hints that preference was due for relegation from the 'blue paper' proposals. In which case, said Chamberlain, he would resign. Wrapped up in a vain attempt to get Balfour to define specifically what he meant by 'fiscal freedom', however, most cabinet members took this statement as a bargaining threat, not a definite intention based on secret arrangements over the specific content of cabinet policy. On this, Balfour refused to allow any firm decision, and the next few days saw much to-ing and fro-ing as a result. Ritchie, Hamilton, and Lord Balfour felt they had no option but to resign, but Devonshire, though sending off his own resignation, had been hooked on Balfour's line. He sought clarification of what might publicly be said, 'if not by you, by the next important Member of the Cabinet'. Was he to expect, that is, Chamberlain's recantation, or his resignation? After increasingly clear hints, culminating on the 16th in the private revelation of a resignation letter Chamberlain had sent in, the Duke was finally induced to stay. The price of keeping his office, however, was total secrecy over Chamberlain's letter. The free traders were thus given no chance to withdraw, and over the next two days Balfour was able to announce that the two extreme wings of his cabinet had both handed in their notice.

Ritchie's group were furious. Since their aim was to block Chamberlain, they, like Devonshire, would have agreed to almost any policy to stay on and consolidate their victory. They suspected a Balfour–Chamberlain conspiracy to split their forces and isolate them as extreme conservatives, a suspicion reinforced by the nature of Chamberlain's resignation letter and Balfour's reply. Chamberlain's letter was dated 9 September from Birmingham but, as Julian Amery has revealed,[29] his copy of it, written on paper bearing his London address, displays little resemblance to the actual letter sent from Birmingham on the 9th. Nor in that was there any reference to an enclosed resignation letter. It seems unlikely that Chamberlain would have thus committed himself before knowing the outcome of the 14 September cabinet, but backdating a resignation probably drawn up finally on the 15th had obvious advantages: it implied that Ritchie and co. had resigned not against a possible cabinet acquiescence in Chamberlain's policy but against a policy which Chamberlain had already rejected. They were thereby made to appear far more conservative and intransigent than had ever been their intention.

The content of the Chamberlain–Balfour dialogue made for an even thicker plot. Chamberlain accepted that public re-action to food taxes made preference unacceptable at the moment, though a policy of tariff negotiations backed by threats of retaliation was viable as an official policy. 'Accord-ingly I suggest that [Balfour] should limit the present policy . . . to the assertion of our freedom in the case of all commercial relations with foreign countries', while he himself was resigning to preach the gospel of imperial unification. Balfour in reply accepted the desirability of closer imperial fiscal relations, but agreed that public opinion was not ripe for food taxes: Cham-berlain was right to acknowledge that this should not hinder other necessary fiscal changes though, regrettably, this had entailed his resignation.

The two men thus agreed on each other's course of action, accepted each other's policy—though Balfour expressed scepti-cism at converting the colonies from protection—and believed that Chamberlain's departure was likely to 'serve the interests of Imperial unity'; the dating of Chamberlain's letter showed that the free-traders had been sloughed off to compensate for his departure; and, in the subsequent reshuffle, Austen was promoted to the Exchequer, and all Chamberlain's men re-mained in cabinet with a right of independent utterance. The old duumvirate appeared still intact, separated only by the formal barrier of office.

As so often with Chamberlain's manœuvres, reality was rather different. 'If we had been united, if the timid ones could have seen that boldness was the best policy, I would have gone confidently to the next General Election on the whole pro-gramme, and although we might have been beaten next time, we should have had a clear run afterwards,' was his later comment,[30] which admitted, whatever appearances might be, that he had lost the cabinet battle. He had wanted prime ministerial approval for the new policy and an acknowledge-ment of his personal authority, but Balfour chose to back Devonshire's reservations and force Chamberlain into the role of sacrificial lamb to 'appease those opponents in our own ranks who were rapidly becoming personal and violent'.

There were, of course, other alternatives which Chamberlain could have taken, and it is not entirely clear why resigning in this way attracted him. Austen was later to offer the view that Balfour had 'encouraged my father to go out' with promises to shift government policy gradually towards preference. 'Really, one rubs one's eyes,' J. S. Sandars, Balfour's secretary, commented on this.[31] He in turn suggested that Chamberlain had in fact been anxious to get out of government—a view partly supported by Chamberlain's reference in the 9 September letter to his desire for relief from the strains of office, and a contemporary story of his passing bitter comments on a row of red boxes awaiting attention. His frustration at being tied to a waning ministry must have been greatly reinforced by eagerness to exploit the popular acclaim which his May speech had brought. There was, however, an alternative way to achieve this—to stand by his principles and work for the government's disintegration by threatening withdrawal with Austen, Selborne, and the three or four other ministers who supported him. This, after all, was the outcome he had often angled for in similar circumstances during Gladstone's 1880 ministry. A straight government split might have entailed its resignation and the election he wanted: victory in that with his new programme, whether authorized or not, would strengthen him significantly—defeat would allow him a period of opposition to restructure the party as he had tried after 1874, 1885, and 1892. Affection for Balfour, and his consequent desire to ease Balfour's position as much as possible, offers one, though a rather implausible, explanation of why he rejected this line, for it was not generally Chamberlain's style to put personal before political considerations. Austen's comment quoted above made a valid point—Balfour had studiously cultivated the impression that he did, and would continue to, take Chamberlain's side, and that the sacrifice was only temporary, made more in sorrow than in anger to appease the 'timid ones'.

It is probably more reasonable, however, to see that Chamberlain took the line of going into the wilderness and leaving Balfour and his government largely intact because he believed it if not the best, at least the best possible political outcome. As he had said of Liberalism in the period 1885–6, his aim was not to split the party, but gradually to ease out its more conservative leaders. To break the government might ruin Unionism as a viable political force in the future, and perhaps open up the dangerous possibility of a free trade, centrist coalition based on Devonshire and right-wing Liberals. In September 1903, too, he had had little chance to assess his own support in Parliament and the country—even in cabinet, alignments were unclear because Balfour had managed to avoid a formal vote—and, with his past reputation for disruption hanging like an albatross round his neck, he might not be lightly forgiven by the average loyal Unionist for such drastic action. Mass resignation by the tariff reformers was thus a dangerous course of action. To 'pour water in his wine', accept Balfour's definition of fiscal reform as retaliation and thereby perhaps keep the free traders as well as Devonshire, was no better. This would not only be seen as a personal defeat, leaving him with little room to manœuvre in the future, but might perpetuate indefinitely the political stalemate in a weak government whose uncertain policy would be open to constant debilitating sniping from the opposition. It was also pointless, since 'If my judgement is correct it will not be very long before the whole programme is accepted by the country, and I regard this as certain if we are approaching a time of commercial depression.'[32] Recovering his freedom of action while retaining Balfour's blessing, which was readily conferred to avert the possibility of an open attack, became the best available option. Chamberlain's calculations, however, were almost certainly based on the premise that, whether willingly or not, Balfour would be forced to move in his direction and that the government's life would now be severely curtailed. Already Chamberlain had made one mistake. It might have been possible in July 1902 for him to insist on taking the Exchequer, but he had calculated that the key task was negotiating agreements with the colonies and retained his old office. In doing so, he underestimated Treasury resistance. Now he underestimated Balfour's desire to oppose encroachment on his control of the party, his capacity to do so, and his determination to hang on to office as the most important weapon in his armoury. And, in the running fight in which they were to engage for control over Unionism during the next three years, Balfour won hands down every time.

This at first did not appear likely, despite the inspired improvizations which he had devised after Chamberlain's May speech. On 1 October he delivered to the Conservative Union conference at Sheffield a statement of official government policy on lines laid down in his letter to Chamberlain. A motion approving it was passed, but the occasion was an unhappy one. Chaplin, Chamberlain's agent at the meeting and the long-standing advocate of agricultural protection, decided not to propose the full programme because of uncertain support, but Balfour's expressed scepticism of the popularity of food taxes was received in silence, and his pronouncement that he, and he alone, would lead the party was ruined by Leo Amery's intrusive and warmly applauded cry 'What about Joe?' A major consequence of the speech was Devonshire's decision to resign, ostensibly because Balfour's speech was too protectionist. In reality it had been partly enforced by a threat from Ritchie to publish an account of the cabinet crisis critical of the Duke's 'betrayal', and perhaps also Devonshire's belated realization that Balfour was intent on preserving peace with Chamberlain rather than regrouping his cabinet, with Devonshire as the main prop, to resist the tariff reform onslaught. Balfour was furious at this upset to his plans, but the impact of the resignation was mitigated by its lateness, and overshadowed by Chamberlain's first autumn speech.[33]

Chamberlain had a big programme in mind for the winter of 1903–4. After an initial statement of the general policy in Glasgow and Greenock on 6 and 7 October, he planned to tour Britain's major commercial and industrial centres—the North East, Liverpool, Birmingham, South Wales, Leeds, and the City of London. It was a unique campaign in British politics—a single-handed attempt by an ex-minister to convert the nation to one man's dream of its future.

The early speeches in Scotland contained the nub of his arguments, and laid down parameters for the debate to be held by politicians on and off over the next two decades. He began by claiming that he and Balfour shared broadly identical aims, 'the maintainance and increase of the natural strength and the prosperity of the United Kingdom . . . Then . . . the realization of the greatest ideal which has ever inspired statesmen in any country or in any age—the creation of an Empire such as the world has never seen.' Strengthening imperial trade links was a vital prerequisite, and, more immediately, was needed to counter the threat to British exports from European and American tariffs, compensated for only by increased colonial custom. The moral was that 'if that trade declines, or it does not increase in proportion to our population and to the loss of trade with foreign countries, then we sink at once into a fifth rate nation.' The colonies dared not risk their infant industries by full free trade, but 'outside this there is still a great margin . . . which has given us this enormous increase of trade'. In addition, he appealed to the colonies to make sacrifices for Britain: 'there are many things which you do not now make, many things for which we have a great capacity of production—leave them to us as you have left them heretofore.' Only by 'commercial union, reciprocal preference', a 'practical tie which will prevent separation', was the ideal achievable; and 'in return for a very moderate preference [the colonies] will give us a substantial advantage', which would increase domestic employment and job security, though this 'will be described by the Leader of the Opposition as a squalid argument'.

The nature of this 'practical tie' could be settled only after detailed commercial negotiations, but he offered possible outlines of Britain's offer: a two-shilling import duty on corn and flour, completely remitted to the colonies; a five per cent tariff on meat and dairy produce, also with preference; no duties on maize and bacon, since these were cheap foods for the poor; preference on colonial wines and possibly fruits; and counterbalancing reductions on tea, coffee, cocoa, and sugar duties. On the most pessimistic calculations, he claimed, this would not alter the living standards of the average industrial worker, and make the agricultural worker marginally better off. The changes, however, would reduce public revenue, and, to compensate, there should be a ten per cent flat duty on foreign manufactures, used to reduce other taxes or to back tariff negotiations. Balfour had earlier told Devonshire that the general tariff was a proposal which Chamberlain had abandoned, and the revenue argument for it cloaked its real rationale, noted earlier in the Glasgow speech when figures had been produced to argue that manufactured imports were a major feature of British economic life, many of them supplied at below-market price through subsidies or 'dumping'. The protectionist implications of the policy were spelled out more clearly at Greenock.

Here he declared himself a firm free trader whose beliefs had been shattered by the economic successes of protectionist nations. Further, 'I want to have exchange with all the nations of the world, but if they will not exchange with me, then I am not a Free Trader at any price.' The existing system was inequitable when British goods were undercut by foreign products unencumbered by high wages and the costs of protecting the working conditions of labour; free trade, industrial health, and welfare legislation were incompatible, and one would have to go. This bid for working-class support was extended; foreign industrial growth and free imports benefited primarily the middle-class consumer and recipient of foreign investment dividends, while the British workman paid for them with his job. The trends were there for all to see:

Greenock was one of the great centres of the sugar trade . . . then came foreign competition, aided by bounties . . . Agriculture, as the greatest of all trades and industries of this country, has been practically destroyed. Sugar has gone; silk has gone; iron is threatened; wool is threatened; cotton will go! . . . Do you think that the same causes which have destroyed some of our industries, and which are in the course of destroying others, will not be equally applicable to you when your turn comes?

The free trade argument that labour would shift to more productive employment was no answer to the unskilled, redundant middle-aged worker, and in any case socially undesirable: 'Sugar has gone. Let us not weep for it—jam and pickles remain. Now of all those . . . independent artisans who were engaged in refining sugar and making machinery for sugar refining . . . I would like to know how many have found rest and wages and comfort in stirring up jam-pots and bottling pickles.' Claiming Balfour's agreement, he asked: 'What is the remedy? . . . Let us get rid of the chains which we ourselves have forged, and which have fettered our action. Let us claim some protection like every other civilized nation.' Foreign retaliation was no danger since 'we are the best customers of all those countries . . . It is absolutely absurd to suppose that . . . keenly competitive among themselves, [they] would agree among themselves to fight with us when they might benefit at the expense of their neighbours.' Since British imports from each exceeded her exports to each, in a war of tariffs she must inevitably win. But protection was not enough. The Empire offered an alternative, expanding market; American prosperity was based on a home market of seventy million consumers —the Empire offered 350 million, fifty of them in the white dominions.

These arguments were paraded throughout his winter speeches, with the insertion of particular appeals. The corn tax, removed from his programme in September, returned to appeal to the agricultural interest; in Liverpool he stressed the protection of shipping and ship-building, and Lancashire industries generally; the metal industries were selected at Birmingham on 4 November—coal and steel at Cardiff on the 20th. Liverpool received a powerful appeal to the working class: though the TUC had recently condemned his policy, trade unionism, the protection of labour, he claimed, had as its inevitable corollary protection of labour's products, and the choice lay between the 'demon of cheapness', and employment and high wages. The campaign concluded with a rousing imperial speech in the City of London on 19 January. 'The struggle for life, the struggle for existence in future will not be between cities or even between kingdoms. It will be between mighty empires; and the minor states will come off badly if they are left to be crushed between the gigantic bulk of these higher organizations.' Britain must abandon a narrow conception of nationalism and 'Learn to think imperially'.

It was a grand vision, parallel in many ways to that of modern European integrationists—the amalgamation of nations into a single economic, political, and military unit, powerful in world affairs and transcending parochial national boundaries. Its inspiration was the imperial and economic success of the German and American federations, and the desire to ensure that Britain held her own in a world dominated by these new powers. But American unification was inspired by a war of liberty—German unification under threat of two great powers on her flanks and by Prussian military might—'Europe' has arisen out of fear of a mighty Russia in the East, and of reliving two world wars and the greatest economic depression of recent times. Did comparable conditions exist for imperial union? Chamberlain believed so—his opponents called him alarmist, and claimed Britain's economic health and imperial strength to be still firmly grounded. With some justification, he was accused of wanting to deny autonomy to the colonies which they would not accept. And though messages of support reached him from the colonies, he did publicly exaggerate the extent of their commitment to the 'imperial idea'. The conflict between imperial centralization and colonial fiscal and political independence had been thrashed out at successive conferences, and invariably tilted towards the latter. Chamberlain did not believe the problems insurmountable, and Commonwealth co-operation during two world wars and the depression showed the validity of this belief. But he did see largely what Empire would do for Britain, and exaggerated what it would do for the colonies.

Would the Empire, however, help Britain? There was a wide agreement that military co-operation would, but the chief problem was economics. Here Chamberlain had, confusingly, to deliver appeals for national sacrifice to promote long-term benefits with the promise of immediate gains to British industry and agriculture from tariffs. Otherwise the election would be lost. On this he sowed the wind, and soon found he had reaped a whirlwind. Academic economists and financial experts launched against him; Liberal politicians denounced a policy of what Lloyd George called 'dear food and cheap offal', and Asquith made his reputation by pursuing Chamberlain round the country to counter his arguments in detail. The crude statistics of the time were used and abused by both sides to argue over the problems of Britain's trade balance—Chamberlain sinned greatly by taking invalid years for comparison and exasperated Hewins, his chief economic adviser, by refusing to have figures checked in advance. Opponents argued that retaliation or protection would only marginally affect the trade balance because most British imports were of raw materials which Balfour had declared would not be taxed, and that Chamberlain had exaggerated the compensation provided by colonial markets for declining foreign exports—many goods had gone to specific areas for temporary reasons like the now flagging mining boom in South Africa. Trade to the colonies was still minute in comparison with total exports and, critics argued, certainly not worth an upheaval in Britain's policy. Chamberlain was forced to present his programme as a set of minor changes having major implications, but if the condition of the nation was so bad, and imperial relations at a turning point, would minor changes help? If they solved the problem, could the danger be as great as Chamberlain claimed? If they did not, would there not be an irresistible slide down the slope of protection, as Devonshire had claimed? Were not declining industries simply unprofitable and inefficient? Dumping was, by its nature, a temporary phenomenon (though 'I don't suppose I can hold Mr. Asquith's head under water for ever—but I can hold it there long enough to drown him'). Chamberlain claimed to be looking to the future, but was he not clinging to a past ideal of Britain as workshop of the world? Asides against 'jam and pickles' were no response to the problem of coping with changes in consumer taste and industrial techniques. Unemployment, Liberals stressed increasingly, was best tackled through labour exchanges and industrial retraining, and working-class welfare by land, tax, educational and temperance reforms, thereby turning Chamberlain of the 1880s and 1890s against Chamberlain of the 1900s. He claimed that juggling with tariffs would avoid cost of living increases, but this appeared a tendentious claim, and, with the price index rising, was not controlling prices of more immediate interest to the poor worker and fixed-salary middle classes?

Contemporary judges concluded that Asquith got the better of his detailed intellectual debate with Chamberlain. But the debate had wider significance. At its heart lay a conflict of interpretation over Britain's industrial future, and over the need for direct government intervention in economic exchange rather than adherence to free exchange in a protectionist world. Chamberlain's was a too-simple panacea for the problems of decline in Britain's old staple industries; it neglected the possibility of the new consumer durable industries taking their place, and understated the problems of dislocation involved in shifting, however gradually, an economy so tied to general world-wide trade towards an imperial system. Yet he saw a problem in Britain's future where his opponents saw none, or which they were inclined to underestimate; like modern Europeans of the 1970s, Chamberlain forecast Britain's inevitable decline into an aged industrial backwater and regarded economic integration as the only available option, whatever its difficulties. Perhaps his problem was that he foresaw this too clearly, and too early; British workers and the British electorate still regarded the world as their oyster, and Chamberlain's campaign was to polarize opinion largely against imperial integration before the full impact of Britain's economic weaknesses became manifest in the wake of two world wars.

That this would be the outcome was not obvious in the winter of 1903–4: 'Joe's electric strength carries all before it,' Churchill commented after Glasgow.[34] The Unionists attached to the Free Food League were in major difficulties. They were united against Chamberlain, but on little else. Many wanted a good fight, and Winston Churchill and Hugh Cecil ventured into Birmingham as Lord Randolph and Lloyd George had done earlier, to retreat almost as rapidly. But Devonshire, though accepting the Presidency of the League, insisted, with only partial success, that there should be no opposition to the government or the retaliation policy. He wanted to be a 'drag on the wheel', he claimed. Beach, under pressure in his Bristol constituency, went even further and joined Balfour on the same platform in mid-November. Free traders were furious at the opportunity presented for Chamberlain to welcome growing party unity on tariff reform, Devonshire particularly so since Beach was pre-empting the role of sympathetic critic he wished to play. It also led Campbell-Bannerman to the welcome observation that the free traders were 'time-servers almost to a man'.[35] Lord James and Churchill, in severe difficulties with his Oldham party and a shrewd observer of his father's career, were the chief advocates of closer relations with the Liberals to carve out a Devonshire–Rosebery alliance which would place them in the centre of the arena. Devonshire was brought into negotiations during the winter, but they proved unsuccessful. Hugh Cecil observed in December that, apart from a few exceptional cases, 'no free trade Unionist is likely to be returned to the next Parliament unless by the help of the Opposition', and was angling to vote with the Liberals in a division. But Campbell-Bannerman,

unlike Salisbury in 1886, could not be pushed to give the necessary electoral guarantees, wary, as Salisbury had once been, of
being dished in a realignment of the Centre. Though tempting
dissident Unionists, he was waiting to see 'how many of the 53
are really in earnest and have the courage of their opinions',
in the belief that 'we are under no necessity to go to them and
indeed cannot go to them: it is they who must come to us.'[36] As
subsequent parliamentary events were to show, only half of the
'53' were 'in earnest'—a number insufficient, unlike 1886, to
warrant Opposition moves in their direction when Campbell-
Bannerman was regaining control through the growing unity
over free trade.

Chamberlain meantime was gaining in strength. Vince's
pamphlets were flooding the Unionist grass roots, and Chaplin
noted in late November that elections to the Conservative
Union executive had produced a Chamberlainite majority. A
Liberal Unionist area conference at Newcastle, meeting just
before Chamberlain's speech there, had ignored an appeal
from Devonshire to reject a Chamberlainite motion. The party
was slipping away from him, and he tried to check it by reaffirming a 'neutrality' pact he and Chamberlain had agreed
upon in June. But, when he and forty free traders met on 10
December and issued a statement urging Unionist voters not
to support by-election candidates advocating the full programme, Chamberlain determined to challenge him. Three
December by-elections were won with good majorities by adherents to his policy, a major boost after eighteen months bad
results, and throughout the new year he fought to wrest control
of the Liberal Unionist Party. On 18 May he finally secured a
definite vote from its council in favour of a democratic reorganization of the party and the withdrawal of support from
any candidate opposed to government policy on tariffs.
Devonshire and his allies had been turned out of their own
party, and refused to join the reorganized association. Chamberlain became President, with Selborne and a reluctant
Lansdowne as vice-Presidents. The latter tried to persuade him
to be content with a moderate programme, but at its first mass
meeting on 14 July 1904 the full imperial preference policy was
approved. The Tariff Reform League was meanwhile building
a powerful organization with huge funds, and being used to

good effect. Of the by-elections Chamberlain had noted that 'Pearson [its chairman] told the agents of the candidates that, unless the latter made a strong declaration, the whole Tariff Reform machinery would be removed, the offices closed, and the meetings abandoned.'[37]

Even by early 1904, however, the campaign was beginning to falter. Though Tariff Reform frequently presented itself as a new political movement, in reality it always remained a Unionist pressure group, and its advocates were inevitably dragged down by the problems and rapidly fading appeal of the government. The fillip Liberalism had received from the educational and tariff controversies was bolstered by the un-popular 1904 Licensing Act, and by the new agitation over that 'terminological inexactitude', Chinese Slavery—the importa-tion of unskilled Chinese labour into the South African mines, a policy rejected by Chamberlain when Colonial Secretary but accepted by his successor, Alfred Lyttelton, and exploited by Labour and Liberal politicians to imply that Britain would be the next target for cheap immigrant workers. Chamberlain himself had abandoned the platform for discussions on a com-mission he had established to formulate a 'scientific tariff', and from February to April he was abroad resting after warnings about his health. In February he had suffered a serious per-sonal blow with the loss of his close friend Powell Williams, whose death, Chamberlain feared, had been brought on by the enormous increase in work imposed upon him as his chief political agent on all the tariff reform committees. Chamber-lain had also banked for electoral success on a development of the economic recession which set in during 1902, but trade figures early in 1904 foreshadowed a growth in activity which lasted until 1906. Further, the atmosphere of international crisis, so important in generating appeals for imperial solidarity, was no longer being reinforced by the alarums and excursions of the 1890s, and the German ambassador commented that 'if all the signs are not misleading, England is in full reaction against the Jingoism of the Chamberlain epoch.'

Chamberlain had said that, if he resigned on the full pro-gramme, he believed the government would be forced to move in his direction. The crucial question, therefore, was how Bal-four would react to the winter campaign. Austen soon found the answer. Pressing Balfour to denounce the free-fooders' by-election letter in December, he was warned that their flirtation with the Liberals made the moderate Sheffield programme vital, and at Manchester in January Balfour appealed for party unity, tolerance for its 'weaker brethren', and reasserted the present impracticability of preference. He had not become leader of the Unionist Party to preside over its disintegration, and, so he said later, was determined to retain office to ensure that the vital measures of army reform, *entente* with France and Japan, educational reform, and an imperial defence committee were implemented. These, though plausible reasons, were also useful. If the government fell and went into opposition or returned with a reduced majority, Chamberlain's position would be strong—delay might allow his campaign to run out of steam and rally moderate enthusiasts to the official leadership. In this, Devonshire's loss proved to be an asset. He provided a figurehead for moderate free-traders who would oppose the government only if it went for the full programme. A Liberal motion on tariffs brought an early division in the 1904 Parliament from which Balfour was conveniently absent, ill, and ministers made conflicting policy statements. The nominal majority of 100 fell to fifty-one, with twenty-seven free-traders voting against it and twelve abstaining. J. S. Sandars could point the lesson that 'only Sheffield save us. If we avoid frightening or irritating these 25 Unionists [free-trade government supporters] we shall carry on. If we alarm or annoy them on the fiscal question they can turn us out at a moment's notice.'[38]

Chamberlain was in fact encountering strong resistance. The Whips and Central Office were 'more Balfourite than Mr. Balfour himself', said Mrs Chamberlain, the latter refusing to accept inclusion of a Tariff Reform League representative and firmly resisting its pressure on local associations. Chamberlain-ite MPs had behaved well in the parliamentary division, said Sandars, which persuaded the Whips to counter a further Liberal motion in March with an amendment rejecting food taxes, protection, and preference. This, however, Chamberlain's followers could not take. After strong protest, the amendment was withdrawn and, though Beach supported the government, twenty-four Unionists voted against.

The disturbing implications of this were not lost on Chamberlain, resting abroad at the time. Noting that worsening by-election results were undermining his supporters' morale, he also observed that Balfour had 'plainly pledged himself to go to the country on retaliation and *nothing more*': yet, 'In no case am I going to fight against Balfour's government. I would much rather go out of politics'.[39] This decision was in fact dictated by circumstances. His cabinet adherents were settling down to the business of governing, and he was soon complaining that 'not one' was now willing to withdraw on his account—a tribute to Balfour's careful wooing of Austen to detach him from his father. In the Commons and the country, he could command a large force only by promising Balfour's ultimate conversion to a 'whole-hog' policy once the free traders were destroyed, but if he attacked Balfour it would split down the middle, and leave him weakened and isolated; and, as he readily acknowledged, there was 'nowhere else to go'.

How, then, was he to deal with Balfour's unwillingness to move beyond retaliation? The answer to this was also an answer to the problems of declining Unionist popularity and the danger of gradually losing the initiative. It was to bring the government down, and use the now anticipated period of opposition to restructure the party. But, given the costs involved in doing this himself, his only choice lay in making the free-traders do it for him, and this meant pinning Balfour to a statement of policy—any statement of policy, whether encompassing the 'full' programme or not—which would unite the free-traders in a division. Conversely, of course, Balfour had to rebuff his attempts without alienating moderate tariff reformers. As in 1886, the years 1904–5 were to see a process of 'diamond cut diamond'.

A discussion with Balfour in mid-April after his return from resting abroad convinced Chamberlain of his earlier judgement, and in speeches throughout 1904 he sought to consolidate his forces to apply pressure on Balfour with claims that 'victories in politics are like victories in war: they are won by enthusiasm; they are lost by timidity', and that 'a fighting policy will have the best chance and . . . the whole-hogger will beat the half-hearter.' Privately he was canvassing the view that 'the Unionist Party will be defeated next time [and] my efforts and hopes are directed to the election after next', while publicly building up support for a view that 'the general election . . . is coming within a reasonable time, and I do not myself think that it ought to be delayed beyond a reasonable time.' The question of colonial preference, he claimed, 'is ripe, at any rate, to be submitted to the people of this country.'[40]

In August and September Austen, too, was pressing for an early election, and also for Balfour's adoption of a plan, suggested by his father in an earlier Commons debate, for the calling of a Colonial Conference free to discuss preference. This he claimed as a 'bridge' over which to move closer to Chamberlain. Sandars commented that it was 'Not a bridge for the great mass of the party . . . Personally I think . . . Joe has failed. Austen's letter shows that he knows he has, and that he wants to save what he can at some price.'[41] Balfour was more wary of Chamberlain's strength, and also shrewder in recognizing that the request was too reasonable and moderate for outright refusal, but that, since such a conference would inevitably support preference, the free-traders would be compelled to reject the proposal on principle. He retaliated by accepting the scheme, but insisting that it required a 'double election'—one giving a mandate for the conference, the other for its decisions. Chamberlain protested at this 'insincere' suggestion, and Austen meekly threatened resignation were it adopted. But Balfour must have relished this product of his ingenuity, which moved in the direction of preference without entailing definite pledges, put off the controversial food tax question, and outbid Chamberlain's democratic rhetoric with an even more democratic proposal. He announced it at Edinburgh on 3 October as a programme capable of restoring party unity.

Chamberlain was furious, but, determined 'to put my own interpretation on Balfour's words and to accept them in the sense which I give to them', at Luton two days later he welcomed Edinburgh as a great advance towards his own position. The pledge of a double election was the 'only blemish', and this over simply 'perhaps a point of tactics'. Free-traders were thrown into confusion, but eventually reconciled themselves to Balfour's principle despite Chamberlain's deliberate attempt to antagonize them. The amusing consequence was that when they put up the Edinburgh principle as an amendment to a tariff reform motion at the Conservative Union conference, it was rejected, and Balfour only covered his embarrassment with a speech wholly ignoring the tariff question.

Chamberlain meanwhile was engaged on a second great campaign in the country. At Welbeck in August, Luton in October, and Gainsborough in February he pressed a strong protectionist line to largely agricultural audiences; in December at Limehouse he coupled industrial protection with the protection of labour by immigration restrictions; at Preston in January he tried to convince Lancashire not to anticipate continued prosperity for its cotton industries. His mood was now swinging erratically between optimism and despair; his health was suffering, and a further blow came with the death of his daughter Ethel. Balfour's sophistical treatment of the tariff question became increasingly frustrating.

The new year saw a further chance to break the *impasse*. In reply to a taunt from Morley to summarize his ambiguous fiscal policy, Balfour did so on 'a half-sheet of notepaper' as four principles—fiscal freedom, closer imperial commercial relations, an open colonial conference, and no rise in domestic food prices. Omission of the double election pledge dangled tempting bait before Chamberlain and he nibbled, writing Balfour on 12 February 1905 to request a private meeting to discuss policy—only their second since his resignation. To strengthen this appearance of a reconciliation, he reiterated in the Commons on 16 February his claim that their differences were 'on a point of method and not . . . of principle', and reasserted his desire for an early election.

He and Balfour met on the next day, and extended their discussions in subsequent correspondence. Chamberlain's line was aggressive, criticizing Balfour's flaccid policy and Central Office interference in by-elections, and stressing the advantages of advocating a general tariff rather than simply 'fiscal freedom'. The points were evaded or rebuffed, clearing the ground for the crucial double election issue. Chamberlain hankered after a clear disavowal which would drive the free-traders into opposition, and Balfour admitted that Chamberlain's approach 'seems incomparably simpler, more convenient, and more effective than mine'. But he reiterated an earlier objection that the colonial governments themselves would want an electoral decision on any conference agreements, and emphasized the point with which Chamberlain had never really come to grips: 'The prejudice against a small tax on food is not the fad of a few imperfectly informed theorists; it is a deep-rooted prejudice affecting the large mass of voters, especially the poorest class', and it was this, not Central Office pressure, which influenced by-election candidates. Edinburgh was vital to allay electoral fears until the *pros* as well as the *cons* of preference could be presented to the country. Chamberlain could respond only with his standard argument that the 'half-hearters' acquired all the opprobium for advocating fiscal reform without being able to counter with a 'whole-hog' cry, and 'In my experience the ordinary voter never cares for details. He seizes upon a principle or large issue'.[42]

Despite the worries of free-traders, the discussions came to nought, leaving the Commons situation still fluid and the Opposition with fine opportunities to attack. Churchill, now sitting on the Liberal benches after an adverse decision from his local party, put down a motion on tariffs in early March, followed later in the month and in early April by further Liberal ones designed to fragment Unionism. Chamberlain was for taking a strong line to help them do this. He demanded a direct negative to Churchill's motion and, when the government rejected this tactic in favour of moving the previous question, insisted on the same treatment for the four subsequent ones. Balfour and the Whips, claiming that on at least two this would entail defeat, initially hoped to satisfy everyone by allowing a free vote, and, despite a rearguard action from Austen in cabinet, finally decided to solve the government's problems with the humiliating technique of total abstention from all four votes.

Chamberlain's fury knew no bounds, though he had made sure of avoiding direct embarrassment to himself by taking a rest cure from 'flu in Folkestone. Consequent adverse press comment on the government's tactics, and strong pressure from his militant supporters, decided him upon a tougher line. Calling together his parliamentary followers on 13 April, he won support for a memorandum to Balfour containing a breakdown of the factions in the House, which claimed 172 professed preferentialists, 98 retaliationists, some possibly for preference,

73 for preference if it were official policy, 27 free-traders, most about to retire, and 4 others. Criticizing Balfour's failure to take a firm stand, it further approved the 'half-sheet of notepaper' principles but called for greater 'clarity' through definite commitment to a general tariff, direct assistance to agriculture, preference, and the abandonment of the double election pledge.

Balfour set out to meet this strong challenge with a danger-ous tactical exercise. Summoning a meeting for 16 May with Chamberlain, Lansdowne, and Herbert Maxwell, a leading Chamberlain supporter but also a loyal Unionist MP, he made the devastating offer that fiscal reform, with preference and a general tariff, should be '*the* foremost article in the programme submitted by the Unionists at the approaching General Elec-tion'. Maxwell then suggested a way to escape the double election commitment: the next regular colonial conference, due in 1906, should constitute the 'open' conference on tariffs, with an election delayed until afterwards to provide the man-date on its decisions. How Maxwell came to formulate this plan is unclear, though it had been suggested in a speech on 12 May by Broderick, a pro-Balfour minister. Its adoption, however, might benefit both sides. Since Chamberlain would now have the official policy he wanted, Balfour would have the tariff re-formers tied firmly to keeping him in office for at least a year. Conversely, and perhaps more important for Chamberlain, it might force the free-traders to turn the ministry out immedi-ately He tried to seal the arrangement by offering to re-enter the government in an office without salary or portfolio.

Balfour had other things in mind than being swallowed by Chamberlain's Leviathan. Questioned in the Commons on whether the Edinburgh pledge still held, he insisted on his free-dom to hold a colonial conference on preference if the govern-ment were still in existence. Uproar, and a suspended sitting, ensued when he refused to clarify this further. A censure motion was put down by the Liberals, and the free-fooders threatened to vote with them. Equally promptly, Balfour decided he could not keep to his new agreement. Chamberlain, formerly elated, became deeply depressed. His inclination was to walk out of the censure debate until supporters, more impressed than he by Balfour's apparently conciliatory moves, persuaded him that a statement from Balfour abandoning the double election pledge, together with the idea of a pre-election conference, might be satisfactory.

Further illness on Balfour's part delayed the censure motion and his planned speech on 2 June at the Albert Hall became the test. Once again he hedged. Meandering through his speech were proposals for a free conference, 'some power to negotiate effectively' with protectionist countries, and a statement that electoral defeat would undermine the rationale for a double election on preference. Austen welcomed this as a major advance—his father saw it as a further wet blanket. And, though on the following day at St. Helens he translated Balfour's points into the clear statements of the 16 May agreement, and was later supported in this by Lansdowne, Balfour publicly rejected having his speeches interpreted for him.

He had in fact emerged, ill and exhausted, but triumphant. His conciliatory gestures had divided Chamberlain's forces and averted open attack without allowing the free-fooders to unite against him. Chamberlain was reduced to frustrated inactivity for the next few months, though taking a swipe at Balfour before the massed Tariff Reform League in July by claiming that the reformers were 'not a party organization . . . We are outside party considerations', and scathingly denouncing those 'afraid to commit themselves prematurely' who would later take advantage of the advance guard's success. The government he believed 'worn out—they stumble at every step', but, though wanting 'a dissolution this summer', 'I must not . . . be quoted as holding this opinion' for fear of appearing disloyal.[43] His attitude to the government was one of sullen non-co-operation, a refusal either to quarrel with it and to 'put Balfour with his back to the wall', or to seek further compromise.

In October Balfour passed on the information that he was intent on engineering the government's resignation soon after the beginning of the 1906 session. But, not content with having fended off Chamberlain's assaults, he was also now seeking to rally party unity by dishing him altogether. Rumours that free-fooders were intent on delivering divisive speeches from Liberal platforms in the winter must have convinced him that an early dissolution was inevitable; it also led him to call for united opposition to the dangers of socialist and Home Rule legislation from the Liberals. Lord Londonderry, who, according to Chamberlain, was 'stupid', put the implications of this bluntly by calling publicly for the relegation of tariff reform behind a negative campaign against the Liberal menace. Chamberlain denounced this line on 3 November, and used it to castigate the government's tactics in the recent session, and thereby to bully it into an early resignation. His speech did in fact lead to a cabinet row, though the combatants were eventually persuaded, in Sandars's words, 'to remain bound in the gossamer web of the chief's dexterities'. Balfour extended a further friendly hand to Chamberlain, but it was rebuffed, and his appeal for unity at the Tory party conference in the face of a pro-Chamberlain motion fell on stony ground. Chamberlain's retaliation at his own party conference that 'No army was ever led successfully to battle on the principle that the lamest man should govern the march of the army' perhaps convinced Balfour that he dare not face a new session. Influenced by corresponding discord between Campbell-Bannerman and Rosebery on Irish policy, he handed in his resignation on 4 December. The Liberals successfully formed a new government and dissolved.

Chamberlain's electoral campaign was built around the full programme and the League effectively acted as an alternative headquarters to Central Office for many Tory candidates. His own activities were confined almost entirely to the Midlands, in the hope of averting at least here what was now being anticipated as a Liberal landslide. He refused to discuss the possibilities of joint action with Balfour, who developed his recent line of thought by relegating tariff reform to second place in his election address behind opposition to Liberal measures. He spoke alongside Unionist free-traders, and backed his cousin Robert Cecil against opposition from even moderate fiscal reformers to his candidacy for Marylebone.

The state of Unionism in the election showed Chamberlain's initiative of May 1903 to have been only partially successful. He had planned to give the party, after seventeen years of power and fourteen of office, a new rationale for its existence. Opposition to Home Rule was no longer adequate, and militant imperialism clearly needed after its crescendo in 1900 a correspondingly strong domestic appeal. Apart from its intrinsic merits, tariff reform was to provide an image of Unionism as modern, dynamic, professional, replacing what Chamberlain considered the amateurism of old-fashioned whiggery and high-Toryism. In May 1903 he had banked on a swift surgical operation to eject his hard-line conservative opponents, a rapid reorientation of policy, and an early election while the radical adventure provided a glamorous aura with which to isolate old-fashioned Liberalism. Instead, Balfour and Devonshire had worked to block his progress and force his retirement. They had then turned what Chamberlain hoped would be a rapid propagation of his unauthorized programme, leading to an early election, into a prolonged period of trench warfare. The impetus of his campaign began to flounder. Even in 1904 Hewins, Amery, and Garvin had founded an association of Compatriots to preserve the pristine state of the imperial vision against tendencies towards protectionism and crude economism —what Balfour called 'Joe's method of bribing every class of the country in turn' and symbolized by Chamberlain's increasing emphasis on a general tariff and measures to assist agriculture—imposed by the need to preserve the dynamic of the campaign. The 'men who were in earnest' controlled the Liberal Unionist Party and the Conservative Union, and might count on up to 200 MPs; but, as the electoral fortunes of the party slumped and the conflict between Chamberlain and Balfour grew, Balfour could consolidate his hold on what Chamberlain called the 'university classes' among whom he had never been strong, and capitalize on the worries of those who came to believe Chamberlain 'more a fanatic than a statesman'. Balfour bluffed, temporized, twisted and turned to keep intact the balance of forces in the old Unionist Party, and let his government slide into contempt and electoral disaster. The country was seething for change, Garvin had observed in 1902, and Balfour had been appointed by the ruling Tory families precisely to control it: after 1903, to preserve the kind of party which would keep him as leader, he allowed it to crumble under his feet.

Chamberlain's contribution to this disintegrative process was not simply in offering a challenge to a fiscal orthodoxy held with almost religious fervour and to Britain's popular cheap-food policies: an election in 1904 on fiscal reform might well

have been just won, or at least succeeded by victory within a
few years given the weakness of contemporary Liberalism. It
was rather that Chamberlain was too powerful and too controversial a figure for any dramatic initiative of his to be
evaluated without rousing strong personal and political an-
tagonisms among senior Unionists, and hence too weak to
carry the initiative through except at great cost. There is an
interesting contrast to 1903 in later Conservative history. In
1960 the Prime Minister Harold Macmillan faced two problems
—Britain's economic and financial difficulties, and how to
maintain popular support after three successive election victories for the party. Within two years he had disbanded the old
Empire and committed Britain to European integration,
abandoned *laissez-faire* domestic policies for moderate *dirigisme*,
and sacked his Chancellor and a third of his cabinet to promote
a band of young professional politicians. Chamberlain had
attempted a comparable feat in the context of early twentieth-
century politics to 'modernize' his party, but he created havoc
where Macmillan only just failed. Macmillan's advantage lay
in holding the premiership, and his ostentatiously Balfourian
public manner symbolized his recognition of Balfour's view
that, in the context of a rather unadventurous Tory party,
necessary radical changes had to be undertaken from a position
well to the right of centre. Unlike Macmillan, though, Balfour
had a Chamberlain with which to contend. Always in danger
of having his own radicalism compromised by Chamberlain's
overenthusiastic advocacy, he was compelled to pay far more
deference to conservative elements in the party than he would
otherwise have wished. And of course, it was precisely because
the 'old guard' feared Chamberlainite enthusiasm and could
not accept him as one of their own that Chamberlain was
never in the running for the premiership which ultimately he
needed to carry through his plans.

CHAPTER 10

Radicals and Reactionaries. 1906–1914

The election of January 1906 devastated the Unionist Party. From 334 seats, its representation fell to 157. Birmingham itself was hard-pushed to maintain the seven Unionist MPs. The new government could command 401 Liberals and Lib-Labs in a majority independent of its uncertain allies, the 83 Nationalists and 29 Independent Labour members. Chamberlain had sought a mandate for tariff reform, and been rebuffed on an over 80 per cent poll. Inevitably, the losers began to search for explanations for this overthrow of twenty years' right-wing hegemony in British politics.

To Balfour and the free-fooders the reason was clear: Chamberlain's persistence with radical fiscal reform had restored Liberal unity and morale after a decade of stagnation and disharmony, divided Unionism, and alienated not only the moderate centre of politics but also formerly loyal supporters. The result was not so much a vote for Liberalism, as one against Chamberlain, delivered by a working-class electorate fearing food price increases and by the middle classes of the spas, the suburbs, and the counties, apprehensive of unpredictable consequences from an economic upheaval. To these charges Chamberlain reacted with predictable vehemence. Party divisions, he agreed, had contributed, but here 'the uncertainty as to Balfour's views has handicapped us seriously and has prevented our new policy from being put forward with the conviction and earnestness which alone could have made it a strong steadying influence.' He had to admit, though, that his own supporters had fared little better than those of other factions. Balfour, his brother, Gerald, and members of the Cecil connection were all defeated, but so too were Chamberlainites like Bonar Law and Lyttleton. It was calculated that the party now comprised 109 Chamberlainites, 32 Balfourites, 11 Free Fooders and 5 waverers—Balfour's men being squeezed out particularly in marginal seats where they thought ambivalence would pay. Chamberlain, however, insisted that 'my information is uniformly to the effect that the new proposals . . . were the only ones that excited keen interest and enthusiasm on the part of our supporters.' Furthermore, 'Even among our opponents many were convinced of the necessity of a change, but they were not sufficiently won over to make it the sole issue or to vote with the party to whom on so many other grounds they were strongly opposed.' Education and 'Chinese Slavery' headed his list of issues deflecting electoral interest—which of course avoided the fact that it had been in part precisely to avert attack on such issues that tariff reform had been initially mobilized.[1]

Chamberlain attributed defeat most of all to electoral repugnance at a party which had grown increasingly stale during its long tenure of office. Certainly Unionism's 'image' had suffered badly in recent years, and Campbell-Bannerman had successfully exploited the pessimistic post-war mood of national self-examination to contrast the erratic performance of a waning ministry with the promise of a revitalized Liberal leadership aiming at the secure, dependable goals of 'Peace, Retrenchment, Reform'. This, however, was not the whole story. In the huge turnout of 1906, the Liberals doubled their vote of 1900 to three million, but Unionism gained 800,000 votes for a total of two and a half million. Technical and organizational reasons partly help explain this, but it is hard to see apathy and disillusion as defeating Unionism. What indeed the government of 1900 had done was to realize an objective that Chamberlain had set himself as long ago as the 1870s, though greatly to its cost. By its actions it had subsumed the distinct debates which had formerly characterized campaigns in individual local constituencies to a national debate on a few select questions around which the whole general election had pivoted. For the first time, virtually every seat was disputed by the two main parties. The era of the modern election had begun.

Chamberlain might take heart from the fact that, if tariff reform had yet to prove itself an election winner, there was no reason to believe that it had not rallied extra support for his party. But he could not ignore the implications of views held by Balfour. Balfour had latterly sought to reunite the party in the face of the menace of Radical and Socialist legislation; subsequently he accounted the advent of independent Labour MPs as the major event of the election. This pointed to two factors: in 1906 Unionism's working-class electorate was decimated, much to Labour's advantage; and, just as Liberalism's electoral gains represented a conservative reaction against Unionist challenges to the *status quo* in fiscal, education, and trade-union affairs, so Unionism's increased poll might represent a conservative reaction to more radical changes threatened from the left.[2] The political strategy entailed by any such pessimistic assessment of the electorate's radicalism was 'wait and see', and it was one which Chamberlain himself in practice readily acknowledged: 'The disaster has been complete,' he told Field-Marshal Roberts, 'but I agree with you that there must be a speedy reaction. For the present we can do nothing but give our opponents rope. They will soon be able to put their theories into practice and if we are right they will soon display their inherent weakness.'[3] Fiscal reform and imperial integration were for the moment dead and buried—the government's huge majority, its hostility to the programme, and the contemporary strength of the economy made this certain. Other items would now monopolize the political agenda. It had, however, one last task to perform. With his supporters dominant in the Unionist rump and Balfour ejected from his seat, Chamberlain now held the whip hand in the Commons. But, pressed to seize the party leadership, he eschewed fighting Balfour out in the open 'both on personal grounds and also because I feel that without his influence I could not hope in what remains to me of active life to restore the Party to its old efficiency and predominance.'[4] In believing that the game of ousting Balfour would not have been worth the candle if it generated a hostile 'cave', Chamberlain, not for the first time since 1886, was perhaps being over-cautious: a clean, open, break in 1906 might have proved more satisfactory for the party than the debilitating and ultimately unsuccessful attempts of the next five years to paper over the cracks. As it was, Chamberlain, presumably believing that Balfour would now have to pay the full price for remaining leader, set out to re-create unity through reconciliation, and even compelled reluctant supprters to back Balfour's candidacy for a by-election in the City.

His campaign to secure an acknowledgement of his new position of authority opened with a letter to Balfour while the election was yet in progress recommending a party meeting to elect a temporary leader during Balfour's absence from the House.[5] Intent on avoiding this, Balfour replied inviting Chamberlain into the shadow cabinet, noting that he was the only possible stand-in, but rejecting the idea of a meeting which would effectively provide the formal Unionist approval of Chamberlain and his policy he had fought to avert for three years. Chamberlain was insistent. He threatened not to join the shadow cabinet were a meeting refused, and raised the further issue of amalgamating Liberal Unionist and Conservative organizations, of which 'one result would be that we should be able to democratize local Conservative associations by introducing our system of voluntary workers chosen from the working classes and getting rid of the existing system of privilege for subscribers and so-called men of influence'. Balfour was warned, as were the management committees of the League and the Liberal Unionists in early February, that a split was inevitable unless the parliamentary party were given its opportunity to decide between the 'official' and 'unofficial' programmes in the latter's favour.

At a meeting of 2 February he and Balfour failed to reach agreement. Balfour, opposing both organizational reform and a party meeting, argued for the creation of party unity by demoting fiscal issues and concentrating on straight opposition to government policy, but, while privately acknowledging the inevitability of this course, Chamberlain was determined on first securing public recognition of his achievements over the previous three years. He began threatening a secession of his group, though warning supporters against turning the issue into an explicitly personal battle between himself and Balfour.

This was hard to avoid with speculation on a fight for the leadership rife in the press. As the assailant, Chamberlain was under pressure to close ranks in defeat, and his demand for innovatory procedures to decide policy and party organization were poorly received in a party of strong hierarchical traditions.

He eventually felt compelled to discard his strongest threat against Balfour with an open letter declaring himself 'not a candidate' for the leadership, insisting, however, on the price of party reorganization and a clear decision on fiscal policy. Balfour, too, was becoming anxious to avoid an open conflict. On 6 February he wrote accepting the demand for a party meeting, though quibbling with the suggestion that peers and defeated candidates should attend, which would strengthen Chamberlain's support and compel his own attendance and acquiescence in its decisions. He also posed a pertinent question: what would the procedure be for a meeting whose traditional role was to secure party acceptance for leadership policies? Chamberlain, claiming that 'I do not think that we could allow ourselves to be guided by precedent,' replied that 'I take it that, as matters stand, and assuming—*if I must assume* —that we can come no nearer, the choice lies between the "half sheet of notepaper" and the Glasgow programme.'[6] The appeal for prior agreement contained in italics was reinforced by the suggestion that decisions made would not be binding on the leadership but 'merely taken for information'.

With this and the publication of Chamberlain's letter disavowing leadership ambitions, Balfour set out to exploit his concessions. The meeting would have the task of expressing only 'general aspirations' on the organization question, he said, since he was establishing a party committee to consider it. In addition he observed that a choice between their policies would effectively be one between alternative leaders. He himself could not carry on if defeated and Chamberlain's position subsequently, he warned, would be equally embarrassing. Chamberlain responded to the threat, pleading for an agreed policy and offering a draft resolution for the meeting which declared fiscal reform to be the 'first constructive work' of the party. Details of the policy need not yet be settled, but the general aims were fair trade and imperial commercial union, with a general tariff and corn duties in principle unobjectionable. He, Austen, Balfour, Gerald Balfour and the party managers agreed to meet in anticipation of the party meeting arranged for 15 February, two days after Parliament's reassembly. Here, however, Balfour dug in his heels, refusing to have a vote which formally disavowed his own previous policy and hence inevitably excommunicated free-food and retaliationist opinion.

Austen came up with the solution. On 14 February an exchange of letters between Chamberlain and Balfour—the 'Valentine's Day compact'—was published expressing their policy agreement, which left the meeting with the task only of noting the correspondence and expressing confidence in Balfour's continued leadership of the party.

Contemporary comment on the procedure invariably pointed to it as Chamberlain's triumph. Balfour's public letter contained a full statement of Chamberlain's policy, and in fact repeated almost word for word Chamberlain's draft of 10 February for a resolution, with the caveat that tariffs should not be imposed 'for the purpose of' raising prices or protecting specific industries, and a declared intention that fiscal policy should cease any longer to divide the party. Moreover, while Chamberlain privately described the letter as less 'definite' than he would have liked, he was soon eagerly telling supporters that 'we have arrived at what is now the programme, the definite official programme of the party.' Cynics observed that, though Balfour remained leader and the party had not officially voted for a 'whole-hog' policy, the leadership was held on sufferance and the Tariff Reform League was in effective control of the Unionist Party. In practice, however, given that Balfour emerged from the election weaker than almost any other modern British party leader, he had proved remarkably resilient in defence. By a dogged refusal to stand down or to approve a formal vote on policy, he had thrown Chamberlain himself on the defensive; by conceding in advance the outlines of Chamberlain's programme, he bound the tariff reformers formally to declare their confidence in him, certain in his mind that he could continue walking the tightrope of 1903–6 and, by exploiting the post-election situation, regain his authority over the party and devalue the significance of his chief colleague.

The first few months of the new government, however, confirmed Chamberlain in his position of strength. Before Balfour's return to the House in mid-March he commanded the defeated party as temporary leader in a fighting style welcome to the dispirited backbenchers. Balfour's own first speech on returning

proved disastrous to his reputation as the most skilful parliamentarian of his generation, when Campbell-Bannerman dismissed his convoluted tactics over fiscal policy as 'foolery'. The
same debate also showed Unionism to be as divided and uncertain as in previous sessions when Balfour rejected Chamberlain's suggestion to meet a government motion on the tariff
question with a statement of the alternative policy and offered
instead a bromide resolution aimed at maximizing the
Unionist vote.

As expected, however, fiscal questions soon gave place on the
political agenda to others. The Unionist leaders were determined to meet the government's programme with the tactics of
1892–5, and the Lords were soon busy emasculating its
measures. For Chamberlain, however, this negative approach
was as unsatisfactory as it had been in that earlier period. As
always, he was intent on offering a forceful statement of that
'secular, materialist' ideology which he believed modern
parties must possess to remain in contact with the mass electorate. His first success had been over the government's 1906
Education Bill which denied denominational schools their
special status under the 1902 Act. It was a Nonconformist-
inspired Bill which produced immediate reaction from Anglican and Catholic interests. Yet Chamberlain successfully
persuaded leading Anglican supporters and MPs, and eventually Balfour himself, not to stand simply by the 1902 principle,
but to accept the principles on which he had operated Birmingham's schools from 1873–6—secular rate-aided education,
with religious teaching left to private arrangements out of
school hours. Popular among Unionists because it would keep
religious teaching away from Nonconformist local authorities
and school managers, the proposal was employed by Chamberlain to display the Bill's narrow sectarian bias, and made it hard
for the government to proceed further after the Lords applied
its surgeon's knife.

Education, however, was not Chamberlain's chief worry.
Rather it was that Liberalism would build a reputation by
pursuing those social reform policies which Unionists had so
long advocated, and so long neglected. His party had to regain
the image which he had provided for it in the mid-1890s if it
were not to be stranded in the next election, and in 1906 he

strongly criticized Lloyd George's Merchant Shipping and Workmen's Compensation Bills for their restricted application, and Asquith's retrenchment budget for failing to use the surplus to finance old age pensions. Pensions, indeed, was again becoming a key issue for him. Soon after the election Beatrice Webb heard that he was asking round for recent information on the subject,[7] and in the budget debate he revived the link of 1903, which was to emerge as a key issue in 1909, that funding social reform involved either tariffs or the 'socialist' methods of higher death duties and land taxation. In mid-June he delivered a major statement of the plans which he had for Unionism's future ideological development:

We must not make the mistake of thinking that we can or ought to ride back to power on a policy of mere negation . . . The policy of resistance, of negation, is not sufficient answer to that Socialist opinion which is growing up among us—that Socialist opinion the objects of which are, after all, worthy of earnest and even favourable consideration. But the means by which those objects are promoted are open to serious objections. We can only meet Socialism . . . by pointing out in all true sympathy the impossibility, the impracticability of the methods chosen, and by suggesting other and better methods for securing all that is good in the object sought for.[8]

If after 1906 Unionism was set on employing the destructive parliamentary tactics of 1892–5, Chamberlain himself was set on redeploying his ideological gambit of that period. Liberalism was to be outflanked with a populistic appeal to the disenchantment of working-class voters, and the middle classes wooed back into the fold by warnings of social instability and a threat to property. Over the next two years it did appear that Liberalism would tread its previous sorry path, but after 1908, Asquith and Lloyd George proved able to introduce a new dynamic with pensions and a 'socialist' budget which had proved beyond Rosebery, Harcourt, and Morley. Whether with Chamberlain's assistance Unionism could have challenged the government more effectively is a debatable point: the possibility, however, did not arise.

Many years before, he had said that, if he failed to enter Parliament by his fortieth year, he would abandon the idea of a career in national politics. In 1876 he met the deadline with only days to spare, and July 1906 was the seventieth anniversary of his own birth and the thirtieth of his parliamentary life. For the past few years the strain of an active career had begun to tell. His periods of energetic exertion still astonished friends, but the intervals of rest became longer, though still too short for advisers who warned that minor heart troubles could not be ignored, and certainly not cured by his continuing addiction to good wine, food, and black cigars. The last few years, too, had been marred by paralysing headaches which brought a halt to any work in progress for days on end. To his declining health the anniversary celebrations of July 1906 provided the final straw. For two days there were celebrations in Birmingham surpassing even those of Gladstone's 1877 visit and Bright's jubilee of 1883. On 8 July Chamberlain delivered a great speech in the Bingley Hall which he knew so well, presenting an *apologia pro vita sua*, an exaltation of Birmingham and its past political role, and a call for the nation to transmit the imperial ideal even were he himself no longer alive to promote it. Three days later he was found by his wife at Highbury struggling to move after a sudden stroke. This paralysed his right side, gradually affected his eyesight and speech and so weakened him that walking for any distance without support or working for other than very brief periods proved impossible. The public was not informed of the severity of his attack, and even close allies and friends had not seen him by mid-1907—Balfour took to eliciting medical opinion on his condition from photographs. Chamberlain held his Commons seat until 1914, for much of the time entertaining hopes of a return to politics, but his active career was over. As John Morley said, 'his ardent spirit should have gone to heaven in a chariot of fire and not in a bath chair.'

His presence, however, still continued to haunt the Unionist Party, and on occasions his active intervention played a marginal role in the politics of the next eight years. Austen replaced him as leader of the Tariff Reform movement and Liberal Unionist party, and developed the programme of linking tariff and social reform which Chamberlain had initiated until Asquith's non-contributory pensions proposals of 1908 threw Unionism into disarray. Radical Chamberlainites had opposed Austen's succession, and their prediction that his respect for Balfour and inclination always to play the game would enhance

Balfour's control over the party and the movement proved accurate. The 'Confederates' secretly worked behind a façade of party unity to attack free-fooders and moderate fiscal reformers, but with only limited effect.[9] And, without Chamberlain's threatening personality to contend with, Balfour found it possible to move towards the more extreme fiscal programme. The government's refusal to countenance tariff discussions at the 1907 Colonial Conference gave him an opportunity to launch a major attack on its imperial and fiscal narrow-mindedness, and at the party conference later that year, held symbolically in Birmingham, he gave strong hints that tariff reform would be the party's next great election issue.

Lloyd George's 1909 budget, greeted by Chamberlain with 'rueful admiration', brought the still existing tensions within Unionism to the fore. The party's sectional interests—landlords, large property owners, and the drink trade—wanted tough opposition to 'confiscatory' and 'socialist' taxation, but Balfour and Lansdowne, leader in the Lords, hesitated at resisting such measures with outright opposition. It was partly under Chamberlain's influence that the tide of opinion began to turn. In May 1909 he published a declaration of policy which was the natural consequence of his June 1906 speech: however desirable social reform was, more important was the question of whether it should be financed by taxation which would adversely affect economic enterprise or by tariffs which would promote it. His journalist followers, Garvin and Leo Maxse, developed this line in the press, stressing that Unionism must resist the budget, but that it would lose the fight without a constructive alternative. The choice had to be presented as 'Tariff Reform or Budget': and with the economy moving once again into a downturn, and after recent scare campaigns over Britain's international and defence position, the fiscal radicals believed that they could weld their policy on to the reaction to Lloyd George's proposals.

During 1909 Chamberlain, now slightly recovered and with his mind still fully active, was much consulted by Unionist leaders over tactics, and in late September at a public meeting held in Birmingham Balfour accepted the dichotomy between fiscal reform and budget, and called for an election to decide the issue. Chamberlain and his followers took this as Balfour's

final determination to rally the party around their policy, but
their welcome proved premature. It soon became clear that
Balfour wanted to produce a united front against the budget
not, as Chamberlain, opposition to the budget to promote
fiscal reform.[10]

Tactical differences had already emerged. It was universally recognized that only action by the Lords could check
the government, and Chamberlain sent a message to the
Birmingham meeting calling upon them to fulfil their constitutional duty and force an appeal to the electorate. Balfour,
though accepting this privately as the logical implication of
Unionist policy, shied away from public support of an action
which clearly flouted the convention of money Bills being un-
touchable by the Upper House. In November 1909 Chamberlain moved to London to become a centre for Unionist cabals
in the events which led to rejection of the budget in the Lords
and the subsequent election.

The result in January 1910, giving 273 seats to the Liberals'
275, with 40 for Labour and 82 for the Nationalists, proved
non-committal. Lloyd George and Chamberlain had each
hoped for clear majorities from their respective programmes,
and the stalemate could not be viewed by either with equanim-
ity. With the decisive position of the Nationalists, the price of
Liberal rule became restriction of the Lords' powers and
Home Rule. Leaders of the main parties were thrown back on
a political agenda they had consigned to cold storage a decade
and a half before. Chamberlain avowed of the result that he was
'well satisfied although I wish we had more to tell', and could
take comfort from the virtual elimination of the free-food
Unionists: but in reality it created something like despair in the
tariff reform camp, driving the most active adherents towards
increasingly intransigent postures. For, despite Balfour's earlier
statement, it was debate over the budget and the role of the
Lords which had dominated the campaign, and the fiscal issue
had played a subordinate part. In the new House a tariff reform motion was defeated by only thirty-one votes, but the
desire of radical Unionists to exploit the uncertain parliamentary balance and eject the government was frustrated by
Austen's adherence to Balfour's policy of 'wait and see'. This
was in clear opposition to Chamberlain's insistent demands for

tactics which reflected his old fighting spirit—to attack a weak government, whatever the issue, and force it to meet the electorate weak and discredited. By the time that Balfour had gone on the attack in March, the government had consolidated its position and reached firm agreement with the Nationalists.

The product of this—the Parliament Bill of 1910 curbing the veto powers of the Lords—distracted attention further from fiscal questions. Furthermore, the marginal defeat of January had determined many reformers to amend the programme in the hope of guaranteeing a future Liberal defeat. Garvin and Bonar Law initiated a move to attract working-class voters, particularly in Lancashire, by abandoning food taxes, and in November, to the fury of Chamberlain and Austen, Balfour exploited the tariff reformers' confusion to declare that preferential food taxes would never be imposed without a prior referendum. The December election, however, suggested that little had been gained. Primarily constituting a mandate on the position of the Upper House, the results retained the party balance with Liberals and Unionists each taking 272 seats, Labour and the Nationalists improving by two each. Unionism's results in Lancashire had improved, but there were losses elsewhere, particularly in rural areas where hopes of agricultural protection had been deflated even further.[11]

Within the party open conflict finally broke out over the government's ability to proceed with reform of the Lords. The decision of Balfour and Lansdowne to allow passage of the Parliament Bill under threat of a massive creation of peers produced open rebellion among die-hard 'Ditchers' led by Lord Halsbury, and their stand gained support from an important quarter. Though the tariff reformers were divided, Austen, Garvin, Leo Amery, and F. E. Smith, with Chamberlain's own full support, urged continued resistance to the Bill, and Balfour's 'betrayal' inspired the formation of a Halsbury Club (joined by many of them, though by Austen with reluctance), and Leo Maxse's parallel campaign that 'Balfour Must Go'. With a message to a meeting of the 'Ditchers' in July 1911, commending Halsbury 'because in the crisis of [his country's] fate he has refused to surrender his principles', Chamberlain put his reputation behind the campaign, and in the autumn, while Austen was seeking to restrain the attack, he pressed his son to seize the initiative and grasp for the leader-ship.

Chamberlain always professed a real affection for Balfour, but, unlike Austen, he was capable of putting this aside in moments of major political importance. Mid-1911 was one such. Balfour's conception of Unionism had always been one of a broad coalition, its factions linked through his own flexible personality, and appealing to moderate centrist opinion in the country. Much of his solid support, however, had resided among the old Tory county families who saw him as Salisbury's heir in providing a bastion against a Chamberlainite take-over of the grand old party. By 'hedging' over the Lords in 1911 Balfour, to prevent Unionism becoming identified solely with a reactionary defence of privilege, just as earlier he had fought to avoid it becoming the single-issue party of protectionism, had broken his own stronghold. The tariff reform leaders had from the beginning gathered extreme right-wing or backward-looking elements in the party among their support; by their consistent stand in 1909–11, adopted by some at least as much to increase their links with the 'old guard' as to maintain a strong fighting stance against Liberalism, they vastly increased their pool of support among conservative Unionists. Lord Salisbury, and his brothers Hugh and Robert Cecil, even began flirting with the Chamberlainite view that adopting fiscal reform might be necessary to keep Radical and socialist destruction at bay. The time was ripe, as Chamberlain recognized and had perhaps anticipated, for Balfour to be deposed. In November 1911, acknowledging the impossibility of his position, Balfour finally resigned, squeezed out, as Randolph Churchill and Lord Salisbury had squeezed out Sir Stafford Northcote in 1885, by a coalition of radicals and conservatives in the party.[12]

The result of the succession crisis little pleased Chamberlain. Austen was by this point the obvious replacement, but obstruc-tive tactics from Balfour's followers in supporting Walter Long caused problems. To his father's utter contempt, Austen once more played the game to stand down in favour of the compro-mise, Bonar Law. Law's history as a tariff reformer proved a fair prediction of his treatment of Chamberlain's great cause. In November 1912 he abandoned Balfour's referendum pledge but, under pressure to maximize Unionist cohesion in the contemporary battle over Home Rule, returned three months later to Balfour's earlier 'double election' principle for the introduction of food taxes. Such remained the state of tariff reform when Ireland and then war came to dominate the political arena and occupy the minds of its leading actors.[13]

Joseph Chamberlain himself died six days before his seventy-eighth birthday and soon after announcing finally his intended resignation from Parliament, in the year 1914 which was to harbinger the collapse of the world of which he and the causes for which he had fought were such typical products. Bitterness and frustration had made him in his final years an even more difficult person to deal with than ever, and his wife had increasingly sought support from a Nonconformist minister whom, despite family opposition, she married soon afterwards. Periodic discussions with leading political figures were not sufficient to keep Chamberlain contented. His influence counted most among minor political actors—Amery, Garvin, Maxse—and the chief participants had made their calculations independently in a world from which his disabilities excluded him. Austen, in whom he had put much faith for the perpetuation and final triumph of the Birmingham dynasty, increasingly ploughed his own furrow, and after 1911 appears to have been given up by his father as a lost cause.

If, however, he was left a lonely old man on the sidelines of politics, indirectly Chamberlain cast a long shadow over the Unionist Party, then and for the next two decades. For many years the leading personnel of the party consisted of those who could consider themselves Chamberlain men of the generation of 1906; and, despite continual hedging, ambiguity, and outright back-tracking, they had inherited what the Right in British politics had not possessed since Disraeli abandoned Protection in the 1850s—a positive programme and ideology for which to work. Commitment to the panacea persisted. Free trade was killed, as Lloyd George observed, by its own supporters when the Liberal Chancellor of the First World War, Reginald McKenna, in effect acknowledged Chamberlain's argument that exceptional times demanded exceptional measures by imposing commercial duties, and in 1923 Stanley Baldwin could find no better way to establish his authority over the Conservatives and frustrate the re-formation of Lloyd

George's post-war coalition than raising tariff reform as an election issue. The inter-war collapse of Britain's staple industries gave additional strength to the argument and, in the great depression after 1929, Neville Chamberlain found his chance posthumously to satisfy his father's demands by settling preferential tariffs at the Ottawa Commonwealth Conference. That, in the long run, these arrangements failed to create the mighty cohesive Empire his father hoped to build does not refute Chamberlaim's claims: 'too little, too late' had been his perennial comment on the politics of his own time, and the Ottawa agreements fully live up to it.

If Chamberlain's last great campaign influenced the personnel and policy of British conservatism, it also, perhaps more significantly, affected its style, certainly in the period before Baldwin's ascendancy. Too much has been made of the years of the last Liberal government as a period of violence, sudden change, and the breakdown of Liberal values: relating obstruction from the Lords, Unionist hints at violent resistance over Ireland, international tension, strikes, and militant feminism is an interesting but unfruitful pastime.[14] Nor should too much be made of a sudden extremism overwhelming Unionist reaction to Liberal measures: the Lords had precedents for their obstreperousness in the years 1892–5, and vague threats had been levelled over Ireland in 1886 and 1893. Yet the smashing defeat of 1906, followed by Asquith's 'unfair' victories of 1910, had laid a far more truculent mood upon Unionism to which Chamberlain's influence had contributed. As leaders, Salisbury, Balfour and later Baldwin were all careful to prevent the die-hard wing of their party alienating the 'floating balance' among the electorate, while simultaneously controlling radical elements like Randolph Churchill or Chamberlain whose opportunistic initiatives to strip the opposing party of its reformist garb might throw the party into utter confusion. By his initiative in 1903 Chamberlain severely undermined the continuity of this tradition.

Tariff reform as an ideology not only cut across the distinction between Conservative and Liberal Unionist: it transcended the classical division between left and right within the whole Unionist Party. It gave those who wanted progress and change a mechanism for financing social reform, modernizing the industrial structure, improving the standard of living of the workers and moderating class divisions, and bringing an aura of professionalism into the government system; for them, it made Liberalism appear the conservative and not the progressive force, and Chamberlain represented their views in describing Lloyd George's great budget as 'the last effort of Free Trade finance to find a substitute for Tariff Reform' in legislating for necessary and desirable social reforms. With its protectionist appeal, however, its ultra-nationalist overtones, and wider connotations that the 'rights' of 'the people' were less important than the duties they owed to the imperial collectivity, and to those rulers who had come to govern it on their behalf, tariff reform contained a strong, traditionalist, right-wing message. Increasingly since 1886, as has been observed in earlier chapters, Chamberlain himself had associated his objectives with traditional 'Tory' values as a mechanism for solidifying a progressive Unionist Party: after 1903, as tariff reform continually failed in its task of driving Liberalism back into the political ghetto it had inhabited in the years after 1886, Chamberlain and his followers come to define their rejection of its policies in conservative terms. In 1894 Chamberlain had recommended a Unionist overhaul of the Lords to counter Liberal attacks—by 1911 he was defending its existing powers to the hilt: he firmly backed the struggle of Edward Carson and Bonar Law to humiliate the government over Ulster, despite a comment to Margot Asquith in 1910 that 'he had always been a Home Ruler', and that 'nothing could be done till the difficulties of Ireland were settled'.[15] Increasingly, the supposed 'progressiveness' of tariff reform became a cloak for the absorption of the tradition of Tory Democracy into a defence pure and simple of the *status quo*, fought after 1910 with a determination seen before but infrequently in British politics. Chamberlain had always been a ruthless partisan protagonist, but he had come far from the heady days of the 1870s when he had anticipated the early advent of a Republic and the final end to social and political privilege in Britain.

A Concluding Essay

They were practical, political men. But at the same time they were
thinking men, who had an insight into the requirements of the time—
into what was ripe for development.

G. W. F. Hegel, on 'great historical figures'.

Despite Joseph Chamberlain's reputation as a straightforward
practical man of affairs, the complexities and sharp contrasts of
his career have proved a source of vigorously contested evalua-
tions from contemporaries and later historians. The reasons are
clear. In contrast to his loudly-proclaimed aspiration to make
great constructive changes in public policy, he steered on to the
statute book no major innovatory legislation save the isolated
Acts on industrial accidents. He claimed the credit for electoral,
education and land tenure reforms, but the claim is at least
questionable. If any popular mythology of him survives in the
modern day, it is likely to associate him first with the imperial
frenzy of the Boer War—a humiliating, and perhaps ultimately unnecessary, adventure. Chamberlain moreover set out
to acquire, and often claimed to wield great personal power:
yet he filled only minor offices of state, voluntarily renounced
claims on the Unionist leadership in 1902 and 1906, and in 1886
threw over any chance of inheriting naturally Gladstone's control of Liberalism. Having entered politics as the champion of
radical-democracy, he departed as its most intransigent opponent—he appeared, as Winston Churchill commented,
'first Fiery Red, then True Blue'.[1] He seized his first government post as a prominent Little Englander, and resigned his
last to pursue a campaign of grandiose militant imperialism
that ruined his health and thereby drove him from political
life. Intent on building in his lifetime a great progressive governing party, he proved the most destructive wrecker of party

relations in his generation. In so many respects, alongside the vibrant energy which permeated his projects and the commanding, if controversial, reputation, he acquired, there lies an aura of failure—a sense of grand plans and ambitions, stridently promoted, and subsequently abandoned or brought to nothing.

The precise degree of success and failure has been differingly assessed and variously explained. Contending views can perhaps be approached through Chamberlain's own comment to Edward Russell in 1881: 'Many politicians nowadays are guided by what I must call hand to mouth considerations . . . you and I both try to keep fast hold of certain general principles. Like all Englishmen we are more or less opportunistic, but I hope we do not sacrifice everything to such considerations.'[2]

The quotation invites radically contrasted judgements on his significance. One school of thought, presented most forcibly by the biographers J. L. Garvin and Julian Amery, has largely embraced the view Chamberlain offered in his Birmingham *apologia* of 1906: his career was one of consistent, dedicated patriotic service to the cause of social improvement and enhanced national strength. Apparent changes of tack reflected not abandoned principles but primarily a flexibility of method and growing maturity of perception: whereas the 1886 split marked his recognition of Liberalism's incapacity to tackle the central issues of national cohesion and social reform, the vision embodied in tariff reform proved the logical culmination of all his previous work. Uniquely alive to the implications of Britain's new democratic polity and changed international environment, he devoted his life to devising imaginative solutions to contemporary problems, but foundered continually upon the resistance offered by exclusive ruling élites, the 'timid ones' and those whose priorities were out of step with the modern world.

His critics have been less generous towards Chamberlain's 'opportunistic' streak. Arthur Balfour was surprised to hear him comment in 1886 that 'in politics, there is no use looking beyond the next fortnight'—a view he identified with Lord Randolph Churchill rather than the master-strategist of Radicalism. Salisbury's reaction, which matched contemporary Gladstonian criticism of Chamberlain as the 'prince of opportunists', was to identify his chief political weakness in the fact that he had 'not yet persuaded himself that he has any convictions.'[3] For many commentators, Chamberlain has remained at the level of cabinet intriguer and parliamentary conspirator, a man who mastered the arts of popular demagogy and caucus management, and professionally dedicated himself to building a secure place in the sun of Westminster politics. Liberal and Nationalist writers have seen the failed *putsch* of 1886 as a point at which pragmatic adventurousness turned into cynical ambition as he sold his Radical soul for a mess of Tory pottage— Conservatives have questioned whether, with his egocentrism, oversensitive antennae and vivid political imagination, the façade of hard-bitten realism did not conceal serious defects in his grasp of the 'art of the possible'. On these views, his career smacks of vaulting ambition, the absence of great practical achievements reflecting both the narrow horizons of his statesmanship and basic failings in his comprehension of the real limitations within which political leadership must inevitably act.

Though the images of Chamberlain as great statesman and dramatic careerist clearly confront each other as partisan stereotypes, no complete portrait can afford to do without either. Throughout this book I have tried to locate his development of various programmes and ideological postures firmly within the context of ambitions and strategies which turned upon the great issues of the day, for no more than any other politician was he able to contemplate the celestial realm of political ideals free from his own human limitations and the constraints of his immediate environment. At the same time, there were issues and ideas which he stood for and which must be considered in a far wider perspective than we have so far attempted. In this concluding essay, my aim is to tie up these loose ends, and provide a more general interpretation and evaluation of what has been recounted in earlier chapters.

There is a very real sense in which Chamberlain embodied, if we can use the phrase, the spirit of his age. His political fortunes, not to say his subsequent reputation, were rooted in his association with the great movements and ideas of the period between 1867 and 1914. The advent of mass democracy; a dramatic expansion in the role of the state; the growth of an organized working class movement; imperial expansion and its impact upon the consciousness of the British people; the growth of Irish Nationalism; the uncertainties created by challenges to Britain's roles as workshop and policeman of the world: all these phenomena which menaced and later undermined the stable certainties of mid-Victorian liberal England were identified successively by Chamberlain as objects for creative and imaginative political action. At worst he reflected many of the lowest commonplace prejudices of the time—chauvinism, both national and sexual, the cult of racial superiority towards blacks, Irish, and Jews, the cultural philistinism of the English middle classes; at best, he challenged the cosy complacency of the dominant ideologies, bringing into the forefront of politics the unpleasant realities of urban industrial life and identifying the strains and tensions which threatened the foundations of Britain's domestic and imperial stability.

No great intellectual system or insight supported his political objectives, and, unlike Gladstone and Bright, he had no universal moral principles to guide him through the maelstrom of public life. Chamberlain was an imaginative businessman, with an urge for action and for wordly success. 'You do not believe that the great things of the world are done by the intellect. You decide first and then find reasons,' Professor Hewins said to him during a conversation in 1908;[4] Chamberlain fully agreed. Open to conviction on any case, he yet seized hold of policies, programmes and ideological stances, not because of their inherent intellectual coherence, but because, with the instincts of a born political strategist, he felt them to be the right sort of material for the time and the place. The 'social politics' of 1883–5, reforms in Ireland, social reform and imperial development were all taken up because they appeared to be the coming issues with which anyone interested in change and progress had to identify. Utterly incapable, as he admitted, of grasping the essentials of academic economics, he swung towards imperial preference in 1902 when his official brief foundered in the face of well-constructed arguments from Canadian officials, and fumbled badly many of the early arguments over fiscal reform—an innocent in international affairs, he had to learn the hard way, in his dealings with Germany, the skills of diplomacy and the complexities of foreign relations.

An intellectual magpie, he picked up ideas where he could from the popular journals and periodicals of the time. William Harris, Dilke, Morley, Collings and others were used mercilessly in the early years to clarify and work through the implications of his schemes. The Gothenburg temperance proposal and workmen's compensation were measures he drew from other MPs and then popularized, while Winston Churchill claimed to find the whole Glasgow fiscal programme in old Fair Trade pamphlets among his father's possessions.

The failure of so many of these proposals to be put into effect makes it hard accurately to assess the validity of his instincts. Among them, Gothenburg, the Irish Central Board and pensions might well have been pushed through by a determined government with great advantage, but they stood little chance once their fate was left to hang upon the prior creation of a broad consensus among interested parties. Workmen's compensation, free education, and, to a lesser extent, land reform proved more successful to the extent that the alternatives had for one reason or another been tried and failed. Of the most controversial issues with which he was associated a more extensive discussion is in order.

Perhaps Chamberlain's main claim to prescience about the politics of the future was his attempt in 1885 to redirect Liberalism towards problems of poverty and redistribution. Lloyd George commented during debate over his notorious budget that had 'Chamberlain not been driven from the party, there would be little for us to do today'. An intriguing if ultimately insoluble historical puzzle is whether the growth of an independent Labour Party might have been forestalled if Chamberlain's attempt to turn Liberalism into a party of social reform with a clear pro-labour programme had succeeded. Certainly, as I have suggested in earlier chapters, Labour faced serious difficulties competing against the two main parties in the period up to the Liberal split during the First World War, the reformism of Asquith and Lloyd George proving a serious obstacle. Much would have depended on whether Chamberlain could have mobilized earlier that massive working-class electorate which registered and voted for the first time in 1906, and thereby compensated for the inevitable flight of more conservative elements in the party.

The experience of the 1885 election provides insufficient evidence.

As I have also noted earlier, it is important not to exaggerate the originality of his 1885 programme. There was little in the way of deep reflection or an ideological revolution in the various issues he was canvassing at this time. In particular, social reform was largely encompassed by the prospect of agrarian reform in the campaign, and the logic of his argument over this was open to question. Partly it had a social and political objective—to replace a parasitic landowning class by a class of productive farmers, whether as owners or tenants of the local authority, who would repopulate the land with a race of independent yeomen and provide Radicalism with a firm rural base. But if land was a central issue in Ireland, and to a lesser extent in Scotland and Wales, in England the old rural élites had little difficulty after 1885 in fending off Radical promises of a new heaven and a new, redistributed, earth. Land hunger, and the impetus for the *jacquerie*, were no longer forces capable of being harnessed. Among his Radical successors after 1886, too, there was a waning faith in the possibility of an agrarian revolution through Chamberlain's plans for land purchase *via* the local county councils; nationalization and 'confiscatory' taxation were increasingly regarded as the only serious threat to the 'land monopoly'.

The economic purpose behind his plans—the restoration of a prosperous competitive agricultural sector by repopulating the countryside, raising productivity and lowering prices while reducing urban unemployment—was even more dubious. In the absence of protective tariffs, this would undoubtedly have made little headway in the face of falling import prices, while the basis of Britain's efficient modern agricultural industry has been laid by massive government aid for more intensive cultivation of a much restricted rural sector. The classic Radical policy of 'free land' which Chamberlain initially espoused had behind it the sound economic sense of providing better prospects for growth among more efficient farmers; in 1885 he was drawn by the political need to give Radicalism new foundations in the counties towards hinting at the mass allocation of smallholdings to the landless agricultural labourer. In the short run, the economic consequences could have been disastrous. To expect, additionally, major economic benefits for the towns and cities was pure utopianism.

A second major theme in Chamberlain's career is his attitude towards national and imperial strength and unity. In 1902 he told his Birmingham audience that 'the days are for great Empires, not for little states'. Quite the reverse has proved true in our century. He derided Little Englanders and those like Gladstone and Salisbury who questioned the benefits of expanding imperial control: they have since had the last laugh. Incapable of bearing the costs of empire against local nationalist élites, Britain, not alone among the advanced capitalist states, has hastily disbanded a colonial system inherited from the Chamberlain era and returned to the less ostentatious mid-Victorian practice of economic exploitation of resources in the underdeveloped world under a cover of loose and informal political influence. Chamberlain's imperialist ideology undoubtedly weakened his judgement of what would best benefit the interests of the imperial system: there was much to be said for Salisbury's view that less aggressive postures in South Africa, for instance, would have done less damage to the cause at home and abroad.

That petty nationalism was an ideology of the past, not of the future, was a misconception shared by many of Chamberlain's generation, but many critics of Chamberlain's tortuous relations with the Irish Nationalists have failed to appreciate how little in sympathy with their aspirations he really was. It is a well-cultivated myth that in 1886 Gladstonianism reasserted the primacy of a great Liberal principle, that of aiding nations 'struggling rightly to be free', and was defeated by some conservative atavistic urge to maintain dominance over a subject people. However, in the essay *On Representative Government* by John Stuart Mill, that paragon of mid-Victorian Liberalism, was to be found a view that national self-determination might be the only answer for a people subjected to imperial tyranny, but that where, as in Ireland, an imperial government was gradually extending to subject nationalities the civil, political and economic rights enjoyed by the dominant people, then continued unity within a common state was much to be preferred. In 1885 Gladstone was converted to the view that Anglo-Irish relations should be considered under the first rather than the second category, but this was a matter of judgement not of principle. Those like Chamberlain who were concerned above all else with 'improvement' and with social and economic reform were less convinced, just as in the 1970s the strongest opponents of Welsh and Scottish nationalism have been found as much on the left as on the right of British politics.

The return of nationalist politics to Britain in the 1970s, as well as growing worries about administrative over-centralization, have led some commentators to reconsider Chamberlain's interest in provincial councils and federalism in the 1880s. Was this a lost opportunity to deal with the distinct regional patterns of the United Kingdom and the centrifugal forces to which they are still capable of giving rise? Alone among leading contemporary politicians Chamberlain took the notion of a major constitutional overhaul seriously—extending the Central Board scheme for Ireland into the national councils proposal of the 1885 election was logical, but politically it was a quite unnecessary complication of the contemporary issue. Its rapid disappearance from his campaign programme, though, invites further comment. However inherently desirable he may have felt federation or systematic devolution to be, after 1885 the prime role of such schemes was to stymie Gladstonian Home Rule. His ideas were well publicized, but Chamberlain never placed them high on the list of measures with which he attempted to impose progressive politics upon different party leaderships. Just as in 1885 he rapidly discarded national councils as an election issue when they encountered Nationalist opposition, so thereafter he did little to press his arguments in the face of hostility from Conservatives and Ulster Unionists. Unionist leaders took to his suggestion of land purchase in Ireland because it fitted their own conception of a satisfactory pacification programme: effectively he resigned himself to accepting their cowardice about tackling political reform. One further factor does need noting. Almost all Unionists identified the loyalist population of Ulster as a central objection to any plans for an internally self-governing Ireland. Invariably, though, the argument was used to block any form of Home Rule, rather than providing an incentive for thought about how the Irish minority could be catered for. Almost alone, Chamberlain in the 1880s grappled with the idea of separate assemblies for Dublin and Belfast, the Irish 'solution' into which politicians stumbled by default in the years 1914–22. This might, until a decade ago, have been considered a mark of high statesmanship: today it is more tempting to observe his propaganda efforts in the 1880s and 1890s to consolidate Radical and Liberal opinion in Ulster within the Unionist coalition, which led to the ascendancy of that defensive political alliance whose conduct of local affairs since self-government has always proved sadly wanting.

In relation to the histrionic jingo imperialism with which Chamberlain came to be identified in the 1890s, it is difficult, today, to rouse sympathy for either the fears or the ideals of that generation. The horrors of world war and of the 'civilizing mission' have been too fully explored. Retrospective criticism can, however, be misleading. Alternatives to Chamberlain's bellicose imperialism were hard to find. Gladstonian internationalism had foundered in Egypt in the 1880s, and thereafter little could be found capable of binding together a concert of nations to maintain perpetual peace. Salisbury pessimistically forecast a great war, but could not bring himself to prepare for it, hoping that diplomatic juggling might substitute for the imperial consolidation and abandonment of non-alignment needed to survive a great trial of national strength. In a world where brag, bluster, and blackmail were being universally elevated into principles of international statesmanship, men like Chamberlain were inevitably called forth who could play the game effectively by its new rules. His hope that Germany might prove a sound partner in crime in the age of imperialism was always over-optimistic; his view on the inevitability of co-operation with America to defend an increasingly insecure *pax Britannica* proved much more prescient, a surer guide for action in relation to that sensitive republic than the Foreign Office's offhand and patronizing manner.

Whether tariff reform, implemented in Chamberlain's lifetime, rather than in the more unfavourable conditions of the 1930s economic depression, could have laid the basis of a firmer imperial economic and political system remains a much disputed question. Economic historians continue to debate whether real advantages did accrue from protection and imperial preferences in that later period. Chamberlain's opponents rightly claimed that he had done no exact cost-benefit analysis on his proposed changes—they rested more on his sense of the paradox involved in maintaining a free-trade Britain in a protectionist world, benefiting from small colonial preferences yet refusing to reciprocate. Opposition, however, rested just as much on presupposition as fine calculation. Deepseated prejudices against government interference in free exchange were reinforced by myths about the inevitability of corruption entering the political arena once detailed decisions about trade and commerce had to be taken by ministers. As Chamberlain noted, it seemed incongruous to adopt a classical Liberal stand on tariffs when trade unions and welfare legislation already presented major inroads into the free market. An obsession with the 'bane of cheapness' also hindered serious thought about the long-term prospects of Britain's existing pattern of world trade and industrial productivity. The descendants of Chamberlain's opponents on this matter, spiritually and often even genetically, were those hostile to Britain's entry into the EEC in the 1970s; their desire was the continued acquisition of cheap food and raw materials from a world market where the best buys were usually to be found among the remnants of that colonial trading system which Chamberlain's son had founded under his father's inspiration in the 1930s.

There were two economic puzzles, however, to which Chamberlain never gave fully satisfactory answers. He was always inclined to justify tariffs both as a protective measure and a source of revenue for social reforms. Yet, to the extent that tariffs barred imports, to that extent revenue would not be collected; while if imports were to provide revenue, they would have to be allowed into the Empire to compete at comparable rates against domestic products, thereby minimizing the protectionist part of the programme.

The second matter was finance capital. It has often been argued that many of Britain's twentieth-century economic problems originated in a failure to modernize industry during this period, due partly to entrepreneurial failures, partly also to the massive diversion of capital abroad, creating markets for British exports, but denying funds to less profitable domestic industries and making the overseas balance heavily dependent on dividends from abroad. Increasingly, Britain was turning from workshop to rentier of the world. Yet the imperial commercial system Chamberlain envisaged would have fared badly without a concentration of capital within it to maintain a level of productivity comparable to that of its competitors. As Colonial Secretary, he had, of course, taken steps to make colonial investments more attractive; yet he never seriously challenged the ideology of free trade in capital emanating from the City of London as he did that of free trade in commodities, perhaps out of timidity, perhaps anticipating that higher imperial growth rates would attract the necessary funds. The implication was there, of course; and some writers have seen tariff reform as a deeply divisive factor between 'finance capital' and 'industrial capital' in Edwardian England, the former apprehensive at the curbing of its lucrative world-wide interests.[5] If the picture is overdrawn—the as yet secure cotton and coal industries were less impressed than hard-pressed engineering concerns in the Black Country, while many financial interests had a big stake in colonial expansion—it remains true that the City as an institution remained largely insensitive to Chamberlain's programme.

His interest in the co-ordination of a powerful imperial military and defence structure through tariff reform was to some extent furthered by Balfour and his successors. The main ambition, however, was never realized. So long as the tensions posed by the various colonial nationalisms were not contained within a single confederal structure, he believed, they would always tempt foreign powers to chance their arm against one or other of Britain's overextended commitments. And though the goal was always a distant prospect, the years immediately following the Boer War were as favourable a time as any for working gradually towards it. Chamberlain's inability to carry the cabinet and the electorate made it virtually impossible for imperial consolidationists in the colonies to make any real headway with their own people. All that could be hoped for thereafter was close but pragmatic co-operation between distinct nation states.

These comments suggest that it is no easy task to evaluate the value and importance of Chamberlain's contribution to the formulation of public policy during his career. Nor is it any more simple to place his approach to contemporary issues within a broader framework.

The central theme which appears to dominate his viewpoint, and which marks him so distinctively as a politician of the twentieth rather than the nineteenth century, is his identification with 'collectivism' and the growth of an interventionist state in reaction to the classical *laissez-faire* ideology which dominated mid-Victorian public policy. Even if we acknowledge that the traditional picture of the nineteenth-century minimal state has frequently been overdrawn, it is still valid to identify Chamberlain with that growing reaction to the inhumanities and 'contradictions' of classical liberal social and economic policies which has ushered in a new era of state regulation. Municipal socialism, free compulsory education, 'constructionist' Radicalism, social reform, consolidationist imperial policies and finally the challenge to free trade were in this respect all cut from the same cloth.

The breadth and coherence of any such collectivist urge should not be overstressed. Though Chamberlain's starting point was invariably the inadequacy of classical Liberalism in dealing with a whole range of contemporary problems, this should not obscure the fact that his reaction to it took a variety of forms. If the democratic Radicalism of his early days was rooted in a belief that the extension of citizenship implied not merely a right to vote, but a right to the basic security and minimum standards of welfare enjoyed as yet only by the more privileged, the later Unionist promised increased welfare as a by-product of faster economic growth through imperial unification, both of them required by the need for greater national strength and unity. In all this, as we have earlier observed, there was little in the way of socialism, whether democratic or national. It was untainted by the administrative scientific socialism of the Fabians, or the religious, moral, or aesthetic revulsion from modern industrialism which permeated both sections of the contemporary Left and the more romantically Disraelian strands of the Tory party. Even the paternalistic philanthropy of the Nonconformist conscience, perhaps the most obvious inspiration for his ideas as well as an important prop of his political power, was more often a political liability than a practical guide for action.

Chamberlain's faith lay in the progressive civilizing force of individualistic competitive capitalism, but it was associated with a pragmatic view on the role of the state in fulfilling necessary programmes of social reconstruction. In direct line of descent from Jeremy Bentham's school of Philosophic Radicals, he continually justified his proposals by their contribution to 'the greatest happiness of the greatest number'. Rationalizing and modernizing society's values and institutions was the hallmark of this approach, with state regulation and public utilities employed to maximize social welfare where private initiative could not or would not do so. If the traditional Benthamite enemies—mass ignorance, tradition, religious prejudice, the land monopoly, and caste privilege—were inappropriate appendages to Chamberlain's insecure position within Unionism in the 1890s, he set out to redefine its basic secular and materialistic objectives in terms of rationalizing industrial relations, providing state incentives for the thrifty and hard-working to buy and improve housing and to protect themselves from the consequences of injury and old age, assisting colonial development, and modernizing Britain's trading and diplomatic relationships.

'Collectivism' is something of a misnomer for all this. 'Municipalization' was the furthest he ever departed from the private ownership of property, both in Birmingham's domestic affairs and the wider national issues of land tenure and temperance reform; disestablishment, peasant proprietorship, and devolution ran counter to the trend; by 1902 he was way out of step with the tendencies towards greater centralization and rationalization of the education system; and tariff reform emerged as a form of minimal government interference in the market to fend off the threat of more drastic intervention from the left. Chamberlain's instincts were rooted not so much in any collectivist inspiration as in a rather more flexible and amorphous concept of social and political modernization applied over a wide range of contemporary problems.

Questions of public finance inevitably raised by his scepticism towards a universal faith in *laissez-faire* highlights the change in his general political orientations. As Birmingham's mayor he found little difficulty in raising loans for his municipal projects, funding them and still reducing the rates, but other

tasks were less amenable to such treatment. True to his political
heritage in these early years, he favoured retrenchment on
wasteful military expenditure and further cuts in indirect taxation. The rich were thus an obvious target. Disendowment of
the Church offered an obvious source of funds for educational
improvements; reducing the ratepayer's liability for housing
improvements led him in the early 1880s to devise ways of
throwing the burden more on the urban landlord; and from
this period until Harcourt's imposition of death duties in 1894
he strongly favoured a more progressive tax structure. Soon,
however, his confidence in the viability of even mildly redistributive financial mechanisms was on the wane. As President of the Local Government Board in 1886 he had empowered
local authorities to provide public works in times of high unemployment, though within strict financial limits—a valuable
innovatory measure continued by his successors; in 1892 he
met demands for an extension of the facility with the argument
that employment was better secured by greater colonial trade
than by such costly palliatives. His opposition at this time,
shared by all Unionists, to Progressive control of the London
County Council centred around objections to what was considered its squandering of the rates upon unnecessary or undesirable social improvements. At the national level, his
imperialism came to preclude retrenchment on defence, and
finance came to be sought less from the taxpayer and more
from new sources—the Suez Canal shares, colonial contributions to the naval budget, new taxes in the dependencies. The
story on domestic matters was similar. Pensions and accident
compensation, unlike education, were to be contributory
schemes, and by 1902 he had come to accept the Treasury
belief that further taxation on wealth and income was both
politically impossible and likely to prove counterproductive in
terms of incentives for future investment. Indirect taxes on the
consumer and high growth rates from tariff reform thus became his answer to the tightening strait-jacket on public
finance. By 1909 he had clarified the choices available to satisfy
the insatiable demands of the modern state. 'Tariff Reform or
Budget' presented the alternatives of state-assisted economic
growth, and income redistribution, on the ideologies of
which competition between conservative and reform parties

has largely centred in twentieth-century Britain. It is a measure of Chamberlain's historical significance that he articulated in its primitive form at the different stages of his career each of these alternative philosophies. In this respect, he demonstrated clearly that the preconceptions which had dominated the nineteenth century were on the way out.

The development of Chamberlain's financial preoccupations clearly corresponded to the change in his wider social philosophy associated with the shift from Liberalism to Unionism. It can also be related to another major interpretation of his career —that his changed political loyalties reflected the changed allegiances of the English industrial bourgeoisie in late Victorian and early Edwardian England. Julian Amery has described him as an aggressive Radical agitator when the class enemy was Church and aristocracy, a defender of the 'national heritage' when the bastions of power had been seized and Lloyd George was launching a new challenge to the *status quo*.[6] Peter Fraser, we have seen, interpreted Chamberlain's Unionism in the 1890s as a reaction to industrial unrest and socialist ideas, a view partly complementing, partly at odds with, the proposition that, even in the early 1880s, he was on the defensive against threats to private property posed by English and Irish popular movements. R. C. K. Ensor in two classic articles[7] surveyed Chamberlain's career in the light of his business origins, arguing in particular for the Liberal Unionist breakaway of 1886 as a defensive nationalistic response among the bourgeoisie to Irish agrarian discontent, with Goschen representing financial capital, Chamberlain the industrialists, and Hartington, though an aristocratic landowner, keeping 'close to the bourgeoisie's point of view'.

The tendency towards an alignment of politics on national class lines rather than on sectarian allegiance or pure localism is one of the striking features of Chamberlain's lifetime, if often exaggerated: both Liberalism and Unionism were 'bourgeois' parties; each at the same time had significant support among what was still, because of the tight franchise requirements, a restricted working-class electorate; and the strength of each party was highly regionalized—Liberalism was largely confined to the Celtic fringe, South Yorkshire and the North East. Chamberlain himself undoubtedly symbolized the classic

career pattern of the successful self-made industrial bourgeois—
commercial success provided a place in local society and
politics, which opened the door into national political life
where he fraternized on terms of social inferiority with longer-
established layers of the English upper classes, ultimately integrating his sons through the public schools and old
universities. Politically he symbolized in the 1890s Unionism's
offer of a 'historic compromise' between the traditionally
distinct religious and ideological affiliations of the propertied
classes in the face of domestic and international uncertainty.
And undoubtedly he aspired throughout his career to provide
a new dynamic professional middle-class leadership for Britain's antiquated political structures—whether recruited from
a Dissenting Radicalism processed by the Liberal Federation,
or the industrial-farming complex schooled in the Tariff
Reform League.

How usefully his activities can be explained in detail in class
terms is less clear. Ensor's view of the 1886 crisis particularly
leaves much to be desired, ignoring as he did any analysis of
the contrasting motives of the chief actors and implicitly
accepting Gladstone's nonsense that the issue had pitched 'the
masses' against 'the classes'. Most significant here was precisely
Chamberlain's failure to take with him the bulk of that
bourgeois Radicalism with which he was so closely identified,
and which instead remained with Gladstone to dominate a
popular-based middle-class party. Middle-class Liberalism,
even its Radical section, had undoubtedly been shaken by
events in the early 1880s. Chamberlain, reflecting its mood over
Irish disruption and international tension, as well as recognizing that the posture of a left-wing minister in a broad political
alliance had to be rather different from that of the Republican
agitator he had been but a decade before, came to articulate
more conventional attitudes towards popular politics. In his
exposed position, the line between himself and organizations
far more critical of the *status quo* had to be clearly defined. This
tendency should not, however, be misinterpreted. Though
many of the more histrionic partisans on the left and the
right were, and have since been, inclined to see the politics of
the 1880s in terms of a clash between socialism and capitalism,
the masses and the classes, subversion and order, the central

question for Liberalism was whether it should take the idea of mass citizenship seriously and explicitly respond to popular and working-class demands, or whether, as Goschen, a variety of Whigs and, occasionally, Hartington implied, resistance or sullen hostility should characterize its response. On this question, Chamberlain remained on the attack. Most significantly, his articulation of the broad view in 1885 proved him to be far more radical than those classes in the electorate from which he originated. Amery's claim that before 1886 Chamberlain represented a bourgeoisie aggressive and challenging of the Church and the landlords precisely obscures the complexities of his position—the minority position of bourgeois Radicalism, flourishing as a complement rather than an alternative to Liberalism, ambiguous over whether it wished to supplant the territorial aristocracy or participate with it in furthering peace, retrenchment and reform, and rooted in social groups already firmly integrated into the state with the early concessions of citizenship, free commercial activity, and the elimination of autonomous working-class movements in the 1840s and 1850s.

Equally ambiguous was the role of the commercial classes within Unionism. Their more adventurous spokesmen's obsessions with the reconstruction of industrial and imperial relations cut little ice with the ratepayers, rentiers, farmers, landlords, and salaried professional classes who formed the electoral backbone of Salisbury and Hartington's party, whole sections of which ultimately turned and fled from the disturbing implications of fiscal reform. If Chamberlain's social conservatism in the later years should not be underestimated, Winston Churchill's characterization as 'True Blue' is in large part unhelpful. Tariff reform, as we have suggested in earlier chapters, made its impact precisely because it promised to mobilize certain commercial interests in a subversive assault upon the entrenched leadership of a party which appeared insufficiently attentive to their view of the needs of industry and agriculture. On this view, the pragmatic conservative alliance of land, trade, and finance which had dominated British politics since 1886 was no longer an adequate instrument of government; yet the attempt to give it sharper definition with the idea that a radical break with the *status quo* must be made if the security of the British state was to be maintained never convinced a sufficiently large section of the bourgeoisie and middle classes. This is only to say that, in certain fundamental respects, as Denis Judd has stressed in a recent biography, Chamberlain remained a radical in temperament and approach even into later life.[8] The one danger in making this assertion, however, is that it obscures and confuses distinct senses of the word 'radical'. Chamberlain may have remained permanently convinced of the inherent virtues of unorthodox policies and methods, but the distinctive concerns and ideology of Radicalism as a political movement had by the time of tariff reform long since been rejected as an adequate response to the twentieth century.

If the characterization as a bourgeois politician does little to explain Chamberlain's distinctiveness among contemporary politicians, that as the man who had grasped the essence of the new world of democratic politics remains one of the most powerful and persistent myths surrounding him. It was the commonplace of the age, among both advocates and opponents of democracy, that the franchise reforms of the 1860s and 1880s had put a mass working-class electorate up for grabs, and that power would ultimately be inherited by those who could turn the sheer weight of numbers to their advantage. Chamberlain offered himself throughout his life as the great interpreter of the popular mind and the leading expositor of its varying passions and aspirations. Undoubtedly by the end of his life this democratic garb was fraying at the edges. Electoral reform, redistribution, destruction of the Upper House's powers, votes for women, extensive local self-government for the Celtic fringes and the other paraphernalia of his Radical days had been discarded, and tariff reform brought him into alliance with reactionary and anti-democratic elements among Toryism, not to say the more unfamiliar meritocratic authoritarianism of those like Milner who aspired to impose viceregal forms of government upon an unruly domestic political arena. Yet the classic Chamberlain style persisted. Accusations levelled since his Birmingham days were continually revived—that he was pitching the ignorance, prejudice and hysteria of the many-headed monster against the accumulated wisdom of parliamentary leaders, 'Americanizing' British politics through the caucus, committee wire-pullers and populist demagogy. Whatever their other differences, Gladstone and Salisbury represented a commitment to perpetuate aristocratic government into the era of democracy—and each extended his political career precisely to resist the threat which Chamberlain's politics and that of his imitators, with its insistence on open government and public debate, the mobilization of party rank and file and the electorate around social and economic questions, posed to sound government. Chamberlain here laid the foundations of the future. He initiated techniques and principles which have become central elements of the modern party system—the mass party with its centralized organization and host of small subscribers and activists, the electoral manifesto and its role as the provider of a mandate for action by a successful party, and the discipline imposed on parliamentarians to subsume their individual consciences to the dictates of party loyalty.

With the tradition of liberal parliamentarianism in Britain Chamberlain had little sympathy. He was, so he had said in the 1870s, a 'Radical autoritaire', a believer in discipline and leadership as necessary elements in democratic practices. Parliament's traditional role, he told Balfour in 1886, had been to resist the overbearing influence of Kings and their ministers; its traditional freedoms were superfluous when The People were the masters. The constitutional checks and balances so dear to Liberal theorists were redundant in a world that needed disciplined majorities to uphold leaders who had captured a popular mandate. And throughout his career Chamberlain took little stock of the nuances of parliamentary management. Periodic cabals with backbenchers and attempts to deploy skills of parliamentary manipulation always came second in his early career to activity on the public platform—as Colonial Secretary his strength rested far more upon his public than his parliamentary speeches. It is no accident that he terminated his active career as he began it—undisputed master of an extra-parliamentary movement designed to undermine policy agreed within a cabinet which had majority support in the Commons.

Ambiguities over the notion of democracy inherent in this approach remain within modern practices. Institutions ostensibly designed to make the ordinary voter a force in democratic decision-making act rather more successfully to curb initiative from the bottom and provide party leaders with an instrument for governing in the face of a multitude of inchoate demands and pressures arising out of the electorate. Chamberlain aimed to challenge what he considered to be a socially exclusive Whig and Tory oligarchy by bringing The People into government; once he had entered the inner circles of power, his democratic rhetoric and practices were deployed as instruments of manipulation with which he could play tactical games for personal control over policy within a largely unreconstructed system of parliamentary politics.

Nor were his claims to speak for The People without risk of challenge. However successfully he captured the mood of the times, on the two occasions of 1885 and 1906 when he sought to convert it into electoral majorities, the result was a flop. Historians, in addition, have widely rejected his excessive claims to have created through the new caucus the Liberal victory of 1880, and the popularity of both social reform and imperialism in the 1890s among the working-class electorate to which they were ostensibly addressed has been strongly disputed.[9] Like any other politician, he was inclined to read from the public mind only what he himself had already written there, and, despite his extensive information network throughout the constituencies, to take his soundings primarily in a restricted political arena. The complexities of public opinion in the Black Country, which throughout the time of his national prominence was undergoing a dramatic second industrial transformation, were what he best comprehended. But, as Mundella had warned in 1883, 'Sheffield is the very political antipodes of Birmingham'[10]—a message with which Balfour, after his ejection from Manchester, might well have wished to counter Chamberlain's Birmingham majorities of 1906. As Member of Parliament after 1885 for the industrial seat of West Birmingham, Chamberlain invariably adopted the posture of spokesman for the ordinary working-class voter. Yet no more than Gladstone or Salisbury did he fraternize with the lower orders, and it was easy to deride his claims, emanating as they did from the comfortable drawing rooms of Highbury. When he promoted the parliamentary ambitions of working-class candidates like Henry Broadhurst and Joseph Arch in the early days, and later tried to integrate trade unionists into the Tariff Reform League, this was more significant as a move to attract new faces to old causes than to promote a distinctive Labour voice. Labour, like Irish Nationalism, he was always inclined to see as a sectional interest—not without justification in the context of the time. He was undoubtedly sympathetic to conditions among the poor, a liberal donor to charities, and periodically a champion of paternalistic legislation to alleviate social distress; in the early 1890s his views on industrial relations were far in advance of almost every other leading politician of the day. But he anticipated a degree of political deference for the dynasty he founded in his city such as any Whig or Tory landlord of old would have assumed among his tenantry.

The interpretations of Chamberlain's politics we have so far considered, which attempt to use his 'collectivist' views, social background, and democratic methods as a guiding thread through the convulsions of his career, are all inclined to undervalue his sheer originality and creativity as a political actor. His personal dynamism; an urge to 'get things done', and to associate himself with great constructive achievements; the restless pursuit of domination over men and events which was both a personal need and, he believed, the precondition for imposing rational solutions upon contemporary problems: all these drove him in continual search of ways to reconstruct existing political alignments and forge new political agencies capable of handling the complexities of public affairs. The central political question of the period was whether two competing coalitions of landed, industrial and professional wealth could keep their grip on the unstable allegiances of a broad middle and working class electorate which was capable of responding in diverse and uncertain ways to the impact of democracy, Empire and economic change; and Chamberlain exploited in succession a whole variety of forces and pressures to which this problem gave rise in order to create the governing alliance that would give him real control of affairs. Paradoxically for a man who disavowed ever being the victim of abstract ideological considerations, and whose most devastating criticism of any person or proposal was 'impractical', Chamberlain proved one of the most systematic creators in modern British politics of ideologies designed to define the significance of, and provide the political force to carry, his policies. Though many died with the demise of the immediate circumstances for which they were devised, others had more lasting effect.

In the Birmingham mayoralty he proved able to find the right style to give him that personal ascendancy and ability to carry through his plans for which ever afterwards he craved. The powerful appeal of 'Municipal Socialism', which identified middle-class philanthropy with a slogan of which no progressive working class leader could complain, forged a powerful popular alliance, which proved the cost-effectiveness of its policies, and was made respectable by Chamberlain's skilful personal diplomacy in attracting local notables, municipal leaders elsewhere, and even royalty, to place a seal of approbation upon the work. In spirit it was rooted in a long established tradition of municipal improvement, and accomplished little that was wholly new. Yet the dramatic impact of the slogan, and the original political organization created to carry it, made a lasting impression, inspiring new schools of urban reformers— the Fabians, Progressives on the reformed London County Council and the first generation of Labour politicians—to draw out its implications for a far wider set of tasks than Chamberlain's generation had been prepared to consider.

The fate of his search in national politics for a comparable instrument was less happy. The idea of a new national 'Party of Progress', a popular alliance defined in opposition to social privilege and armed with a flexible programme of reforms, never came near to its aspiration of sweeping aside the outmoded Whig and Tory oligarchies. Reform organizations refused to perform like the network of associations and committees through which Chamberlain continued to manipulate Birmingham's internal politics; and, though the hope of building such a party permeated his thoughts until 1886, it was sublimated after 1876 in successive attempts to wrestle with the different pillars of Gladstone's dominance over the Liberal alliance. Nonconformity in the Bulgarian affair, the urban elector in 1885, and right-wing Liberals over the various imperial questions, culminating with Ireland in 1886, became targets for his propaganda to shape Liberalism in a new image.

The 'social politics' of the years after 1883 represented his most significant redefinition of Gladstonian Liberalism. Moulding old Radical opposition to privilege into the call for a national effort to tackle problems of poverty, it offered a conjunction between grievances arising out of the new democracy and the benevolence or long-term self-interest of the middle classes, whereby the wealth of the few would support a new positive role for the state. Rooted in a belief that the politics of Whiggery were 'played out', and that the classic ideological framework of the Nonconformist conscience provided an insufficient basis for a party which thereby had to move significantly to the left, this new initiative, though it laid down seeds for the future, failed to provide him with the leverage he needed to dominate the party. As yet it was not ready to have its traditional concerns openly challenged by the sort of campaign Chamberlain employed to impose his will. Furthermore, his disenchantment with the obsessions of the Liberal left, much increased after 1886, underestimated the electoral force which still lay in them. The next two decades were lean times for Liberalism radicalized by Irish policy, but it retained a mass following in the urban areas and the decisive electoral victory of 1906 showed that life still remained in the old causes. Campbell-Bannerman's leadership perhaps, however, revealed the accuracy of Chamberlain's forecast: under it latter-day Gladstonianism degenerated into a combination of ritualistic high-minded reaffirmation of moral fundamentals and low political cunning, to maintain a fragile cohesion of the sectional groups.

If Chamberlain's initiative in 1885 proved for the moment unsuccessful, his contorted response to Irish Home Rule was disastrous. There was undoubtedly consistency, not to say common sense, in his view that the modernization of Ireland required good government, not self-government; but much more lay behind his actions. He appears to have believed that if the melting-pot of political loyalties, heated by the indecisive election result of 1885, could be brought to the boil, there would rise to the surface a man who could traverse the political arena with Unionist commitments and the Radical policies required to face up to the great crisis over Ireland. It proved a misconception to set in motion that 'patriotic alliance' with Hartington with which he had flirted over the previous few years once

Gladstone set out to monopolize the progressive position on Ireland. Furthermore, Conservatism proved unexpectedly able to steal Chamberlain's clothes, forcing through the economic reforms which he believed that the country would ultimately have to call on him to implement. Radical Unionism, always a faction with overblown aspirations to become an instrument for transcending the traditional pattern of party politics, became first a mechanism for Chamberlain's personal manœuvres between Toryism and Liberalism as occasion demanded, and finally the rationalization for integrating an insecure regional alliance into the grand coalition of Unionism.

The central image of this coalition was opposition to fundamental social and political change threatened by Liberal subversion. The caricature of Liberalism was plainly misleading, for it was precisely that party's *immobilisme* which allowed Unionism to play simultaneously the twin cards of permanence and stability, and action and reform. To the extent that its leaders, Salisbury and Hartington, symbolized the former, Chamberlain felt he had ample scope to launch a drive for control over party policy with programmes of social and imperial change to resolve the problems of industrial unrest, economic uncertainty and unstructured colonial management. This contained a significant ideological reformulation. 'The People', identified in his old Radical mythology by its united opposition to dominant sectional interests, became transformed into 'One Nation' pitted against the sectional interests of contemporary Liberalism. Disraelian and Churchillian roots were tapped mercilessly to support the symbiosis of nationalism and social reform. There was a further adjunct. Much in Tory Democracy rhetoric had formerly been made of a confrontation between on the one hand Church, Peers and People, and on the other the hypocrisy of a Whig 'Venetian oligarchy' allied to the narrow material self-interest of the 'millocracy'. Chamberlain now set out to rationalize the sudden growth of commercial and financial wealth within Unionism as a new inspiration for progressive change. In doing so he made a major contribution towards creating the modern ideology of Conservatism which, alongside its appeals to tradition and social deference, has idolized the manager and owner of commercial wealth as the mainspring of the national life and the true embodiment of its long-term interests. Only with the post-war collapse of Liberalism did modern Conservatism become fully defined, but Chamberlain laid the seeds for identifying it with an ideology of a reformist capitalism which has proved its central modern image.

His perception of political relationships on the Right also shrewdly anticipated later events. At three major crisis points in British politics during the twentieth century—1915–16, 1931 and 1940—Conservatism reasserted its control over the political process, preparatory to a radical remodelling of state policy, by deft manœuvres. It either replaced its leadership with a former rebel like Winston Churchill, or appropriated from the left someone like Lloyd George or Ramsay MacDonald, to provide the linchpin of an apparently national coalition. Chamberlain anticipated that Conservatism in the late 1880s and 1890s would likewise need him. And undoubtedly he proved an asset for Salisbury, tolerated and occasionally even encouraged when more reactionary elements made noises which threatened to give the party a bad name. Yet Salisbury much preferred the image of masterly inactivity associated with his Whig captives than the dynamic bustle offered by Chamberlain.

When the extent of the 1895 victory emerged it was clear, too, that his importance to Unionism had declined dramatically. A majority of 152 seats was the most effective counter to any view that Unionism needed progressive leaders with progressive policies. The coherent programme of social reform which Chamberlain had sketched out to direct the new government's strategy became deflected into the sheer grind of making a minor government department work effectively.

The ideology which Chamberlain constructed to make the Colonial Office the hub of a great imperial enterprise contributed perhaps as much as any other force to defining the spirit of imperialism with which the latter years of Victoria's reign are associated. The combination of aggressive national self-confidence, symbolized by the gigantic displays of imperial exhibits at the Queen's Diamond Jubilee, and an underlying sense of tension and crisis in the international arena which threatened the foundations of this new civilization, were superbly played upon by the Colonial Secretary in his public speeches to create a climate suitable for dramatic changes in Britain's overseas relations. Convinced increasingly that he alone could provide the strong national leadership needed in this new era, he intervened continually in the conduct of foreign policy to lay the foundations of a new imperial strategy. As it happened, even in the crisis of the Boer War he was unable to establish his claims to leadership. Milner, Salisbury, and Rosebery all carried as much weight in the popular imagination as the man who had bungled the crisis of 1895 and ultimately involved Britain in a messy, controversial colonial skirmish. That important sections of Unionism thought his most useful role after 1900 would be that of cleansing the Augean Stables of the War Office added insult to injury in the face of his inability to get a grip on the broad structure of government policy-making.

Tariff reform marked the climax, and the great disappointment, of Chamberlain's life. His last attempt to realize the ambition of political ascendancy through a great political cause, it became a crusade to win over the hearts and minds of the British people. Formulated initially to break through the dead end into which Unionism appeared to be running after 1901, tariff reform offered in outline a simple policy which would lay the foundations of greater national strength, but one with extensive ideological overtones. Identifying the interests of almost every economic group in Britain with the transcendence of Liberal internationalism abroad, and Liberal financing at home, Chamberlain's movement promised a Rosebery-like programme of national efficiency and reconstruction, spanning the radical populism of men like Garvin and the anti-democratic élitism of those like Milner. Tariff reform owed something in character to Bismarckian authoritarian nationalism; something to neo-Benthamite ideas of national reconstruction; something to old-fashioned Tory protectionism; and a lot to pure economic self-interest. It has also been identified with later, and even more disreputable, phenomena—the various fascisms of the inter-war period. Undoubtedly, there are parallels. With its appeal beyond normal parliamentary channels to an ultra-nationalistic mass movement, denunciation of the debilitating forces of Liberalism and Socialism, its support from sections of big business and the

landed interest, and, most significantly, its character as the
creation of a charismatic leader, the tariff reform movement
provided early lessons in how the European Right could respond to political and economic crisis after the First World War.
These parallels must not be pressed too hard. Even if a Tory
party remodelled under Tariff Reform League pressure did
teeter on the brink of unconstitutional action over Ulster in the
pre-war years, neither Chamberlain, let alone most of his
followers, were willing to challenge the normal processes of
parliamentary competition. This was precisely the source of
those complexities Chamberlain faced from 1903 to 1906. Nor
was he inclined to find a genuinely authoritarian solution to
the problems he identified. Tariff reform was designed precisely to create economic circumstances which would avert
that confrontation with organized Labour which lay at the
heart of most later fascist doctrines.

Chamberlain's inability to convince the party and the electorate that a great national crisis was imminent and had to be
faced through a radical break with past philosophies must
stand as a testimony to his whole career. Throughout it he
flourished in an atmosphere of rancour and bitter political discord. He offered himself as a man with the clear-sighted
determination to steer a steady path through the complexities
of public affairs, yet could make his voice heard only by
dramatizing the sense of crisis, and compounding the problems.
As Salisbury once observed, when a Chamberlain speech was
due, 'you may look out for squalls.' He offered a succession of
dramatic proposals in the face of what he identified as national
lethargy towards pressing problems, and, if what he had to
offer frequently bore fruit later, at the time it could well be
characterized as a gross overreaction rooted in his own transient political aspirations. When all is said and done, deep-seated
changes in Britain's social and political life caused little overt
disruption in the years after 1867. Rising standards of living
and emigration allowed middle-class politics to flourish despite the advent of democracy and organized Labour; the
effects of Britain's waning economic and imperial hegemony
were obscured by the reluctance of increasingly powerful competitors to offer open challenge before they felt secure of their
own position; even Ireland was a thorn in the side of the

British state rather than any dangerous internal threat. The governing classes, after surviving past tribulations which had shattered or transformed out of recognition their counterparts on the continent, retained a self-confidence in their ability to deal with the modern world. After 1918 many chickens came home to roost. Ireland proved a breeding ground for civil war, the economy frighteningly vulnerable, the Empire a hollow shell, Labour tentatively flirting with class war, and the great Liberal tradition doomed to crumble in the face of full-blooded social democracy and a Tory party which took up *dirigisme* with a vengeance.

Among admirers of 'strong men', those in the tradition of social reforming Liberalism and nationalist, *étatiste* Conservatism, Chamberlain came to be presented as the man of unfulfilled promise, continually cast aside by contemporaries who could not make the imaginative leap necessary to anticipate the future. Against this can be posited the picture of someone who simply failed to grasp that the political structures of his own time had no place for the unorthodox policies and ideologies he put forward.

In this respect, the limitations of Chamberlain's character and style should not be regarded as negligible factors. For a politician who devoted such time and energy to the detailed mechanics of politics, he proved singularly inept in his handling both of men and political tactics at important points in his life. Birmingham could never produce the sort of wizardry which his successor to the leadership of popular Radicalism, Lloyd George, imported from Wales. Invariably his chosen weapon was the bludgeon rather than the rapier. He once said, 'On every committee of thirteen, there are twelve who go to the meetings having given no thought to the subject, and prepared to accept some one else's lead. One goes having made up his mind what he means shall be done. I always make it my business to be that one.'[11] Birmingham might prove responsive to this railroading—though Schnadhorst and Morley were testament to the fact that even the worm will one day turn—but Gladstone, Salisbury, Germany, Kruger, and Balfour each in succession showed that they were not prepared to submit to such treatment lying down. They destroyed his plans, either by unexpected open resistance in defence of their deepest be-

liefs, or by an ingenious subtlety of which Chamberlain ultimately proved himself incapable; after 1903 he contemplated
Balfour's manœuvres with increasingly blank incomprehen-
sion. His judgement on his friends was often no better than that
on his opponents: he lost credibility by using men like O'Shea
and Labouchere, he allowed his family's financial interests to
compromise his public position as Colonial Secretary, and he
placed far too much faith in the political sensibilities of Milner
and the South African gang. The personal animosity which in-
fected so many of his political dealings was not only in itself an
unattractive characteristic, but an extra source of opposition
when honeyed words might have proved more effective. The
ruthlessness with which he pursued various Nationalists and
Radicals after 1886 on the not wholly justified grounds of personal betrayal was perhaps all part of the political game; but
it was no help in influencing Gladstone's cabinets that he
showed such contempt for his colleagues, nor that he should prepare Balfour's government for a new initiative by returning
from South Africa with a foul temper and in open resentment at
their conduct of affairs. Pride and self-importance were be-
setting sins. A personal or political snub risked driving him into
an exaggerated response which political wisdom would not
have dictated: 'Chamberlain was nothing if not a fighter,'
Michael Hurst has observed, 'and sometimes capable of bringing up a twenty-five pounder to shatter a pane of glass.'[12] On
the other hand, studious attention paid to his opinions could
lead him seriously to overestimate his importance: Salisbury
and Balfour's willingness to cultivate Chamberlain on more
personal terms than Gladstone had conceived necessary allowed
them to manipulate him far more successfully.

Many historians have attempted the ultimately fruitless task
of providing Chamberlain with perfect consistency throughout
his career. With the view that he can be identified as always a
social reformer, and at least a latent imperialist, we have dealt
earlier. Chamberlain himself was often ready enough to announce that he had changed his mind, but this does not get to
the heart of one of the central problems of his political style.

Chamberlain's unorthodox policies might have been tolerated more readily had he not proved so unpredictable and unreliable. Those who worked with him could never fully depend

on his loyalty or his capacity to respond in consistent ways across a series of political issues. Over many of the important controversies of his career, a major difficulty was that he was never fully in sympathy with the forces with which circumstances forced him to work closest—Nonconformity, Gladstonian Liberalism and Unionism all in his view possessed fundamental defects which had to be obliterated. Yet he was all too ready to rally allies to the standard, and then lead them off in very different directions. Ostensible spokesman of the Nonconformist conscience in the 1870s, he used it to force his way into the Liberal élite and then devoted his energies to wriggling out of the political strait-jacket it imposed; the idea of a Radical party which yet favoured the Union became an instrument for turning Radicals into Unionists; social reformers of the 1890s had their support for his aspirations channelled into a costly war of aggression; idealistic imperialists found themselves after 1903 backing an increasingly narrow campaign of insular protection. Gifted with a highly original political instinct, it was never entirely clear when he would decide that the time was ripe to change his former identity, set something new in train and dangerously unsettle the tenuous balance of political relationships.

For his cabinet colleagues, it was an unwillingness to play the game of high politics according to accepted conventions which proved the source of greatest suspicion. If he provided but the largest hole in the leaky sieve of Gladstone's second ministry, a comment from Lady Frances Balfour on his role in the Salisbury cabinets ('Joe never has understood the ordinary rules of cabinet cohesion. It is not that he is disloyal, but he does not understand or observe the rules of the game'[13]) suggests that old habits died hard. Undoubtedly, though, that glittering array of landed wealth, professional and social status which dominated the governments of which he was a member had false expectations of the self-made screw manufacturer from the provinces. Men of commerce had been a feature of cabinets long before Chamberlain, but they had been expected to tolerate their position as dependents of the real men of power, or get out. Chamberlain was the first popular tribune seriously to attempt to impose his will upon the inner circles of senatorial power, and, like all poachers turned gamekeeper, was prepared to use all his hard-learned popular skills to maintain an insecure position from which all too many would gladly have dislodged him. The danger he posed was not just that of rocking the boat, but his capacity to do so in a way which made it hard to right the balance by ejecting him. Though he was frequently accused of a predilection for the politics of extremism and schism, had this been the full story, his career would have been easier to describe, and certainly far shorter. That penchant for 'smashing up the whited sepulchre' which had characterized him in the mid-1870s was not part of his subsequent style. He took most of the blame for breaking his party in 1886 and 1903, but there were mitigating circumstances. In the latter case, the cabinet had actually accepted the principle of tariff preference in 1902, and Chamberlain's move in the following year was designed to prevent it systematically backtracking on its commitments. Over Home Rule, the real revolt was that of the 'Whigs', and Chamberlain's move can be seen at one level as an attempt to show that far greater disruption than even Gladstone had anticipated would result from following up the sudden conversion. Ultimately, it was Gladstone who destroyed his party by pressing the issue to a parliamentary vote when it was clear that he simply could not get a majority, and then taking it to the country with the organization in disarray. In both cases, Chamberlain resigned not on overt matters of principle which would entail an irreconcilable breach, but on matters of detail and timing which could be compromised, though it is also fair to say that there was present the tactical flair with which he had conducted the education controversy of the 1870s, when he had shifted between demands for minor revisions of policy and major changes of principle as the audience, the occasion, and the climate of opinion dictated.

Even so, there were elements of Chamberlain's politics which justified the basic charge. Chamberlain belonged to that breed of politicians whose ambitions were set higher than being merely *primus inter pares* in the cabinet room, and modern British politics is littered with the shattered aspirations of Gladstones, Churchills, Lloyd Georges, Mosleys, and Powells who felt they had a unique capacity to mould political life by appealing over the heads of their immediate colleagues or outside the normal framework of party competition. Chamberlain chanced his arm in this respect on many occasions, and the surprise is that he was never reduced to the same political ineffectiveness until the very end of his active career. The nature of his intentions, however, was sufficiently suspect to ensure a permanent watchdog on his activities, thereby always constraining his own freedom of manœuvre.

Ultimately, so typical a product of the Victorian city, and so eloquent an articulator of the central political questions that taxed his generation, Chamberlain proved a misfit, unable to accommodate himself entirely to the main ideological forms in terms of which party debate proceeded, and incapable of operating successfully within the institutional structures available. Though, to paraphrase Gladstone, 'destined to a great historical part', he lacked the material on which to work his will.

In our own time, too, he maintains a peculiar fascination for historians, but among the propagandists of modern political movements his place is far less secure. Liberals, rationalizing their own political impotence, have idolized Gladstone's apparent preference for principle over office in 1886, and remained suspicious of, if not hostile to, his opponent. Labour and socialist writers would identify him primarily with the evils of monopoly capitalism, imperialism, and 'grinding the poor' with dear food. Conservatism has proved more ambiguous. Ready to allocate him a minor role beside Disraeli and Randolph Churchill in developing 'Tory Democracy', their desire to obliterate the memory of 1906, kick over the traces of imperialism, and obscure the identity with big business make him an uncomfortable figure to place in the galaxy of party heroes. Chamberlain left his mark on the future, but the distinctive characteristics of Chamberlainite politics have had few imitators. He may have merited much of the bad press he received; assessed against the great objectives of Radicalism and imperialism he espoused at the different stages of his life, his career was a failure. I hope, however, to have shown that he was more than a mere historical curiosity, and offered genuine alternatives to the eventual course of British politics.

Appendix

Chamberlain and the Crawford–Dilke Divorce Case

The Dilke scandal, like the Jameson Raid and the origins of the Parnell Commission and divorce case, poses problems for students of Chamberlain's career which can never be fully resolved. These are the main facts:

On 17 July 1885 Mrs Virginia Crawford, sister-in-law to Dilke's late brother, Ashton, confessed to her husband, Donald, an adulterous relationship she had had with Dilke some years previously. The confession, arising out of Donald's receipt of the latest in a line of anonymous letters chiding him about his wife's infidelity, contained details of their often ingenious love-making activities, which enlivened proceedings at the uncontested divorce case brought by Donald on 2 February 1886. Dilke was cited as co-respondent, but denied the allegation. The judge granted Crawford a decree nisi, but the case against Dilke was dismissed, with costs, on the grounds that Mrs Crawford's allegations were uncorroborated by other evidence. The apparent paradox of a decision which found against the wife, and left blameless the only co-respondent cited, roused rather mixed comment in the columns of the press and the tittle-tattle of Society. W. T. Stead, editor of the *Pall Mall Gazette* and one of the most effective muck-rakers of the period, highlighted the case, making great capital out of Dilke's failure to enter the witness box to disprove the allegation: further, the Queen's Proctor, a Crown agent empowered to intervene before the granting of a decree absolute, began investigating the affair. Eventually Dilke decided to attempt to clear his name by moving for the Queen's Proctor to challenge the previous decision. This second case was heard between 16 and 23 July 1886. From the start it threatened to backfire on Dilke. The case was designed to prove that Mrs Crawford had *not* committed adultery with Dilke, a far more difficult task than the reverse; Dilke himself was not a direct party to the case, but a witness, and hence could not call on the advice of Council; the President of the court was hostile,

and occasionally incompetent in admitting illegitimate questions and
evidence; and Dilke's defensive, circumlocutory style, and his long-
standing habit of mutilating his diary, entries in which were a key
part of the case against any liaison with Mrs Crawford, made him a
good target for Henry Matthews, Crawford's aggressive Counsel and
the new MP for East Birmingham. The jury's verdict upheld the
earlier decision. From Dilke's point of view, the case had been useful
in establishing Mrs Crawford as a liar in her earlier denials of
liaisons with other men; it did not establish, however, that Dilke had
not been one of her paramours.

The interest of the case for Joseph Chamberlain's career is twofold.
On the one hand, it ruined his closest political ally. Dilke was
always a man of rather insecure temperament who, on his first wife's
death in 1874, had suffered virtually a complete mental breakdown
—in sharp contrast to Chamberlain's reaction to such events in his
own life. The psychological impact of the case excluded him from a
large part of the unauthorized campaign in 1885; the scandal precluded his admission to office in February 1886; it exacerbated
difficulties in his Chelsea constituency, which he lost in the 1886
election; and it kept him ever after from the front rank of politics. On
the other hand, many contemporary and later commentators have
considered Chamberlain a major suspect (Lord Rosebery being
another) as instigator of a conspiracy to ruin Dilke's career.

Right from the start Dilke believed in a conspiracy against him, and
this view was not entirely paranoid. Among Mrs Crawford's lovers
was Captain Henry Forster, whom she was particularly hoping to
marry. At least one of the anonymous letters to her husband appears
to have come from her hand, designed to free herself for such a marriage, and much of the case against Dilke smacked partly of a transference of events from the Forster affair and partly a smokescreen for
it. In the second law case, information about some of Dilke's own past
affairs was made public. Among his lovers were Virginia Crawford's
mother, Mrs Eustace Smith, and Mrs Rogerson, to whom, it was
said, Dilke was virtually engaged in 1884–5 while being involved
simultaneously with Mrs Emilia Pattison (whom he eventually
married during the course of the scandal). In their vengeful role as
women scorned, both appear to have played a part in instigating the
action against Dilke.

The case against Chamberlain is partly *a priori*, in part based on
circumstantial evidence. If Chamberlain was set in 1885 on succeeding Gladstone as the leader of Liberalism, as he always said he was,
then Dilke was his chief rival on the left for the post. Gladstone himself was reported to have named Dilke as a promising candidate, and

undoubtedly all the factors which had made him the front-runner for cabinet office in 1880 applied even more in 1885. Chamberlain is said to have accepted this state of affairs (which of course tells us nothing): but one can also offer reasons why Dilke's fall would not entirely rebound to Chamberlain's advantage. One is that, when mud is flung, it tends to fly indiscriminately. Chamberlain was Dilke's closest friend and ally, and Stead was not the only person who attempted the predictable ploy of using the association against him. Politically, too, if Dilke was likely to prove acceptable to a broader span of opinion in the party, and Dilke's main interests lay in foreign affairs, it might have seemed much safer for Chamberlain to accept Dilke's leadership, control domestic policy, and play *éminence grise*, rather than bidding for the leadership in the face of much tougher opposition. Deciding between these two views partly depends upon an appreciation of their recent political relationship, which provides equally ambivalent conclusions. Dilke, for instance, had taken an independent, occasionally antagonistic, line on the redistribution issue in 1884 and over the resignation threats of early 1885: yet he had readily followed Chamberlain's initiative on the Irish Central Board and the election strategy. It was clear that he would not be Chamberlain's minion—but then it always had been; the two were political allies, and close friends—Dilke, indeed, always discounted the charge against Chamberlain because his ally's 'genius for friendship', as Morley once described it, would never have allowed him to indulge in such foul play as the divorce case—but they also had their own minds. If Chamberlain was concerned to eliminate competition, it was certainly premature with so much to play for in the winter of 1885–6. Dilke ultimately broke politically with Chamberlain over Home Rule, but not until after the divorce case had kept him from office, and a strong Chamberlain–Dilke alliance during this period might have proved far more effective than Chamberlain's isolated stand.

If the *a priori* reasoning produces inconclusive results, so too does the circumstantial evidence. Stead, for instance, claimed that Chamberlain had pushed Dilke into fighting the charges when his best tactic might have been to lie low and hope that the matter would blow over. In the second court case, this is not wholly accurate: Chamberlain initially advised against pursuing the matter, though, when Stead began attacking Chamberlain himself, he does appear to have taken up Stead's suggestion of bringing in the Queen's Proctor. In relation to the first court case, Dilke later commented that, through Mrs Pattison, Chamberlain 'overpersuaded' him to fight when his own instincts were to lie low. This does not establish

that Chamberlain was intent upon creating maximum publicity
against Dilke. Dilke always claimed that, whatever his past indiscretions, he was innocent of the charges laid, and in his correspondence
and conversation Chamberlain always supported him when he might
well have found it useful to reinforce suspicions about the claim. If
Dilke was telling the truth, Chamberlain's 'overpersuasion' is readily
explicable in terms of his own universal instinct to fight back when
attacked rather than meekly submit.

A second charge was that Chamberlain had persuaded Dilke not to
enter the witness box in the first case, a decision which raised the
greatest suspicion about his innocence. The charge is unfounded. It
was Dilke's legal advisers who took the decision—one which was
approved of by the judge in the case because there was no corro-
borated evidence against him—and Chamberlain merely conveyed
the decision to Dilke personally.

A third set of events emerged later. On the evidence of a private
detective engaged by Crawford, it appears that Mrs Crawford
turned up at Chamberlain's house in Princes Gardens, London, two
days before her confession to her husband. Chamberlain was not at
home, but why she was there, even more why she was admitted in his
absence when she was supposedly unknown to Chamberlain and to
his servants, is, to say the least, decidedly odd. Chamberlain did not
tell Dilke of the visit at the time, though some years later he was able
to recall the event without being able to offer any explanation.
Added to this is the fact that the anonymous letter, possibly written
by Mrs Crawford herself, which precipitated the marital crisis, was
posted in Princes Gardens, though almost certainly some time after
the incident described. These two events certainly place the begin-
nings of the scandal literally on Chamberlain's doorstep: no one has
ever explained them, and they are the strongest reason for believing
that Chamberlain might at least have had prior dealings with Mrs
Crawford, though their precise nature remains uncertain.

A final matter is Chamberlain's concern to present as a witness one
Fanny Gray, a former servant of Dilke whom Mrs Crawford implicated as his former mistress and a participant in tripartite sexual
activities, but who mysteriously disappeared for both court cases.
Chamberlain, according to his biographer, J. L. Garvin, was anxious
to find her to disprove the accusations; but Garvin also tells us that
she might have proved a rather unreliable witness, which seems to
cast doubt on Chamberlain's ostensible reason for desiring her
presence.

The charge against Chamberlain is thus not proven, and probably
unproveable either way. In his political, financial and personal

dealings, Chamberlain certainly showed himself capable throughout his life of considerable sharp practice: he was an ambitious man, and, it must be said, not a very nice one, who could readily excite against him the sort of charges which have been levelled in connection with the Dilke case. If true on this occasion, they would represent one of the greatest betrayals of personal trust in modern British politics, and undoubtedly justify the 'Judas' epithet which Liberals readily applied after 1886 to Chamberlain's break with Gladstone over Home Rule.

(For more detailed treatment of the events, see R. Jenkins, *Sir Charles Dilke: A Victorian Tragedy* (1958); B. Askwith, *Lady Charles Dilke* (1969); and also her fictionalized account, *The Tangled Web* (1960).)

Notes

Wherever possible, I have attempted to refer to published works available to the reader rather than to unpublished letters and memoranda. I am grateful, particularly, to Birmingham University Library for assistance in consulting the Chamberlain papers. These papers are cited in the notes as JC PP.

Chapter 1

1. On Chamberlain's family, see J. L. Garvin, *The Life of Joseph Chamberlain* (1932–69), I, ch. 1 and D. H. Elletson, *The Chamberlains* (1966).
2. Salisbury—Balfour (quoting *Pall Mall Gazette*), 29 Mar. 1886: B. E. C. Dugdale, *Arthur James Balfour* (1936), I, 101.
3. T. R. Tholfsen, 'The Origins of the Birmingham Caucus', *Historical Journal*, II, 2 (1959).
4. See J. R. Vincent, *The Formation of the Liberal Party* 2nd ed. (1976), and D. A. Hamer, *Liberal Politics in the Age of Gladstone and Rosebery* (1968).
5. Gladstone—Granville, 1 June 1877: A. Ramm (ed.), *The Political Correspondence of Mr. Gladstone and Lord Granville, 1876–1886* (1962), I, 43.
6. Theodor Herzl, quoted in J. Amery, *The Life of Joseph Chamberlain*, IV, 259.
7. M. Asquith, *Autobiography* (1920), I, 133.

Chapter 2

1. W. H. G. Armytage, *A. J. Mundella, 1825–1897* (1951), ch. 3.
2. T. Wemyss Reid, *Life of W. E. Forster* (1888), I, 463 ff., on Forster's sharp analysis of the alternatives. M. Hurst, *New Outlook*, Jan. 1971 assesses Forster.
3. Garvin, *Life*, I, 105.
4. Chamberlain—Morley, 19 July 1873, on the need for at least a dozen 'Irreconcilables': JC PP.

5. On the character of the League's campaign, see P. C. Griffiths, 'Pressure Groups and Parties in Late Victorian England: The National Education League', *Midland History*, III, 3 (1975).
6. 'The Liberal Party and its Leaders', *Fortnightly Review*, 1 Sept. 1873.
7. J. P. D. Dunbabin, 'The Revolt of the Field', *Past and Present*, 26 (1963).
8. M. C. Hurst, 'Liberal versus Liberal: Bradford and Sheffield in the General Eelection of 1874', *Historical Journal*, XV, 4 (1972).
9. Mundella—Leader, 20 June 1876: Armytage, *Mundella*, 167.
10. A. Briggs, *Victorian Cities* (1963), ch. 5.
11. 12 Mar. 1876: JC PP.
12. H. M. Pelling, *Popular Politics and Society in Late Victorian Britain* (1968), 3.
13. Armytage, *Mundella*, 130.

Chapter 3
1. 19 Aug. 1873: JC PP.
2. 13 Mar. 1874: JC PP. Garvin, *Life*, I, 218–19, misquotes this as 'Free Church and Free Land'.
3. Gladstone—Lord Harrowby: J. Morley, *The Life of W. G. Gladstone* (1903), II, 501.
4. 12 Oct. 1874: JC PP. D. A. Hamer, *John Morley* (1968), ch. 7, clearly reveals this anti-sectarianism.
5. 25 Dec. 1874: Garvin, *Life*, I, 223.
6. 'The Right Method with Publicans', *Fortnightly Review*, May 1876. See B. H. Harrison, *Drink and the Victorians* (1971), on contemporary debates within the temperance movement.
7. Birmingham, 26 Sept. 1876: JC PP.
8. *The Trouble Makers* (1957), 69. R. T. Shannon, *Gladstone and the Bulgarian Agitation, 1876* (1963), brilliantly analyses attitudes to the campaign.
9. 19 Dec. 1875: Garvin, *Life*, I, 223.
10. Chamberlain—Morley, 13 Jan. 1878: Garvin, *Life*, I, 246.
11. 10 Oct. 1876: Garvin, *Life*, I, 240. Also, A. G. Gardiner, *The Life of Sir William Harcourt* (1923), I, 312.
12. Armytage, *Mundella*, 173.
13. Birmingham, 2 Oct. 1876: JC PP.
14. 'Free Schools', *Fortnightly Review*, Jan. 1877.
15. F. H. Herrick, 'Origins of the National Liberal Federation', *Journal of Modern History*, XVII, 2 (1945).
16. 'A New Political Organisation', *Fortnightly Review*, July 1877; 'The Caucus', ibid., Sept. 1878.

17. 21 May 1877: A. Ramm (ed.), *Political Correspondence, 1876–1886*, I, 41.
18. Sheffield, 25 Nov. 1875: JC PP.
19. S. Gwynn and G. M. Tuckwell, *Life of Sir Charles W. Dilke* (1917), I, 273.
20. Chamberlain—Collings: Garvin, *Life*, I, 247.
21. Gwynn and Tuckwell, *Life of Dilke*, I, 294.
22. 4 Apr. 1880: Garvin, *Life*, I, 291–2.
23. B. McGill, 'Francis Schnadhorst and Liberal Party Organisation', *Journal of Modern History*, XXXIV, 1 (1962), and T. Lloyd, *The General Election of 1880* (1968), assess the Federation's real significance.

Chapter 4

1. 29 Apr. 1880: D. W. R. Bahlman, *The Diary of Sir Edward Hamilton, 1880–1885* (1972), I, 4.
2. 10 Apr. 1880: D. A. Hamer, *Liberal Politics*, 86.
3. 19 May 1883: JC PP.
4. T. W. Heyck, *The Dimensions of British Radicalism* (1974), analyses Radical opinions on Ireland.
5. Chamberlain—Morley, 25 Jan. 1880 (quoted by P. Fraser, *Joseph Chamberlain* (1966), 34), shows that Chamberlain meant by Home Rule the devolution of local control, not national self-determination.
6. 27 Oct. 1880: JC PP.
7. 17, 19 Dec. 1880, 16 Jan. 1881: Bahlman, *Hamilton's Diary*, I, 89, 91, 99.
8. Gwynn and Tuckwell, *Life of Dilke*, I, 368.
9. D. M. Schreuder, *Gladstone and Kruger* (1969), shows the interaction of Irish and South African affairs in these years.
10. 24 June 1881: JC PP.
11. Chamberlain—Schnadhorst, 15 Feb. 1881: JC PP (later published in *The Times*).
12. Chamberlain—Dilke, 12 Oct. 1881: Garvin, *Life*, I, 341.
13. 4 Oct. 1881: JC PP.
14. 12 Apr. 1882: JC PP.
15. 23 Apr. 1882: Joseph Chamberlain, *A Political Memoir, 1880–1892*, ed. C. H. D. Howard (1953), 40.
16. J. L. Hammond, *Gladstone and the Irish Nation* 2nd ed. (1964), 275.
17. See A. Thorold, *The Life of Henry Labouchere* (1913) 161 ff., for some of these communications.
18. R. Robinson and J. Gallagher, *Africa and the Victorians* (1961), ch. 4, for interrelations between Egyptian and Irish problems.

19. 1 Feb. 1882: A. Ramm (ed.), *Political Correspondence, 1876–1886*, I, 338.
20. Joseph Chamberlain, *A Political Memoir, 1880–1892*, 71.
21. Gwynn and Tuckwell, *Life of Dilke*, I, 448.
22. Cabinet memo, 18 Oct. 1882: JC PP.
23. D. A. Hamer, *John Morley*, 148.
24. Chamberlain—Dilke, 19 Oct. 1882: Gwynn and Tuckwell, *Life of Dilke*, I, 546.
25. Granville—Spencer: Lord E. Fitzmaurice, *The Life of Granville* (1906), II, 266.
26. Chamberlain—Dilke, 4 Feb. 1883: JC PP.
27. 29 Jan. 1883: JC PP.
28. Chamberlain—Edward Russell, 18 Apr. 1883: JC PP.
29. Chamberlain—Russell, 22 Jan. 1883: JC PP.
30. Joseph Chamberlain and others, *The Radical Programme* (1971), ed. D. A. Hamer.
31. Chamberlain—Dilke, 6 Nov. 1883: JC PP.
32. P. Fraser, *Joseph Chamberlain* (1966), 46.
33. A. Jones, *The Politics of Reform, 1884* (1972), is authoritative on the franchise question.
34. Chamberlain—Bunce, 11 May 1884: JC PP.
35. Labouchere—Chamberlain, 20 Dec. 1883: JC PP.
36. Chamberlain—Bunce, 29 Mar. 1884: JC PP.
37. Chamberlain—Bunce, 11 May 1884: JC PP.
38. Garvin, *Life*, I, 491, fn. 3.
39. See Robinson and Gallagher, *Africa and the Victorians*, 73.
40. 26 Sept. 1884: JC PP.
41. Quoted in part, Garvin, *Life*, I, 529–30.
42. 5 Jan. 1885, Birmingham: JC PP.
43. D. A. Hamer, *John Morley*, 162.

Chapter 5
1. Garvin, *Life*, I, 538.
2. A. G. Gardiner, *The Life of Sir William Harcourt*, I, 514, 515.
3. Chamberlain—Dilke, 3 Jan. 1885; Dilke—Chamberlain, 1 Jan. 1885: JC PP.
4. A. B. Cooke and J. Vincent, *The Governing Passion* (1974), 27–8.
5. Gladstone—Granville, 22 Jan. 1885: J. Morley, *Life of Gladstone*, III, 171.
6. 15 Feb. 1885: JC PP.
7. 12 Sept. 1884: JC PP.
8. 17 Dec. 1884. The full text, along with contrasting views on the Board scheme, are presented in C. H. D. Howard, 'Joseph

Chamberlain, Parnell and the Irish Central Board Scheme',
Irish Historical Studies, 8 (1953).

9. Chamberlain—Morley, 21 Jan. 1885: *A Political Memoir*, 141.
10. Chamberlain—O'Shea, 21 Jan. 1885: Garvin, *Life*, I, 586.
11. Edward Hamilton Diary, 16 May 1885: R. R. James, *Rosebery* (1963), 167.
12. See Gladstone—Hartington, 30 May 1885: Morley, *Life of Gladstone*, III, 196.
13. Cooke and Vincent, *The Governing Passion*, 230–43, cover these complex relationships in some detail.
14. L. P. Curtis, *Coercion and Conciliation in Ireland, 1880–1892* (1963), ch. 3.
15. *A Political Memoir*, 152.
16. 18 July 1885: JC PP.
17. Morley, *Life of Gladstone*, III, 174.
18. C. H. D. Howard, 'Joseph Chamberlain and the "Unauthorised Programme"', *English Historical Review*, LXV (1950).
19. B. Holland, *The Life of Spencer Compton, Eighth Duke of Devonshire* (1911), II, 71–2.
20. Chamberlain—Harcourt, 9 Oct., 25 Sept. 1885: Garvin, *Life*, II, 102–3.
21. 9 Sept. 1885: A. Ramm (ed.), *The Political Correspondence*, II, 392–3.
22. Chamberlain—Dilke and Collings, 20 Sept. 1885: JC PP.
23. Gladstone—Granville, 29 Sept., 5 Oct. 1885: A. Ramm (ed.), *The Political Correspondence*, II, 400, 403.
24. Gladstone—Chamberlain, 22 Sept., Chamberlain—Gladstone, 23 Sept. 1885: *A Political Memoir*, 130, 131.
25. E. J. Feuchtwanger, *Gladstone* (1975), 230–1.
26. Gladstone—Chamberlain, 26 Sept., Chamberlain—Gladstone, 28 Sept. 1885: *A Political Memoir*, 161–2.
27. For these negotiations, J. L. Hammond, *Gladstone and the Irish Nation*, ch. 22.
28. Chamberlain—Labouchere, 20 Oct. 1885: JC PP.
29. 25, 26 Oct. 1885: *A Political Memoir*, 131–3, 162–3.
30. Gladstone—Grosvenor, 27 Nov. 1885: Hammond, op. cit. 398.
31. 6 Dec. 1885: JC PP.
32. Brett, 9 Dec.; Chamberlain, 4 Dec.; Labouchere, 6 Dec. 1885: JC PP.
33. See M. Barker, *Gladstone and Radicalism* (1975), 28 ff.
34. W. S. Churchill, *Lord Randolph Churchill* (new ed. 1952), p. 411.
35. 17, 19 Dec. 1885: JC PP.
36. N. M. Marris, *Joseph Chamberlain* (1900), 234. For similar, more

recent, views: Garvin, *Life*, II, 180; J. W. Derry, *The Radical Tradition* (1967), 329; P. Fraser, *Joseph Chamberlain*, 82; F. S. L. Lyons, *Ireland since the Famine* (1971), 185.

37. E. Strauss, *Irish Nationalism and British Democracy* (1951), ch. xviii; a view criticized by C. C. O'Brien, *Parnell and His Party* (1957), 109–14.

38. 6 May 1886: Gwynn and Tuckwell, *Life of Dilke*, II, 222.

39. 3 Jan. 1886: Garvin, *Life*, II, 161.

40. Hammond, op. cit. 341.

41. R. R. James, *Lord Randolph Churchill* (1959), 227.

42. 13 Feb. 1886: JC PP.

43. 29 Jan. 1883: JC PP.

44. Chamberlain—Labouchere, 24 Dec. 1885: Garvin, *Life*, II, 145.

45. For details see Appendix.

46. 2 Jan. 1886: A. Ramm (ed.), *The Political Correspondence*, II, 420.

47. *A Political Memoir*, 177–8.

48. 'A Radical View of the Irish Crisis', *Fortnightly Review*, 1 Feb. 1886.

49. e.g. in the *Fortnightly Review* article, and Chamberlain—Morley, 28 Dec. 1885, quoted in P. Fraser, *Joseph Chamberlain*, 84.

50. This seems the implication of Balfour—Salisbury, 22 Mar. 1886: Dugdale, *Balfour*, I, 101.

51. House of Commons, 16 Apr. 1886: copy JC PP.

52. M. C. Hurst, *Joseph Chamberlain and West Midland Politics* (1963), 15–20.

53. R. R. James, *Lord Randolph Churchill*, 240.

54. Labouchere—Chamberlain, 1 May 1886: JC PP.

55. 5 May 1886: Garvin, *Life*, II, 224.

56. Viscount Chilston, *Chief Whip* (1961), 71 ff.

57. On the changing character of the Federation, see P. C. Griffiths, 'The Caucus and the Liberal Party', *History*, 61 (1976), and A. W. Roberts, 'Leeds Liberalism and Late-Victorian Politics', *Northern History*, V (1970).

58. Cooke and Vincent, *The Governing Passion*, 428.

59. J. L. Hammond, *Gladstone and the Irish Nation*, 489.

60. N. Blewett, *The Peers, The Parties and The People* (1972), 21.

Chapter 6

1. Harcourt—Morley, 20 Nov. 1886: D. A. Hamer, *Liberal Politics*, 228.

2. Blanche Dugdale, *Arthur James Balfour*, I, 101.

3. Mrs Dilke's Diary, 5 Feb. 1887: M. Hurst, *Joseph Chamberlain and Liberal Reunion* (1967), 382–3.

4. Balfour—Salisbury, 21 Dec. 1886: R. R. James, *Lord Randolph Churchill*, 292.
5. 30 Mar. 1887: Garvin, *Life*, II, 304.
6. 16 Aug. 1887, 18 Sept. 1887: JC PP.
7. 13 Mar. 1888: JC PP.
8. Chamberlain—Miss Endicott, 8 May 1888: Garvin, *Life*, II, 356. For extensive treatment of the local situation in this period, M. Hurst, 'Joseph Chamberlain, the Conservatives and the succession to John Bright, 1886–89', *Historical Journal*, VII, 1 (1964), and *Joseph Chamberlain and West Midland Politics, 1886–1895*.
9. C. Green, 'Birmingham Politics, 1873–1891: the Local Basis of Change', *Midland History*, II, 2 (1973).
10. See A. Briggs, *History of Birmingham* (1952), II, ch. 3.
11. 1 Feb. 1888: Garvin, *Life*, II, 417.
12. H. Harrison, *Parnell, Joseph Chamberlain and Mr. Garvin* (1938), presents a hostile, though suggestive, account of Chamberlain–O'Shea relations.
13. Viscount Chilston, *Chief Whip*, 203.
14. Contrasting views on the extent and value of this factionalism can be found in D. A. Hamer, *Liberal Politics*, and M. Barker, *Gladstone and Radicalism*.

Chapter 7
1. Quoted in R. R. James, *Lord Randolph Churchill*, 257.
2. Gwynn and Tuckwell, *Life of Dilke*, II, 284.
3. 29 Jan. 1892: JC PP.
4. P. Fraser, *Joseph Chamberlain*, 44.
5. 24 July 1892: Dugdale, *Arthur James Balfour*, I, 211.
6. 22 June 1892: JC PP.
7. 21 Apr. 1893: JC PP.
8. W. C. Mallalieu, 'Joseph Chamberlain and Workmen's Compensation', *Journal of Economic History*, X, 1 (1950), and D. G. Hanes, *The First Workmen's Compensation Act* (1968), cover this subject in greater detail.
9. See B. B. Gilbert, *The Evolution of National Insurance in Great Britain* (1966).
10. P. Fraser, *Joseph Chamberlain*, ch. 7.
11. 9 Nov. 1894, Birmingham: JC PP.
12. K. Young, *Local Politics and the Rise of Party* (1975), 61–3, 67, notes that Chamberlain was much involved in an attempt to weld a progressive programme upon the reorganized Unionist groupings in London, which represented a major expansion beyond his

Midlands base. Young also notes Salisbury's determination to resist him.

13. Salisbury—Chamberlain, 9 Nov. 1894, Chamberlain—Salisbury, 15 Nov. 1894: JC PP.

13a. But see also the recent study by P. Marsh, *The Discipline of Popular Government: Lord Salisbury's Domestic Statecraft, 1881–1902* (1978).

14. 13 Nov. 1894: see P. Fraser, 'The Liberal Unionist Alliance: Chamberlain, Hartington and the Conservatives', *English Historical Review*, LXXVII (1962).

15. R. Taylor, *Salisbury*, 155.

16. Chamberlain—James, 11 Dec. 1894; Chamberlain—Mrs Chamberlain, 28 Feb. 1895: JC PP.

17. See A. P. Thornton, *The Imperial Idea and its Enemies* (1959).

18. Jan. 1892: JC PP.

19. See S. B. Saul, *The Myth of the Great Depression, 1873–1896* (1969).

20. 22 Jan. 1879; NLF conference, Leeds: JC PP.

21. V. Bérard, *British Imperialism and Commercial Supremacy* (1906), 54–90, followed by B. Semmel, *Imperialism and Social Reform* (1960), ch. 4.

22. 24 Dec. 1887, *The Times* interview in Ottawa: JC PP.

23. Chamberlain—Balfour, 19 July 1892: JC PP.

24. Chamberlain—Austen Chamberlain, 16 July 1887: JC PP 5/12/1.

25. A. P. Thornton, *The Imperial Idea and its Enemies*, 100–1.

Chapter 8

1. Peter Fraser, *Joseph Chamberlain*, 281.

2. See S. M. Hardy, 'Joseph Chamberlain and some Problems of the "Under-developed Estates"', *University of Birmingham Historical Journal*, XI (1968).

3. See generally, R. V. Kubicek, *The Administration of Imperialism* (1969), ch. 4.

4. 24 Nov. 1897, ibid. 76.

5. R. E. Dummett, 'Joseph Chamberlain, Imperial Finance and Railway Policy in British West Africa in the Late Nineteenth Century', *English Historical Review*, XC (1975).

6. Margot Asquith, *Autobiography*, I, 133.

7. D. C. M. Platt, *Finance, Trade and Politics in British Foreign Policy* (1968), discusses the economic significance of South Africa.

8. Gwynn and Tuckwell, *Life of Dilke*, II, 272: Chamberlain—Miss Endicott, 3 May 1888, Garvin, *Life*, II, 349.

9. According to A. G. Gardiner, *The Pillars of Society* (1914), 38.

10. Said to Lady Lugard; Garvin, *Life*, III, 83.

11. E. Pakenham, *The Jameson Raid*, and E. Drus, 'The Question of

Imperial Complicity in the Jameson Raid', *English Historical Review*, LXVIII (1953) cover the events and the roles of different actors in the Raid.

12. Chamberlain—Salisbury, 26 Dec. 1895, quoted by Garvin, *Life*, III, 78, shows how little the government collectively knew of the preparations.

13. 4 Jan. 1896, Garvin, *Life*, III, 95.

14. 21 Jan. 1896, Queensland Dinner; 13 Feb. 1896, House of Commons.

15. See J. Butler, *The Liberal Party and the Jameson Raid* (1968).

16. Chamberlain—Salisbury, 8 Apr. 1897: Garvin, *Life*, III, 140.

17. Kubicek, *Administration of Imperialism*, 155.

18. B. H. Brown, *The Tariff Reform Movement, 1881-95* (1943), 124 ff.

19. See J. E. Kendle, *The Colonial and Imperial Conferences, 1887-1911* (1967).

20. J. A. S. Grenville, *Lord Salisbury and Foreign Policy* (1964), is the invaluable guide to the period.

21. Cooke and Vincent, *The Governing Passion*, 206.

22. See J. E. Flint, *Sir George Goldie and the Making of Nigeria* (1960), ch. 12.

23. Chamberlain—Selborne, 29 Sept. 1897; Garvin, *Life*, III, 211.

24. 1 Dec. 1897: JC PP.

25. Chamberlain—Selborne, 1 Dec. 1897: Garvin, *Life*, III, 213.

26. R. Taylor, *Lord Salisbury* (1975), 179.

27. G. M. Young, *Portrait of an Age* 2nd ed. (1953), 81.

28. See I. H. Nish, *The Anglo–Japanese Alliance, 1894-1907* (1966).

29. 3 Feb. 1898: Dugdale, *Balfour*, I, 252-3.

30. Chamberlain memo, 29 Mar. 1898: JC PP.

31. See Balfour—Salisbury, 14 Apr. 1898: Dugdale, *Balfour*, I, 258-61.

32. 29 Apr. 1898: Garvin, *Life*, III, 278-9.

33. George Curzon, quoted in Grenville, *Lord Salisbury*, 171.

34. On the negotiations, see Grenville, ibid., ch. 8.

35. Chamberlain—Balfour, 19 Aug. 1898: JC PP.

36. 23 Aug. 1898: JC PP.

37. Eckardstein's report, 4 Nov. 1898: Garvin, *Life*, III, 231-2.

38. Spenser Wilkinson—Chamberlain, 12 Mar. 1898: JC PP.

39. C. Headlam, *The Milner Papers* (1931), I, 220-4.

40. Chamberlain—Milner, 16 Mar. 1898: ibid. I, 229.

41. Chamberlain—Salisbury, 30 Nov. 1898: Garvin, *Life*, III, 380.

42. Milner—Selborne, 31 Jan. 1899: Headlam, *Milner Papers*, I, 301-2.

43. J. S. Marais, *The Fall of Kruger's Republic* (1961), 243 ff., details the manœuvres.

44. 28 April 1899 memo. for 2 May cabinet: JC PP.
45. Comments quoted in E. Stokes, 'Milnerism', *Historical Journal*, V, 1 (1962).
46. G. H. L. LeMay, *British Supremacy in South Africa* (1965), 22, and ch. I generally.
47. 4 Sept. 1897: JC PP.
48. Quoted in Stokes, art. cit.
49. J. S. Marais, op. cit. 274.
50. See also Selborne—Milner, 25 June 1899: Headlam, op. cit. I, 445.
51. 11 July 1899: G. E. Buckle (ed.), *Letters of Queen Victoria, 1886–1901* (1930–2), III, 382–4.
52. 24 Aug. 1899: R. H. Wilde, *Joseph Chamberlain and the South African Republic* (1956), 134.
53. Salisbury—Lansdowne, 30 Aug. 1899: Lord Newton, *Lord Lansdowne* (1929), 157.
54. Cabinet memo, 6 Sept. 1899: JC PP.
55. Chamberlain—Hicks Beach, 7 Oct. 1899: JC PP.
56. W. L. Langer, *The Diplomacy of Imperialism* (1951), 791–2, contrasts the two approaches.

Chapter 9

1. See J. P. Cornford, 'The Parliamentary Foundations of the Hotel Cecil', in *Ideas and Institutions of Victorian England*, ed. R. Robson (1967), for discussion of the phenomenon.
2. Garvin, *Life*, III, 158.
3. B. B. Gilbert, *The Evolution of National Insurance in Great Britain* (1966), chronicles the fate of pensions in this period.
4. H. Stretton, *The Political Sciences* (1969), chs. 1, 2, illustrates general problems of historical explanation through the medium of some interesting comments on Chamberlain's change of heart.
5. 16 Sept. 1901, summarized in Lady Victoria Hicks Beach, *Life of Sir Michael Hicks Beach* (1932), II, 150 ff.
6. Garvin, *Life*, III, 515.
7. Amery, *Life*, IV, 140.
8. Grenville, *Lord Salisbury*, ch. 15.
9. H. W. Koch, 'The Anglo–German Alliance Negotiations: Missed Opportunity or Myth?', *History*, LIV (1969), assesses the issues.
10. Chamberlain—Minto, 6 Oct. 1899: Garvin, *Life*, III, 531–2.
11. For further details, see J. E. B. Morrison, 'The Unionist Coalition and Education, 1895–1902', *Historical Journal*, 20, 3 (1977).
12. R. B. McDowell, *British Conservatism* (1959), 160.

13. Chamberlain—Selborne, 29 May 1902: Amery, *Life*, V, 34.
14. J. S. Sandars memo to Balfour, 25 Feb. 1902: Dugdale, *Balfour*, I, 337.
15. Amery, *Life*, V, 49.
16. A. Gollin, *Balfour's Burden* (1965), 27 ff.
17. 22 Sept. 1902: B. Holland, *Duke of Devonshire*, II, 284.
18. Le May, *British Supremacy*, ch. 3.
19. See Headlam, *Milner Papers*, II, ch. 12.
20. Campbell-Bannerman—Bryce, 26 Jan. 1903: John Wilson, *CB: A Life of Henry Campbell-Bannerman* (1973), 395.
21. Lord Onslow (Chamberlain's Parliamentary Under-Secretary) —Chamberlain, 13 Mar. 1903: Amery, *Life*, V, 140.
22. Balfour—Devonshire, 27 Aug. 1903: quoted by Amery, *Life*, V, 427.
23. Ibid. See D. Judd, *Balfour and the British Empire* (1968), for a broader analysis of Balfour's views.
24. Chamberlain—Collings, 18 July 1903: Amery, *Life*, V, 307.
25. Gollin, *Balfour's Burden*, 84–8, 196 ff.
26. 27 Aug. 1903: Amery, *Life*, V, 378–9.
27. Gardiner, *Life of Harcourt*, II, 557.
28. Amery, *Life*, V, 391.
29. Ibid. V, 416, fn. i.
30. Chamberlain—Selborne, 23 Sept. 1903: ibid. V, 435.
31. Sir Austen Chamberlain, *Politics from Inside* (1936), 22 ff.
32. Chamberlain—Pearson, 17 Sept. 1903: Amery, *Life*, V, 427.
33. See Gollin, op. cit., ch. XI.
34. Churchill—Rosebery, 9 Oct. 1903: R. S. Churchill, *Winston S. Churchill*, II companion, pt. i (1966–9), 227.
35. Campbell-Bannerman—Harcourt, 27 Nov. 1903: Gardiner, *Life of Harcourt*, II, 559.
36. For a detailed account of the tariff reform crisis with particular concern for the free-trade Unionists, R. Rempel, *Unionists Divided: Arthur Balfour, Joseph Chamberlain and the Unionist Free Traders* (1972).
37. Chamberlain—J. Parker Smith, 12 Jan. 1904: Amery, *Life*, VI, 512.
38. Gollin, *Balfour's Burden*, 223.
29. Chamberlain—Austen Chamberlain, 11 Mar. 1904: JC PP.
40. For the average MP, by-election results suggested less cause for such aggression: R. Rempel, *Unionists Divided*, 121–2.
41. 14 Sept. 1904: Gollin, *Balfour's Burden*, 232.
42. Amery, *Life*, VI, 655–60.
43. Chamberlain—J. Parker Smith, 24 June 1905; JC PP.

Chapter 10

 1. Chamberlain—J. Parker Smith, 27 Jan. 1906; Chamberlain—Alfred Deakin, Prime Minister of Australia, 26 Apr. 1906: Amery, *Life*, VI, 793, 889.
 2. For assessment of the election, A. K. Russell, *Liberal Landslide: The General Election of 1906* (1973).
 3. 27 Jan. 1906: Amery, *Life*, VI, 793–4.
 4. Chamberlain—Mrs Endicott, 30 Jan. 1906: ibid. VI, 799.
 5. For further analysis, P. Fraser, 'Unionism and Tariff Reform: The Crisis of 1906', *Historical Journal*, V, 2 (1962).
 6. 7 Feb. 1906: Amery, *Life*, VI, 827.
 7. B. Webb, *Our Partnership* (1948), 330.
 8. 25 June 1906, inaugural dinner of 1900 Club: Amery, *Life*, VI, 893.
 9. See N. Blewett, 'Free Fooders, Balfourites, Whole Hoggers: Factionalism within the Unionist Party, 1906–10', *Historical Journal*, XI, 1 (1968).
10. K. Young, *Arthur James Balfour* (1963), 288 ff.
11. See N. Blewett, *The Peers, The Parties and The People* (1972).
12. See P. Fraser, 'The Unionist Debacle of 1911 and Mr Balfour's Retirement', *Journal of Modern History*, XXXV, 4 (1963).
13. R. Blake, *The Unknown Prime Minister: The Life and Times of Bonar Law* (1955), 115–16.
14. G. Dangerfield, *The Strange Death of Liberal England* (1936).
15. M. Asquith, *Autobiography*, II, 133.

Concluding Essay

 1. W. S. Churchill, *Great Contemporaries* (1937), 53.
 2. 1 Nov. 1881; JC PP.
 3. Blanche Dugdale, *Balfour*, I, 101 ff.
 4. *Apologia of an Imperialist* (1929), I, 227.
 5. B. Semmel, *Imperialism and Social Reform* (1960), ch. VII.
 6. J. Amery, *Life of Chamberlain*, VI, 994.
 7. 'Joseph Chamberlain', *Spectator*, 3 July 1936: 'Some Political and Economic Interactions in late Victorian England', *Transactions of the Royal Historical Society*, XXXI (1949).
 8. D. Judd, *Radical Joe* (1977), xiv.
 9. See, for example, H. Pelling, *Popular Politics*, chs. 1, 5, and R. Price, *An Imperial War and the British Working Class* (1972).
10. Mundella—Chamberlain, 18 Dec. 1883: JC PP.
11. A. G. Gardiner, *Pillars of Society*, 43.
12. M. Hurst, *Joseph Chamberlain and West Midland Politics*, 36.
13. Lady Frances Balfour, *Ne Obliviscaris* (1930), I, 404.

Bibliographical Note

I have not wished to give a list of the works mentioned in the notes to each chapter. The range of books consulted in preparing this study has been extensive, and only those have been referenced which have provided the most useful sources, or have been influential in forming opinions put forward in the text.

J. L. Garvin and J. Amery, *The Life of Joseph Chamberlain* (Macmillan, 1932–69), is packed with information, even when interpreted in a manner unduly favourable to Chamberlain. It superseded all the earlier biographies. P. Fraser, *Joseph Chamberlain: Radicalism and Empire, 1868–1914* (Cassell, 1966), provides a somewhat unbalanced narrative, and, while many of its ideas are provocative, they are frequently misleading when placing Chamberlain within the context of contemporary ideas. H. Browne, *Joseph Chamberlain: Radical and Imperialist* (Longman, 1974), is a brief account, with documents for discussion in schools. D. Judd, *Radical Joe* (Hamish Hamilton, 1976), provides a full account, although it is insufficiently critical and does little to provide an overall assessment of Chamberlain's methods and historical importance. J. Enoch Powell, *Joseph Chamberlain* (Thames and Hudson, 1977), is disappointing given its authorship. Superb photographs do much to convey the atmosphere of the Chamberlain era, but the text is slight, and too inclined to transfer the author's concepts of nationhood on to his subject. Viscount Milner *et al.*, *Life of Joseph Chamberlain* (1912), comprises a set of essays by leading contemporaries, most interesting for the differing attempts of Milner, Ramsay MacDonald, and L. S. Amery to interpret Chamberlain as the sort of person they would have liked him to be. There are many short essays. That by A. G. Gardiner, *The Pillars of Society* (J. M. Dent, 1914), remains a splendid pen-portrait, while R. C. K. Ensor, 'Joseph Chamberlain', *Spectator*, 3 July 1936, presents his distinctive conception of Chamberlain's career. R. R. James, 'Radical Joe', *History Today*, VII, 9 (1957), and M. C. Hurst, 'Joseph Chamberlain and Late-Victorian Liberalism', *Durham University Journal*, 1973–4, treat the early period of his life, the latter with rather more acuity and respect for his political methods.

There are many books useful for different aspects of Chamberlain's career. J. T. Bunce, *History of the Corporation of Birmingham* (Birmingham, 1885), and F. Dolman, 'Joseph Chamberlain's Municipal Career', *Fortnightly Review*, June 1895, are informative on the mayoralty, and A. Briggs (ed.), Francis Adams, *History of the Elementary School Contest* (Harvester Press reprint, 1972), on the Education League. The content of R. S. Watson, *The National Liberal Federation* (London, 1907), is self-explanatory. Other works referenced on the Federation should be supplemented by H. J. Hanham, *Elections and Party Management* (Longman, 1959). E. C. Gullie, *Joseph Chamberlain and English Social Politics* (Columbia U. P., 1926), amasses considerable material on Chamberlain's domestic reforms, but shows too little discrimination and exaggerates continuities and consistency. W. Strauss, *Joseph Chamberlain and the Theory of Imperialism* (Public Affairs, 1942), tackles the story in relation to overseas affairs, with perhaps too much emphasis on immediate economic determinants and racial beliefs as explanations of Chamberlain's actions. Sir W. Maycock, *With Mr Chamberlain in the United States and Canada, 1887-8* (Chatto, 1914), has some interesting material. R. H. Wilde, *Joseph Chamberlain and the South African Republic, 1895-99* (Archives Yearbook for South African History, I, 1956, Cape Town), is detailed and in places acute, though to some extent now superseded. C. V. Kubicek, *The Administration of Imperialism: Joseph Chamberlain at the Colonial Office* (Duke U. P., 1969), mixes new interesting material on the methods of administration with fairly conventional interpretations of events, while S. B. Saul, 'The Economic Significance of "Constructive Imperialism"', *Journal of Economic History*, xvii (1957), remains a sound assessment of imperial development.

S. H. Zebel, 'Joseph Chamberlain and the Genesis of Tariff Reform', *Journal of British Studies*, VII, 1 (1967), considers contending explanations of the 1903 political crisis. Early chapters of M. Beloff, *Imperial Sunset. Vol. I: Britain's Liberal Empire* (Methuen, 1969), clarify the sense of crisis in imperial relations felt around the turn of the century, and G. R. Searle, *The Quest for National Efficiency, 1899-1914* (Blackwell, 1971), considers some of the responses in the domestic arena. W. A. S. Hewins, *Apologia of an Imperialist* (Constable, 1929), and L. S. Amery, *My Political Life* (Hutchinson, 1953), provide the best revelations of what tariff reform meant to its most intelligent spokesmen. A. Sykes, *Tariff Reform in British Politics, 1903-1913* (OUP, 1979), unpublished at the time of writing, promises to be valuable in explaining the movement. H. C. G. Matthew, *The*

Liberal Imperialists (OUP, 1973), is useful on those Liberals closest in ideas to Chamberlain in the later years, and B. Porter, *Critics of Empire* (Macmillan, 1968), on those most radically opposed.

R. C. K. Ensor, *England, 1870–1914* (Oxford, 1936), and E. Halevy, *A History of the English People in the Nineteenth Century*, V, VI, (E. Benn, 1952), are indispensable general textbooks for the period, with R. R. James, *The British Revolution. Vol. I: From Gladstone to Asquith, 1880–1914* (Hamish Hamilton, 1976), perceptive on the men of the time, R. T. Shannon, *The Crisis of Imperialism, 1865–1915* (Paladin, 1976), on the ideas and the problems.

Chamberlain's personal—and partial—account of events in the 1880s is published: C. H. D. Howard (ed.), *A Political Memoir, 1880–1892* (Batchworth Press, 1953). Unfortunately neither his play, nor his articles for various journals (over two dozen in all), have been reprinted, though there are various collections of speeches. C. W. Boyd, *Mr Chamberlain's Speeches* (Constable, 1914), *Home Rule and the Irish Question. Speeches 1881–7* (1887), *Foreign and Colonial Speeches* (1897), and H. W. Lucy (ed.), *Speeches of the Right Hon. Joseph Chamberlain* (1885), present in different ways selected and rather one-sided pictures of Chamberlain's pronouncements: *The Radical Platform. Speeches 1885, Speeches on the Irish Question, 1887–1890* (1890), and *Imperial Union and Tariff Reform. Speeches May to November, 1903* (1903), cover more limited periods of time.

Index